TRENDS IN POSTTRAUMATIC STRESS DISORDER RESEARCH

Trends in Posttraumatic Stress Disorder Research

Thomas A. Corales

Editor

Nova Science Publishers, Inc.

New York

Editorial Production Manager: Donna Dennis
Senior Production Editor: Susan Boriotti
Office Manager: Annette Hellinger
Graphics: Andrea Charles, Magdalena Nuñez and Annemarie VanDeWater
Editorial Production: Marius Andronie, Maya Columbus, Keti Datunashvili, Joan Flynn, Andrew Kallio, Vladimir Klestov, Lorna Loperfido, Joann Overton and Rusudan Razmadze
Circulation: Ave Maria Gonzalez, Vera Popovic, Luis Aviles, Alexandra Columbus, Raymond Davis, Cathy DeGregory, Melissa Diaz, Marlene Nuñez, Jeannie Pappas, Lauren Perl and Katie Sutherland
❋

Library of Congress Cataloging-in-Publication Data
Available Upon Request

ISBN: 1-59454-135-3

Copyright © 2005 by Nova Science Publishers, Inc.
             400 Oser Ave, Suite 1600
             Hauppauge, New York 11788-3619
             Tele. 631-231-7269   Fax 631-231-8175
             e-mail: Novascience@earthlink.net
             Web Site: http://www.novapublishers.com

Printed in the United States of America

CONTENTS

PREFACE

Posttraumatic Stress Disorder, or PTSD, is a psychiatric disorder that can occur following the experience or witnessing of life-threatening events such as military combat, natural disasters, terrorist incidents, serious accidents, or violent personal assaults like rape. People who suffer from PTSD often relive the experience through nightmares and flashbacks, have difficulty sleeping, and feel detached or estranged, and these symptoms can be severe enough and last long enough to significantly impair the person's daily life.

PTSD is marked by clear biological changes as well as psychological symptoms. PTSD is complicated by the fact that it frequently occurs in conjunction with related disorders such as depression, substance abuse, problems of memory and cognition, and other problems of physical and mental health. The disorder is also associated with impairment of the person's ability to function in social or family life, including occupational instability, marital problems and divorces. PTSD is associated with a number of distinctive neurobiological and physiological changes. PTSD is treated by a variety of forms of psychotherapy and drug therapy. This new book presents leading research from around the world.

Recent treatment development efforts across health care settings have begun to focus on Post-Traumatic Stress Disorder (PTSD) including it's burden, disability, and link with comorbidities. PTSD is a common and debilitating consequence of exposure to a traumatic event. Up to 90% of the general population in the United States has been exposed to a traumatic stressor such as interpersonal violence, traffic accidents, man-made or natural disasters, or wartime combat at some time in their lives. According to data from the National Comorbidity Study the lifetime prevalence of PTSD among traumatized individuals is 8% in men and 20% in women. Veterans tend to have higher rates of PTSD (15%-30) and the prevalence of PTSD is thought to be in excess of 50% in trauma victims who seek non-psychiatric medical treatment for the after-effects of the trauma. The nature of PTSD is that of a chronic disorder that impairs functioning in many, if not all, areas of life for those that are affected. Among the general population PTSD is associated with nearly the highest rate of medical visits and other service use, and therefore is a very costly disorder. The psychiatric, physical, and functional impairments associated with this disorder extend beyond the individual and impact family members and society as a whole. Given the morbidity and cost, prompt recognition and treatment for PTSD are important public health measures. Chapter 1 will summarize current progress in research related to the recognition, diagnosis and treatment for PTSD.

In PTSD, the hypothalamic-pituitary-adrenocortical (HPA) system is disturbed with increased negative feedback inhibition of cortisol secretion. Recent findings point to the possibility that another steroid hormone, dehydroepiandrosterone (DHEA) or its sulphated metabolite DHEAS might be increased in peripheral blood of PTSD subjects. During the last decades, new findings regarding DHEA have emerged. DHEA is one of the principal steroid molecules in the body and has anabolic properties. It has been shown that it is a neurosteroid; i.e. it can be produced in the brain and it shows non-genomic actions on receptors. The receptor effect which is best characterised till now is a non-competitive blockade on the GABA$_A$ receptor, but other receptors are involved as well. Neuroprotection by DHEAS against cell death and behavioral deficits has been shown in different animal models of stress. In chapter 2, a brief review of the neurosteroids is presented along with published studies and preliminary reports on DHEA/DHEAS in PTSD. The possible interpretations and hypothetical implications are presented, such as the possibility that cognitive dysfunction in PTSD might be explained by increased levels of DHEA/DHEAS in the nervous system. While it is far too early to conclude that DHEA or DHEAS are of any patophysiological importance in PTSD, the findings point to a possibility of confounding by trauma or PTSD in studies of neurosteroids in depression and other psychiatric disorders. They also point to a need of studying an array of steroid molecules in psychiatric and stress research. Possible research strategies in order to elucidate the putative role of DHEAS and other neurosteroids in PTSD are outlined.

A revised associative functional analysis (AFA) model of posttraumatic stress disorder (PTSD) is outlined in chapter 3. In terms of the AFA model currently elicited respondent mechanisms, and dysfunctional cognitive and behavioral responses reciprocally influence each other, and interact with a representational memory network of corresponding factors in determining the development and maintenance of PTSD. The present AFA model combines cognitive, behavioral and network models into a unified framework. In the present AFA model a special emphasis is put on the influence of pleasurable and mastery respondent learning mechanisms incompatible to the respondent trauma-related learning. It is proposed that in order to achieve recovery the former should be elicited in the context of fully elicited trauma-related respondent mechanisms. Prolonged exposure counterconditioning (PEC), a new treatment for PTSD, aims at reinforcing an individuals incompatible respondent learning mechanisms and utilizing them in order to counter the numbing symptoms, increase the trauma exposure tolerance and weaken respondently learned trauma-related emotions. Important theoretical and methodological issues related to the PEC treatment are reviewed. In the discussion section additional issues related to the present AFA model and the PEC treatment for PTSD are outlined.

The persistent symptoms of a head injury after an accident may be mis-attributed to traumatic brain injury, symptom exaggeration, or emotional factors, when brain injury cannot be documented. In fact, there can be unhealed somatic injuries causing dysregulation of the structures supplying chemical signals to the brain and other structures through the liquid internal environment. This reflects persistent reactions of the hormonal, immune, and inflammatory systems. The persistent physiological effects of an unhealed injury and impairment are reflected in mood disorders, cognitive dysfunctions, and impairment which are discussed in chapter 4. The physiological mechanism is dysregulation as a consequence of extended effects of unhealed injuries after trauma. The regulatory systems are feedback mechanisms, homeostasis and allostasis, circadian rhythms, and such brain structures as the hypothalamus. The effectors are the hormonal axes, immune and inflammatory systems, autonomic and enteric nervous systems, and also hypothalamic integration and output. Chemical signalling systems through the blood, vagus nerve, and cerebrospinal fluid are participate along with the nervous system. Common symptoms are accounted for by this model: Fatigue, exhaustion, and burnout, illness behavior, loss of appetite, apathy, social withdrawal, inactivity, and sleepiness, sexual dysfunction, and dysfunction of pediatric sexual development. Thus, the stress reaction to an accident causing bodily injury is far more extensive than the familiar PTSD.

In chapter 5, two cohorts of Cuban refugee children and adolescents who migrated with their parents by sea and were later confined to refugee camps were assessed for symptoms of Post-traumatic stress disorder during refugee camp confinement. A third cohort of children and adolescents was assessed for Posttraumatic Stress Disorder four to six months after release from the refugee camps, and assessed for the presence of internalizing and externalizing behaviors by their teachers. A clinic population of 285 children and adolescent refugees who had left Cuba by sea in the summer of 1994, undergoing their sixth month of confinement, was assessed in the military field hospital inside the camps for the presence of PTSD with the Posttraumatic Stress Disorder Reactive Index. A second cohort of 79 children and adolescents who had taken an alternative exit route out of Cuba and had been transferred from a camp in another country were assessed using DSM-III-R criteria for PTSD. A third cohort of 87 children and adolescents were assessed for PTSD with the PTSDRI, and for the presence of internalizing and externalizing behaviors by their teachers, using the Child Behavioral Checklist-Teacher Report Form. The majority of children and adolescents in the clinic population reported very severe symptoms of PTSD. The rates of pre-existing medical conditions such as Asthma and Epilepsy, and pre-existing psychiatric conditions such as Learning Disabilities and Behavior Dis-control Problems, were found to be double than those found in the general population. The type of posttraumatic symptoms and the effects of particular stressors showed variations by sex and gender. The subjects that were transferred from a camp situated in another country also showed elevated rates of PTSD symptoms. However, these were not as sever as those found among the clinic population. The majority of the children and adolescents that were studied after release from the refugee camps reported moderate to sever PTSD symptoms. The most common symptom clusters were avoidance, regressive behaviors, re-experiencing the traumatic events somatic symptoms and hyper-arousal. A statistically significant dose-effect relationship was found between the number of stressors and the severity of self reported PTSD symptoms. Teachers' overall ratings of internalizing and externalizing behaviors did not produce clinically significant findings. The psychological effects of multiple stressors on child and adolescent refugees are discussed. The role of mental health professionals in treating child and adolescent refugees and their families during refugee camp confinement, the psychological effects on mental health workers, the role of political agendas and the adaptation issues of the refugees to the host country are also addressed. PTSD symptoms among refugee children and adolescents may continue unabated after the stressors have been removed. The symptoms may be experienced subjectively and go unnoticed by adults.

The long-term effects of Holocaust survivors who were children during the war is the focus of chapter 6. The data will be based on two previous quantitative and qualitative studies: The first study examined the psychological distress, Posttraumatic Stress Disorder (PTSD), Quality of Life (QoL), Self-identity and Potency among 170 Holocaust survivors who were born after 1926. This sample was divided into four groups based on the setting of their experience during the Holocaust: Catholic Institutions, Christian foster families, concentration camps, and hiding in the woods and/or with partisans. The second study assessed posttraumatic stress disorder (PTSD) symptoms, subjective quality of life (QoL), psychological distress and potency in a group of child Holocaust survivors who did not know their true identity. Twenty-three such survivors were compared to a matched group of 23 child Holocaust survivors who knew their identity. The results of the first study showed that survivors who had been with foster families scored significantly higher on several of the measures of distress, whereas survivors who had been in the woods and/or with partisans scored significantly higher on several of the positive measures, QoL, potency, and self-identity. The results of the second study showed that survivors with unknown identity have higher somatization and anxiety scores and lower physical, psychological and social QoL than do survivors with known identity. The discussion will be focusing on the understanding of the different experiences according to developmental theory and sense of control. In addition, the psychological consequences of not knowing one's identity will be discussed in light of the role of resilience. Several illustrations (personal stories of survivors) will be presented.

Chapter 7 rethinks the role of the Posttraumatic Stress Disorder (PTSD) diagnosis in mental health services for refugees. It reviews four research studies conducted with Bosnian refugees in Chicago that investigated services issues related to PTSD. The summary findings were: (1) Persons presenting for services had higher levels of PTSD symptoms, but also depression symptoms and other distinct demographics and service exposure characteristics associated with vulnerability; (2) Assessment and educational activities of providers did not adequately reflect the high prevalence of PTSD in refugee populations; (3) Although nearly all patients treated for PTSD received psychiatric medication and supportive counseling, treatment patterns varied with demographic characteristics; (4) Providers' discourse on refugees was highly oriented towards services issues with a focus on service access problems. Overall, these studies demonstrate that PTSD is an important construct for refugee mental health services, but because PTSD alone does not explain the range or context of refugees' mental health needs, a services perspective on PTSD is necessary. On the basis of empirical evidence, this chapter delineates a *Services Mental Health Approach to Refugee Trauma (SMART)* to facilitate building services for refugees with PTSD and related mental health problems. The major claims of this approach are as follows: (1) PTSD should be regarded as one of multiple causes of suffering amongst a heterogeneous refugee population to be addressed by mental health services; (2) PTSD and mental health related information for communities and families, and training for providers, must be more comprehensive and culturally synchronous in order to facilitate better help seeking and services; (3) Provision of specific interventions in refugee mental health services should be guided by scientific evaluation and clinical observations of targeted outcomes in real life contexts; (4) Refugee mental health services should have as a primary goal facilitating access to a range of mental health, health, social, occupational, child, and family services. Specific implications for interventions and policy-aimed research regarding mental health services for refugee trauma are described.

Posttraumatic stress disorder is frequently seen among refugees who have been exposed to violence. Delayed onset following migration triggers recurrent nightmares, flashbacks, emotional detachment, and difficulty trusting others. Some people suffer from a pattern of alcoholism, family violence, and somatic illness that is rooted in traumatization. Long-term therapy is rarely practical for overwhelmed clients with multiple needs. Chapter 8 describes an eclectic brief treatment that takes into account cultural factors. The importance of psychodiagnostic assessment is explored. A 4-stage treatment process involving specific tools is described. Contraindications for short-term therapy are also outlined.

A brief review on the impact of trauma on domains of psychosocial functioning (occupational, social, recreational/leisure, sexual) will be offered in chapter 9. Typically, improvements in these areas of psychosocial functioning of trauma exposure may be considered in a tertiary manner or even anecdotally reported in large treatment outcome trials. The authors will then examine the impact of two empirically validated treatments (Prolonged Exposure and Cognitive Processing Therapy) on impairments in domains of psychosocial functioning of trauma exposure. Specifically, they will explore the effects of these two evidence-based treatments on the various domains of psychosocial functioning (occupational, social/recreational, sexual). Clinically, as will be discussed, changes in these domains are often reported as the most meaningful to the patient.

A multiple casualty/multiple fatality incident in a medical/surgical hospital setting will present many challenges to a Critical Incident Stress Management (CISM) Team Coordinator supervising the CISM team's response, as well as to hospital administrators. Mental health professionals, who have not had the opportunity to work in this type of healthcare facility, will likely be unfamiliar with the work environment and agency culture as it exists within these settings. In particular, knowledge of "Code Blue" responses will be crucial to proper assessment of the event's impact on hospital employees and subsequent CISM response planning. In addition, although hospital administrators are skilled in managing hospital operations, including medical and surgical treatment of crime victims, they probably will be unprepared for any situation in which a number of their employees have been injured or killed as the result of a violent crime committed on the premises. Some of the issues that they will face will include the shock that such an event has occurred in their facility, frantic and/or grieving family members, traumatized and/or grieving employees, heightened concerns for safety and security on behalf of frightened employees and their family members, the unprompted arrival of well-meaning but not always properly trained mental health professionals, and a throng of media representatives. The initial hours following the event will be chaotic (at best) and the collaborative efforts of both the hospital's administration, the CISM Team Coordinator and off-site Employee Assistance Program (EAP) and/or Crisis Response Organization (CRO) support personnel will be needed to facilitate the recovery process. Chapter 10 will review these issues as well as important considerations in the initial and ongoing assessment of a critical incident in a hospital setting, team member selection, logistics concerns unique to these settings, and the subsequent planning of the CISM response.

There is uncertainty in the literature as to whether childhood history of severe physical abuse or neglect meets the requirement of a traumatic event (Criterion A) for establishing a diagnosis of adult posttraumatic stress disorder (PTSD). The purpose of chapter 11 was to examine associations between two forms of recalled childhood maltreatment (physical abuse and serious neglect), and 19 different adult psychiatric disorders, comorbidity of disorders, and suicide variables in a large nationally representative mental health survey. Participants were from the National Comorbidity Survey. Those who reported childhood physical abuse or childhood serious neglect and indicated physical abuse and neglect as the *most upsetting* traumatic event they had experienced in their lifetime were included ($N = 146$). DSM-III-R psychiatric disorders were assessed by the *Composite International Diagnostic Interview*. Lifetime prevalence of the psychiatric disorders and odds ratios were calculated by comparisons between physical abuse and neglect (PAN) respondents and the remainder of the NCS sample (N = 5731), which served as a normative general population comparison group. The appropriate statistical weight was applied and standard errors were re-estimated to reflect the complex sampling design of the NCS. Almost 76% of the PAN respondents had at least one lifetime psychiatric disorder and almost 50% had three or more disorders. Logistic regressions demonstrated several large significant positive associations between PAN and prevalence of psychiatric disorders, comorbidity, and risk of suicide ideation, planning, and attempts, when compared to the remainder of the NCS sample. The largest effects (odds ratios) were observed for PTSD, the presence of three or more lifetime disorders, and suicidal ideation and attempts. General population findings suggest individuals who experience PAN may be at a greater risk for subsequent development of psychiatric disorders, particularly multiple comorbid disorders, and elevated risk of suicidal behaviors later in adulthood, even though many of them do not meet current formal diagnostic criteria for PTSD.

Many studies have shown that cognitive-behavior therapy (CBT) is generally effective in reducing posttraumatic stress disorder (PTSD). However, CBT is far from universally efficacious, and so various efforts have been made to enhance or modify treatment protocols. Chapter 12 discusses seven important areas that are currently being investigated, and remain to be further studied, in order to improve the efficacy and availability of cognitive-behavioral interventions for PTSD: (a) To identify the active ingredients of CBT interventions, so that the most effective interventions may be emphasized in treatment packages, while the less effective interventions are de-emphasized or dropped altogether. (b) To develop algorithms for selecting, sequencing, and integrating cognitive-behavioral and other interventions. (c) To better understand and limit the occurrence of side effects and other adverse outcomes. (d) To improve methods for PTSD prevention or early intervention. (e) To enhance treatments for special populations such as children and the elderly. (f) To improve the dissemination of CBT. (g) To draw on new developments in the basic sciences, particularly neuroscience, to guide the refinement of cognitive-behavioral theory and treatment. In the coming years the findings from basic and clinical research are likely to lead to important advances in the treatment of PTSD.

In: Trends in Posttraumatic Stress Disorder Research
Editor: Thomas A. Corales, pp. 1-28

ISBN 1-59454-135-3
© 2005 Nova Science Publishers, Inc.

Chapter 1

PROGRESS IN THE IDENTIFICATION, DIAGNOSIS AND TREATMENT OF POSTTRAUMATIC STRESS DISORDER

Hani Raoul Khouzam[*]
Veterans Affairs Central California Health Care System
Bita Ghafoori[**]
Director of Research, UCSF-Fresno, Assistant Clinical Professor, UCSF-Fresno
Clinical Psychologist, VACCHCS
Robert Hierholzer[**]
Associate Chief of Staff(ACS) for Resaerch and Education, VACCHCS
Clinical Professor of Psychiatry, UCSF Fresno

ABSTRACT

Recent treatment development efforts across health care settings have begun to focus on Post-Traumatic Stress Disorder (PTSD) including it's burden, disability, and link with comorbidities (Boughton, 2003). PTSD is a common and debilitating consequence of exposure to a traumatic event. Up to 90% of the general population in the United States has been exposed to a traumatic stressor such as interpersonal violence, traffic accidents, man-made or natural disasters, or wartime combat at some time in their lives (Breslau, Kessler, Chilcoat, Schultz, Davis and Andreski, 1998). According to data from the National Comorbidity Study (1995) the lifetime prevalence of PTSD among traumatized individuals is 8% in men and 20% in women. Veterans tend to have higher rates of PTSD (15%-30%; Kulka, Schlenger, Fairbank, Hough, Jordan, Marmar and Weiss, 1990) and

[*] Staff Psychiatrist,Medical Director,Chemical Dendency Treatment Program(CDTP), Veterans Affairs Central California Health Care System(VACCHCS), Fresno, California. Associate Clinical Professor of Psychiatry, Univsrsity of California,San Francisco,Fresno Meical Education Program, Fresno,California(UCSF) Fresno. Clinical Instructor in Medicine. Harvard Medical School - Boston, Massachusetts. Visiting Lecturer - Department of Psychiatry and Behavioral Sciences. University of Oklahoma - College of Medicine - Oklahoma City, Oklahoma. Central California Health Care System - 2615 E. Clinton Ave., Fresno, California, 93703; Phone: (559) 225-6100 Ext. 4128; Fax: (559) 241-6494; E-Mail: hani.khouzam2@med.va.gov
[**] This work was supported in part by a grant from the Institute for Research on Unlimited Love

the prevalence of PTSD is thought to be in excess of 50% in trauma victims who seek non-psychiatric medical treatment for the after-effects of the trauma (Schnurr, Friedman, and Bernardy, 2002). The nature of PTSD is that of a chronic disorder that impairs functioning in many, if not all, areas of life for those that are affected. Among the general population PTSD is associated with nearly the highest rate of medical visits and other service use, and therefore is a very costly disorder. The psychiatric, physical, and functional impairments associated with this disorder extend beyond the individual and impact family members and society as a whole. Given the morbidity and cost, prompt recognition and treatment for PTSD are important public health measures. This review will summarize current progress in research related to the recognition, diagnosis and treatment for PTSD.

PRELUDE

Traumatic circumstances always affect more people than the victims and the immediate survivors. The ripple effects of traumatic events strike other individuals, families, communities and even whole countries. This has been true from the beginning of time as we read in the book of Genesis when Cain murdered his brother Abel and suffered painfully disturbing consequences, including guilt, shame leading to his isolation, and alienation from his grieving family and subsequently ended by becoming a restless wanderer on the earth (Genesis 4:12).

In his conclusion of the Lord of the Rings trilogy and epic, the author J.R.R. Tolkien, who himself suffered and experienced the horrors of being a soldier during WW-1, describes his accounts of his traumatic events through his main hero Frodo. To defeat the Dark Lord, the accursed Ring of Power had to be destroyed by the fires of Mount Doom. But the way was impossibly hard and Frodo was weakening. Weighed down by the compulsion of the Ring, he began to despair. In the battle that follows, the Ring is destroyed and the power of evil is broken. But the triumph of good is never absolute, and no one can yet say whether men will find wisdom and courage to destroy their Ring of Power or whether they will be destroyed by it (Tolkien, 1956).

INTRODUCTION

Posttraumatic stress disorder is a common psychiatric condition. Recent and ongoing world events including the September 11/2001 terrorist attack have focused attention on the diagnosis, identification, treatment and management of this complex psychiatric condition. This chapter will review the progress and advances made in the areas of research ,clinical management and treatment of PTSD. It is our hope that this review will inform further research efforts with the ultimate goal of improving the lives of the people who suffer from PTSD.

DIAGNOSING PTSD

Since its inception as a formally recognized Diagnostic and Statistical Manual (DSM) mental disorder in 1980, the body of literature on PTSD has grown rapidly (Saigh, 1992). The diagnostic criteria set forth by the Diagnostic and Statistical Manual of Mental Disorders-Forth Edition Text Revised (DSM-IV TR) (American Psychiatric Association, 2000) clearly describes the multifaceted nature of trauma and how trauma impacts various aspects of functioning.

PTSD represents the development of characteristic symptoms that result from a traumatic event that is outside the range of normal human experience (Pearce, Schauer, Garfieled, Ohlde and Patterson, 1985). Individuals who experience the trauma develop symptoms of distress which may include: persistent reexperiencing of the traumatic event (Criterion B of DSM-IV TR); persistent avoidance of stimuli associated with the trauma and numbing of general responsiveness (Criterion C of DSM-IV TR); and persistent symptoms of increased arousal not present before the trauma (Criterion D of DSM-IV TR [American Psychiatric Association, 2000]). Other symptoms may include: recurrent and intrusive recollections of the event; recurrent distressing dreams; markedly diminished interest in usual activities; and increased arousal, including sleeping difficulty, difficulty concentrating, and hypervigilence (DSM IV-TR, [American Psychiatric Association, 2000]). Some or all of these symptoms follow exposure to a traumatic stressor that was perceived as threatening to the self and the person's response involved intense fear, helplessness, or horror (Criterion A of DSM-IV TR [American Psychiatric Association, 2000]). Often times distressed and unstable interpersonal relationships are significant problems that result from the after effects of trauma. Traumatized individuals may experience overwhelming feelings of anger, sadness, shame, fear, hopelessness, and helplessness.

THE NATURE AND IMPACT OF TRAUMATIC STRESS

Exposure to a traumatic event is common. Up to 90% of the general population in the United States has been exposed to a traumatic stressor such as interpersonal violence, road traffic accidents, man-made or natural disasters, or wartime combat at some time in their lives (Breslau, Kessler, Chilcoat, Schultz, Davis and Andreski, 1998). The percentage of those exposed to traumatic stressors who then develop PTSD can vary depending on the nature of the trauma. Kessler and colleagues (1995) found that approximately one in 12 adults experiences PTSD at some time during their life, with women being twice as likely as men to develop PTSD following exposure to traumatic events. According to data from the National Comorbidity Study (1995), the lifetime prevalence of PTSD among traumatized individuals is 8% in men and 20% in women. Among treatment seeking populations, however, the prevalence of PTSD is thought to be higher, sometimes reported to be in excess of 50% among individuals who are not seeking specialized trauma care (Schnurr, Friedman and Bernardy, 2002).

Men and women tend to differ in the traumas they are likely to experience. Men are more likely to experience physical attack, combat, captivity, kidnapping, and being threatened by a weapon (Schnurr, Friedman and Bernardy, 2002). Women are more likely to experience rape, sexual molestation, and childhood abuse (Schnurr et al., 2002). Schnurr and colleagues (2002) have suggested that differences between traumas experienced may provide a possible explanation for the gender differences in PTSD prevalence. Other risk factors, such as younger age, lower education, pre-existing psychiatric disorder, early conduct problems, childhood adversity, personality pathology, family history of a psychiatric disorder, severity of initial reaction, peritraumatic dissociation, and poor social support after a trauma have all been found to be associated with increased risk for developing PTSD (Schnurr et al., 2002).

PTSD, COMORBIDITY, AND HEALTH

PTSD is often accompanied by other psychiatric conditions as well as other medical conditions and general impairments of psychosocial functioning (Kulka, Schlkenger, Fairbank, Hough, Jordan, Marmar and Weiss, 1990; Schnurr, 1999; Schnurr, Friedman and Bernardy, 2002). The most common comborbid psychiatric diagnosis among individuals with PTSD is major depression (Schnurr, Friedman and Bernardy, 2002). Other commonly occurring combordid diagnoses include: dysthymic disorder (dysthymia), mania, generalized anxiety disorder, panic disorder, simple phobia, social phobia, agoraphobia, alcohol abuse/dependence, drug abuse/dependence, and conduct disorder (Kessler et. al, 1995; Schnurr, Friedman and Bernardy, 2002).

Individuals with PTSD identify higher rates of medical comorbidity than those without PTSD (Schnurr and Jankowski, 1999; Weisberg et al., 2002; Schnurr and Jankowski 1999) reviewed the literature on the relationship between physical health and PTSD and concluded that "PTSD is associated with poor self-reported health and increased utilization of medical services". Compared to patients not diagnosed with PTSD, patients with PTSD report higher rates of health complaints and medical moribidity and mortality including diabetes, cardiovascular problems, respiratory difficulties, musculoskeletal problems, and neurological problems (Boscarino, 1997; Kulka, Schlkenger, Fairbank, Hough, Jordan, Marmar and Weiss, 1990; Schnurr and Jankowski, 1999; Weisberg, et al, 2002).

In addition to reports of specific physical conditions, individuals with PTSD also tend to report poorer health status and lower health related quality of life (Schnurr, Spiro, Aldwin, Stukel, 1998; Norris, Weisshaar, Conrad, Diaz, Murphy, Ibanez, 2001; Sundquist, Bayard-Burfield, Johansson, Johansson, 2000). Data from the National Vietnam Veteran Readjustment Study (Kulka et al., 1990) found that PTSD was associated with poorer perceived health status for both men and women. PTSD was found to be associated with diminished well being and physical limitations for males, and PTSD was associated with one or more bed days for a physical health problem within the prior three months for females. Golding and colleagues (1997) conducted a meta-analysis of health perceptions among individuals with a sexual assault history and found that sexual assault was associated with poor subjective health across men, women, and various ethnic groups. Several studies among individuals who present to primary care with trauma histories have found that trauma is associated with a greater number of physical symptoms and lower health related quality of life (Dickinson, DeGruy, Dickinson and Candib, 1999; McCauley, Kern, Kolodner, Derogatis and Bass, 1998).

PSYCHOBIOLOGY OF PTSD

Research on the systems affected by PTSD, specifically the human stress response system, may serve as a context to understand psychobiological abnormalities, which may contribute to the complex manifestation of PTSD. Stress is a normal part of the human experience, and our "fight or flight" response is necessary for escaping acute danger. The activated sympathetic nervous system stimulates the release of adrenal hormones that results in physiological changes such as increased heart rate, breathing, and blood pressure. These physiological changes subside quickly under normal conditions; however, chronic stress, including post-trauma stress, may keep the nervous system perpetually aroused. Prolonged stress has been found to be associated with medical illness and immune system changes in both human and animal models (Chiaramonte, 1997). Specifically, neurobiological abnormalities (continuously elevated SNS and adrenergic function; dysregulation of HPA function; abnormal startle response system) and psychological factors (depression, hostility, negative health behaviors, and poor coping) are associated with increased medical illness. Schnurr and colleagues (2002) reported that PTSD may play a mediational role in the relationship between trauma and physical health considering some of the correlates of PTSD.

SERVICE UTILIZATION AND COST

Not surprisingly, those with PTSD report using substantial medical services and mental health services (Calhoun et al., 2002; Kulka, Schlkenger, Fairbank, Hough, Jordan, Marmar and Weiss, 1990; Marshall, Jorm, Grayson, O'Toole, 1998; Hankin, Spiro, Miller, Kazis, 1999 Schnurr and Jankowski, 1999). Given that trauma survivors frequently experience a variety of medical symptoms, including headaches, nausea, diarrhea, vomiting, muscle aches, chest pain, restlessness, tremors, sweating, and general fatigue (Dahl, 1989), they tend to be great utilizers of general medical care, including primary care and the emergency department, compared to individuals without PTSD (Walker et al., 1999; Walker et al., 2003; Calhoun et al, 2002). For example, the National Vietnam Veteran Readjustment Study found that Vietnam veterans with PTSD report more lifetime and current use of VA health care services for physical health problems than those without PTSD (Kulka, Schlkenger, Fairbank, Hough, Jordan, Marmar and Weiss, 1990). Another recent VA study (Calhoun, 2002) found that although veterans use substantial mental health services, they used "more services in traditionally nonmental health clinics". Calhoun (2002) found that patients with PTSD made a median of seven health care visits for mental health care services and a median of 18 visits for general physical health care services. Patients younger than 52 with PTSD had an estimated 124% higher use rate of outpatient physical health care services than younger patients without PTSD and also used mental health care services at a 97% higher rate (Calhoun, 2002). PTSD symptoms such as anger, irritability, and concentration difficulties often interfere with medical treatments and contribute to problems with noncompliance. In a study of HMO enrollees, Walker and colleagues (1999) found that sexually abused women had higher primary and outpatient costs and more frequent emergency department visits in comparison with women who were not abused. Similar trends have been found in individuals who developed PTSD following exposure to a natural disaster (Abrahams, Price, Whitlock and Williams, 1976; Adams and Adams, 1984; Bennet, 1968).

CURRENT PSYCHOTHERAPY OUTCOME RESEARCH

Many treatments have been utilized for PTSD sufferers including hypnotherapy (Brom, Kleber and Defes, 1989; Jiranek, 1993; Kingsbury, 1988; Leung, 1994; MacHovec, 1983; Peebles, 1989; Spiegel, 1988, 1989), psychodynamic psychotherapy (Bart, 1975; Grigsby, 1987; Marmar, Horowitz, Weiss, Wilner and Kaltreider, 1988; Roth, Dye and Lebowitz, 1988), eye movement desensitization and reprocessing (Montgomery and Ayllon, 1994; Shapiro, 1995, 1991, 1989a, 1989b; Wolpe and Abrams, 1991), as well as other psychosocial treatments and pharmacological treatments. Although hundreds of reports of various treatments for the aftermath of exposure to a traumatic stressor have been published, few systematic empirical studies which provide empirical evidence for the efficacy of a treatment exist. The majority of published studies of PTSD treatment are case reports which offer support for almost every psychosocial and pharmacological treatment available. Nonetheless, the studies focusing on systematic testing of treatment efficacy for PTSD primarily focus on three treatment approaches: psychodynamic psychotherapy, pharmacotherapy, and Cognitive Behavioral therapy.

PSYCHODYNAMIC THERAPY

Psychodynamic psychotherapy is a widely used treatment approach for PTSD in inpatient and outpatient settings. Most of the literature on psychodynamic therapy consists of case studies and a few attempts at systematic empirical studies. Horowitz has perhaps provided the most theoretical and empirical data regarding psychodynamic psychotherapy for the treatment of PTSD. Horowitz (1976) described the emotional reactions of traumatized individuals as the result of discrepancies between internal and external information. He stated that traumatized individuals tend to experience either denial or partial amnesia, which activate the PTSD symptom clusters of avoidance and emotional numbness (Solomon and Johnson, 2002). Horowitz's (1976) treatment approach consists of a brief dose-related psychodynamic treatment that has many similarities to cognitive-behavioral treatment.

Most of the systematic studies of psychodynamic psychotherapy tend to lack methodological rigor. In addition, the empirical studies that have been conducted on psychodynamic psychotherapy usually compare psychodynamic therapy to another form of therapy. For example, Boudewyns and colleagues (Boudewyns and Hyer, 1990; Boudewyns, Hyer, Woods, Harrison and McCranie, 1990) compared flooding (imaginal exposure) to "conventional therapy" and found significantly more inpatient treatment successes received flooding therapy. A limitation in the studies by Boudewyns and colleages (Boudewyns and Hyer, 1990; Boudewyns, Hyer, Woods, Harrison and McCranie, 1990) was that they used no blind assessments and no standardized assessments. Cooper and Clum (1989) also studied imaginal flooding as an adjunct to standard psychosocial and pharmacological treatment in 14 veterans with combat related PTSD. Results indicated addition of imaginal flooding was beneficial; flooding augmented symptoms such as nightmares by 96% versus 15% with standard treatment alone, and it augmented anxiety symptoms by 33% versus 18% with standard treatment alone. A limitation of the Cooper and Clum (1989) study was low sample size as well as a lack of methodological precision. Overall, the psychodynamic psychotherapy groups tend to be less effective at reducing distressing PTSD symptoms than other forms of treatment.

COGNITIVE-BEHAVIORAL THERAPY

A common element across successful approaches to PTSD treatment act on the emotional response syndromes of fear. Fear, a normal reaction to threat, is combination of a network of responses including feelings, thoughts, behaviors, and physiological events (Marks and Dar, 2000). Treatment focused on reducing fear may focus on one or more of the network of responses within the emotional response syndrome. The Cognitive-Behavioral Therapies (CBT) have received considerable attention and empirical support for their ability to reduce fear and other distressing symptoms in PTSD sufferers (Foa et al,. 1999; Foa and Rothbaum, 1998; Foa, Rothbaum, Riggs and Murdock, 1991).

Cognitive-Behavioral Treatment of Post-Traumatic Stress Disorder may include a variety of treatment strategies including exposure procedures, cognitive therapy, stress inoculation training, and their combinations. CBT often involves a relaxation/meditation component, the identification and monitoring of negative thoughts, the evaluation of those thoughts by Socratic questioning, cognitive restructuring, and either imaginal or in vivo exposure (Marks and Dar, 2000). Some studies have suggested that dismantling strategies are necessary to determine if full CBT packages are comparable to specific cognitive therapy components. In addition, dismantling CBT components may elucidate fear reducing mechanisms.

Prolonged Exposure (PE) is a type of therapy originating from learning theory, and it has been particularly influenced by Mowrer's two-factor theory (Mowrer, 1960). In accordance with Mowrer's conceptualization, habituation of a feared stimulus is thought to occur when the fearful individual confronts feared situations, thoughts, feelings, and memories without encountering the feared aversive consequences. Many individuals with PTSD mistakenly view the process of remembering their trauma as dangerous, and spend much time actively avoiding thinking or processing the trauma. PE was designed to help patients activate their traumatic memories in order to modify the pathological aspects of the memories (Foa and Rothbaum, 1998). PE often begins with psychoeducation, and then it gradually introduces behavioral exposure, either imaginal or in vivo, to reminders of the trauma and trauma memories (Resick et al., 2002).

The studies that have investigated exposure therapy for PTSD in veterans have generally produced positive results. Most of the treatments, however, failed to include a control group, lacked methodological precision, lacked sufficient power, or had other limitations. In addition, exposure therapy has not consistently demonstrated a superiority on a broader range of functioning (e.g. somatic complaints, quality of life, health care utilization). For example, Keane and colleagues (1989) compared implosive therapy (imaginal exposure) to a wait list control in 24 Vietnam veterans with a diagnosis of PTSD. The authors found that treatment seemed to reduce fear (40% reduction in flooding group vs. 33% increase in controls) and depression (39% and 0% reduction, respectively) as well as some symptoms of PTSD. The Keane (1989) study primarily focused on symptom reduction. It also had several methodological flaws and limitations, such as a lack of blind evaluators, and an inability to determine conclusively whether the improvements noted represented true treatment effect or a result of therapist or patient expectancies. Boudewyns and colleagues (Boudewyns and Hyer,

1990; Boudewyns, Hyer, Woods, Harrison and McCranie, 1990) published two reports on Exposure Therapy for veterans with PTSD. They compared flooding (imaginal exposure) to "conventional therapy" and found significantly more inpatient treatment successes received flooding therapy. A limitation in the studies by Boudewyns and colleages (Boudewyns and Hyer, 1990; Boudewyns, Hyer, Woods, Harrison and McCranie, 1990) was that they used no blind assessments and no standardized assessments. In addition, this study also focused on symptom reduction and failed to assess other areas of functioning. Cooper and Clum (1989) also studied imaginal flooding as an adjunct to standard psychosocial and pharmacological treatment in 14 veterans with combat related PTSD. Results indicated addition of imaginal flooding was beneficial; flooding augmented symptoms such as nightmares by 96% versus 15% with standard treatment alone, and it augmented anxiety symptoms by 33% versus 18% with standard treatment alone. A limitation of the Cooper and Clum (1989) study was low sample size as well as a lack of methodological precision. Thus, the contribution of exposure therapy to the improvement of symptoms and broader areas of functioning in veterans s unclear.

Foa and colleagues (Foa and Rothbaum, 1989) have suggested that PE alone can be considered the treatment of choice for PTSD, but PE alone may not be suitable for all trauma victims, especially veterans of war. When the major problem lies in the dysfunctional thoughts that produce guilt and shame or debilitating anger, cognitive restructuring may be an effective technique (Foa and Rothbaum, 1998). Cognitive restructuring emerged from cognitive theory, which was originally developed for the treatment of depression by Beck and colleagues (e.g. Beck et al., 1985). Cognitive Therapy, and cognitive restructuring in particular, emphasizes the influence of core assumptions and beliefs as mediating the development and maintenance of pathological anxiety. Cognitive restructuring involves psychoeducation and teaching patients how their thoughts, feelings, and behaviors are linked in order to identify dysfunctional thoughts and common thinking errors. Other goals in a cognitive restructuring treatment program include teaching the patient more rational responses and methods of reappraising beliefs and attributions about themselves, the trauma, and the world. After being helped to identify negative automatic thoughts, the therapist may use Socratic questioning to challenge the thoughts and may ask the patient to monitor the thoughts with a daily diary. The patient is then taught to appraise and modify distorted beliefs about themselves, the traumatic event, the world, and the future. Patients are routinely given homework to facilitate the cognitive restructuring approach.

Most studies comparing cognitive restructuring and prolonged exposure have been conducted on sexual assault survivors (Foa, Hearst-Ikeda, Perry, 1995; Foa, Rothbaum, Riggs, Murdock, 1991; Krakow, Hollifield, Johnston, Koss, Schrader, Warner, Tandberg, Lauriello, McBride, Cutchen, Cheng, Emmons, Germain, Melendrez, Sandoval and Prince, 2001; Resick, Nishith, Weaver, Astin, Feuer, 2002; Resick and Schnicke, 1992). To date, only one controlled study has been conducted by Marks and colleagues (1998) in which cognitive-behavioral treatment of four groups of outpatients with chronic PTSD resulting from various traumatic stressors were compared. Marks and colleagues compared exposure therapy, cognitive restructuring, exposure combined with cognitive restructuring, and relaxation training, and looked at some predictors of treatment outcome. The authors found that cognitive restructuring group, the exposure group, and the combined group were more effective in reducing PTSD symptoms than the relaxation group; however, no major differences between the three treatments were found. The authors also found that there were no differences between types of treatment on the following moderator variables: gender, PTSD duration, or whether the initiating trauma was personal or impersonal.

Although it has been established that CBT is an effective treatment for PTSD (Resick, 2001), research is still necessary to establish what specific CBT techniques is most effective for specific populations. In her review of the literature for Cognitive Therapy for PTSD, Resick (2001) has stated "It is too early to say whether cognitive therapy is effective across all trauma populations or whether cognitive therapy alone is as effective as therapy combined with exposure."

SPIRITUAL AND RELIGIOUS INTERVENTIONS IN PTSD

Contemporary psychotherapy is of integral nature. It is a part of integral medicine and of the integral viewpoint in science. There can be no doubt about it, sub-specialisation deepens the insight, simultaneously narrowing the efficiency of any activity. Integration is mandatory in any treatment approach of PTSD. Biological, psychological, social, and religious standpoints of an individual make the appropriate form of that approach. A comprehensive treatment approach need to be directed towards this integral way of thinking (Gruden, Gruden and Gruden-Pokupec, 1999). Trauma affects all levels of a person's physical, mental, social and spiritual being. When the spiritual component is recognized and acknowledged, it resonates with PTSD patients and additional treatment possibilities emerge for their recovery (McBride, 2002). The events of September 11, 2001 triggered a widespread national response that was two-fold: a posttraumatic stress reaction and an increase in attendance in religious services and practices immediately following the tragic events. A research study on religious coping, illustrated the benefits of seeking religious comfort for managing postdisaster stress responses (Meisenhelder and Chandler, 2000).

And although religious psychotherapy is not conventionally practiced in the U.S.A., the effects of religious and spiritual beliefs on the treatment and improvement of PTSD has been reported in the literature (Khouzam and Kissmeyer, 1997; Khouzam, 2001; Fontana and Rosenheck, 2004).

In a recent research it was found that one of the most pervasive effects of traumatic exposure is the challenge that people experience to their existential beliefs concerning the meaning and purpose of life. Particularly at risk is the strength of their religious faith and the comfort that they derive from it. In this study the interrelationships among veterans' traumatic exposure, PTSD, guilt, social functioning, change in religious faith, and continued use of mental health services were examined (Fontana and Rosenheck, 2004). The data were drawn from studies of outpatient (N=554) and inpatient (N=831) specialized treatment of PTSD in Department of Veterans Affairs programs. Structural equation modeling was used to estimate the parameters of the model and evaluate its goodness of fit to the data. The model achieved acceptable goodness of fit and suggested that veterans' experiences of killing others and failing to prevent death weakened their religious faith, both directly and as mediated by feelings of guilt. Weakened religious faith and guilt each contributed independently to more extensive use of VA mental health services. Severity of PTSD symptoms and social functioning played no significant role in the continued use of mental health services. This research concluded that veterans' pursuit of mental health services appears to be driven more by their guilt and the wekening of the relisious faith rather than by the severity of their PTSD symptoms or their deficits in social functioning. The specificity of these effects on service use suggests that a primary motivation of veterans' continuing pursuit of treatment may be their search for a meaning and purpose to their traumatic experiences. This possibility raises the broader issue of whether spirituality should be more cental to the treatment of PTSD, either in the form of a greater role for pastoral counseling or of a wider inclusion of spiritual issues in traditional psychotherapy for PTSD.

In a case report individualized treatment which incorporated spiritual awakening was found to be beneficial in addressing survivor guilt in a Vietnam was veteran with PTSD and major depression (Khouzam and Kissmeyer, 1997).

With the current shift to include positive outcomes of trauma, a research was designed to explore factors that allow growth to occur. Structural equation modeling was used to test a model for understanding posttraumatic growth. This research concluded that facilitation of posttraumatic growth is crucial to all helping professions (Cadell, Regehr and Hemsworth, 2003).

The therapeutic purposes and effects of specially designed ceremonies in the treatment of persons with posttraumatic stress disorder were evaluated in Vietnam war combat veterans. The ceremonies were compartmentalized to review the trauma experiences and , to provide symbolic enactments of transformation of previously shattered relationships, and reestablish conncections among family members and society in general. The ceremonies focused on the themes of separation from and return to the family, forgiveness of the living, and releasing the dead. The rituals and ceremonies were found to be highly efficient vehicles for accessing and containing intense emotions evoked by traumatic experiences. The Vietnam war combat veterans involved with their families in these ceremonies considered them to be the most effective components of PTSD treatment (Johnson, Feldman, Lubin and Southwick, 1995).

PTSD AND ITS PHARMACOLOGICAL TREATMENT

Almost every group of psychotropic medications have been tried either in double -blind placebo control studies, open trials and in case studies

The psychopharmacological treatment of PTSD, regardless of the specific medications used, generally requires a longer treatment period than in some other psychiatric conditions. (Jacobs and Dalenberg,1998) High doses, and a combination of various agents may be needed for targeting the complex symptoms of PTSD.

Selection of medication depends upon specific symptoms and the coexisting psychiatric conditions (Eriksson and Lundin, 1996). Symptoms of PTSD which may respond to medications include anger, hostility, violent impulses, anxiety, poor concentration, sleep disturbances, nightmares, violent dreams, depressed mood, recurrent intrusive recollections (flashbacks) and avoidance behaviors (DSM-IV TR) (American Psychiatric Association,2000).

The Pharmacological treatment of PTSD include pharmacological treatment of co-morbid psychiatric conditions if present, as well as treatment of PTSD in the absence of co-morbid psychiatric conditions.

Pharmacological agents for the treatment of co-morbid psychiatric conditions should be carefully selected to complement other medications in reducing additional effects of PTSD symptoms (Roth, Newman, Pelcovitz, et al, 1997; Yehuda, Kahana, Schmeidler, et al, 1995).

Patients without psychiatric comorbidity may still often require multiple pharmacological agents in order to achieve relief from specific groups of PTSD symptoms. The various pharmacological agents that have been used for the treatment of PTSD are summarized in the following section.

Antidepressants

The most widely used pharmacological agents include:

Selective (specific) Serotonin Reuptake Inhibitors (SSRIs)
The first two medications that received the US Federal Drug Administration(FDA) approval for PTSD treatment were the SSRIs antidepressants sertraline and paroxetine (Brady, Pearlstein, Asnis, 2000). Although SSRIs have achieved significant amelioration of PTSD symptoms,they are not always effective in all patients. Future research should then attempt to be more specific in finding which serotonergic agents could produce better results in most patients (Friedman, 2002).

The SSRIs are selective inhibitors of serotonin reuptake at the presynaptic terminal, leading to an increase in the concentration of 5-hydroxytryptamine (5-HT) in the synaptic cleft (Friedman, 2002). In general, SSRIs effectively manage target symptoms of PTSD including intrusive thoughts, flashbacks, hyperarousal, irritability, angry outbursts, difficulty with concentration and associated depression and anxiety. SSRIs are also used for the treatment of dissociative symptoms(Friedman, 2002; Reich, 1999) .Table 1 outlines some of the various SSRIs and dosages. About 50% of patients will experience some adverse effects to the SSRIs including gastrointestinal disturbances (GI), nausea or diarrhea, headache, restlessness and sexual dysfunction. Although these represent class effects, some distinct side effects do differentiate the individual SSRIs (Labbate, 1999).GI disturbances are more common with sertraline, somnolence and dry mouth are more common with paroxetine, initial restlessness is associated with fluoxetine, sedation is more common with fluvoxamine, and nausea is frequent with citalopram. SSRIs are capable of inhibiting the hepatic cytochrome P450 11D6 isoenzyme system. Knowledge of other medications affected by this enzyme system will allow the prescriber to predict potential drug-drug interactions. The use of SSRIs can be encouraged since they are relatively simple in their dosage, safe and they yield favorable outcomes for many patients.

Table 1. The Selective (specific) Serotonin Reuptake Inhibitors (SSRIs)

SSRI	Starting dose (mg/day)	Average dose (mg/day)	Maximum dose (mg/day)
Citalopram Celexa®	20	20-40	60
Escitalopram Lexapro®	20	10-20	40
Fluoxetine Prozac®	10-20	20-50	80
Fluvoxamine Luvox®	50	100-250	300
Paroxetine Paxil®	10-20	20-50	60
Paroxetine CR=Paxil CR®	25	25-60	62.5
Sertraline Zoloft®	25-50	50-150	200

Tricyclic Antidepressants (TCAs)

The TCAs have documented some efficacy in the treatment of several PTSD symptoms including intrusive thoughts, flashbacks, anxiety and panic-related hyperarousal, loss of interests, sleep disturbances, irritability and depressed mood affecting concentration and contributing to feelings of shame and guilt. (Othmer, Othmer and Othmer, 1998) The daily average dose of amitryptiline is 150mg, of nortriptyline is a 100mg, while both doxepin and imipramine daily average dose is 200mg. TCAs produce their therapeutic effects largely by inhibiting norepinephrine (NE) and 5-HT reuptake in the central nervous system (CNS). They also exert effects on other neurotransmitter systems including adrenergic, histaminergic, muscarinic and cholinergic receptors, so both their therapeutic and adverse effects are associated with their actions. Adverse effects of the TCAs include sedation, blurred vision, dry mouth, constipation, urinary retention, postural hypotension, tachycardia, cognitive dysfunction and weight gain. (Othmer, Othmer and Othmer, 1998; Friedma, 2002). Interaction with other sedating and anticholinergic medications potentiates their adverse effects (Kaplan and Sadock, 1998). Prior to the advance of newer antidepressants (especially the SSRIs), TCAs were first-line agents in treating PTSD, now they are considered secondary agents because of their potentially life-threatening cardiotoxicity, especially following overdose attempts.

Trazodone

Trazodone is an antidepressant with anxiolytic properties, chemically unrelated to the TCAs (Viola, Ditzler and Batzer,1997). Its mechanism of action is not fully understood, it is believed to inhibit 5-HT reuptake and to act as a 5-HT2 partial antagonist. Trazodone can ameliorate chronic insomnia and decrease the intensity of nightmares. It is also effective in the management of aggressive behaviors. (Viola, Ditzler and Batzer,1997). Trazodone dosages can vary depending on patients' response with a maximum daily dose of 600mg. Although it possesses minor anticholinergic effects, trazodone is quite sedating, can cause orthostatic hypotension and in a small percentage of male patients, causes priaprism requiring surgical intervention. Trazodone is relatively safe medication in normal physically healthy individuals and is considered to be -lethal unless combined with other sedative or hypnotic medications and alcohol or drugs during intentional and unintentional overdose.

Atypical (Novel) Antidepressants

Antidepressants with atypical modes of action can also be considered for the treatment of PTSD in patients unable to tolerate the adverse effects of TCAs, trazodone and the SSRIs. The role of these newer antidepressants in treating PTSD has not yet been fully studied. These agents, include nefazodone, venlafaxine, mirtazapine and bupropion.

Nefazodone

Nefazodone is structurally related to trazodone, acting as a 5-HT2 antagonist inhibiting the reuptake of both NE and 5-HT (Dopheide, Stimmel and Yi,1995). Nefazodone can be used for decreasing intrusive thoughts, flashbacks, depression, anxiety, panic symptoms, avoidance behaviors, irritability and angry outbursts. Nefazodone can also be beneficial in decreasing hyperarousal, hypervigilance and startle reactions. Nefazodone dose should not exceed a maximum daily dose of 400mg. Its most common adverse effects include asthenia, somnolence, nausea, constipation and dry mouth. It is less likely than trazodone to cause orthostatic hypotension or priaprism.(Dopheide, Stimmel and Yi, 1995).Because nefazodone is a potent inhibitor of cytochrome P450-3A4, it is contraindicated with the commonly used antihistamines astemizole or terfenadine, and in patients treated with cisapride (which can lead to fatal cardiac arrhythmias). Nefazodone also increases the plasma levels of alprazolam, triazolam, haloperidol and digoxin, and can decrease the plasma level of propranolol. Nefazodone association with cases of life- threatening hepatic failure has been added in its prescription package,so patients with any degree of liver function impairment should not take nefazodone (Lader,1996). The manufacturer of nefazodone has recently decided to no longer market this medication in Europe or in the USA.

Venlafaxine

This antidepressant inhibits both NE and 5-HT uptake; it is also a weak inhibitor of dopamine (DA) reuptake. It can be used for symptomatic relief of severe depressive symptoms associated with PTSD, the control of anxiety, phobic reactions and panic symptoms (Khouzam, Mahdesian and Donnelly, 1998). The maximum daily dosage of venlafaxine is 225mg. Side-effects include nausea, headache, nervousness, anxiety, anorexia, sweating and insomnia. At high doses, a small percentage of patients experience increased diastolic blood pressure; a smaller percentage may have increased heart rate and serum cholesterol levels. Venlafaxine, when used as recommended,has no effect on any of the cytochrome P450 isoenzymes (Lader, 1996). Venlafaxine is available in tablet formulation and extended-release capsules. The tablets and the extended-release capsules are equally potent, and persons stabilized on one form can be switched from one form to another at equivalent dose.

Mirtazapine

This antidepressant is a tetracyclic compound acting as a potent antagonist of 5-HT2 and 5-HT3 receptors. It is also a potent antagonist of histamine (H1) receptors and a moderate antagonist of muscarinic receptors (De Mello, 1999). It's sedating properties can be beneficial in sleep disturbances and in decreasing hyperarousal in PTSD (Hageman, Andersen and Jorgensen, 2001). Mirtazapine can also be an alternative medication for comorbid treatment-resistant depression. Mirtazapine's maximum daily dose is 60mg. The main side effects of mirtazapine are somnolence, dizziness and increased appetite with weight gain. It can interfere with cognitive and motor performance because of its sedating effects. As with other tetracyclics, there is a risk of agranulocytosis, so patients should pay particular attention to any flu-like or other symptoms suggesting infection (De Mello, 1999).

Bupropion

The precise neurochemical mechanism of action of bupropion is still not fully understood but is known to affect noradrenergic and dopaminergic systems. Its effects on treating PTSD symptoms are not well known, but it has shown some beneficial effects in patients with comorbid depression and anxiety who could not tolerate adverse effects to other antidepressants (Friedman and Southwick, 1995). Bupropion is available in tablets and sustained- release tablet, the total daily dose should not exceed 450 mg of immediate release formulation or 400mg of sustained release form. The main adverse effects of bupropion include headache, nausea, agitation and insomnia. Bupropion may be associated with the risk of inducing seizures in doses exceeding 300mg, and it is absolutely contraindicated in patients with seizure disorders and in patients with anorexia and bulimia. (Friedman & Southwick,

1995). Bupropion is marketed under two different trade names; Wellbutrin which is indicated for treatment of depression and Zyban which is indicated as an adjuctive pharmacological agent for treatment of smoking cessation.

Monoamine Oxidase Inhibitors (MAOIs)

The MAOIs, are a class of medications that block the degradation of the DA, NE and 5-HT. Phenelzine was found effective in decreasing intrusive thoughts and avoidant behaviors (Hageman, Andersen and Jorgensen, 2001). It also shows effect in treating atypical depressive symptoms characterized by hypersomnia, hyperphagia and comorbid symptoms of anxiety. Although phenelzine's maximum daily dose is 60mg, some patients may tolerate up to 90mg daily dose. MAOIs are associated with anticholinergic side effects including dry mouth, urinary retention, constipation and blurred vision. They can also cause orthostatic hypotension and sexual dysfunction. Because of their irreversible inhibition of MAOI's, they require a tyramine free diet and can cause a fatal hypertensive crisis if ingested with food containing tyramine (Lader, 1996) The potential for drug-drug and alcohol interactions with MAOIs precludes their use in PTSD patients with substance abuse comorbidity.(Friedman, Donnelly and Mellman, 2003) and in patients using a wide range of other medications, including antidepressants and pain medication such as meperidine (Stack, Rogers and Linter, 1988).

Mood Stabilizers

The mood stabilizers, lithium, valproic acid, and lamotrigine,have been used in patients with prominent symptoms of hyperarousal, hyperactivity, hostility, irritability and angry outbursts (Friedman, Donnelly and Mellman, 2003). These agents can be added in case of partial response to the antidepressants or used as first line treatment for patients having both PTSD and comorbid bipolar disorder (Jacobs and Dallenberg, 1998)

Lithium

Lithium is a monovalent cation with antimanic, antipsychotic, and antidepressant activity, that alters sodium transport in the nerve and muscle cells, and affectings a shift toward intraneuronal catecholamine metabolism (Lader,1996). Lithium decreases NE reuptake and increases serotonin receptor sensitivity. Side effects of lithium include fine hand tremor, polydipsia, polyuria, nausea, vomiting, drowsiness, muscle weakness, poor coordination, giddiness, ringing or buzzing in the ears and blurred vision. Lithium affects the thyroid, so monitoring of thyroid function tests is necessary. Lithium interacts with other medications including haloperidol, chlorpromazine, TCAs and calcium channel blockers. The angiotensin enzyme (ACE) inhibitors and nonsteroidal anti-inflammatory agents (NSAIDs) can lead to an increase in the serum levels leading to lithium toxicity. Due to its effects on the kidneys lithium should be judicially administered with loop diuretics and should not be given with a salt-free diet, to prevent the development of hyponatremia (Friedman & Southwick, 1999). Due to the narrow therapeutic/toxic lithium levels, serum lithium levels should be monitored at frequent intervals.

Valproic Acid and Derivatives

This group includes valproic acid, sodium valproate (the sodium salt) and divalproex sodium. These anticonvulsants and mood stabilizers increase the levels of γ-aminobutyric acid (GABA) as well as increasing GABA receptor site sensitivity. The rationale for using them in PTSD is related to limbic kindling (Post, Weiss and Smith, 1995). It is hypothesized that increased GABA levels interfere with the kindling process, thus diminishing the clinical symptoms of flashbacks, nightmares and hyperarousal. Side effects include GI upset and throat or mouth irritation, which occur if the tablets or capsules are chewed. Patients who have difficulty swallowing may benefit from the syrup or the sprinkle forms. Indigestion, sedation, sleepiness, weakness, fatigue, skin rash, diarrhea, stomach cramps, constipation, Valproic acid can lead to elevation of liver enzymes, thus requiring regular liver funtion monitoring in PTSD patients,and problems with muscle coordination and weight gain can also occur (Friedman et al., 2003).

Lamotrigine

This anticovulsant medication has been recently approved by the FDA for treatment of Bipolar mood disorder Type I especially in treating the depressed phase of this illness, has shown effects in reducing intrusive thoughts, avoidance and the numbing symptoms of PTSD (Hertzberg, Butterfield, Feldman,et al,1999) Lamotrigine has anticovulsant effects similar to carbamazepine, it also modestly increase the serotonin plasma concentration and is a weak inhibitor of of serotonin 5-HT 3 receptors. It also exhibits an antipsychotic effects in patients with epilepsy (Petroff, Hyder, Rothman and Mattson, 2001).

The most reported adverse effects that warranted an FDA warning is lamotrigine association with the development of potentially life-threatening skin conditions, such as toxic epiepidermal necrolysis and Steven-Johnson syndrome which occur in 0.1 percent of adults and 1 to 2 percent of children (Petroff et al., 2001).

Anticonvulsants

Carbamazepine

Carbamazepine is an anticonvulsant that seems to reduce polysynaptic responses and block post-tetanic potentiation (Viola, DitzlerBatzer, et al, 1997). It can be useful in some PTSD patients with sleep disturbances because it can decrease sleep latency and is non-disruptive to rapid eye movement sleep (REM). It is also effective in treating agitation, rage attacks, poor impulse control, violent behavior and angry outbursts.. According to the "kindling" model, periodic brain stimuli that are initially too low to produce stimulation of the limbic system may progressively induce bioelectrical changes ultimately leading to abnormal limbic sensitization manifested by periodic mood swings, agitation and violence (Post, Weiss and Smith,1995).

Carbamazepine has been reported to modulate the kindling effects which have been documented to occur in PTSD (Iancu, Rosen, and Moshe, 2003). Carbamazepine side effects include drowsiness, dizziness or blurred vision. Carbamazepine is a hepatic enzyme inducer which can initially decrease its own plasma levels and influence the plasma levels of other drugs that are affected by the same hepatic pathways. Severe adverse effects of carbamazepine involve hepatotoxicity and the development of blood dyscrasias,requiring periodic monitoring of liver function tests and blood counts. Additionally, it is important to monitor serum carbamazepine levels at intervals of every three to six months regardless of patient's stability and absence of adverse effects (Khouzam and Donnelly, 2001).

Other Anticonvulsants

The approved antiseizure medications, gabapentin, and topiramate have been documented in case studies and used in the treatment of PTSD patients, however, their usage have not yet been fully studied in larger sample of case controlled studies(Friedman, 2002; Petroff et al, 2001).

Antianxiety Medications

Antidepressant medications have useful anxiolytic properties, (Stahl, 1999) but some PTSD patients may require the adjunctive use of antianxiety agents to treat acute, severe and debilitating symptoms of fear, panic, avoidance, hyperarousal, hypervigilance, startle reactions and sleep disturbances. (Friedman, Donnelly and Melleman, 2003) This section will focus on the benzodiazepines and buspirone.

In general, benzodiazepines should be discouraged from being used in the PTSD population due to their potential for inducing physiological dependence, inter-dose rebound or breakthrough anxiety symptoms. Primary care providers need to avoid the routine use of benzodiazepines in PTSD patients, considering that antidepressants have favorable effects on both anxiety and depression.

Benzodiazepines

The benzodiazepines are widely used as anxiolytic agents that warrant careful consideration in the treatment of PTSD. Abuse potential, along with an exacerbations of PTSD symptoms during their withdrawal, limits long-term use. In selecting benzodiazepines, the clinician should be aware of any comorbid substance abuse disorder and consider the possibility of paradoxical disinhibition which can precipitate impulsive and hostile behaviors. The depressive symptoms frequently emerge during PTSD treatment have also been associated with benzodiazepines (Braun, Greenberg, Dasberg and Lerer,1990). Despite their potential usefulness, considerable research is needed to discern the role and impact of benzodiazepines on the overall pharmacological treatment of PTSD (Gelpin, Bonne, Peri, Brandes and Shlev,1996).

Buspirone

Buspirone is a nonbenzodiazepine anxiolytic. It has a high affinity for serotonin 5-HT1A receptors. It has no significant affinity for benzodiazepine receptors and does not affect GABA bindings. Buspirone has moderate affinity for D2 dopamine receptors and appears to act as a presynaptic dopamine agonist. Because of its efficacy in the management of anxiety disorders it can play a role in the treatment of hyperarousal and startling responses (Khouzam and Emes, 2002). Buspirone does not cause sedation or cognitive impairment; it can cause dizziness, nausea, headache, fatigue, nervousness, light-headedness and excitement. PTSD patients need to be alerted to the possibility of these side effects early in treatment so as not to interpret these effects as an aggravation of preexisting symptoms. Buspirone has been reported as effective in the management of the SSRIs induced sexual dysfunction (Clayton, Warnock, Kornstein, et al, 2004).

Antipsychotic Medications

Traditionally, conventional antipsychotics were generally characterized as being irrelevant in the treatment of PTSD due to their adverse effects and potential for inducing tardive dyskinesia (TD) (Butterfield and Becker, 2002). The recent introduction and availability of newer atypical antipsychotics which pose a much lower risk of side effects and TD, however, now make them useful adjunctive therapeutic agents in the treatment of PTSD, especially in treating comorbid hallucinations and delusions (associated with suspiciousness and paranoia) (Khouzam, 2000). Irritability, nightmares and vivid sensory flashbacks withauditory, visual, olfactory and tactile hallucinations, although possibly related to episodes of dissociation and reexperiencing of actual traumatic events, might respond to a short course of treatment with antipsychotics. The association between PTSD and bipolar disorder may also indicate the need for adjunctive use of antipsychotics (Khouzam and Donnelly, 2001). The risk of extrapyramidal side effects (EPS), tardive dyskinesia (TD) and worsening of anhedonia was a major obstacle to using antipsychotics in PTSD . With the advancement of the atypical antipsychotics, however, these risks have markedly decreased. Atypical antipsychotics can be considered for brief low-dose therapy targeting specific symptoms (Hageman, Andersen and Jorgensen, 2001).

Adrenergic Medications

Adrenergic abnormalities are well-established in PTSD research,such knowledge has spurred some adrenergic medications trials. These agents primarily act by decreasing autonomic hyperactivity in PTSD patients which manifests as general anxiety, hyperarousal, hypervigilance and startle reactions. These symptoms may respond to the judicial use of agents like clonidine, guanfacine, propranolol and prazosin.

Clonidine and Guanfacine
These α 2-adrenergic agonists have shown to reduce symptoms of hyperarousal and to sometimes potentiate the effects of TCAs. The most common side effects are dry mouth, drowsiness and sedation. Constipation, dizziness, headache and fatigue are also common but usually diminish within 4-6 weeks (Khouzam and Donnelly, 2001; Horrigan, 1996).

Propranolol
This is a β adrenergic blocker with demonstrated anxiolytic effects in decreasing symptoms of hyperarousal, restlessness, startle reactions, and autonomic hyperactivity. It is usually given in a daily divided dose of 120-160mg. Other beta-adrenergic blockers like atenolol and nadolol have been also been reported as beneficial. The availability of long-acting propranolol (Inderal LA®) in once daily dosage offers the advantage of convenient scheduling and better compliance (Famularo, Kinscherff and Fenton, 1988; Vaiva et al, 2003). The main side effects of the beta-adrenergic blockers include tiredness, weakness, bradycardia, dizziness, breathing difficulty, bronchospasm, sleeplessness and male

impotence.maintained on beta-adrenergic blockers require frequent monitoring of blood pressure and pulse rate for early detection of hypotension and bradycardia.

Prazosin
This Alpha1-adrenergic antagonist have been reported to ameliorate nightmares in combat veterans suffering from PTSD (Raskind, Dobie, Kanter, et al, 2000).

Sedative Hypnotics

The antihistamines and the hypnotic agents zolpidem and zaleplon, can be used as adjunctive hypnotic agents in the management of chronic sleep disturbances associated with PTSD.

Antihistaminic Agents

Hydroxyzine, diphenhydramine and cyproheptadine can be temporarily used to induce drowsiness and sleep.Their main side effects include drowsiness, anticholinergic effects like dry mouth, constipation, urinary retention, exacerbation of asthma and breathing difficulties. Additive CNS depressant effects may occur when antihistaminics are combined with other sedating pharmacological agents.(Friedman, 2002) Some reports, however, suggest that this class of medications might cause stimulation and hyperexcitability in the PTSD population (Clark, Calais, Qualls, et al, 1999).

Hypnotic Agents

Zolpidem
Zolpidem is an imidazopyridine chemically unrelated to benzodiazepines, barbiturates or other hypnotic agents, but selectively binds to the benzodiazepine type I site. The usual dose is 10mg immediately before bedtime. Downward adjustment of the dose may be necessary when given with other CNS depressants (Khouzam, Mahdasian and Donnelly, 1999).

Zaleplon
Zaleplon is a pyrazolopyrimidine nonbenzodiazepine hypnotic, which differentially binds to the benzodiazepine type I site (Elie, Ruther, Farr, et al, 1999).It exerts sedative, anxiolytic, muscle-relaxing and anticonvulsant properties A ten-milligram dose is recommended for adults and five milligrams for geriatric patients.

Both zolpidem and zaleplon have shown efficacy in treating short-term insomnia in both PTSD and non-PTSD patients, however, such efficacy in tracking long-term insomnia as well as other PTSD symptoms have not yet been studied (Khouzam and Donnelly, 2001).

Other Pharnacological Agents

Medications and the Opioid Systems

Numbers of reports have shown that a disregulation of the opioid systems occur in PTSD particularly in the beta-endorphin and in the methionine enkephalin level (Friedman, 2002) .It appears that that narcotic agonists and antagonists can produce clinically variable effects on the exccacerbation or amelioration of PTSD symptoms..There are pharmacological trials of using opioid antagonists like naltrxone in the treatment of PTSD and comorbid chemical dependency (Yehuda, 2000). With the current progress achieved in relationship to opid fuctioning opiod receptors and the multitude of opioid pharmacological agents, this will be an important area for future PTSD research.

Glutamatergic Systems

Research have documented that glutamatergic mechanisms involving N-methyl-D-aspartate NMDA and the non NMDA metabotropic glutamatergic modulators are altered in PTSD (Fiedman, 2002). Preclinical and clinical evidence suggests that PTSD symptoms could be alleviated following enhancement of neurotransmission mediated at the N-methyl-D-aspartate (NMDA) subtype of glutamate receptors. Research conducted on the glycine regulatory site of the NMDA receptor with the partial agonist D-cycloserine at 50 mg daily dose, showed improvement in PTSD symptoms.This finding may be a promising and relevant focus for future pharmacological interventions in PTSD (Heresco, Kremer, Javitt, et al, 2002).

Substance P

Substance P is the primary neurotransmitter in the sensory neurons and the striatonigral pathway.Based on substance P neurons anatomic distribution and their reciprocal interactions with the noradrenergic systems, it is likely that they become activated during the human stress response.Safe substance P antagonist labeled as MK-869 has been synthesized. And was found to be as effective as SSRIs antidepressant medications in alleviating PTSD symptoms (Friedman, 2002).

Research with this class of medications seems to offer possible future advances for the treatment of PTSD.

Corticotropin-Releasing Factor (CRF)

Since the entire cascade of human stress response seems to be related to the activation of CRF,the normalization of CRF functioningmay lead to therapeutic relief of PTSD symptoms.At the present time CRF antagonists are being developed and researched with the hope of being safe pharmacological agents for PTSD treatment (Yehuda, 2000).

Neuropeptide Y

The neuropeptide Y(NPY) is heavily concentrated in the brain stem, amygdala, hypothalamus and cortex. Originally NPY have been shown to stimulate appetite, however NPY enhancers are believed to function as endogenous anxiolytics. Preclinical studies have shown that injections of NPY into the central neucleus of the amygdala lead to a central anxiolytic action and attenuated the CDF actions and other stress-released peptides (Morgan, Wang, Southwick, Rasmusson, et al, 2000). Pharmacologic agents that that could promote higher NPY levels may provide protection agaist exssessive CRF secretion which could occur in PTSD.

Hypothalamic-Pituitary-Adrenocortical (HPA) Axis

In PTSD, HPA disregulation has been described as a distinctive abnormality.The profile of PTSD patients is unique because it is associated with lower cortisol levels, up-regulation of glucocorticoid receptors and supersuppression to dexamethasone. A novel and possibly effective approach to normalizing the HPA abnormality in PTSD is to attempt to down-regulate glucocorticoid receptors with prednisone or other glucocorticoid medications.This pharmacological approach is still considered experimental and has not yet been accepted as a main stream approach of treating PTSD (Friedman, 2002).

Thyroid System

Due to the fact that PTSD has sometimes been associated with excessive thyroid activities especially elevated triidothyronine (T3) and Throxine (T4), the thyroid system is of interest in the treatment of PTSD. Researcher also found a linear relationship between PTSD symptoms and free T3 levels. The increased thyroid functioning was attributed to the HPA axis activation and as a result most pharmacological interventions at this point of time focus on the normalization of HPA system rather than treating the thyroid function abnormalities (Yehuda, 2000).

PTSD MIND-BODY AND SPIRITUAL CONNECTIONS

Religious behavior varies widely among individuals. There is increasing support for the view that such individual differences can be explained by biological and genetic factors (Borg, Andree, Soderstrom and Farde, 2003). The serotonigic system may serve as a biological basis for spiritual experiences. It has been speculated that the several-fold variability in the serotonin 5-HT$_{1A}$ receptor density may explain the great variability in people's spiritual zeal (Borg, et al, 2003).

Psychological stress can alter the expression of the acetylcholinesterase gene to generate at least 3 alternative proteins that are implicated in a wide variety of normal mind-body functions, as well as pathologies. These range from early embryological development, plasticity of the brain in adulthood, posttraumatic stress disorder (PTSD), and stress-associated dysfunctions of the central nervous, endocrine, and immune systems, to age-related neuropathologies. Such s... ...duced alternative gene splicing has been proposed as a major mind-body pathway of p... ...genomics affecting the modulation of gene expression by creative psychological, s... ...ltural processes. Research are now needed to investigate how stress-induced alte... ...ing of the acetylcholinesterase gene may play a pivotal role in the deep psyc... ...f psychotherapy, meditation, spiritual rituals, and the experiencing of positi... ...tic values that have been associated with mind-body medicine connections, ...passion, beneficence, serenity, forgiveness, and gratitude (Rossi, 2004).

CONCLUSION

PTSD is a severe and chronic psychiatric condition. Because of the complexity of symptoms, no single treatment modality can effectively address all PTSD symptoms. The multidisciplinary treatment approach to PTSD treatment, needs to address the biological, psychological, social and spiritual dimensions of this condition.

A review of the recent literature indicates psychosocial approaches, and CBT in particular, are promising in that initial empirical results indicate short term and long term reduction of distressing symptoms. Future research focusing on dismantling strategies may provide valuable information regarding what components of psychosocial treatments are most beneficial in reducing PTSD symptoms and improving quality of life.

Pharmacological interventions are also effective for symptomatic relief of PTSD. Psychopharmacological agents can be beneficial in the management of other comorbid psychiatric conditions.

Given the unique pathophysiology of PTSD, future medications for its treatment need to be designed and selected to address the psychobiological abnormalities associated with this condition. Research that addresses PTSD-related human stress response abnormalities may provide valuable informations about appropriate biological treatment of PTSD. Future research need to be conducted with newer pharmacological agents that are PTSD specific rather than medications , that were orifinally designed as antidepressants, anxiolytics,mood stabilizers,, anticonvulsants, antipsychotics, adrenergic agents or sedative hypnotics.

Interventions related to the psychosocial impact of PTSD have also yielded important findings about the importance of incorporating the religious and spiritual dimensions in diagnosing and treating PTSD.

It is hoped that this review will provide the latest informations and research findings necessary for the initiation and the maintenance treatment of PTSD.

AKNOWLEDGEMENTS

The authors are thankful to Dr Avak Howsepian for his inspiring remarks , Drs Nestor Manzano, Craig Campbell, Scott Ahles, William Cahill and Geoffrey Twitchell for their ongoing academic support, Mr Alan Perry for his administrative leadership, Mr. Leonard D. Williams for his encouragement, Ms. Emma E.A. Nichols for her technical input and Mr Javier Garza for his computer assistance.

REFERENCES

American Psychiatric Association *The diagnostic and statistical manual of mental disorders (4th edition)*. Text Revision DSM-IV TR (2000) Washington, DC: American Psychiatric Association.

Bartzokis G., Liberman, R.P. and Hierholzer, R.: Behavior therapy in groups. In Kutash, I.L. and Wolf, A. (eds): *Group Psychotherapist's Handbook: Contemporary Theory and Technique*. New York: Columbia University Press, 1990.

Beck, A.T. and Steer, R.A. (1993). *Beck Anxiety Inventory manual*. San Antonio, TX: Psychological Corporation.

Beck, A.T., Steer, R.A., (1987). *Beck Depression Inventory Manual*. San Antonio: The Psychological Corporation.

Beck, A.T., Ward, C.H., Mendelson, M., Mock, J., & Erbaugh, J. (1961). An inventory for measuring depression. *Archives of General Psychiatry*, 4:561-571.

Blake, D.D., Weathers F.W., Nagy L.M., Kaloupek D.G., Gusman F.D., Charney D.S., Keane T.M. (1995) The development of a Clinician-Administered PTSD Scale. *Journal of Traumatic Stress,* 8:75-90.

Borg, J., Andree, B., Soderstrom, H., and Farde, L. (2003). The serotonin system and spiritual experiences. *American Journal of Psychiatry*, 160:1065-1969.

Boscarino, J.A. (1997). Diseases Among Men 20 Years After Exposure to Severe Stress: Implications for Clinical Research and Medical Care. *Psychosomatic Medicine*, 59:605-614.

Brady, K., Pearlstein, T., Asnis, G., et al. Efficacy and safety of sertraline treatment of posttraumatic stress disorder: A randomized controlled trial. *JAMA*. 2000;283:1837-1844.

Braun. P., Greenberg, D., Dasberg, H., Lerer, B. (1990) Core symptoms of posttraumatic stress disorder unimproved by alprazolam treatment. *Journal of Clinical Psychiatry* 51:236-238.

Brende, J.O., Dill, J.E., Dill, B. and Sibcy, G.A. (1998). Integrated diagnostic and treatment approach for the medical patient who has had psychological trauma. *Southern Medical Journal*, 92(4): 442-443.

Breslau, N., Kessler, R.C., Chilcoat, H.D., Schultz, L.R., Davis, G.C. and Andreski, P. (1998). Trauma and posttraumatic stress disorder in the community: the 1996 Detroit Area Survey of Trauma. *Archives of General Psychiatry*, 55(7): 626-632.

Butterfield M.I, Becker M.E.(2002) *Posttraumatic stress disorder in women:assessment and treatment in primary care.* 29:151-170.

Cadell, S., Regehr, C., and Becker, M.E. (2002). Posttraumatic stress disorder in women: Assessment and treatment in primary care. *Primary Care* 29:151-170.

Calhoun, P.S., Bosworth, H.B., Grambow, S.C., Dudley, T.K. and Beckham, J.C. (2002). Medical Service Utilization by Veterans Seeking Help for Posttraumatic Stress Disorder. *American Journal of Psychiatry*, 159:2081-2086.

Carver, C.S., Scheier, M.F. and Weintraub, J.K. (1989). Assessing coping strategies: a theoretically based approach. *Journal of Personal and Social Psychology*, 56(2):267-283.

Cautela, J.R. (1977). *Behavior analysis forms for clinical interventions.* Champaign, IL: Research Press.

Chiarmonte, D.R. (1997). Mind-body therapies for primary care physicians. *Primary Care*, 24(4):787-807.

Clark, R.D., Calais, L.A., Qualls, C., Brugger, R.D. and Vosburgh, T.B. Cyproheptadine treatment of nightmares associated with posttraumatic stress disorder (Letter). *J Clin Psychopharmacol.* 1999;19(5):486-487.

Clayton, A.H., Warnock, J.K., Kornstein, S.G., Pinkerton, R., Sheldon-Keller, A., and McGarvey, E.L. (2004). A placebo-controlled trial of bupropion SR as an antidote for selective serotonin reuptake inhibitor-induced sexual dysfunction. *Jounal of Clinical Psychiatry*, 65:62-67.

Dahl, S. (1989). Acute response to rape, a PTSD variant. *Acta Psychiatr Scand*, 80(suppl): 56-62.

De Mello MF. Mirtazapine effectiveness in a patient with refractory psychotic depression. *International Journal of Psychiatry in Clinical Practice.* 1999;3(2):141-142.

Derogatis, L.R. *SCL-90-R Administration, Scoring, and Procedures Manual*, Third Ed. Minneapolis: National Computer Systems, Inc. 1994

Dolpheide, J.A., Stimmel, G.L., Yi, D.D. Focus on nefazodone: A serotonergic drug for major depression. *Hospital Formulary*. 1995;30(4):205-212.

Elie, R., Ruther, E., Farr, I., Emilien, G., Salinas, E. (1999) Sleep latency is shortened during 4 weeks of treatment with zaleplon, a novel nonbenzodiazepine hypnotic. *Journal of Clinical Psychiatry*. 60:534-544.

Endicott, J., Spitzer, R.L., Fleiss, J.L., and Cohen, J. (1976). The Global Assessment Scale: A procedure for measuring overall severity of psychiatric disturbance. *Archives of General Psychiatry*, 33.

Famularo, R., Kinscherff, R., Fenton, T. (1988). Propranolol treatment for childhood posttraumatic stress disorder,acute type.A pilot study. *American Journal of Disease of Children*, 142:1244-1247.

Foa, E.B. & Rothbaum, B.O. (1998). *Treating the trauma of rape: cognitive behavioral therapy for PTSD*. New York: Guilford Press.

Fontana, A. and Rosenheck, R. (2004) Trauma, Change in Strength of Religious Faith, and Mental Health Service Use Among Veterans Treated for PTSD. *J Nerv Ment Dis*. 192: 579-584.

Friedman M.J. (2002). Future pharmacotherapy for post-traumatic stress disorder: Prevention and treatment. *Psychiatric Clinics of North America*, 25:427-441

Friedman, M.J., Donnelley, C.L., Mellman, T.A. (2003) Pharmacotherapy for PTSD, *Psychiatric Annals*, 33:57-62.

Friedman, M.J., Southwick, S.M. Towards pharmacotherapy for post-traumatic stress disorder. In: Friedman MJ, Charney DS, Deutch AY, eds. *Neurobiological and clinical consequences of stress: From Normal Adaptation to PTSD*. Philadelphia: Lippincott-Raven; pp, 465-481, 1995.

Frisch, M.B., Cornell, J., Villanueva, M. and Retzlaff, P.J. (1992). Clinical validation of the Quality of Life Inventory: A measure of life satisfaction for use in treatment planning and outcome assessment. *Psychological Assessment*. 4.

Gelpin, E., Bonne, O., Peri, T., Brandes, D., Shalev, A.Y. (1996). Treatment of recent trauma survivors with benzodiazepines:a prospective study. *Journal of Clinical Psychiatry;* 57:390-394.

Green, B.L. (1996). Trauma History Questionnaire. In B.H. Stamm (ed.) *Measurement of stress, trauma, and adaptation*, pp. 366-369. Lutherville, MD: Sidran Press.

Gruden, V., Gruden, Z., and Gruden-Pokupec, S.J. (1999). An integral approach to the victims of war. *Coll Antropol*. 23:603-5.

Gustaf-Eriksson N, Lundin T. (1996). Early traumatic stress reactions among Swedish survivors of the m/s Estonia disaster. *British Journal of Psychiatry*. 169:713-716.

Hageman, I., Andersen, H.S., Jorgensen, M.B. (2001). Post-traumatic stress disorder:a review of Psychobiology and pharmacotherapy. *Acta Psychiatrica Scandinavia*. 6:411-422.

Hamilton, M. (1967). Development of A Rating Scale for Primary Depressive Illness. *British Journal of Social and Clinical Psychology*, 6.

Hankin, C.S., Spiro, A., Miller, D.R. and Kazis, L. (1999). Mental disorders and mental health treatment among U.S. Department of Veterans Affairs outpatients: the Veterans Health Study. *American Journal of Psychiatry*, 156(12):1924-1930.

Hellman, C.J., Budd, M., Borysenko, J., McClelland, D.C., & Benson, H. (1990). A study of the effectiveness of two group behavioral medicine interventions for patients with psychosomatic complaints. *Behavioral Medicine*, 16(4):165-173.

Heresco-Levy, U., Kremer, I., Javitt, D.C., Goichman, R., Reshef, A., Blanaru, M., Cohen, T. (2002). Pilot-controlled trial of D-Cycloserine for the treatment of post-traumatic stress disorder. *International Journal of Neuropsychopharmacology*, 5:301-307.

Hertzberg, M.A, Butterfield, M.I., Feldman, M.E., Beckham, J.C., Sutherland, S.M., Connor, K.M., Davidson, J.R. (1999). A preliminary study of lamotrigine for the treatment of posttraumatic stress disorder. *Biological Psychiatry*, 45:1226-1229.

Hierholzer, R.W. (2002). Suicide in dementia: case studies of failure as a risk factor. *Clinical Gerontologist*, 24:159-163.

Hierholzer, R.W., and Liberman, R.P. (1986). Successful living: A social skills and problem-solving group for the chronic mentally ill. *Hospital and Community Psychiatry*, 37:913-918.

Hierholzer, R.W., Munson, J.L., Peabody, C.R., and Rosenberg, J. (1992). The clinical presentation of PTSD in World War II combat veterans. *Hospital and Community Psychiatry*. 43:816-820.

Hierholzer, R.W., and Thornbrough, M.: The transitional unit of the Albuquerque VAMC. in Corrigan P and Liberman RP (eds): *Behavior Therapy in Psychiatric Hospitals*. New York: Springer Publishing Company, 1994.

Horrigan, J.P., Guanfacine for PTSD nightmares. *Journal of the American Academy of Child and Adolescent Psychiatry*. 1996; 35:975-876

Iancu I., Rosen, Y., and Moshe, K. (2002). Antiepileptic drugs in posttraumatic stress disorder. *Clinical Neuropharmacol*. 25:225-229.

Jacobs WJ, Dalenberg C. Subtle presentations of post-traumatic stress disorder. *The Psychiatric Clinics of North America*. 1998;21(4):835-845.

Jankowski, K. (2003). A National Center for PTSD Fact Sheet. http://www.ncptsd.org/facts/specific/fs_physical_health.html

Johnson, D.R., Feldman, S.C., Lubin, H., and Southwick, S.M. (1995). The therapeutic use of ritual and ceremony in the treatment of posttraumatic stress disorder. *Journal of Traumatic Stress*. 8:283-98.

Kabat-Zinn, J. (1982). An outpatient program in behavioral medicine for chronic pain patients based on the practice of mindfulness meditation: theoretical considerations and preliminary results. *General Hospital Psychiatry*, 4:33-47.

Kabat-Zinn, J. (1990). *Full Catastrophe Living: The program of the Stress Reduction Clinic at the University of Massachusetts Medical Center*. New York: Dell

Kabat-Zinn, J., Massion, A.O., Kristeller, J., Peterson, L.G., Fletcher, K.E., Pbert, L., Lenderking, W.R. and Santorelli, S.F. (1992). Effectiveness of a meditation-based stress reduction program in the treatment of anxiety disorders. *American Journal of Psychiatry*, 149(7):936-943.

Kaplan HI, Sadock BJ, eds. *Synopsis of Psychiatry*. 8th ed. Baltimore: Williams & Williams; 1998:1083-1092.

Kessler, R.C., Sonnega, A., Bromet, E., Hughes, M. and Nelson, C.B. (1995). Posttraumatic stress disorder in the National Comorbidity Survey. *Archives of General Psychiatry*, 52: 1048-1068.

Khouzam, H.R. and Kissmeyer, P. (1997). Antidepressant treatment, posttraumatic stress disorder, survivor guilt, and spiritual awakening. *Journal of Traumatic Stress*. 10:691-696.

Khouzam H.R., Mahdasian, J.A. and Donnelly, N.J. (1998). Three psychiatric medications. *Patient Care*. 32(15):27-31.

Khouzam H.R. (2000). Treatment of depressive mood in schizophrenia with the atypical antipsychotic quetiapine. *Depression and Anxiety*. 11:80-82.

Khouzam, H.R. (2001). Religious meditations and its effects on posttraumatic stress disorder in a Korean war veteran. *Clinical Gerontologist*. 22 (3/4):125-131.

Khouzam, H.R, and Donnelly, N. J., (2001). Postraumatic stress disorder , Safe, effective management in the primary care setting. *Postgraduate Medicine*; 110:60-78.

Khouzam, H.R., Emes, R. (2002). The use of buspirone in primary care. *Journal of Psychosocial Nursing and Mental Health Services*. 40:34-41.

Kristeller, J.L. and Hallett, C.B. (1999). An exploratory study of a meditation-based intervention for binge eating disorder. *Journal of Health Psychology*, 4:357-363.

Kroenke, K. and Mangelsdorff, A.D. (1989). Common symptoms in ambulatory care: incidence, evaluation, therapy, and outcome. *American Journal of Medicine*, 86:262-265.

Kubany, E.S., McKenzie, W.F., Owens, J.A., Leisen, M.B., Kaplan, A.S., & Pavich, E. (1996). PTSD among women survivors of domestic violence in Hawaii. *Hawaii Medical Journal*, 55(9):164-165.

Kulka, R.A., Schlenger, W.E., Fairbank, J.A., Hough, Jordan, Marmar and Weiss. (1990). *Trauma and the Vietnam War generation: Report of findings from the National Vietnam Veterans Readjustment Study*. New York, Brunner/Mazel, Inc., 1990.

Labbate LA. Sex and serotonin reuptake inhibitor antidepressants. *Psychiatric Annals*. 1999;29(10):571-574.

Lader, M.H. (1996) Tolerability and safety:essentials in antidepressant pharmacotherapy. *Journal of Clinical Psychiatry* 57 (supple 2):39-44

Lehrer, P.M., & Woolfolk, R.L. (1993). Specific effects of stress management techniques. In P.M. Lehrer & R.L. Woolfolk (Eds), *Principles and practice of stress management* (pp.481-520). New York: Guilford.

Linehan, M.M. (1993). *Skills training manual for treating borderline personality disorder*. New York: Guilford.

Marks, I., & Dar, R. (2000). Fear reduction by psychotherapies. *British Journal of Psychiatry*, 176:507-511.

Marmar C.R., Weiss D.S., Metzler T. (1998) Peritraumatic dissociation and posttraumatic stress disorder. In: Bremner J.D., Marmar C.R., (eds.). *Trauma, memory, and dissociation*. Washington DC: American Psychiatric Press, pp. 229-52.

Marshall, R.P., Jorm, A.F., Grayson, D.A. and O'Toole, B.I. (1998). Posttraumatic stress disorder and other predictors of health care consumption by Vietnam veterans. *Psychiatric Services*, 49(12):1609-1611.

McBride, J.L. (2002). Spiritual component of patients who experience psychological trauma: Family physician intervention. *JABFP*. 15:168-169.

McLellan, A.T. (1985). New data from the Addiction Severity Index: Reliability and validity in three centers. *Journal of Nervous & Mental Disease*, 173:412-423.

McLeod, C.C., Budd, M.A. and McClelland, D.C. (1997). Treatment of Somatization in Primary Care. *General Hospital Psychiatry*, 19(4):251-258.

Meisenhelder, J.B. and Chandler, E.N. (2000). Faith, prayer and health outcomes in elderly Native Americans. *Clinical Nursing Research*, 9:191-203.

Moody, L.E., Faser, M. and Yarandi, H. (1993). Effects of guided imagery in patients with chronic bronchitis and emphysema. *Clinical Nursing Research*, 2:478-486.

Morgan C.A.3rd, Wang, S., Southwick, S.M., Rasmusson, A., Hazlett, G., Hauger, R.L, Charney, D.S. (2004). Plasma Neuropeptide-Y concentration in human exposed to military survival training, *Biological Psychiatry*, 47:902-909.

Najavits, L.M. (2002). *Seeking Safety: A Treatment Manual for PTSD and Substance Abuse*, New York, NY: The Guilford Press.

New International Version (1988). *The Holy Bible*. Wheaton, IL:Tyndale House Publ.

Othmer E, Othmer P, Othmer S. Brain functions and psychiatric disorders. *Psychiatric clinics of North America*. 1998;21(3):517-566.

Petroff, O.A., Hyder, F., Rothman, D.L, Mattson, R.M. (2001). Topiramate rapidly raises brain GABA in Epilepsy patients. *Epilepsia*, 42:543-548.

Post, R.M., Weiss, S.R.B., Smith, M.A. Sensitization and Kindling: Implications for the evolving neural substrates of post-traumatic stress disorder. In: M.J. Friedman, D.S. Charney, and A.Y. Deutch eds. *Neurobiological and clinical consequences of Stress: From Normal Adaptation to PTSD*. Philadelphia: Lippincott-Raven; (pp 203-224) 1995.

Raskind, M.A., Dobie, D.J., Kanter, E.D., Petrie, E.C.,Thompson, C.E., Peskind, E.R. (2000). The alpha-adrenergic antagonist prazocin ameliorates combat trauma nightmares in veterans with posttraumatic stress disorder:a report of 4 cases. *Journal of Clinical Psychiatry*. 61:129-133.

Rees, B.L. (1995). Effect of relaxation with guided imagery on anxiety, depression, and self-esteem in primiparas. *Journal of Holistic Nursing*, 13:255-67.

Reich J. (1999). Comorbid anxiety and depression and personality disorder: A possible stress-induced personality disorder syndrome. *Psychiatric Annals*. 1999;29(12):707-712.

Resick, P.A. (2001). Cognitive Therapy for Posttraumatic Stress Disorder. *Journal of Cognitive Psychotherapy: An International Quaterly*, 15(4):321-329.

Rossi, E.L. (2004). Stress-induced alternative gene splicing in mind-body medicine. *Adv Mind Body Med*. 20(2):12-19.

Roth, S., Newman, E., Pelcovitz, D., Kolk, Bvd, Mandel, F.S. (1997) Complex PTSD in victims exposed to sexual and physical abuse: Results from the DSM-IV field trial for posttraumatic stress disorder. *Journal of Traumatic Stress*. 10:539-555.

Rothbaum, B.O., Meadows, E.A., Resick, P. and Foy, D.W. (2000). Cognitive-behavioral therapy. In E.B. Keane, M.J. Freidman (Eds.), *Effective treatments for PTSD: Practice guidelines from the International Society for Traumatic Stress Studies*. (pp. 320-325). New York, NY: Guilford Press.

Schnurr, P.P., Friedman, M.J., Foy, D.W., Shea, M.T., Hsieh, F.Y., Lavori, P.W., Glynn, S.M., Wattenberg, M. and Bernardy, N.C. (2003). Randomized trial of trauma-focused group therapy for posttraumatic stress disorder: results from a department of veterans affairs cooperative study. *Archives of General Psychiatry*, 60(5):481-489.

Schnurr, P.P. and Jankowski, M.K. (1999). Physical Health and Post-traumatic Stress Disorder: Review and Synthesis. *Seminars in Clinical Neuropsychiatry*, 4:295-304.

Schnurr, P.P., Friedman, M.J. and Bernardy, N.C. (2002). Research on Posttraumatic Stress Disorder: Epidemiology, Pathophysiology, and Assessment. *Psychotherapy in Practice*, 58(8):877-889.

Shapiro, S.L., Schwartz, G.E. and Bonner, G. (1998). Effects of mindfulness-based stress reduction on medical and premedical students. *Journal of Behavioral Medicine*, 62:613-622.

Skinner, H.A. and Sheu, W.J. (1982). Reliability of alcohol use indices: The Lifetime Drinking History and the MAST. *Journal of Studies on Alcohol*, 43:1157-1170.

Spitzer, R.L., Williams, J.B., Gibbon, M., & First, M.B. (1992). The Structural Clinical Interview for DSM-III-R SCID: I. History, rationale, and description. *Archives of General Psychiatry*, 49:624-629.

Stack, C.G., Rogers, P., and Linter, S.P. (1988). Monoamine oxidase inhibitors and anesthesia. *Br J Anesth*, 60:222-227.

Stahl S.M. (1999). Antidepressants: The blue-chip psychotropic for the modern treatment of anxiety disorders. *Journal of Clinical Psychiatry*. 60:356-357.

Teasdale, J.D., Segal, Z.V. and Williams, J.M.G. (1995). How does cognitive therapy prevent relapse and why should attentional control (mindfulness) training help? *Behaviour Research and Therapy*, 33:225-39.

Teasdale, J.D., Segal, Z.V., Williams, J.M.G., Ridgeway, V., Soulsby, J. and Lau, M. (2000). Prevention of relapse/recurrence in major depression by mindfulness-based cognitive therapy. *Journal of Consulting and Clinical Psychology*, 68:615-623.

Tolkien, J.R.R. *The Return of the King*. Houghton Mifflin Ballantine Books, New York, NY. 1956.

Vaiva, G., Ducrocq, F., Jezequel, K., Averland, B., Lestavel, P., Brunet, A., Marmar, C.R. Immediate treatment with propranolol decreases posttraumatic stress isorder two months after trauma. *Biological Psychiatry*, 54:947-949

VandenBos, G., & DeLeon, P. (1984). The use of psychotherapy to improve physical health. *Psychotherapy*, 25, 335-343.

Viola J, Ditzler T, Batzer W, Harazin, J., Adams, D., Lettich, L. and Berigan, T. (1997) Pharmacological management of post-traumatic stress disorder: clinical summary of a five-year retrospective study, 1990-1995. *Mil Med.* 162(9):616-619.

Walker, E.A., Katon, W., Russo, J., Ciechanowski, P., Newman, E. and Wagner, A.W. (2003). Health Care Costs Associated With Posttraumatic Stress Disorder Symptoms in Women. *Archives of General Psychiatry*, 60:369-374.

Ware, J.E., Kosinski, M. and Keller, S.D. (1994). *SF-36 Physical and Mental Health Summary Scales: A User's Manual*, Health Assessment Lab, Boston.

Weisberg, R.B., Bruce, S.E., Machan, J.T., Kessler, R.C., Culpepper, L. and Keller, M.B. (2002). Nonpsychiatric Illness Among Primary Care Patients With Trauma Histories and Posttraumatic Stress Disorder. *Psychiatric Services*, 53(7):848-854.

Weiss, D.S., Horowitz, M.J. and Wilner, N. (1984). The Stress Response Rating Scale: A clinician's measure for rating the response to serious life events. *British Journal of Clinical Psychology*, 23:202-215.

Wickramasekera, I. (1989). Somatizers, the health care system, and collapsing the psychological distance that the somatizer has to travel for help. *Professional Psychology: Research and Practice*, 29:105-111.

Wilkinson, P. and Mynors-Wallis, L. (1994). Problem-solving therapy in the treatment of unexplained physical symptoms in primary care: A preliminary study. *Journal of Psychosomatic Research*, 38(6):591-598.

Witvliet, C.V., Phipps, K.A., Feldman, M.E. and Beckham, J.C. (2004) Posttraumatic mental and physical health correlates of forgiveness and religious coping in military veterans. *Journal of Traumatic Stress*. 17:269-273.

Wolpe, J. (1958). *Psychotherapy by reciprocal inhibition*. Stanford, CA: Stanford University Press.

Yehuda, R., Kahana, B., Schmeidler, J., Southwick, S., Wilson, S., Giller, E. Impact of cumulative lifetime trauma and recent stress on current posttraumatic stress disorder symptoms in Holocaust survivors. *Am J Psychiatry*. 1995;152(12):1815-1818.

Yehuda, R. Biology of posttraumatic stress disorder. *Journal of Clinical Psychiatry*, 2000; 61(suppl 7):14-21.

Zachariae, R., Oster, H., Bjerring, P. and Kragballe, K. (1996). Effects of psychological intervention on psoriasis: A preliminary report. *Journal of American Academy of Dermatology*, 34(6):1008-1015.

In: Trends in Posttraumatic Stress Disorder Research
Editor: Thomas A. Corales, pp. 29-43
ISBN 1-59454-135-3
© 2005 Nova Science Publishers, Inc.

Chapter 2

REVIEW OF DHEAS IN PTSD: A PUTATIVE ROLE FOR DEHYDROEPIANDROSTERONE IN POSTTRAUMATIC STRESS DISORDER?

Hans Peter Söndergaard and Töres Theorell

National Institute for Psychosocial Factors and Health – IPM, Stockholm, Sweden

ABSTRACT

In PTSD, the hypothalamic-pituitary-adrenocortical (HPA) system is disturbed with increased negative feedback inhibition of cortisol secretion.

Recent findings point to the possibility that another steroid hormone, dehydroepiandrosterone (DHEA) or its sulphated metabolite DHEAS might be increased in peripheral blood of PTSD subjects.

During the last decades, new findings regarding DHEA have emerged. DHEA is one of the principal steroid molecules in the body and has anabolic properties. It has been shown that it is a neurosteroid; i.e. it can be produced in the brain and it shows non-genomic actions on receptors. The receptor effect which is best characterised till now is a non-competitive blockade on the $GABA_A$ receptor, but other receptors are involved as well. Neuroprotection by DHEAS against cell death and behavioral deficits has been shown in different animal models of stress.

In this paper, a brief review of the neurosteroids is presented along with published studies and preliminary reports on DHEA/DHEAS in PTSD.

The possible interpretations and hypothetical implications are presented, such as the possibility that cognitive dysfunction in PTSD might be explained by increased levels of DHEA/DHEAS in the nervous system.

While it is far too early to conclude that DHEA or DHEAS are of any patophysiological importance in PTSD, the findings point to a possibility of confounding by trauma or PTSD in studies of neurosteroids in depression and other psychiatric disorders. They also point to a need of studying an array of steroid molecules in psychiatric and stress research. Possible research strategies in order to eludicate the putative role of DHEAS and other neurosteroids in PTSD are outlined.

BACKGROUND PTSD

Posttraumatic stress disorder (PTSD) has been recognised as a psychiatric disorder since 1980 when it was introduced in DSM-III. The research has been intensive and covered a broad range of issues from epidemiology to neurobiology as well as treatment.

The prevalence of PTSD among different populations varies to a great extent depending on the exposure to trauma. Studies have shown a significant prevalence of PTSD [1-3] among adolescents living in inner-city areas in the United States, and generally, the lifetime prevalence has been found to be 5-6 % among males and roughly the double among females [4]. The prevalence is substantially higher in countries where war or severe oppression are the rule [5]. Among refugees, studies are scarce but the prevalence is probably at least 15-25 % [6].

Neurobiological research on PTSD has been extensive. One of the theories that have been investigated is a hypothesis about hippocampal dysfunction [7, 8] based on the prevalent cognitive problems of the patients as well as the peculiar form of fragmented and intrusive memories of the traumatic events that is characteristic of PTSD [9-11]. Also, animal studies pointing to hippocampal damage after different forms of stress paradigms have stimulated this development [12]. Several cross-sectional studies have shown reduced hippocampal volume in PTSD subjects compared to exposed and unexposed individuals without PTSD [13-18], but it is still unclear whether this volume reduction is preexisting or reversible because of lack of longitudinal studies.

Another field that has been studied extensively is the finding of a changed pattern of cortisol in PTSD. The hypothalamo-pituitary-adrenal (HPA) axis has been shown to be changed, most probably in the following fashion [19-28]; in the brain, corticotrophin-releasing factor (CRF) is excreted in increased amounts, leading in turn to a blunted ACTH response and lower basal cortisol excretion. Also, feed-back inhibition of cortisol excretion is normally exaggerated in PTSD leading to increased suppression after dexametasone challenge. An increased number of glucocorticoid receptors have been found in lymphocytes in PTSD [23, 29-31].

Cortisol belongs to the family of steroid hormones. Curiously, until recently very few other steroid hormones have been studied in PTSD and in psychiatric disorders generally. The reason for this is probably that cortisol has been firmly established as *the* "stress" hormone. It prepares the organism for "fight and flight"; on the other hand it has been demonstrated that prolonged stress and increased cortisol secretion are associated with a wide range of health problems, including psychological malfunction in previously healthy individuals [32-36].

The other steroid hormones have been studied to a much lesser extent. Recently, studies have been published which report changes in PTSD of dehydroepiandrosterone (DHEA) in its sulphated form in blood (DHEAS), which will be reviewed and developed further here.

BACKGROUND ON STEROIDS AND 'NEUROSTEROIDS'

The family of steroid molecules are synthesised in the body from cholesterol, which is converted into pregnenolone, which can be further metabolised to DHEA [37]. From pregnenolone and DHEA, a number of steroid molecules are synthesised in the adrenals and gonads. They are normally classified into four main groups, the gonadal steroids or sex hormones, mineralocorticoids governing the water/salt metabolism, the anabolic steroids, of which DHEAS is one of the most important, and the glucocorticoids, of which cortisol (hydrocortisone) is the principal one humans.

The secretion of steroid hormones is generally governed by releasing factors, activating release of a superordinate hormone (in the example of the HPA-axis above, CRF leads to release of ACTH which stimulates cortisol production and excretion). Cortisol in turn exerts negative feed-back on CRF release. This feed-back system has been studied by inhibition by the synthetic glucocorticoid dexametasone. After dexametasone, non-suppression of cortisol has been found in endogenous depression, while increased suppression has been found in PTSD, i.a.

The normal mechanism of action of the steroid molecules is generally that they activate intracellular receptors leading to DNA transcription, a *"genomic"* mechanism of action [38]. This in turn leads to RNA production and protein expression. Such proteins are generally enzymes that facilitate metabolic actions, such as the production of cortisol leading to increased amounts of glucose or free fatty acids in the bloodstream. Other examples are the gonadal steroids which govern spermiogenesis in the male via testosteron and estrus and ovulation in the female by estrogen and progesteron.

Diseases caused by anomalies of excretion of steroid hormones can take many forms, such as Cushing's disease caused by hypersecretion of cortisol or Addison's disease in hypofunction of the adrenal with lack of cortisol, to mention a few.

In psychiatric disorders, cortisol excretion is increased in "classical" endogenous depression [39-41] and often lowered in a number of conditions such as chronic fatigue syndrome [42-44], fibromyalgia [45], and PTSD. In these disorders it seems that the cortisol pattern will characteristically become – more or less - normalised with remission of symptoms, at least in depression [46].

DHEA AND DHEAS

As mentioned above, few other steroid hormones than cortisol have been studied until recently in psychiatric research. One that has been studied to some extent is DHEA/DHEAS [37].

DHEA denotes the hormone synthesised and found in lipophilic surroundings, while DHEAS denotes the sulphated watersoluble form occuring in blood. Similarly, the precursor pregnenolone is sulfated and is then called pregnenolone sulfate (PS).

An observation which has inspired research on DHEA was the observation of Baulieu and others that while rodents normally do not produce DHEA or DHEAs in their adrenals, nonetheless it could be found in the rodent brain after adrenalectomy [37] and thus there should be a mechanism of producing it in the brain or at least concentrating it there. Many studies have confirmed that such a phenomenon indeed exists in glial tissues [47-51], i.e. the supportive tissue of the nervous system. The exact biochemical pathway in glial tissue is unknown but there are indications that it might differ from the pathway in adrenal tissue [52-54].

The possible releasing factors governing synthesis of DHEA in the brain are unknown. However, in animals increased levels of both pregnenolone and DHEA are found 30 minutes after stimulation with both CRF and ACTH, both in whole brain and in plasma [55]. In the frog, a neuropeptide ODN which is an endogenous ligand at the benzodiazepine receptor has been shown to induce conversion of pregnenolone into other neurosteroids [56]. In humans, CRF stimulates increased amounts of serum DHEA with a peak value after 30-60 minutes [57].

Studies of human brain cell lines have shown that pregnenolone is synthesised in oligodendroglia and can be converted into DHEA in both oligodendroglia and astrocytes. Amyloid and oxidative stress did also stimulate formation of DHEA [54]. In macrophages, pathways of "downstream" steroid metabolism from DHEAS have been demonstrated as well, indicating that an array of tissues might share the capacity to metabolise steroids [58].

One of the known facts about DHEAS is that it decreases with age [37] and also in a number of chronic medical conditions such as arthritis or immunological diseases [59-63]. It has been studied in Alzheimers disease where it is lowered in most of the brain but not in the amygdala where it is increased [64], and suggestions have been made to treat memory problems in aging people by medication with DHEAS.

In 1986, Majewska published an important finding regarding DHEAS [65]. The background for this research was probably to gain an increased understanding of the effects of abuse of anabolic steroids, since DHEA is the naturally occuring anabolic steroid. The surprising finding was that DHEAS exerted a *non-genomic* effect on certain receptor systems. The effect was a *non-competitive* blockade of the $GABA_A$ (gamma-aminobutyric acid) receptor [37, 66]. This finding was important, not the least because this implies that the blockade exerted by DHEAS could not be competed with by other naturally occurring or synthetic ligands; in other words, DHEAS might block the effects of agonists or antagonists on this receptor. Gammaaminobutyric acid – GABA- is one of the most abundant neurotransmittors in the brain, and almost all neurons possess GABA receptors. In the GABA receptor complex, a number of receptors are embedded, thus what has been termed the "benzodiazepine" receptor and the receptors for the excitatory amino acids NMDA ("aspartate") and glutamate are at times described as substructures of the GABA receptor complex [38].

It has been shown that DHEA and DHEAS protect cultured hippocampal neurons against excitatory amino acid-induced neurotoxicity [67, 68]; e.g. aspartate (NMDA) and glutamate. It further protected mice against suffocation stress-induced behavioral deficits induced by exposure to carbon monoxide [69].

The protective effect exerted by DHEAS in these experiments was in a range which imply that these mechanisms could be relevant not only to pharmacology but even to normal physiology as well as patophysiology, since the concentrations of DHEAs which showed such an effect were close to naturally occuring concentrations.

NEUROACTIVE STEROIDS

As implied above, naturally occuring steroids apart from cortisol can affect the brain; hence, the term neuroactive steroids. A number of steroids have such effects, these are 17-estradiol, progesterone, 3α,5α-THP, 3α,5α-THDOC, pregnenolone sulphate (PS), and DHEAS [38].

NEUROSTEROIDS

The term neurosteroids has been coined to describe steroids which beyond neuroactive properties also seem to undergo metabolisation or even de novo synthesis inside the nervous system. Presently, the order of neurosteroids includes pregnenolone, DHEA / DHEAS, and at least the 3α-reduced metabolites of progesterone and deoxicorticosterone; 3α,5α-THP, and 3α,5α-THDOC [38]. Other authors include a wider range of steroid molecules [70].

According to Baulieu, DHEA and DHEAs are neuroactive. DHEA shows neurotropic effects, which has been confirmed by independent groups [67]. There is binding to synaptosomal membranes, increasing neuronal excitability. DHEAS shows neuromodulatory effects on the GABA$_A$ receptor, as well at the glutamate receptor. At the glutamate receptor, however, pregnenolone shows much stronger effect. Another receptor is the Sigma (σ) receptor, on which aspartate (N-methyl-d-aspartate; NMDA) has the effect of releasing noradrenaline in hippocampal slices [71]. On this receptor, DHEAs and pregnenolone show opposite effects. According to Baulieu, DHEAs acts as an agonist, whereas pregnenolone sulfate acts as an inverse agonist, and progesterone may act as an antagonist [72]. This example might serve to illustrate that neurosteroid modulation might be effected by the *balance* between different neurosteroids.

A neuroprotective effect of DHEAS against neurotoxicity of glutamate (NMDA) [73-75], and kainate has been shown in cultured hippocampal cells from rat [68].

Rupprecht and Holsboer [38] cite modulating effects of neurosteroids on a range of neurotransmitter receptors, but sometimes the experimental concentrations of neurosteroids are too high to be of physiological significance. At the GABA$_A$ receptor, 3α, 5α-THP, 3α, 5β-THP, and 3α, 5α-THDOC are examples of positive modulators, whereas DHEAS and pregnenolone are negative ones.

Thus, some neurosteroids have been associated with excitotoxic effects such as the non-protection by pregnenolone, while others seem to show a protective effect such as DHEAS. On the other hand, this protective effect might be accompanied by an excitatory effect on other systems because the inhibitory effect of GABA on GABA receptors is suppressed.

Another theoretical effect of the neurosteroids might be an opposing effect of cortisol [76].

RELATIONSHIP BETWEEN CENTRAL AND
PERIPHERAL LEVELS OF NEUROSTEROIDS

There are few studies – if any – of a relationship between blood levels of DHEAS and levels in the central nervous system, apart from the findings of parallel increases of DHEA and pregnenolone in animals after stimulation with CRF. These increases happen within a short time frame (30-60 minutes) such that it is unlikely that DHEA or pregnenolone in the CNS are of a peripheral origin.

Is it possible that serum levels of neurosteroids mirror central levels in the CNS? The parallel rise after stimulation with CRF suggests that this is a possibility [55]. Another possibility exists, namely that higher levels centrally could spill over into the blodstream. This is not possible for the sulphated water-soluble derivatives though since they are unlikely to pass the blood-brain barrier; on the other hand, the non-sulphated lipophilic molecules might pass the blood-brain barrier and enter the peripheral pool. The matter must be studied further before any firm conclusions are possible, because the meaningfulness of measurements of peripheral neurosteroid molecules in blood relies on an assumption that they change in a parallel fashion with central ones in the central nervous system.

FINDINGS REGARDING DHEAS IN PTSD

When we planned a longitudinal study of health markers in recently resettled refugees 1996, serum levels of the stress-responsive hormones cortisol, thyroxine, prolactin, and DHEAS were included as markers. Selfrating questionnaires were also included. The selection of hormones was based on the literature. The inclusion of dehydroepiandrosterone sulphate; the sulphated form being the most common one in peripheral blood, relied on the assumption that it would be a marker of health [59-61, 77]. At baseline, subjects were assesed for PTSD with a structured clinical interview, CAPS [78, 79].

Distress or illness in significant others, and a perception of excessive demands in everyday life, were life events associated with increases in serum cortisol and at times even with increases in thyroxine. Events associated with decreased levels of prolactin were typically situations of strain in relation to authorities or individuals to which the subjects were in a position of dependency. DHEAS changed in opposite directions in PTSD and non-PTSD subjects. DHEAS also changed with positive events [80].

In the analysis of the data from the longitudinal study it turned out that DHEAS behaved contrary to expectations in the PTSD group [81]. First of all, subjects diagnosed with PTSD at baseline showed higher levels of serum DHEAS throughout the study. Secondly, subjects with PTSD who reported increased symptoms at last follow-up nine months later, showed rising levels of DHEAS whereas subjects with less symptoms according to self-rating scales showed decreasing levels.

As mentioned above, it turned out that there was an interaction effect of PTSD on changes of DHEAS after self-reported life events; i.e. subjects who reported positive life events had lowered levels of DHEAS after the event if they had PTSD, whereas subjects without PTSD showed increased levels of serum DHEAS. Accordingly, in non-PTSD subjects the expected relationships were found whereas in PTSD subjects the opposite pattern was found.

In the cross-sectional study there also was an interaction effect of depression and PTSD on DHEAS levels [81]. While serum DHEAS was higher in non-depressed PTSD than in non-PTSD without depression, depressed non-PTSD subjects had higher levels of DHEAS than PTSD subjects with depression when correcting for age.

Searching the literature at the time (2000) lead to the following findings; one report was already published regarding DHEAS in PTSD pointing to increased levels of DHEAS in non-depressed soldiers with PTSD compared to controls [82]. Unfortunately this report was not classified correctly on the Medline at the time, the right search term would have been prasterone, the Medline search word for DHEAS, but since the authors of the report used the search term neurosteroid, it was not found immediately. Thus, an increased level of DHEAS in PTSD was actually found independently by two groups.

A study of the effects of glucocorticoid feedback sensitivity in PTSD using metyrapone was negative with regard to DHEA (Kanter et al 2001). In this study, plasma DHEA at baseline was lower among PTSD patients and combat controls than in non-combat control subjects. In this study it was reported that 11 of 13 subjects with PTSD also suffered from dysthymia or depression, whereas none in the two control groups suffered from any Axis I disorder, but this was not analysed further. DHEAS is not reported in this study. No correction for age was carried out; on the other hand cases and controls had the same mean age. In our study, non-depressed PTSD subjects had higher serum levels of DHEAS than depressed subjects with PTSD. In the Spivak et al study, none of the PTSD subjects suffered from depression. It can be argued that the representativity of the populations is of importance since both a high prevalence and a non-occurence of co-morbid depression are hardly typical of a PTSD population.

PRELIMINARY REPORTS

Other reports have been published at conferences. Bremner et al have reported increased levels of DHEAS in women with PTSD related to childhood sexual abuse (personal communication).

Butterfield et al have reported that PTSD subjects who made suicide attempts had increased serum levels of DHEAS; a finding that might be interpreted that severity of PTSD is associated with higher levels of DHEAS (Poster presented at ISTSS annual conference 2003).

Interestingly, Bremner et al have reported a decreased number of benzodiazepine binding sites in post mortem brain from PTSD subjects [83].

Tentative Interpretations

The few studies published till now which have included DHEAS warrant caution in interpretations. Despite this, the findings imply that this hormone as well as the other neurosteroids might be of importance in PTSD.

Firstly, the diagnosis of PTSD, or traumatic events per se, might be a confounder in the larger –but restricted – number of studies analysing DHEA or DHEAS in depression or other psychiatric disorders, for example eating disorders. A number of studies have been carried out, both in depression and other disorders which have not controlled for a possible interaction effect on serum DHEAS concentrations of PTSD or of previous traumatic life events corresponding to the A criterion of PTSD.

Secondly there is a possibility that DHEAS and other neurosteroids might be of importance in understanding the psychopathology of PTSD. Since DHEAS is a non-competitive blocker of GABA-A receptors, among others, it might explain the increased arousal inherent in PTSD, as well as the developmental blocks and the learning difficulties that are observed clinically as well as in research [84] (unpublished data, Emdad et al.).

The cognitive difficulties inherent in PTSD among refugees are currently being studied in our research group. According to preliminary results, general IQ measures as well as years of school do not differ between PTSD subjects and control subjects from the same refugee group. But short-term visual memory tasks and executive functions differ considerably.

The hypothesis of hippocampal dysfunction has been brought forward as a candidate of being a crucial factor in PTSD on the basis of a number of small studies, and because of findings of stress-related hippocampal dysfunction in animal research using different kinds of stress paradigms. The clinical symptoms of PTSD are also in accordance with this hypothesis. But there might be another explanation for the clinical phenomena of PTSD. This points to another explanation of dysfunction of the hippocampus. The symptoms may be caused by receptor effects of increased DHEA or DHEAS levels in the brain.

Bremner et al have published a paper which reported decreased benzodiazepine receptor binding in prefrontal cortex in combat-related PTSD [83]. This might be explained by increased levels of DHEAS in the brain, since the non-competitive receptor blockade on GABA$_A$ receptors could explain a seeming reduction of benzodiazepine receptors, i.e. the agonists might be displaced from the binding sites by DHEAS.

In the larger picture of steroid hormones studied in PTSD, where cortisol has been extensively studied, it is of importance to ask whether the finding of changes in DHEAS is merely an epiphenomenon, or if there might be a specific connotation to this finding. It might be that the inhibition of basal cortisol excretion reported in PTSD could explain the high levels of DHEAS peripherally. On the other hand, the increased serum concentrations of DHEAS in PTSD – if this is corrobated in further studies – might explain a last-line defense in extreme traumatisation. The non-competitive blockade of several receptor systems might be interpreted as a mechanism in order to protect the brain from the effects of other hormones and transmitters such as cortisol.

The implications for the possible role of neurosteroids in PTSD are that the study of neurosteroids is impossible without the relinquishment of commercial routine methods, or the development of new practical large-scale methods. Many publications on the lesser known steroids are based on spectroscopic methods requiring the use of oxime-derivatives of the hormones, which are expensive and time-consuming. Presently, only DHEA and DHEAS can be analysed by commercial immunoassays.

POSSIBLE STUDIES WITH REGARD TO A ROLE FOR DHEAS IN THE SYNDROME OF PTSD

In the study of steroid hormones in relation to PTSD, several methods are of interest.

First of all, replication studies of the putative finding of increased levels of serum DHEAS in PTSD are needed. Especially, studies of identical twins discordant for PTSD could be of interest.

If such studies confirm an association, a number of questions arise.

- Is the increased serum concentration of DHEAS just an epiphenomenon?
- Is it pre-existing, caused by trauma or by PTSD?
- Can the psychopathology of PTSD be explained by effects of DHEAS in the brain?

It is also of interest to include the other known neurosteroids in future cross-sectional studies because of the proposed mechanism of "cross-talk" between genomic and nongenomic actions, and because they seem to show a dynamic equilibrium. Other neurosteroids than DHEAS might also explain e.g. PTSD symptoms, the signs of hippocampal dysfunction, or a reduced hippocampal volume. In chronic fatigue syndrome (CFS), such a study has recently been published [70]. In this study, an array of neurosteroids but first of all isopregnanolone (3β-5α-THP) was increased in CFS.

So far, only serum levels of DHEAS have been studied. It is obviously desirable to study all neurosteroids in the cerebrospinal fluid of PTSD subjects. For instance, DHEAS levels might show a steeper gradient between peripheral and CSF levels in PTSD compared to non-PTSD subjects.

Longitudinal studies, i.e. studies of subjects without PTSD who develop PTSD, as well as the changes in PTSD cases after treatment are also of importance in teasing out a possible role of DHEAS and other neurosteroids in PTSD, see table 1.

Table 1. Suggested interpretations, hypotheses and studies regarding DHEAS in PTSD

Finding	Interpretation	Hypothesis	Study
DHEAS increased in PTSD	The number of studies are too few to conclude anything, and the differences are so small that they hardly can have any clinical significance	The small differences in blood can mirror much larger differences in the brain	More studies of DHEAS in PTSD and controls with control for age and depression. Comparisons of serum DHEAS and CSF DHEAS in patients and controls.
	DHEAS is indeed higher in PTSD	The higher level of DHEAS in PTSD is merely an epiphenomenon caused by higher CRF levels and the down-regulation of cortisol production	Further longitudinal studies of the relationship between symptom load, cortisol, and DHEAS.
		but other neurosteroids might also differ, and the psychopathology of PTSD might be caused by other steroid molecules	Studies of an array of steroid molecules in PTSD and controls.
		Higher DHEAS causes arousal and cognitive symptoms of PTSD by blockade of parts of GABA receptor complex	Correlation studies of cognitive functions and arousal symptoms in PTSD.

CONCLUSIONS

Till now, only four published studies have explored an association between PTSD and DHEAS, whereof one is negative.

Evidently, this is not enough to claim that DHEAS is of any patophysiological significance in PTSD. More studies are necessary. Of these, some will have to focus on the gradient of DHEA and DHEAS in the central nervous system relative to peripheral blood.

These studies might clarify whether the DHEAS concentration is indeed higher in the brain of PTSD subjects.

Other studies should be carried out in order to study the association between psychological trauma and DHEA/DHEAS. Is there a true association between PTSD and DHEAS, or is the underlying association between psychological trauma or stress? Do subjects who react with depression, anxiety or PTSD after traumatic events develop deviating patterns of DHEA/DHEAS longitudinally?

The next question is whether DHEAS might explain the psychopathology of PTSD. For instance, is DHEA/DHEAS in serum or CSF related to cognitive difficulties in PTSD subjects?

Finally, the demonstration that an array of steroid hormones are in fact of importance in a number of mental disorders point to the necessity of studying these hormones, in a much more comprehensive fashion than it has been done until now. Most psychiatric research has quite reasonably focused on pharmacology with the disease as the point of departure, but in the future it will become necessary to study the pathway from life events to disorder in order to prevent the prevailing mental diseases.

REFERENCES

[1]   Giaconia, R.M., et al., Traumas and posttraumatic stress disorder in a community population of older adolescents. *Journal of the American Academy of Child & Adolescent Psychiatry*, 1995. 34(10): p. 1369-80.
[2]   Berton, M.W. and S.D. Stabb, Exposure to violence and post-traumatic stress disorder in urban adolescents. *Adolescence*, 1996. 31(122): p. 489-98.
[3]   Buka, S.L., et al., Youth exposure to violence: prevalence, risks, and consequences. *American Journal of Orthopsychiatry*, 2001. 71(3): p. 298-310.
[4]   Breslau, N., The epidemiology of posttraumatic stress disorder: what is the extent of the problem? *Journal of Clinical Psychiatry*, 2001. 62 Suppl 17: p. 16-22.
[5]   Mollica, R.F., et al., Longitudinal study of psychiatric symptoms, disability, mortality, and emigration among Bosnian refugees.[comment]. *JAMA*, 2001. 286(5): p. 546-54.
[6]   Thulesius, H. and A. Hakansson, Screening for posttraumatic stress disorder symptoms among Bosnian refugees. *Journal of Traumatic Stress*, 1999. 12(1): p. 167-74.
[7]   Sapolsky, R.M., Why stress is bad for your brain.[see comment]. *Science*, 1996. 273(5276): p. 749-50.
[8]   Bremner, J.D., et al., Magnetic resonance imaging-based measurement of hippocampal volume in posttraumatic stress disorder related to childhood physical and sexual abuse--a preliminary report. *Biological Psychiatry*, 1997. 41(1): p. 23-32.
[9]   van der Kolk, B.A. and R. Fisler, Dissociation and the fragmentary nature of traumatic memories: overview and exploratory study. *Journal of Traumatic Stress*, 1995. 8(4): p. 505-25.
[10] van der Kolk, B.A., et al., Dissociation, somatization, and affect dysregulation: the complexity of adaptation of trauma. *American Journal of Psychiatry*, 1996. 153(7 Suppl): p. 83-93.
[11] van der Kolk, B.A., The psychobiology of posttraumatic stress disorder. *Journal of Clinical Psychiatry*, 1997. 58 Suppl 9: p. 16-24.

[12] McEwen, B.S. and A.M. Magarinos, Stress effects on morphology and function of the hippocampus. *Annals of the New York Academy of Sciences*, 1997. 821: p. 271-84.

[13] Grossman, R., M.S. Buchsbaum, and R. Yehuda, Neuroimaging studies in post-traumatic stress disorder. *Psychiatric Clinics of North America*, 2002. 25(2): p. 317-40.

[14] McFarlane, A.C., R. Yehuda, and C.R. Clark, Biologic models of traumatic memories and post-traumatic stress disorder. The role of neural networks. *Psychiatric Clinics of North America*, 2002. 25(2): p. 253-70.

[15] Bremner, J.D., Neuroimaging studies in post-traumatic stress disorder. *Current Psychiatry Reports*, 2002. 4(4): p. 254-63.

[16] Bremner, J.D., Neuroimaging of childhood trauma. *Seminars in Clinical Neuropsychiatry*, 2002. 7(2): p. 104-12.

[17] Gilbertson, M.W., et al., Smaller hippocampal volume predicts pathologic vulnerability to psychological trauma.[comment]. *Nature Neuroscience*, 2002. 5(11): p. 1242-7.

[18] Hull, A.M., Neuroimaging findings in post-traumatic stress disorder. Systematic review. *British Journal of Psychiatry*, 2002. 181: p. 102-10.

[19] Yehuda, R., et al., Low urinary cortisol excretion in patients with posttraumatic stress disorder. *Journal of Nervous & Mental Disease*, 1990. 178(6): p. 366-9.

[20] Yehuda, R., et al., Hypothalamic-pituitary-adrenal dysfunction in posttraumatic stress disorder. *Biological Psychiatry*, 1991. 30(10): p. 1031-48.

[21] Yehuda, R., et al., Enhanced suppression of cortisol following dexamethasone administration in posttraumatic stress disorder. *American Journal of Psychiatry*, 1993. 150(1): p. 83-6.

[22] Yehuda, R., et al., Glucocorticoid receptor number and cortisol excretion in mood, anxiety, and psychotic disorders. *Biological Psychiatry*, 1993. 34(1-2): p. 18-25.

[23] Yehuda, R., et al., Dose-response changes in plasma cortisol and lymphocyte glucocorticoid receptors following dexamethasone administration in combat veterans with and without posttraumatic stress disorder. *Archives of General Psychiatry*, 1995. 52(7): p. 583-93.

[24] Yehuda, R., et al., Low urinary cortisol excretion in Holocaust survivors with posttraumatic stress disorder.[comment]. *American Journal of Psychiatry*, 1995. 152(7): p. 982-6.

[25] Bremner, J.D., et al., Assessment of the hypothalamic-pituitary-adrenal axis over a 24-hour diurnal period and in response to neuroendocrine challenges in women with and without childhood sexual abuse and posttraumatic stress disorder. *Biological Psychiatry*, 2003. 54(7): p. 710-8.

[26] Bremner, J.D., et al., Elevated CSF corticotropin-releasing factor concentrations in posttraumatic stress disorder. *American Journal of Psychiatry*, 1997. 154(5): p. 624-9.

[27] Heim, C., et al., Persistent changes in corticotropin-releasing factor systems due to early life stress: relationship to the pathophysiology of major depression and post-traumatic stress disorder. *Psychopharmacology Bulletin*, 1997. 33(2): p. 185-92.

[28] Smith, M.A., et al., The corticotropin-releasing hormone test in patients with posttraumatic stress disorder. *Biological Psychiatry*, 1989. 26(4): p. 349-55.

[29] Yehuda, R., et al., Lymphocyte glucocorticoid receptor number in posttraumatic stress disorder. *American Journal of Psychiatry*, 1991. 148(4): p. 499-504.

[30] Stein, M.B., et al., Enhanced dexamethasone suppression of plasma cortisol in adult women traumatized by childhood sexual abuse. *Biological Psychiatry*, 1997. 42(8): p. 680-6.

[31] Liberzon, I., et al., Differential regulation of hippocampal glucocorticoid receptors mRNA and fast feedback: relevance to post-traumatic stress disorder. *Journal of Neuroendocrinology*, 1999. 11(1): p. 11-7.

[32] Rahe, R.H., et al., Psychological and physiological assessments on American hostages freed from captivity in Iran. *Psychosomatic Medicine*, 1990. 52(1): p. 1-16.

[33] Smyth, J., et al., Stressors and mood measured on a momentary basis are associated with salivary cortisol secretion. *Psychoneuroendocrinology*, 1998. 23(4): p. 353-70.

[34] Steptoe, A., et al., Job strain and anger expression predict early morning elevations in salivary cortisol. *Psychosomatic Medicine*, 2000. 62(2): p. 286-92.

[35] Kirschbaum, C., et al., Stress- and treatment-induced elevations of cortisol levels associated with impaired declarative memory in healthy adults. *Life Sciences*, 1996. 58(17): p. 1475-83.

[36] Cohen, S., et al., Reactivity and vulnerability to stress-associated risk for upper respiratory illness. *Psychosomatic Medicine*, 2002. 64(2): p. 302-10.

[37] J.H.H.Thijssen, H.N., ed. *DHEA: a comprehensive review*. 1999, The Parthenon Publishing Group: New York.

[38] Rupprecht, R. and F. Holsboer, Neuroactive steroids: mechanisms of action and neuropsychopharmacological perspectives.[see comment]. *Trends in Neurosciences*, 1999. 22(9): p. 410-6.

[39] Linkowski, P., et al., The 24-hour profile of adrenocorticotropin and cortisol in major depressive illness. *Journal of Clinical Endocrinology & Metabolism*, 1985. 61(3): p. 429-38.

[40] Holsboer, F., The dexamethasone suppression test in depressed patients: clinical and biochemical aspects. *Journal of Steroid Biochemistry*, 1983. 19(1A): p. 251-7.

[41] Christensen, L., et al., Afternoon plasma cortisol in depressed patients: a measure of diagnosis or severity? *Life Sciences*, 1983. 32(6): p. 617-23.

[42] Wood, B., et al., Salivary cortisol profiles in chronic fatigue syndrome. *Neuropsychobiology*, 1998. 37(1): p. 1-4.

[43] Scott, L.V. and T.G. Dinan, Urinary free cortisol excretion in chronic fatigue syndrome, major depression and in healthy volunteers. *Journal of Affective Disorders*, 1998. 47(1-3): p. 49-54.

[44] Scott, L.V., S. Medbak, and T.G. Dinan, Blunted adrenocorticotropin and cortisol responses to corticotropin-releasing hormone stimulation in chronic fatigue syndrome. *Acta Psychiatrica Scandinavica*, 1998. 97(6): p. 450-7.

[45] Heim, C., U. Ehlert, and D.H. Hellhammer, The potential role of hypocortisolism in the pathophysiology of stress-related bodily disorders. *Psychoneuroendocrinology*, 2000. 25(1): p. 1-35.

[46] Zobel, A.W., et al., Cortisol response in the combined dexamethasone/CRH test as predictor of relapse in patients with remitted depression. a prospective study. *Journal of Psychiatric Research*, 2001. 35(2): p. 83-94.

[47] Mensah-Nyagan, A.G., et al., Anatomical and biochemical evidence for the synthesis of unconjugated and sulfated neurosteroids in amphibians. *Brain Research - Brain Research Reviews*, 2001. 37(1-3): p. 13-24.

[48] Baulieu, E.E., Neurosteroids: a novel function of the brain. *Psychoneuroendocrinology*, 1998. 23(8): p. 963-87.

[49] Baulieu, E.E., Neurosteroids: of the nervous system, by the nervous system, for the nervous system. *Recent Progress in Hormone Research*, 1997. 52: p. 1-32.

[50] Zwain, I.H. and S.S. Yen, Neurosteroidogenesis in astrocytes, oligodendrocytes, and neurons of cerebral cortex of rat brain. *Endocrinology*, 1999. 140(8): p. 3843-52.

[51] Zwain, I.H. and S.S. Yen, Dehydroepiandrosterone: biosynthesis and metabolism in the brain. *Endocrinology*, 1999. 140(2): p. 880-7.

[52] Brown, R.C., et al., Oxidative stress-mediated DHEA formation in Alzheimer's disease pathology. *Neurobiology of Aging*, 2003. 24(1): p. 57-65.

[53] Cascio, C., et al., Pathways of dehydroepiandrosterone formation in rat brain glia. *Journal of Steroid Biochemistry & Molecular Biology*, 2000. 75(2-3): p. 177-86.

[54] Brown, R.C., C. Cascio, and V. Papadopoulos, Pathways of neurosteroid biosynthesis in cell lines from human brain: regulation of dehydroepiandrosterone formation by oxidative stress and beta-amyloid peptide. *Journal of Neurochemistry*, 2000. 74(2): p. 847-59.

[55] Torres, J.M. and E. Ortega, DHEA, PREG and their sulphate derivatives on plasma and brain after CRH and ACTH administration. *Neurochemical Research*, 2003. 28(8): p. 1187-91.

[56] Do-Rego, J.L., et al., The octadecaneuropeptide ODN stimulates neurosteroid biosynthesis through activation of central-type benzodiazepine receptors. *Journal of Neurochemistry*, 2001. 76(1): p. 128-38.

[57] Attanasio, A., et al., Plasma adrenocorticotropin, cortisol, and dehydroepiandrosterone response to corticotropin-releasing factor in normal children during pubertal development. *Pediatric Research*, 1987. 22(1): p. 41-4.

[58] Schmidt, M., et al., Conversion of dehydroepiandrosterone to downstream steroid hormones in macrophages. *Journal of Endocrinology*, 2000. 164(2): p. 161-9.

[59] Hedman, M., E. Nilsson, and B. de la Torre, Low blood and synovial fluid levels of sulpho-conjugated steroids in rheumatoid arthritis. *Clinical & Experimental Rheumatology*, 1992. 10(1): p. 25-30.

[60] Hedman, M., E. Nilsson, and B. de la Torre, Low sulpho-conjugated steroid hormone levels in systemic lupus erythematosus (SLE). *Clinical & Experimental Rheumatology*, 1989. 7(6): p. 583-8.

[61] de la Torre, B., et al., Relationship between blood and joint tissue DHEAS levels in rheumatoid arthritis and osteoarthritis. *Clinical & Experimental Rheumatology*, 1993. 11(6): p. 597-601.

[62] de la Torre, B., et al., Blood and tissue steroid levels and their interrelationship in men with pathological conditions of the reproductive organs. *International Journal of Andrology*, 1986. 9(4): p. 241-9.

[63] de la Torre, B., et al., A study of the short-time variation and interrelationship of plasma hormone levels reflecting pituitary, adrenocortical and testicular function in fertile men. *International Journal of Andrology*, 1981. 4(5): p. 532-45.

[64] Weill-Engerer, S., et al., Neurosteroid quantification in human brain regions: comparison between Alzheimer's and nondemented patients. *Journal of Clinical Endocrinology & Metabolism*, 2002. 87(11): p. 5138-43.

[65] Majewska, M.D., et al., The neurosteroid dehydroepiandrosterone sulfate is an allosteric antagonist of the GABAA receptor. *Brain Research*, 1990. 526(1): p. 143-6.

[66] Majewska, M.D., Neurosteroids: endogenous bimodal modulators of the GABAA receptor. Mechanism of action and physiological significance. *Progress in Neurobiology*, 1992. 38(4): p. 379-95.

[67] Lapchak, P.A. and D.M. Araujo, Preclinical development of neurosteroids as neuroprotective agents for the treatment of neurodegenerative diseases. *International Review of Neurobiology*, 2001. 46: p. 379-97.

[68] Kimonides, V.G., et al., Dehydroepiandrosterone (DHEA) and DHEA-sulfate (DHEAS) protect hippocampal neurons against excitatory amino acid-induced neurotoxicity. *Proceedings of the National Academy of Sciences of the United States of America*, 1998. 95(4): p. 1852-7.

[69] Maurice, T., et al., Differential effect of dehydroepiandrosterone and its steroid precursor pregnenolone against the behavioural deficits in CO-exposed mice. *European Journal of Pharmacology*, 2000. 390(1-2): p. 145-55.

[70] BE Pearson Murphy, F.V.A., C M Allison, C Watts, A-M Ghadirian, Elevated levels of some neuroactive progesterone metabolites, particularly isopregnanolone, in women with chronic fatigue syndrome. *Psychoneuroendocrinology*, 2004. 29: p. 245-268.

[71] Monnet, F.P., et al., Neurosteroids, via sigma receptors, modulate the [3H]norepinephrine release evoked by N-methyl-D-aspartate in the rat hippocampus. *Proceedings of the National Academy of Sciences of the United States of America*, 1995. 92(9): p. 3774-8.

[72] Baulieu, E.-E., Neuroactive neurosteroids: dehydroepiandrosterone and dehydro-epiandrosterone sulfata, in *DHEA: a comprehensive review*, H.N. J. H .H. Thijssen, Editor. 1999, The Parthenon Publishing Group: New York.

[73] Czlonkowska, A.I., et al., The effects of neurosteroids on picrotoxin-, bicuculline- and NMDA-induced seizures, and a hypnotic effect of ethanol. *Pharmacology, Biochemistry & Behavior*, 2000. 67(2): p. 345-53.

[74] Zou, L.B., et al., Effects of sigma(1) receptor agonist SA4503 and neuroactive steroids on performance in a radial arm maze task in rats. *Neuropharmacology*, 2000. 39(9): p. 1617-27.

[75] Mukai, H., S. Uchino, and S. Kawato, Effects of neurosteroids on Ca(2+) signaling mediated by recombinant N-methyl-D-aspartate receptor expressed in Chinese hamster ovary cells. *Neuroscience Letters*, 2000. 282(1-2): p. 93-6.

[76] Compagnone, N.A. and S.H. Mellon, Neurosteroids: biosynthesis and function of these novel neuromodulators. *Frontiers in Neuroendocrinology*, 2000. 21(1): p. 1-56.

[77] Hertting, A. and T. Theorell, Physiological changes associated with downsizing of personnel and reorganisation in the health care sector. *Psychotherapy & Psychosomatics*, 2002. 71(2): p. 117-22.

[78] Blake, D.D., et al., The development of a Clinician-Administered PTSD Scale. *Journal of Traumatic Stress*, 1995. 8(1): p. 75-90.

[79] Weathers, F.W., T.M. Keane, and J.R. Davidson, Clinician-administered PTSD scale: a review of the first ten years of research. *Depression & Anxiety*, 2001. 13(3): p. 132-56.

[80] Sondergaard, H.P. and T. Theorell, A longitudinal study of hormonal reactions accompanying life events in recently resettled refugees. *Psychotherapy & Psychosomatics*, 2003. 72(1): p. 49-58.

[81] Sondergaard, H.P., L.O. Hansson, and T. Theorell, Elevated blood levels of dehydroepiandrosterone sulphate vary with symptom load in posttraumatic stress disorder: findings from a longitudinal study of refugees in Sweden. *Psychotherapy & Psychosomatics*, 2002. 71(5): p. 298-303.

[82] Spivak, B., et al., Elevated circulatory level of GABA(A)--antagonistic neurosteroids in patients with combat-related post-traumatic stress disorder. *Psychological Medicine*, 2000. 30(5): p. 1227-31.

[83] Bremner, J.D., et al., Decreased benzodiazepine receptor binding in prefrontal cortex in combat-related posttraumatic stress disorder. *American Journal of Psychiatry*, 2000. 157(7): p. 1120-6.

[84] H P Sondergaard, T.Theorell, Language acquisition in relation to cumulative PTSD symptom load over time in a sample of resettled refugees. *Psychotherapy & Psychosomatics*, in press 2004.

In: Trends in Posttraumatic Stress Disorder Research   ISBN 1-59454-135-3
Editor: Thomas A. Corales, pp. 45-66   © 2005 Nova Science Publishers, Inc.

Chapter 3

ASSOCIATIVE FUNCTIONAL ANALYSIS MODEL OF POSTTRAUMATIC STRESS DISORDER

Nenad Paunović

Department of Psychology, Stockholm University, Stockholm, Sweden

ABSTRACT

A revised associative functional analysis (AFA) model of posttraumatic stress disorder (PTSD) is outlined. In terms of the AFA model currently elicited respondent mechanisms, and dysfunctional cognitive and behavioral responses reciprocally influence each other, and interact with a representational memory network of corresponding factors in determining the development and maintenance of PTSD. The present AFA model combines cognitive, behavioral and network models into a unified framework. In the present AFA model a special emphasis is put on the influence of pleasurable and mastery respondent learning mechanisms incompatible to the respondent trauma-related learning. It is proposed that in order to achieve recovery the former should be elicited in the context of fully elicited trauma-related respondent mechanisms. Prolonged exposure counterconditioning (PEC), a new treatment for PTSD, aims at reinforcing an individuals incompatible respondent learning mechanisms and utilizing them in order to counter the numbing symptoms, increase the trauma exposure tolerance and weaken respondently learned trauma-related emotions. Important theoretical and methodological issues related to the PEC treatment are reviewed. In the discussion section additional issues related to the present AFA model and the PEC treatment for PTSD are outlined.

Keywords: associative functional analysis, prolonged exposure counterconditioning, PTSD, theory, treatment.

INTRODUCTION

Cognitive-behavioral conceptualizations of posttraumatic stress disorder (PTSD) have led to the development of cognitive-behavioral therapies (CBT) that have shown good treatment efficacy for this disorder (e.g., Foa et al., 1999; Keane, Fairbank, Cadell, & Zimering, 1989;

Resick, Nishith, Weaver, Astin, & Feuer, 2002; Rothbaum, Meadows, Resick, & Foy, 2000). Cognitive-behavioral models usually focus on correcting dysfunctional cognitive schemas, fear structures in memory, and catastrophic interpretations that are postulated to maintain PTSD (e.g., Ehlers & Clark, 2000; Foa & Rothbaum, 1998; Resick & Schnicke, 1992). In behavioral models negative reinforcement is the primary mechanism that maintains PTSD (e.g., Keane, Zimering, & Cadell, 1985). However, potential limitations of these CBT models include the following. First, since cognitive models postulate that cognitive mechanisms are maintaining PTSD potential maintaining influences of the current environment are not included. Second, in both CBT and behavioral models respondent mechanisms are not viewed as contributing factors in the maintenance of PTSD, despite the use of CBT procedures that supports a respondent conceptualization. For example, breathing retraining and relaxation procedures constitute necessary parts of exposure-based empirically supported treatments for PTSD that are utilized in order to counter trauma-related anxiety and fear (Foa & Rothbaum, 1998; Lyons & Keane, 1989). In addition, extinction and habituation during exposure therapy may often not be due to a decline of trauma-related distress during trauma exposure, but to the therapist soothing the client *after* trauma exposure.

Foa and colleagues have adopted the emotional processing theory in order to explain the maintenance of PTSD (Foa & Rothbaum, 1998; Foa, Steketee, & Rothbaum, 1989). Foa and Rothbaum (1998) describe a pathological trauma memory structure as characterized by erroneous associations between stimuli, responses and their meaning. In addition, extreme positive or negative pre-trauma schemas, and erroneous post-trauma schemas of the self and others characterize it. In order for emotional processing to occur so that the erroneous characteristics of the trauma memory can become modified, a close match between the arousal at the time of the event and the arousal activated during therapy should be accomplished (Foa et al., 1989). In addition, new information that is incompatible to the elements in the fear network must be integrated. Such integration may be indicated by a physiological habituation within and between the sessions and a normal trauma memory (Foa & Rothbaum, 1998). This theoretical model has a couple of potential limitations. First, since it is a cognitive schema model it doesn't include environmental operants as important contributors to the maintenance of PTSD. Second, respondent mechanisms are not viewed as potential maintaining factors in PTSD. Third, it is not clear whether or how the mechanism of negative reinforcement that was viewed as a factor involved in the maintenance of PTSD (e.g., Foa & Rothbaum 1998) is integrated with the pathological trauma memory model. Postulated cognitive and behavioral mechanisms should be parsimoniously integrated into a unified theoretical model.

The first aim of the present paper is to present a revised associative functional analysis (AFA) model of PTSD. The AFA model integrates respondent, cognitive, behavioral, and fear network models in PTSD into a unified framework. It is postulated that each of these mechanisms has a reciprocal influence on each other. However, in the current presentation of the AFA model special emphasis is put on the role of respondent learning mechanisms in the maintenance and recovery of PTSD. First, in order for recovery to occur the currently elicited trauma-related respondent mechanisms must match the most central trauma-related respondent mechanisms represented in a memory network of the traumatic experience. Second, incompatible respondent mechanisms consisting of learned pleasurable and mastery experiences must be fully elicited in the context of fully elicited trauma-related respondent mechanisms so that the former can weaken the latter. Respondent and operant learning mechanisms that are applied in the present AFA model have been adopted from Baldwin and Baldwin's (1986) and Sundel and Sundel's (1999) material. The second purpose of the present paper is to outline important theoretical and methodological issues of prolonged exposure counterconditioning (PEC), a new treatment for PTSD that is based on respondent re-learning mechanisms according to the AFA model. In PEC pleasurable and mastery experiences are imaginally relived in order to counter the numbing symptoms, strengthen the trauma exposure tolerance and respondently weaken the trauma-related respondent learning of fear, anxiety etc. It is also postulated that incompatible respondent mechanisms of pleasurable and mastery experiences can provide a traumatized individual with massive evidence that contradicts trauma-related dysfunctional beliefs, and lead to a diminishment of avoidance behaviors if trauma cues don't elicit distress anymore. Important issues on how to accomplish theoretical and clinical aims in PEC are outlined.

ASSOCIATIVE FUNCTIONAL ANALYSIS (AFA) MODEL OF PTSD

A Revised Associative Functional Analysis (AFA) Model of PTSD

According to the initial AFA model (Paunović, 2003) it was postulated that respondent mechanisms determined a traumatized individuals cognitive and behavioral responses, and that a change in the former would result in a change in the latter. In the present re-formulated AFA model it is proposed that respondent mechanisms, and cognitive and behavioral responses have a reciprocal influence on each other. Respondent re-learning *may* lead to a functional change in dysfunctional cognitive and behavioral responses. However, a functional cognitive and behavioral change may not always occur. Conversely, functional changes in trauma-related cognitive and behavioral responses may not result in a thorough trauma-related respondent re-learning. In terms of respondent re-learning mechanisms it is postulated that two conditions must be met in order to accomplish changes in trauma-related cognitive and behavioral responses. First, the most central details of the trauma-related memory must be elicited. Dysfunctional trauma-related beliefs and a strong motivational tendency to escape from the trauma-related memories and distress should accompany such an elicitation. Second, incompatible respondent learning experiences that fully contradict the trauma-related respondent experience, all of the trauma-related beliefs and escape/avoidance behaviors must be elicited in the context of full trauma response elicitation.

Lang, Bradley and Cuthbert's (1990) motivational structure of emotion is separated into an appetitive system (associated with pleasant emotions and appetitive behaviors) and a defensive system (associated with unpleasant emotion and fight or flight behaviors). The respondent mechanisms in the AFA model that corresponds to these two motivational structures of emotion are divided into trauma-related and pleasurable/mastery learning mechanisms that reciprocally influence each other (see right side of Figure 1).

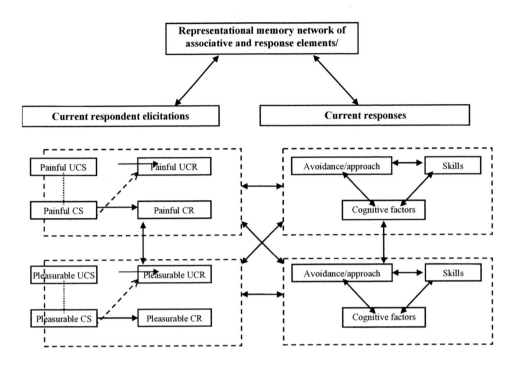

Figure 1. A revised associative functional analysis model of posttraumatic stress disorder and associated psychopathology.

The Interaction between Currently Elicited Respondent Mechanisms and a Representational Memory Network of such Mechanisms

It is postulated that a traumatized individuals representational memory network of dysfunctional trauma-related respondent mechanisms must be fully accessed in order to accomplish recovery in PTSD. Current trauma cues may not be able to access all relevant dysfunctional respondent responses in a trauma memory network. Furthermore, current thoughts about or engagements in valued pleasurable and mastery experiences must be strong enough in order to counter trauma-related respondent responses. An elicitation of incompatible pleasurable and mastery experiences in the context of full trauma response elicitation may lead to recovery if the former is stronger than the latter. It is proposed that representations of respondent pre-trauma, trauma, and post-trauma experiences determine in interaction with representations of incompatible pleasurable and mastery experiences whether psychopathology or recovery from PTSD will follow. In order to accomplish a recovery from PTSD it may first be useful to elicit all strong respondently learned pleasurable and mastery experiences. This may strengthen the trauma exposure tolerance and counter the numbing PTSD symptoms. Second, the most central respondent trauma cues and responses should be elicited in the trauma memory network. Third, in order to integrate representations of respondent trauma-related and pleasurable/mastery experiences the latter should be elicited in the context of the former. A thorough integration should only be possible if the incompatible respondent responses have fully weakened the trauma-related responses. If such a process weakens a trauma-related respondent learning it should be much easier for an individual to reinforce and maintain pleasurable and mastery experiences in everyday life since the latter doesn't become weakened by traumatic intrusions. Pleasurable and mastery experiences may be elicited in two ways. First, past pleasurable and mastery experiences can be imaginally relived. Second, a behavioral activation of pleasurable and mastery experiences in the present time can be pursued in valued directions.

Negative Functions of Intrusions and Trauma-Related Distress

Trauma-related intrusions may have several negative functions when triggered by internal or external trauma cues. First, intrusions may *punish* (a) functional thoughts about previous pleasurable and mastery experiences, (b) present engagements in valued activities related to pleasurable and mastery experiences, and (c) functional beliefs about oneself and other people. Second, intrusions may *respondently weaken* pleasurable and mastery experiences if the former occur in situations that elicit the latter. Such mechanisms may lead to the development and maintenance of numbing symptoms in PTSD. If such respondent weakening occurs in a large variety of situations or if it is excessively strong it may lead to severe numbing symptoms. Third, intrusions may function as *discriminative stimuli* (a) to start engaging in avoidance behaviors that may lead to negative reinforcement and a strengthening of the trauma-related respondent learning, and (b) to catastrophic interpretations of respondent trauma-related stimuli and responses that may in turn reinforce the latter. Fourth, intrusions may *higher-order condition* pleasurable and mastery experiences to trauma-related distress if the former occurs in circumstances of the latter. In this way pleasurable and mastery stimuli may become trauma reminders that are to be avoided.

Currently Elicited Trauma-Related Respondent Stimuli and Responses

In order to fulfill PTSD criteria of a traumatic event emotional responses must include experiences of fear, helplessness or horror during the trauma (American Psychiatric Association, 1994). However, some individuals may respond with other emotions during a traumatic experience such as anger or shame (e.g., Brewin, Andrews, & Rose, 2000). These emotions may become respondently learned and elicited by trauma cues during the trauma sequel in a similar way as emotions of fear, horror or helplessness. Respondent representations of pre-trauma experiences of anger, shame, fear etc. may be elicited during the traumatic experience and may reciprocally influence the trauma-related respondent learning. Distressing respondent posttrauma experiences may also reciprocally reinforce the trauma-related respondent learning.

Trauma-related dysfunctional beliefs (e.g., Ehlers & Clark, 2000) exacerbate the trauma-related respondent learning in PTSD. Catastrophic interpretations may function as positive reinforcers of currently elicited trauma-related respondent stimuli and responses. Catastrophic interpretations may become higher-order conditioned to trauma-related distress and come to function as a respondent trauma cue. The numbing symptoms may also be negatively interpreted. Numbing symptoms may be misinterpreted as signs of irremediable personal inadequacy in a similar way as depressive symptoms. According to Teasdale (1985) the depressive symptoms of a lack of energy, irritability or loss of interest and affection may be viewed as signs of selfishness, weakness, or as evidence that a person is a poor wife or mother. Such interpretations may make the symptoms more aversive and may indicate to the individual that they are going to be very difficult to control. Thus, negative interpretations of numbing symptoms may reinforce these symptoms.

Elicitation of Most Central Respondent Trauma Stimuli and Responses

In terms of the AFA model it was stated that one of the conditions that must be met in order to accomplish full recovery from PTSD was exposure to the most central respondent trauma-related stimuli and responses. Respondently learned trauma-related physical pain may be a stimulus type that at times may be difficult to fully elicit by imaginal and in vivo exposure methods. In order to provide such traumatized individuals with a close match between the exposure medium that is used in therapy and the respondently learned physical pain a use of alternative exposure methods may be warranted. Video movie scenes that match a client's trauma as perfectly as possible can be utilized as an alternative exposure medium.

Obstacles to Current Engagements in Valued Pleasurable and Mastery Experiences

A behavioral activation in pleasurable and mastery activities/experiences can become impeded in several ways. Trauma-related intrusions and dysfunctional avoidance and cognitive responses can dampen thoughts about or engagements in pleasurable or mastery experiences. Pleasurable or mastery activities may be avoided if they become higher-order conditioned to trauma-related distress during the trauma sequel. An avoidance of trauma-reminding pleasurable and mastery activities can become negatively reinforced if the avoidance leads to a decrease in trauma-related distress. A lack of pleasurable or mastery experiences in everyday life may lead to a lack of positive reinforcement. Consequently, numbing symptoms may become exacerbated. Dysfunctional interpretations of intrusions may exacerbate the intrusions that in turn may deplete pleasurable and mastery experiences. Negative interpretations of intrusions during behavioral activation of pleasurable and mastery experiences may punish an individual's engagement in valued activities. Negative interpretations about oneself as an incompetent individual (e.g., ones inability to engage in pleasurable or mastery activities) may exacerbate the trauma-related distress and the numbing symptoms. A lack of social or assertiveness skills in valued situations may result in punishment of valued activities due to the skill deficits. Excessive worries about everyday life issues may impede the elicitation of trauma-related anxiety and fear (e.g., Borkovec, 1994) *and* may dampen or prevent incompatible respondent pleasurable and mastery experiences.

The Relationship between Trauma-related Distress and Dysfunctional Cognitive and Behavioral Responses

The vigor with which individuals with PTSD avoid trauma reminders may be related to the degree of trauma-related distress that intrusions elicit. Individuals who have more severe PTSD symptoms seem to be more vigilant in detecting threat cues in advance in order to avoid them than individuals with less distressing PTSD symptoms (e.g., Leskin, Litz, Weathers, King, & King, 1997). It is hypothesized that if trauma-related respondent emotional responses can be weakened by incompatible respondent emotional responses, this should lead to a decrease in dysfunctional cognitive and behavioral responses. Catastrophic interpretations in PTSD may be more emotional-laden and negative when the trauma-related respondent responses are more distressing than if they are less distressing. If trauma-related respondent emotional responses become weakened by incompatible respondent emotional responses catastrophic interpretations of the trauma and its sequel should dissipate. Likewise, avoidance behaviors should decrease if previously avoided respondent trauma-related stimuli and responses are no longer emotionally distressing.

Mental Defeat as a Cognitive or Emotional Mechanism

Intrusions may be characterized by a repeated reliving of total defeat when an individual totally gave up in his/her mind during the trauma in terms of thinking about how to influence the outcome of the event. This cognitive mechanism is named as *mental defeat* and is associated with inferior outcome in exposure therapy for PTSD (Ehlers et al., 1998). Mental defeat may be viewed as a causal cognitive mechanism in the maintenance of PTSD. However, it is also plausible to view mental defeat as a dependent variable determined by trauma-related respondent emotional mechanisms established during the event. For example, mental defeat may be determined by the degree of fear, horror or helplessness that an individual experiences during a trauma. The stronger the feelings of fear, horror or helplessness are, the more likely it may be that traumatized individuals perceive themselves to be completely defeated during the trauma.

Social Influences on Respondent Mechanisms and Cognitive and Behavioral Responses

Social support may protect traumatized individuals from developing PTSD symptoms (Joseph, Andrews, Williams, & Yule, 1992; Joseph, Dalgleish, Thrasher, & Yule, 1995). However, the mechanisms responsible for the buffering role of social support are unknown. Social support may constitute respondent emotional experiences that counter an individual's social isolation and feelings of alienation from others. Incompatible social-related emotional experiences may strengthen a person's trauma exposure tolerance. Social support experiences may provide a traumatized individual with evidence that there are trustworthy people and that the world is not always a dangerous place.

Individuals with PTSD who live in a hostile and critical environment profit poorly from cognitive and exposure therapies for PTSD. Tarrier, Sommerfield and Pilgrim (1999) found that people with PTSD who live with or have close contact with relatives with high scores on expressed emotion (EE) of high hostility and criticism improve poorly on a range of PTSD symptom measures. Hostile and critical significant others may have various dysfunctional influences on the trauma-related respondent learning, avoidance behaviors and dysfunctional beliefs.

Trauma-related respondent learning mechanisms may be positively reinforced if other people express negative remarks or behaviors to a traumatized individual when the latter is experiencing trauma-related fear or anxiety. Conversely, trauma-related respondent mechanisms may become weakened if other people nurture, verbally praise and show other respectful and loving behaviors when the traumatized individual experiences trauma-related fear and anxiety. Respondently learned pleasurable and mastery experiences can become positively reinforced if other people express positive remarks and behaviors towards a traumatized victim when the latter is behaviorally or experientially engaging in the pleasurable and mastery experiences. Conversely, pleasurable and mastery experiences may become punished if other people express negative remarks and behaviors when a traumatized individual engages in the pleasurable and mastery experiences.

Other people may positively reinforce a traumatized individual's avoidance behaviors and faulty catastrophic interpretations that in turn may lead to a reinforcement of the trauma-related respondent learning. In addition, significant others may discourage a traumatized individual from talking about the trauma or exposing him/herself to imaginal or in vivo trauma cues. Such behaviors may function as punishers to engagements in functional approach behaviors towards harmless trauma cues. Other people may also punish a traumatized individual's functional interpretations of oneself and others by negative remarks and behaviors. A punishment of functional behaviors and cognitions may most probably occur if they are immediately followed by negative remarks from others and if the former promptly decrease after the negative remarks. Functional approach behaviors and cognitions may become extinguished if other people consistently ignore them. Functional responses may abruptly decrease in invalidating environments in which a traumatized individual has learned that nobody is ever listening to what he/she thinks and feels.

Other people may differentially reinforce dysfunctional respondent, cognitive and behavioral responses. Functional respondent, cognitive and behavioral responses can be extinguished (ignored) or punished by negative remarks and behaviors from others. At the same time, dysfunctional respondent, cognitive and behavioral responses can be positively reinforced by nurturing behaviors, positive remarks etc. Conversely, other people may differentially reinforce functional respondent, cognitive and behavioral responses. Functional respondent, cognitive and behavioral responses can be positively reinforced by positive remarks and behaviors and corresponding dysfunctional responses can be ignored or punished.

It is not only the current social environment that may reinforce or punish an individual's functional or dysfunctional respondent, cognitive and behavioral response. Representations of pre-trauma social reinforcing or punishing experiences may be elicited in an individual's memory network. The elicitation of punishing experiences in the network may punish functional respondent, cognitive and behavioral responses. The elicitation of invalidating experiences in memory may abruptly extinguish functional respondent, cognitive and behavioral responses. An elicitation of reinforcing experiences in the memory network may positively reinforce either dysfunctional or functional responses depending upon in which contexts the former is elicited.

The real intention of significant others dysfunctional behaviors towards the traumatized individual may be important to reveal in order to provide the person with realistic information on why people behave as they do. One possible reason of ignoring a victim or expressing negative remarks may be to avoid the emotional pain that significant others themselves experience when reminded of the victim's trauma. Traumatized people may erroneously misinterpret such behaviors as indications of that others do not care about them. On the other hand, if the function of another person's behaviors is to cause harm to a traumatized individual, then such a person should correctly be perceived as harmful and should be avoided.

The Impact of Pleasurable and Mastery Experiences on Beliefs about the Self and Others

Currently elicited pleasurable and mastery experiences may determine an individual's beliefs about him/herself and others. A high degree of current pleasurable and mastery experiences may result in functional beliefs of oneself, other people and the world. A low degree of current pleasurable and mastery experiences may lead to negative beliefs of oneself, others and the world. An imaginal reliving of past pleasurable and mastery experiences may increase an individual's trauma-related functional beliefs. Conversely, a lack of pleasurable and mastery experiences may result in the maintenance of dysfunctional beliefs in PTSD. People who lack pleasurable and mastery experiences in their life need to acquire such experiences in order to combat their dysfunctional trauma-related beliefs. The content of functional beliefs in PTSD comprise of beliefs of oneself as a worthy and competent individual, of other people as trustworthy, and of the world as a relatively safe place (e.g., Foa & Rothbaum, 1998; Resick & Schnicke, 1992). Conversely, dysfunctional beliefs consist of beliefs that oneself is an unworthy and incompetent individual, that other people are untrustworthy, and that the world is an extremely dangerous place.

Pre-trauma Pleasurable and Mastery Experiences

Traumatized people who have had many very pleasurable and mastery experiences before the index trauma are equipped with incompatible respondent learning experiences that can be utilized in order to weaken the trauma-related respondent learning. The incompatible learning experiences can be utilized in order to counter both the trauma-related respondent mechanisms and the concomitant dysfunctional cognitive and behavioral responses. In individuals with PTSD an imaginal elicitation of pleasurable and mastery experiences that occurred before the index trauma may become dampened by intrusions. In addition, people who have had few pleasurable or mastery experiences before the index trauma may not be able to elicit strong enough incompatible experiences in therapy. In order to accomplish recovery from PTSD incompatible respondent experiences should be fully elicited in the context of fully elicited trauma-related respondent responses. Furthermore, the incompatible respondent learning must be equally strong or stronger than the trauma-related learning. In order to make sure that the incompatible experiences are strong enough in order to weaken the trauma they must first elicit intense enough pleasure or mastery emotions. Secondly, they should be relived for a *prolonged time* so that they can weaken the trauma responses and regain their strength after trauma exposure. Such a process may weaken the trauma-related respondent learning and strengthen the incompatible respondent mechanisms.

Avoidance and Approach Behaviors

The function of cognitive and behavioral avoidance behaviors is to decrease trauma-related distress. The relief that follows successful avoidance behaviors *negatively reinforces* the avoidance behaviors *and* the trauma-related respondent learning. Trauma-related thoughts, images and emotions may be suppressed or avoided. Conversations, situations, persons and activities that remind of the trauma may be avoided. Worries about everyday life issues may decrease trauma-related distress and lead to a negative reinforcement of the worry *and* the trauma-related respondent learning. Worry reduces physiological arousal in response to a threatening stimulus (Borkovec & Hu, 1990) and has a negatively reinforcing function (Borkovec, 1994). If substance or drugs abuse is used in order to self-medicate PTSD symptoms it has an avoidant function.

Since the function of cognitive and behavioral avoidance behaviors is to *decrease trauma-related distress*, avoidance behaviors should decrease if trauma-related respondent distress becomes weakened by incompatible respondent emotions. However, avoidance behaviors may persist despite that such process has weakened trauma-related respondent emotions. This may be due to an incomplete weakening of the trauma-related respondent learning. A test that can be used in order to evaluate the extent of the trauma-related respondent weakening is to expose the individual with trauma reminders that fully match the stimulus characteristics of the client's trauma (e.g., violent video movie scenes that will be discussed later) and to ask the person to rate the degree of subjective distress (SUDs).

PROLONGED EXPOSURE COUNTERCONDITIONING

Prolonged exposure counterconditioning (PEC) is a new treatment for PTSD that utilizes incompatible respondent learning experiences in order to accomplish recovery from PTSD (Paunović, 2002, 2003). PEC is based on the AFA model and consists of three parts. First, respondently learned pleasurable and mastery experiences are identified and imaginally relived for a prolonged time. The purpose is to elicit as strong incompatible emotional responses as possible in order to counter the numbing symptoms and to increase the trauma exposure tolerance. Second, respondently learned trauma responses are elicited during a short period of time by a trauma exposure to central details. The aim is to fully elicit the trauma-related emotional responses. Third, when the trauma-related respondent emotional responses have become fully elicited pleasurable and mastery experiences are imaginally relived for a prolonged time. The primary purpose is to weaken the respondently learned trauma responses by incompatible learning experiences. In addition, the respondently learned pleasurable and mastery experiences are reinforced and the numbing symptoms countered in the context of weakened trauma-related responses. The purpose of the second part of this paper is to outline theoretical and methodological issues that are crucial to take into account when the PEC treatment for PTSD is implemented.

The Incompatibility between the Pleasurable/Mastery Reliving and the Traumatic Experience

The pleasurable and mastery reliving in PEC is incompatible to the traumatic experience in several respects. First, a pleasurable reliving that is accompanied by low arousal (e.g., being nurtured by significant others) is physiologically incompatible to anxiety and fear. Second, a pleasurable reliving that is accompanied by high arousal (e.g., enjoyed sporting activities, sexual intercourse) is incompatible to the depressive-like numbing symptoms in PTSD. Third, a pleasurable/mastery reliving is associated with approach behaviors towards valued activities and social transactions whereas the trauma-related learning is related to an avoidance of trauma reminders and valued activities that have become associated with the trauma. Fourth, a pleasurable/mastery reliving provides evidence that supports functional beliefs including that the individual is a worthy and competent individual, that other people are trustworthy, and that the world is a relatively safe place. Conversely, the traumatic experience is associated with dysfunctional beliefs of oneself as a worthless and incompetent individual, of others as untrustworthy, and of the world as a very dangerous place (e.g., Foa & Rothbaum, 1998). Fifth, since PTSD is characterized by an attentional bias towards trauma-related stimuli (e.g., Williams, Mathews, & MacLeod, 1996) a pleasurable/ mastery reliving involves an attention to respondently learned experiences incompatible to the trauma. Sixth, a pleasurable and mastery reliving provides a traumatized individual with evidence that the person is able to experience valued emotions in the present moment in time. Such emotional experiences contradict the numbing symptoms. Seventh, a pleasurable/mastery reliving may increase a client's positive expectations of the future and motivate the individual to behaviorally activate him/herself in valued activities and social transactions in everyday life. Conversely, the traumatic experience may impede positive expectations of the future and may decrease an individual's motivation to engage in valued activities and social transactions in the present moment in time.

Substituting the Associative Technique with Therapist Behaviors

In the current version of PEC the previously used associative technique (Paunović, 2002, 2003) has been replaced by specific therapist behaviors that are higher-order conditioned to the pleasurable and mastery experiences. In the present PEC treatment the quality of the therapists voice is associated with the pleasurable and mastery experiences in the client. The therapist utilizes the same voice quality during both the pleasurable/mastery reliving and the trauma exposure. The purpose of the same voice quality during trauma exposure is to elicit the traumatized individual's respondently learned pleasurable responses in order to increase trauma exposure tolerance, and to positively reinforce the vividness of central trauma details and the elicitation of trauma responses. The previously used associative technique consisted of pairing a tactile stimulus (pressing the top of a client's finger during a short period of time) to the pleasurable/mastery reliving, and eliciting the tactile stimulus during trauma exposure.

However, this technique may be difficult to disseminate to mental health professionals and may be experienced as physically intrusive by some trauma survivors. Also, there is no empirical evidence that supports its usefulness and it is theoretically plausible to assume that it is not a necessary part of the PEC treatment. In addition, pressing a client's finger on repeated occasions may divert the client's attention to the tactile sensations during the treatment process.

Increasing the Client's Engagement in Talking about Pleasurable and Mastery Experiences

It may be important to maximally engage the client in the pleasurable and mastery reliving. An active engagement on the client's part in identifying and re-telling pleasurable and mastery experiences may increase the individual's sense of self-efficacy (e.g., Bandura, 1997, pp. 321-323). A sense of self-efficacy may constitute mastery experiences that have the capability of further reinforcing the client's pleasurable and mastery reliving. Furthermore, self-efficacy may strengthen a client's motivation to engage in a continuous search for potentially more reinforcing experiences. An identification of more reinforcing pleasurable and mastery experiences may provide the therapist with material that is therapeutically more useful. Pleasurable and mastery experiences that are increasingly more reinforcing can elicit increasingly stronger incompatible emotional experiences that can be utilized in order to weaken the trauma-related respondent learning mechanisms.

A Continuous Search for Increasingly More Reinforcing Pleasurable and Mastery Experiences

A client may not initially identify his/her most reinforcing pleasurable and mastery experiences in lifetime. The utilization of initially identified pleasurable/mastery experiences should be considered tentative. Any such experience can be replaced by another if the client or the therapist identifies stronger pleasurable or mastery experiences during the course of PEC treatment.

The nature of the pleasurable and mastery experiences may have a short or a long time span. According to the PEC rationale it is crucial to help the client identify and repeatedly relive peak experiences of pleasure and mastery. Some clients are able to immediately describe their peak experiences of pleasure or mastery without therapist prompting. Other clients may need various amounts of therapist prompting in order to identify and relive their most pleasurable and masterful experiences. If several pleasurable and mastery experiences occurred during the same day, week or month they may contain a series of pleasurable/ mastery events that may be utilized in PEC treatment. Pleasurable and mastery experiences may have occurred during specific time periods such as holidays, weddings etc. They may also have occurred at certain places, with certain people, or in specific situations. Sometimes it may be useful to ask a client to describe several peak experiences of pleasure or mastery that occurred in such circumstances. If several very pleasurable and masterful experiences are identified that are more reinforcing than previously identified experiences they may be utilized in PEC treatment. Sensory-based details of what the client saw, heard, did, what other people did, what happened etc. during the peak of these emotional experiences should be identified for each event and utilized in PEC. In order to elucidate whether a special circumstance (a time period, a specific situation, a significant other etc.) contains several very pleasurable and masterful experiences the therapist can ask the client to remember all of the peak experiences in chronological order. When one event and its central details have been identified the therapist can ask what happened next that was very pleasurable or mastery-laden to the client. The occurrences during which a client felt his/her strongest experiences of pleasure or mastery should be utilized in PEC.

During the course of PEC treatment the client may experience events in everyday life that are more pleasurable and mastery-laden than the ones that are utilized in treatment. Such present day experiences should be utilized in PEC treatment (e.g., imaginally relived) and should replace other less reinforcing pleasure/mastery experiences that are currently utilized in treatment. Stronger reinforcing experiences should be able to more effectively counter the numbing symptoms, increase the trauma exposure tolerance and to weaken the trauma-related respondent learning.

Pleasurable and Mastery Reliving as an Avoidance Behavior and Dysfunctional Reinforcer

Imaginal reliving of pleasurable/mastery experiences can function as an avoidance behavior. If an individual intentionally utilizes pleasurable/ mastery experiences in order to avoid an elicitation of trauma-related distress then the former may become negatively reinforced. Conversely, if pleasurable/mastery experiences are utilized in order to weaken fully elicited trauma-related distress then the former should be considered to be a coping technique. Pleasurable and mastery experiences can function as reinforcers of avoidance behaviors. This should particularly be the case when pleasurable/mastery experiences are consistently relived in response to successful cognitive and behavioral avoidance behaviors. The consequence may be that pleasurable/ mastery experiences positively reinforce cognitive and behavioral avoidance behaviors. *Negative reinforcement becomes positively reinforced.*

The Impact of the Pleasurable and Mastery Reliving on a Client's Cognitions

Trauma-related dysfunctional beliefs of oneself, other people and the world can theoretically be *positively reinforced* by pleasurable/mastery experiences. If the pleasurable/ mastery reliving occurs subsequent to dysfunctional interpretations/ruminations about oneself, others and the world the former may positively reinforce the latter. However, this may depend upon the content of the dysfunctional thoughts vs. the pleasurable/mastery reliving. If the content of the dysfunctional thoughts and the incompatible experiences are unrelated then the latter may function as a positive reinforcer of the dysfunctional thoughts. Conversely, if the content areas overlap, then the pleasurable/mastery reliving may provide the traumatized individual with contradictory evidence to the dysfunctional thoughts. In addition, even if the content areas don't overlap the pleasurable/mastery reliving may provide the traumatized individual with incompatible respondent experiences to the trauma that may contradict the trauma-related beliefs.

Imaginally relived pleasurable and mastery experiences may thus provide the individual with evidence that contradicts trauma-related beliefs. An imaginal reliving of events during which a person experienced other people as very trustworthy may strongly contradict trauma-related beliefs of people as untrustworthy. Also, the dysfunctional belief that oneself is an unworthy individual may be strongly contradicted by imaginal re-experiences of appreciation or love from other people and of events in which the individual experienced mastery. The dysfunctional belief that the world is an excessively dangerous place (i.e., that other people are dangerous) may be strongly contradicted if the client's trauma-related respondent learning becomes weakened by incompatible respondent experiences. As a result, the view of the world may become more realistic and much less dangerous-laden.

Emotions that are re-experienced during the pleasurable and mastery reliving may constitute strong evidence that contradicts a person's negative interpretations of the numbing symptoms. A consistent reliving of pleasurable and mastery experiences may effectively counter the belief that he or she will never be able to enjoy valued activities, be close to other people and experience emotions of happiness or joy.

The pleasurable and mastery reliving in PEC may result in a behavioral activation (i.e., approach behaviors) of valued activities and social transactions. A behavioral activation in valued directions may constitute evidence that the person is a competent individual and that his/her quality of life has increased. A decrease in avoidance behaviors towards trauma reminders may constitute strong evidence that the traumatized individual is competent to face situations that were previously avoided. A behavioral activation in valued activities that were previously avoided because they elicited trauma-related distress may also constitute evidence that the person is a competent individual. An establishment of natural reinforcers in everyday life in combination with the extinction of trauma-related respondent learning may reciprocally reinforce the generation of multiple evidences that may effectively counter dysfunctional trauma-related beliefs.

The Trauma Response Elicitation May Generate an Access to More Reinforcing Pleasurable and Mastery Experiences and Vice Versa

One important topic is whether the trauma response elicitation enables an individual to identify and relive increasingly more reinforcing pleasurable and mastery experiences, and whether the pleasurable and mastery experiences enables the individual to more fully elicit the trauma-related respondent learning. According to the present authors clinical experience there may be a reciprocal influence between the two incompatible respondent learning mechanisms. It is proposed that the pleasurable and mastery reliving may enhance a traumatized individuals access to the most central trauma details and most distressing respondent responses. Conversely, the trauma exposure may enhance an individual's access to increasingly more reinforcing pleasurable and mastery experiences that may be utilized in PEC in order to weaken the trauma-related respondent learning more effectively.

Questions that Elicit Most Reinforcing Pleasurable and Mastery Experiences from the Outset

The initial theoretical assumption of the PEC treatment (Paunović, 2003) was that it is possible to identify a client's most reinforcing pleasurable and mastery experiences from the outset of the treatment. For some clients this seems to be the case. However, other clients don't identify their most reinforcing pleasurable and mastery experiences until after several sessions. One possibility may be that these individuals are not able to identify their most reinforcing experiences until they have accessed trauma-related emotions on several occasions. Other possibilities are that the questions that are used to identify a client's most reinforcing experiences have not been phrased correctly or that other questions may need to be developed. At the present moment in time it is considered more functional to assume that efforts need to be made in order to develop questions that may more effectively tap clients most reinforcing experiences at the outset of a treatment. One criteria on which to judge the usefulness of pleasurable and mastery experiences may be to ask a traumatized individual to judge to what extent each experience strengthens the client to be confronted with the trauma. Other criteria might be to ask the client to evaluate to what extent each experience motivates him/her to become behaviorally activated in valued directions and how much the numbing symptoms are countered. Finally, imaginally relived pleasurable and mastery experiences may be evaluated on the basis of how fast and to what extent they can be relived fully after trauma exposure. However, this is not possible to evaluate until after one or several sessions.

Emotional Regulation Deficits and Pleasurable/Mastery Experiences

An individual's avoidance of valued activities and interpersonal situations may be due to emotional regulation deficits. Traumatized individuals may lack emotional regulation skills. Such individuals may need to train themselves to focus on interpersonal goals instead of feeling states triggered by trauma-related re-experiencing (Cloitre, 1998). An imaginal reliving of pleasurable and mastery experiences may help a traumatized individual to identify and focus on the most valued interpersonal goals.

Pleasurable and Mastery Experiences as an Alternative to Mindfulness

Mindfulness has been described as a technique that can be used as an alternative to ruminations and worries. In mindfulness an individual is trained to attend to present moment experience (Hayes & Wilson, 2003; Teasdale, Segal, & Williams, 2003). The individual is not to manipulate feeling states, but just to mindfully attend to them 'here and now'. With respect to the latter the present author proposes that it may be more therapeutically useful to attend to reinforcing pleasurable and mastery experiences than to present moment experiences in general. An attending to pleasurable and mastery experiences may strengthen an individuals trauma exposure tolerance and counter the numbing symptoms whereas mindfulness training is not intended to do so. Also, it is hypothesized that pleasurable and mastery experiences have effectively weakened trauma-related respondent learning mechanisms in case outcome studies (Paunović, 2002; 2003). It is difficult to conceptualize whether and in what way mindfulness training could weaken respondent trauma responses.

Video Movie Scenes as a Trauma Exposure Medium

Imaginal and in vivo exposure methods may in some cases be unable to match a client's most central trauma stimuli. Consequently, the elicited trauma-related respondent responses may not match the client's most distressing emotional responses during the trauma. An alternative exposure medium such as video movie scenes that fully match the most central stimuli of the client's traumatic event may be able to effectively elicit trauma responses that match those experienced during the peak of the trauma (e.g., Paunović, 2002). However, it is crucial to present very distressing video movie scenes only when the client is able to tolerate such strong exposure medium. Imaginal exposure should be utulized in PEC during the first sessions. Video movie scenes of violent events may be utilized after a couple of sessions when the client's trauma-related respondent learning has become weakened and the client has become emotionally stronger to face such exposure medium.

A Mastery Imagery Technique as Exposure Medium

If the traumatic experience is characterized by helplessness imagery a functional cognitive response may be to replace trauma imagery with mastery imagery of the traumatic situation. This is the purpose in imagery re-scripting (Smucker, Dancu, Foa, & Niederee, 1995; Smucker & Niederee, 1995). However, since imagery re-scripting is characterized by a change in trauma imagery from an observer's point of view the client may in actuality dissociate from the traumatic experience. It is postulated that in order to increase mastery experiences during trauma imagery it is important that the traumatized individual enacts mastery behaviors or perceives how others come to rescue while the client fully relives the traumatic experience. If a client is able to re-experience the trauma and enact mastery behaviors he or she may experience an increase in trauma-related fear related to what could have happened if the individual had resisted the violence. Such a technique may be utilized as an exposure medium in order to elicit a client's most distressing trauma-related fear.

Identification of Neglected Own Needs

Traumatized individuals may neglect their own needs in the pursuit of satisfying other peoples' needs (e.g., Cloitre, Levitt, Davis, & Miranda, 2003). Newman, Castonguay, Borkovec and Molnar (in press) state that interpersonal schemata are most amenable to modification by exposure to corrective experiences when related emotions are activated. Experiencing emotions increases client's awareness of needs about which they were previously unaware and can guide them in choosing behaviors to meet these needs, as well as behaviors to abandon. The trauma exposure and the pleasurable and mastery reliving in PEC may help traumatized individuals to identify their own neglected needs. An identification of neglected needs may motivate an individual to behaviorally activate him/herself in valued directions in order to satisfy the needs.

DISCUSSION

The primary purpose of the present article was to present a revised AFA model of PTSD and to review important theoretical and methodological issues related to the implementation of the PEC treatment for PTSD. In terms of the revised AFA model it is assumed that respondent, cognitive and behavioral mechanisms have a reciprocal influence on each other in the maintenance of PTSD. Furthermore, it is assumed that a representational memory network of respondent, cognitive and behavioral mechanisms interact with corresponding currently elicited factors. The role of respondent mechanisms in the AFA model are particularly stressed since these factors are postulated to be the primary mechanisms in the PEC treatment that is discussed in the second part of the paper. A number of theoretical and methodological issues are outlined relevant to the implementation of the PEC treatment on the basis of the author's clinical experience. It is postulated that this should help clinicians to implement the PEC treatment in accordance with its theoretical intentions. Additional issues relevant to further developments of the AFA model and the PEC treatment for PTSD will be discussed next.

Dysfunctional representational networks of respondent, cognitive and behavioral mechanisms not specifically related to the development of PTSD may be elicited by the traumatic experience. Pre-trauma dysfunctional representational networks may constitute generalized and specific psychological vulnerabilities to develop other anxiety disorders (e.g., Barlow, 2002) that may become elicited by the trauma and PTSD symptoms. That is, a traumatic experience and PTSD symptoms may lead to the development of other anxiety disorders in individuals with generalized and specific psychological vulnerabilities. This issue will be shortly discussed for each type of vulnerability in terms of the AFA model.

A generalized psychological vulnerability to develop anxiety disorders may consist of experiences with overcontrolling, intrusive parents during childhood (Barlow, 2002). A family environment characterized by limited opportunity for personal control is associated with future anxiety and negative affect. In addition, low warmth from parents may be related to depressive symptoms in children (Barlow, 2002). In terms of the AFA model a traumatic experience and PTSD symptoms may elicit a representational memory network of respondent experiences of uncontrollability and beliefs of oneself as an incompetent individual. Furthermore, the traumatic experience and PTSD symptoms may elicit respondently learned emotional experiences of neglect by emotionally cold parents that in turn may exacerbate PTSD numbing symptoms and depression. Respondently learned experiences of uncontrollability and neglect that are established during childhood may be possible to counter by respondently learned experiences of pleasure and mastery. The pleasurable/mastery reliving should be conducted in the context of fully elicited respondently learned experiences of uncontrollability and neglect.

A specific psychological vulnerability to develop panic disorder consists of caregivers often modeling the "dangers" associated with somatic symptoms. Panic disorder patients report a greater frequency of chronic illness and panic-like somatic symptoms in their households when they were growing up than patients with other anxiety disorders or control participants (Ehlers, 1993). Ehlers (1993) state that observing physical suffering can contribute to the evaluation that somatic symptoms are dangerous and that special care is needed. Such experiences may lead to a tendency to focus anxiety on bodily sensations and to develop beliefs about the dangers of these sensations. In terms of the AFA model a traumatic experience and PTSD symptoms may elicit a representational memory network of respondently learned emotional experiences of chronic illness and modeling experiences of panic like symptoms. An elicitation of such a memory network may lead to the development of comorbid panic attacks or panic disorder with/without agoraphobia. A plausible hypothesis is that it may be possible to utilize incompatible respondent experiences of pleasure and mastery in order to weaken respondently learned panic symptoms. One client relived several interpersonal pleasurable experiences that were utilized in order to weaken her imaginally relived first panic episode that occurred in a hospital two hours after her traumatic experience. Her specific psychological vulnerability consisted of experiences with her father who had suffered from a coronary heart disease that subsequently caused him a fatal heart attack. Her PTSD and panic attacks with agoraphobia decreased clinically significantly after PEC treatment.

A potential specific psychological vulnerability to develop social phobia may consist of parents of socially anxious children who spend a great deal of time discussing the potential threatening nature of social situations with their children and reinforce their children's tendency to avoid these situations (Barett, Rapee, Dadds, & Ryan, 1996). People with a psychological vulnerability to develop social phobia who experience a trauma and develop PTSD symptoms may also develop social phobic symptoms. A traumatic experience and PTSD symptoms may elicit a representational network of respondently learned social fear and concomitant dysfunctional cognitive and behavioral responses. It may be possible to weaken respondently learned social fear with respondently learned social experiences of pleasure and mastery. In order to weaken social fear incompatible respondent social experiences should be elicited in the context of fully elicited social fear.

A specific psychological vulnerability in OCD is commonly derived from an early broad sense of responsibility encouraged during childhood and rigid codes of conduct or duty required in school or religious education (Steketee & Barlow, 2002). Extremely high standards imposed during childhood and/or excessively critical reactions from authority figures may contribute to perfectionistic attitudes, feelings of guilt, and extreme beliefs in responsibility. According to Steketee and Barlow (2002) such historical experiences are likely to have special influence when the person experiences an actual increase in duties and responsibility, as in stressful life changes. A traumatic experience and PTSD symptoms may elicit such pre-trauma representational memory network characterized by respondent experiences of excessive responsibility and emotional reactions to critical authority figures. This may result in an attempt to compulsively neutralize distressing trauma-related intrusions (cognitively and/or behaviorally). If the compulsions are excessive and consistent over time a co-morbid diagnosis of PTSD and OCD may be warranted. In terms of the AFA model a respondent learning of excessive responsibility and reactions to critical authority figures may be weakened by incompatible emotional experiences. Pleasure and mastery experiences may be able to weaken both traumatic intrusions and respondent experiences of reactions to authority figures. In order to accomplish this incompatible respondent learning mechanisms must be fully elicited in the context of fully elicited trauma-related distress *and* learned emotional reactions to authority figures.

Individuals who develop generalized anxiety disorder (GAD) often report role-reversed/enmeshed relationships during childhood (Borkovec & Newman, 1998). As children people with GAD tended to take care of the parent rather than the parent taking care of the child. These clients also report greater unresolved feelings of anger and vulnerability toward their primary caregiver. Worry in people with GAD may function as a means of anticipating the needs of, and threats to, significant others in the pursuit of satisfying interpersonal needs. A traumatic experience and PTSD symptoms may elicit a representational memory network in such individuals consisting of respondently learned experiences of excessive care taking and unresolved feelings toward their primary caregiver. In terms of the AFA model pleasurable and mastery experiences may be able to weaken both trauma-related intrusions and respondently learned experiences of excessive care taking and unresolved negative feelings toward their caretaker. In order to accomplish this the incompatible respondently learned experiences should be elicited in the context of fully elicited intrusion-related distress and respondently learned experiences of care taking and unresolved negative feelings toward their caretaker.

The traumatic experience may be characterized by a situation in which the individual felt hopeless and gave up completely in her mind in terms of thinking how to minimize or escape from the dangerous situation. This cognitive style is termed as mental defeat and is associated with inferior results in exposure therapy (Ehlers et al., 1998). An interesting question is whether the inferior results in exposure treatment is due to the *cognitive style* of mental defeat or to *respondently learned emotional experiences* that may underlie the generation of such cognitions. If respondently learned emotions generate the cognitive style of mental defeat then a prolonged pleasurable and mastery reliving may be useful in order to counter the trauma-related respondent learning *and* the cognitive style of mental defeat. Conversely, if the cognitive style of mental defeat is the cause of the inferior results in exposure therapy, then cognitive techniques may be useful in order to combat this dysfunctional cognitive style. In such a case a functional change in the cognitive style of mental defeat should lead to improvements in the *mental defeat experience*.

The phenomenon of *transfer of excitation* (Taylor, 2000) may be useful to have in mind when an imaginal reliving of pleasurable and mastery experiences is conducted. A rationale for using pleasurable/mastery experiences that induce low arousal (e.g., calm, relaxation etc.) before trauma exposure is that they may lower an individual's baseline level of physiological responding. On the other hand, pleasurable/mastery experiences that induce high arousal may be useful when one wants to accomplish a transfer of excitation from the pleasurable to the trauma reliving. Such process may be particularly useful if the client has difficulties in accessing the most central trauma details.

Cognitive and behavioral techniques can be utilized in order to reinforce the respondent re-learning that is hypothesized to take place in PEC. Functional interpretations or verbal statements may reinforce imaginally relived pleasurable and mastery experiences (e.g., "I am a worthy and competent individual", "other people are trustworthy"). A weakening of trauma-related respondent learning provides information that can be verbally reinforced ("I am no longer afraid", "the world no longer seems dangerous"). The pleasurable and mastery reliving may provide information to clients about what their most valued activities are. Behavioral activation in valued directions is useful in helping clients create a behavioral lifestyle that provides them with natural reinforcers in everyday life (Martell, Addis, & Jacobson, 2001).

Clients can utilize questions that may help them to focus on and relive pleasurable and mastery experiences in everyday life. Such questions should include clients' most valued emotional experiences. An individual that labels his/her most valued emotion as happiness can utilize questions that recall self-relived emotional experiences of happiness (e.g., "what am I most happy about in my life?"). The purpose should be to re-experience and reinforce emotions of happiness in everyday life. Same types of questions can be utilized that include other emotional contents. A person that values experiences labeled as security and love may utilize questions that recall self-relived experiences of security and love. Such questions can be utilized on repeated occasions in everyday life in order to reinforce valued emotions. Additional questions may be utilized in order to further elaborate on the valued experiences and to elicit more central details from these experiences (e.g. "what happened during the event that made me most happy?", "what further details do I remember that made me most happy?" etc.). Sensory-specific questions should be utilized in order to extract central stimuli details ("what did I see, hear, do, what did other people do?" etc.). Valued experiences may also be reinforced by questions that help a person focus on emotions of pleasure and mastery ("how do I feel?"). All these questions should be repeatedly utilized with the purpose of eliciting valued emotional experiences in everyday life. An emotional reliving of valued experiences may increase an individual's attempts in valued directions in life. Such a reliving may also constitute contradictory evidence to dysfunctional thoughts about oneself, others and the world. In addition, incompatible respondent experiences in everyday life may counter a traumatized individual's numbing symptoms and intrusions and may increase a person's trauma exposure tolerance.

The purpose of the present article was to present a revised AFA model and to discuss important theoretical and methodological issues relevant to the PEC treatment. In the discussion section additional issues were outlined that may also be useful in a further development of the AFA model and the PEC treatment. Future endeavors should focus on developing the AFA model and the PEC treatment in line with the issues that have been outlined and discussed in the present paper.

REFERENCES

American Psychiatric Association (1994). *Diagnostic and statistical manual of mental disorders* (4th ed.). Washington, DC: Author.

Baldwin, J.D., & Baldwin, J.I. (1986). *Behavior principles in everyday life.* Englewood Cliffs: Prentice Hall.

Bandura, A. (1997). *Self-efficacy: The exercise of control.* New York: W.H. Freeman and Company.

Barlow, D.H. (2002). *Anxiety and its disorders: The nature and treatment of anxiety and panic.* New York: The Guilford Press.

Barrett, P.M., Dadds, R.M., Dadds, M.M., & Ryan, S.M. (1996). Family enhancement of cognitive style in anxious and aggressive children. *Journal of Abnormal Child Psychology, 25,* 187-203.

Borkovec, T:D. (1994). The nature, functions, and origins of worry. In G.D.L. Davey & F. Tallis (Eds.), *Worrying: Perspectives on theory, assessment, and treatment.* New York: Wiley.

Borkovec, T.D., & Hu, S. (1990). The effect of worry on cardiovascular response to phobic imagery. *Behaviour Research and Therapy, 28,* 69-73.

Borkovec, T.D., & Newman, M.G. (1998). Worry and generalized anxiety disorder. In A.S. Bellack, & M. Hersen, *Comprehensive clinical psychology,* (pp. 439-459). New York: Elsevier Science.

Brewin, C.R., Andrews, B., & Rose, S. (2000). Fear, helplessness, and horror in posttraumatic stress disorder: Investigating DSM-IV criterion A2 in victims of violent crime. *Journal of Traumatic Stress, 13,* 499-509.

Cloitre, M. (1998). Sexual revictimization. Risk factors and prevention. In V.M. Follette, J.I. Ruzek and F.R. Abueg, *Cognitive-behavioral therapies for trauma* (pp. 278-304). New York: The Guilford Press.

Cloitre, M., Levitt, J., Davis, L., & Miranda, R. (2003, October). *Bringing a manualized treatment for PTSD to the community.* Concurrent session presented at the 19th Annual Meeting of the International Society for Traumatic Stress Studies, Chicago, IL, USA.

Ehlers, A. (1993). Somatic symptoms and panic attacks: A retrospective study of learning experiences. *Behaviour Research and Therapy, 31,* 269-278.

Ehlers, A., & Clark, D.M. (2000). A cognitive model of posttraumatic stress disorder. *Behaviour Research and Therapy, 38,* 319-345.

Ehlers, A., Clark, D.M., Dunmore, E., Jaycox, L., Meadows, E., & Foa, E.B. (1998). Predicting response to exposure treatment in PTSD: The role of mental defeat and alienation. *Journal of Traumatic Stress, 11,* 457-471.

Foa, E.B., Dancu, C.V., Hembree, E.A., Jaycox, L.H., Meadows, E.A., & Street, G.P. (1999). A comparison of exposure therapy, stress inoculation training, and their combination for reducing posttraumatic stress disorder in female assault victims. *Journal of Consulting and Clinical Psychology, 67,* 194-200.

Foa, E.B., & Rothbaum, B.O. (1998). *Treating the trauma of rape: Cognitive-behavioral therapy for PTSD.* New York: The Guilford Press.

Foa, E.B., Steketee, G., & Rothbaum, B.O. (1989). Behavioral/cognitive conceptualizations of posttraumatic stress disorder. *Behavior Therapy, 20,* 155-176.

Hayes, S.C., & Wilson, K.G. (2003). Mindfulness: Method and process. *Clinical Psychology Science and Practice, 10,* 161-165.

Joseph, S., Andrews, B., Williams, R., & Yule, W. (1992). Crisis support and psychiatric symptomatology in adult survivors of the Jupiter cruise ship disaster. *British Journal of Clinical Psychology, 31,* 63-73.

Joseph, S., Dalgleish, T., Thrasher, S., & Yule, W. (1995). Crisis support and emotional reactions following trauma. *Crisis Intervention, 1,* 203-208.

Keane, T.M., Fairbank, J.A., Caddell, J.M., & Zimering, R.T. (1989). Implosive (flooding) therapy reduces symptoms of PTSD in Vietnam combat veterans. *Behavior Therapy, 20,* 245-260.

Keane, T.M., Zimering, R.T., & Cadell, J.M. (1985). A behavioral formulation of posttraumatic stress disorder in combat veterans. *The Behavior Therapist, 8,* 9-12.

Lang, P., Bradley, M.M., & Cuthbert, B.N. (1990). Emotion, attention, and the startle reflex. *Psychological Review, 97,* 377-395.

Leskin, G., Litz, B., Weathers, F., King, D., & King, L. (1997, November). *Faster stroop reaction times in PTSD.* Poster presented at the 13th annual meeting of the International Society for Traumatic Stress Studies, Montreal, Quebec, Canada.

Lyons, J.A., & Keane, T.M. (1989). Implosive therapy for the treatment of combat-related PTSD. *Journal of Traumatic Stress, 2,* 137-152.

Martell, C.R., Addis, M.E., & Jacobson, N.S. (2001). *Depression in context: Strategies for guided action.* New York: W.W. Norton.

Newman, M.G., Castonguay, L.G., Borkovec, T.D., & Molnar, C. (in press). Integrative psychotherapy for generalized anxiety disorder. To be published in R. Heimberg (Ed), *The nature and treatment of generalized anxiety disorder.* New York: Guilford Press.

Paunović, N. (2002). Prolonged exposure counterconditioning (PEC) as a treatment for chronic post-traumatic stress disorder and major depression in an adult survivor of repeated child sexual and physical abuse. *Clinical Case Studies, 1,* 148-169.

Paunović, N. (2003). Prolonged exposure counterconditioning as a treatment for chronic post-traumatic stress disorder. *Journal of Anxiety Disorders, 17,* 479-499.

Resick, P.A., & Schnicke, M.K. (1992). Cognitive processing therapy for sexual assault victims. *Journal of Consulting and Clinical Psychology, 60,* 748-756.

Resick, P.A., Nishith, P., Weaver, T.L., Astin, M.C., & Feuer, C.A. (2002). A comparison of cognitive-processing therapy with prolonged exposure and a waiting condition for the treatment of chronic posttraumatic stress disorder in female rape victims. *Journal of Consulting and Clinical Psychology, 70,* 867-879.

Rothbaum, B.O., Meadows, E.A., Resick, P., & Foy, D.W. (2000). Cognitive-Behavioral Therapy. In E.G. Foa, T.M. Keane and M.J. Friedman, *Effective treatments for PTSD* (pp. 60-83). New York: The Guilford Press.

Smucker, M.R., Dancu, C., Foa, E.B., & Niederee, J.L. (1995). Imagery rescripting: A new treatment for survivors of childhood sexual abuse suffering from posttraumatic stress. *Journal of Cognitive Psychotherapy: An International Quarterly, 9,* 3-15.

Smucker, M.R., & Niederee, J. (1995). Treating incest-related PTSD and pathogenic schemas through imaginal exposure and rescripting. *Cognitive and Behavioral Practice, 2,* 63-93.

Steketee, G., & Barlow, D.H. (2002). Obsessive-compulsive disorder. In D.H. Barlow (Ed.), *Anxiety and its disorders: The nature and treatment of anxiety and panic.* New York: The Guilford Press.

Sundel, M., & Sundel, S.S. (1999). *Behavior change in the human services: An introduction to principles and applications.* Thousand Oaks: Sage Publications.

Tarrier, N., Sommerfield, C., & Pilgrim, H. (1999). Relatives' expressed emotion (EE) and PTSD treatment outcome. *Psychological Medicine, 29,* 801-811.

Taylor, S. (2000). Understanding and treating panic disorder: Cognitive-behavioral approaches. New York: Wiley.

Teasdale, J.D. (1985). Psychophysiological treatments for depression: How do they work? *Behaviour Research and Therapy, 23,* 157-165.

Teasdale, J.D., Segal, Z.V., & Williams, J.M.G. (2003). Mindfulness training and problem formulation. *Clinical Psychology Science and Practice, 10,* 157-160.

Williams, J.M.G., Mathews, A., & MacLeod, C. (1996). The emotional stroop task and psychopathology. *Psychological Bulletin, 120,* 3-24.

In: Trends in Posttraumatic Stress Disorder Research
Editor: Thomas A. Corales, pp. 67-100

ISBN 1-59454-135-3
© 2005 Nova Science Publishers, Inc.

Chapter 4

POSTTRAUMATIC DYSREGULATION OF THE INTERNAL ENVIRONMENT

Rolland S. Parker

Department of Neurology, New York University School of Medicine

ABSTRACT

The persistent symptoms of a head injury after an accident may be mis-attributed to traumatic brain injury, symptom exaggeration, or emotional factors, when brain injury cannot be documented. In fact, there can be unhealed somatic injuries causing dysregulation of the structures supplying chemical signals to the brain and other structures through the liquid internal environment. This reflects persistent reactions of the hormonal, immune, and inflammatory systems. The persistent physiological effects of an unhealed injury and impairment are reflected in mood disorders, cognitive dysfunctions, and impairment. The physiological mechanism is dysregulation as a consequence of extended effects of unhealed injuries after trauma. The regulatory systems are feedback mechanisms, homeostasis and allostasis, circadian rhythms, and such brain structures as the hypothalamus. The effectors are the hormonal axes, immune and inflammatory systems, autonomic and enteric nervous systems, and also hypothalamic integration and output. Chemical signalling systems through the blood, vagus nerve, and cerebrospinal fluid are participate along with the nervous system. Common symptoms are accounted for by this model: Fatigue, exhaustion, and burnout, illness behavior, loss of appetite, apathy, social withdrawal, inactivity, and sleepiness, sexual dysfunction, and dysfunction of pediatric sexual development. Thus, the stress reaction to an accident causing bodily injury is far more extensive than the familiar PTSD.

INTRODUCTION

This chapter addresses a neglected issue in personal injury: The contribution of unhealed tissue injuries to the internal environment of the brain. The victim of personal injury has a different stress condition than the frightened or threatened person, even when the stressor is extended imprisonment in a concentration camp or prisoner of war status. Accidents causing head injuries, i.e., potential traumatic brain injury (TBI), are usually accompanied by somatic injuries which contribute to systemic disturbances and secondary brain dysfunction through chemical products of the injury and the body's response to it. I hypothesize that after injury, chronic somatic complaints (Parker, 1995; Parker, 2002) may be considered evidence for *unhealed wounds* accompanied by functioning of trauma-related physiological systems long after the initial injury. Common examples (which also add to stress) are part of the postconcussion syndrome (PCS): headaches; pain; restricted range of motion; mood (anxiety, psychodynamic depression; panic; anger); seizures (partial, absence, and generalized; fatigability and loss off stamina, more frequent illness.

In addition to the initial emotional trauma, the post-injury response, is a persistent posttraumatic stress disorder. It is a phenomenon of multiple dimensions: physiological and psychological. Its causes and consequences extend vastly beyond the familiar entity known as posttraumatic stress disorder (PTSD). This has implications for chronic neurobehavioral dysfunctions including mood, cognition, health and loss of stamina. The focus will be upon tissue damage (unhealed wounds) as a source of dysregulation and persistent stress. One significant consequence is dysregulation of bodily functions that creates widespread disorders of body systems, behavioral functioning, stamina, and health. It is assumed that chronic somatic complaints are a marker for continuing dysfunction of particular systems: hormonal, inflammatory, and immune. Since it is not recognized that the dysregulated internal environment disturbs a variety of neurobehavioral functions, chronic complaints (mood and cognition) may be misattributed to traumatic brain injury (TBI), malingering, emotional reasons, etc.

The stress reaction to the acute and chronic effects of injury involves a complex interaction between injured tissue, and the hormonal, inflammatory, immune and nervous systems. Homeostasis, growth, metabolism, development and reproduction are regulated by the interactions of these systems, and their dysregulation accounts for many of the disabling characteristics of the injured person. The endocrine and immunoinflammatory systems augment the nervous system in providing exchange of information between both local and distant cells and tissues. A variety of pathways connect CNS and soma, e.g., neuronal tracts and the vascular system. Nervous and chemical signals may reach targets in widely distributed systems or specific nuclei. The same chemical substance (hormonal, neuroendocrine) can have widely different systemic effects dependent upon the type and number of particular receptors of the target organs. Signals within the internal environment are characterized by multiple messenger, e.g., hormones and other chemicals which stimulate both somatic and neuronal structures. Access to the brain is determined by the blood brain barrier (BBB), effects of trauma upon its permeability, and chemical infiltration through neural structures adjacent to the ventricles in which the BBB is less efficient (circumventricular organs-CVO). Tissue response is determined by the wide variety of receptors within the organ, rather than the particular type of chemical signal. After trauma, the internal environment has greater access to the brain (see blood brain barrier, below).

MICROENVIRONMENT-OVERVIEW OF THE INTERNAL MILIEU

Brain functioning of the organism involves far more than an exchange of information via the CNS: It receives information via the blood and CSF from the body that may be appropriate (contribute to adaptation to external and internal status), or maladaptive (misleading or irrelevant to adaptive considerations). The immune, nervous and the endocrine systems constitute a multisystem *micromilieu* (Jankovic, 1994) or microenvironment, describing the unified immune, nervous and endocrine systems: (1) *lymphoid cells* (T and B lymphocytes); (2) *nonlymphoid cells* (macrophages; epithelial cells, and dendritic cells that interact with lymphocytes and other cells of the microenvironment; (3) *visiting cells* (lymphoid and nonlymphoid which enter the immune milieu and influence the immune network; (4) *neurons* (influencing the microenvironment by neurohumoral activity); (5) *hormones* (released from remote sites by endocrine glands which enter the immune milieu via capillaries and influence the recognition processes; (6) *biologically active substances* (lymphokines, monokines, complement, immunoglobulins) produced by both lymphoid and non-lymphoid cells *in situ* or elsewhere; (7) *neurotransmitters* (numerous types and structures, including the classical types, opioid and other peptides); (8) *membranous and intracellular receptors* (molecules that maintain intercommunication via microenvironmental circuits; (9) *ions* (sodium, potassium, magnesium, calcium, that maintain signals through cell membranes, influencing immune stimulation and inhibition); (10) *electrical, magnetic, and electromagnetic fields* created by differences in ionic concentrations and charged molecules in various compartments of the micromilieu; (11) *higher nervous activity* (mind and psyche) that influences the microenvironment through stress-related, emotional, aggressive and other behaviors.

SIGNIFICANCE OF CHRONIC COMPLAINTS

My thesis is that chronic complaints after an accident reflect unhealed wounds which directly and indirectly disorganize bodily and mental functioning. I assume that chronic complaints after head and body injuries reveals unhealed wounds may have a more extensive range of physiological pathology than those affecting the veterans upon whom the original concept of posttraumatic stress disorder (PTSD) was based. The population under study is primarily persons who have experienced mechanical accidents, with potential effects of unhealed wounds. The stress extends far beyond the initial trauma of the accident. In fact, after an accident, people experience stress from injury and impairment for extended periods which may eventually injure the body or spirit. The consequence is dysregulation of physical or emotional systems resulting in physical or mental disorder. Thus, PTSD as usually described, is an incomplete statement in describing an injured person. In fact, its symptoms are not only ambiguous, they overlap the equally ambiguous postconcussive syndrome (Parker, 2002). Post-accident symptoms, especially when unrecognized or wrongly attributed, may interfere with the quality of life as well as being disabling (Parker, 1995a; Parker, 1995b).

COMPLEXITY OF NORMAL REGULATION

Neurobehavioral activity depends upon a wide variety of subordinate functions: somatic, neurological, and mental. Survival requires bodily functions, physiological and neurobehavioral, be coordinated with each other, that components of a system operate in sequence and with useful signals and manufacture of biologically appropriate products which are maintained with narrow bounds. Normal functioning can be defined as mutual regulation of multiple physiological systems, in order to adapt to environmental necessities, avoid disease and injury, and maintain efficient adaptation in the person's ecological niche, while avoiding pathology and disease. With reference to the internal environment, the process can be abstracted as systemic regulators controlling effector organs participating in the liquid environment that sustains the nervous systems and other organs. This takes place through inter-system bi-directional regulation of ongoing activities. There are countless control systems: genetic, cellular, organs, up to the inter-relations between organs and systems. These systems are in bi-directional signalling relationships with many others, with signals expressed and received in other tissues and the brain. The brain is only one site for receipt and response to chemical and neural messages from distant locations. A multi-system systemic response integrates the organism's holistic response to changes in its external and internal environment.

These systems closely regulate each other by numerous chemical and neurological messengers. Some messengers can stimulate a variety of tissues when they express the appropriate receptors. Other tissues receive stimuli, react to local conditions, and create chemical mediators that are expressed in different tissues including the brain. The brain's reactions in turn influence the periphery for both stress and adaptive functions. Thus, the far flung exchange between the periphery and the center represented by the CNS, autonomic, peripheral, and enteric nervous system has a parallel in the combined chemical domains of the stress, inflammatory and immune systems. These super-systems influence each other. After stress and/or injury the maladaptive results can be calamitous. The effect of different functions and environmental conditions upon physiological and neurobehavioral functions occur both in *real time* and periodically under the influence of numerous circadiam rhythmic cycles of greatly varying length.

Although the familiar description stresses the outflow from the hypothalamic-pituitary-adrenal axis, utilizing hormones carried by the blood, and particular neurotransmitters that activate the adrenal cortex and medulla, the process is more complex. Hormones released by targets of the anterior pituitary gland, and processes caused by tissue destruction and repair, feed back to the hypothalamus and anterior pituitary, creating negative feedback that brings the stress reaction under control. In the event of an accident, the processes of the immune and inflammatory systems not only affect tissues and infiltrate the brain, but their characteristic products are also formed in the brain, and their expression influences the peripheral inflammatory and immune systems. Thus, the brain is merely a portion of a entire-body network functioning through multiple pathways, influencing healing and disease processes, somatic efficiency, moods, and probably cognitive efficiency.

TRAUMATIC DYSREGULATION

Trauma, whether mental or somatic, initiates multiple physiological functions, some of which restrain the specific stress function, heal some tissues, and control other tissues. Two principles are utilized here to understand trauma: (1) Brain and somatic trauma place demands upon the system representing a dysfunction or loss of *autoregulation*; (2) Persistent performance or response demands, even if initially correctable by normal control processes (allostasis), eventually become costly to the individual's capacity to adapt, or even create health problems or permanent system damage (allostatic load). When one or more functional systems can no longer contribute, all cells of the body suffer (Guyton & Hall, 2000, p. 8). These may have deleterious effects upon both soma and the central nervous system (CNS). The reactions of the hypothalamic-pituitary adrenal (HPA) axis and the sympatho-adrenal medullary axis are primary when there is no accompanying injury. Wounds are accompanied by complex somatic responses: interactions of the hormonal, inflammatory, immune and nervous systems; loss of function due to tissue destruction; disturbed functioning of damaged tissue; effects of the healing response and damaged tissue removal processes; and, stress reactions intended to re-establish adaptive regulation. When effects exceed normal homeostatic limits preventing return to set points, or create neurological and physiological consequences remote in place and time from the trauma, pathology substitutes for adaptation.

FEEDBACK CONTROL SYSTEMS (SYSTEMIC AND NEUROLOGICAL)

Neural and chemical feedback loops control the systemic and target organ levels of substances to meet homeostatic or responsive level demands (Molitch, 1995). These include metabolic, environmental, and reproductive cycle functions, by interaction between the hypothalamus, pituitary, and target endocrine glands in closed loop regulatory units that are the core of the endocrine system (Granner, 1993a). After a hormone has elicited an appropriate response, the signal must be terminated. Feedback control is the principal mechanism. Hormonal products of peripheral (systemic) endocrine glands exert negative feedback control over the synthesis and secretion of the stimulatory pituitary hormone.

Types of Feedback Systems

Feedback loops communicate between spatially separated organs. The target hormone level is called the *set point*. Control from outside the system has been described as *feedsideward* (see below). Feedback systems can be described as *positive, negative, and servomechanisms* (Fink, 2000).

Positive feedback increases the output of the stimulator, i.e., "gain". It is less common than negative feedback since it could lead to self-destruction. A physiological example is increased oxytocin secretion, stimulated by pressure of the fetal head on the uterus, leading to uterine contraction which continues until the fetus is expelled. Positive feedback refers to the continuation of a process that has been initiated. While this is sometimes adaptive, it can also be fatal. It is normal for the generation of nerve signals, i.e., stimulation of a nerve fiber initiates a continuous process by which a slight leakage of sodium ions through sodium channels in the nerve membrane is continued to the point of the action potential. Positive feedback occurs when a blood vessel ruptures, and clotting factors within the clot initiates unactivated enzymes in nearby blood. This is an example of how positive feedback is part of a negative feedback process, i.e., maintaining normal blood volume.

Anticipatory or feed-forward mechanisms predict disturbances and utilize pre-programmed responses to maintain stability. The athlete's motions anticipate the future position of the body and ball. The problem with complex and rapid motions is that there is not enough time for nerve signals to travel from the brain to the periphery, back to the brain, and then to the periphery for control and correction of deviant motions. Sensory nerve signals from the moving parts offer information to the brain, after motion occurs, as to whether the programmed motion has been performed correctly. If not, the brain corrects the feed-forward signals that it send to the muscles the next time the movement is required, until no more correction is needed. These anticipatory responses are modified by experience and practice. (*Dyskinesia* is feedback failure when motor responses are disconnected from visual input).

Negative feedback control is critical for homeostasis. The basic stabilizing principle is *negative feedback control system*, i.e., the correction causes changes negative relative to the initiating stimulus. If CO_2 lung excretion of CO_2 is increased, causing reduced fluid concentration of it, the process is slowed down.. If CO_2 concentration is too low, there is a feedback increase in its concentration.

Negative feedback affects two controllers: Pituitary gland and hypothalamus which control and include within their structure critical levels of various chemicals. The hypothalamic factors include both inhibitory and stimulating substances. It affects two controllers: Pituitary and hypothalamus, which control and include critical levels of various chemicals. The hypothalamic factors include both inhibitory and stimulating substances. (Molitch, 1995). The basic stabilizing principle is *negative feedback control system*, i.e., the correction causes changes negative relative to the initiating stimulus. Negative feedback of cortisol and synthetic glucocorticoids on ACTH secretion occurs at the hypothalamic and pituitary levels(Aron et al., 2004).

A *servomechanism* is a closed loop which increases significantly the power of a small signal. An example is prior to human ovulation. Elevated plasma estrogen increase the responsiveness of the anterior pituitary gland to gonadotropin releasing hormone (GnRH) 20-50 times. The estrogen effect is primed by GnRH, which potentiates pituitary responsiveness to itself. This ensures the occurrence of a massive ovulatory gonadotropin response to a small surge of GnRH.

Components of Feedback Systems

A set-point stimulator complex contains a "comparator" or error detector which compares the strength of the feedback signal with a preset level. The strength of the feedback signal above the pre-set level reduces the output of the stimulator, while decrease in the strength of the feedback signal below the preset level results in an increase of output of the feedback signal. An example is maintaining ACTH stimulation within a narrow range. Three components of the feedback system are identified (Reichlin, 1998): A *sensing element* that detects the concentration of the controlled variable; a *reference input* that defines the proper control levels (*set point*); and, an *error signal* that determines the output of the system. *Fast feedback* is sensitive to the rate of change and *slow feedback* that is sensitive to the absolute cortisol level (Molitch, 1995).

BRAIN AUTOREGULATION

Control of Cerebral Circulation

Disturbances of cerebral circulation can be created by head trauma, stress reactions, and mechanical injury to the cerebral and neck vasculature. There are symptoms of the PCS attributable to neck injury (vasculature and nervous system), including alterations of consciousness and balance. Cerebral circulation takes place within a rigid structure, the cranium, so that increase in arterial inflow must be associated with comparable increase in venous outflow. Cranial circulation and content of the intra- and extra-cellular fluids, are vulnerable to trauma of the neck and cranial contents. Interruption of the blood flow for as little as 5 seconds can result in loss of consciousness, while ischemia for a few minutes results in irreversible tissue damage. Sympathetic control of smooth muscle contraction of cerebral vessels is described as both weak and strong, with stress hormones playing a role. Cerebral sympathetic stimulation can constrict the cerebral arteries markedly to prevent high pressure from reaching the smaller blood vessels and causing stroke (Guyton & Hall 1996, p. 785). Contraction of cerebrovascular vessel smooth muscle is primarily under the control of local metabolic factors: CO_2, pH, and K^+, and H^+. The normal pH, or acid/base level is 7.4, i.e., slightly alkaline (Berne & Levy, 1998). The vasomotor center (anterolateral portion of the medulla) has noradrenergic fibers that excite the vasoconstrictor neurons of the SNS, affecting the vasculature of the brain (Guyton & Hall, 1996, pp. 210-211). Sympathetic fibers reach cerebral vessels by these routes: (1) Carotid territory via postganglionic fibers that originate in the superior cervical ganglia (Guyton & Hall, 1996, p. 285). There are no known sympathetic vasodilators to the cerebral vessels. The contractile state depends mainly on local metabolic factors (Berne & Levy, 1998, p. 492). (2) Innervation of the vertebrobasilar territory via fibers that arise from the stellate ganglion (Mathew, 1995) (fusion of first thoracic ganglion with the inferior cervical ganglion of the bilateral sympathetic trunks (Parent, 1996, p. 299). The fibers follow the tunica adventitia of the common and internal carotid arteries, possibly innervating the rostral part of the circle of Willis. Intracerebral arterioles are supplied with perivascular sympathetic nerves, whereas cerebral microvessels, capillaries, and venules may be supplied with or closely associated with intraparenchymal adrenergic nerves. Cerebral blood vessels are also innervated by intraparenchymal fibers which originate from the locus ceruleus.

Cerebral Autoregulation

Normal cerebral autoregulation prevents major changes from sympathetic stimulation. Neuronal integrity is maintained through control of brain metabolism and blood gas level, affected by a variety of metabolic and neurogenic effects (54) (Reis & Golanov, 1996). There are numerous effects of trauma upon cerebral circulation. Cerebral vessels dilate with increase in the CSF (which essentially lacks the blood brain barrier) of hydrogen ion concentration in the CSF, and adenosine (which occurs with reduced oxygen supply, seizures, and increased carbon dioxide) (Berne & Levy, 1998). Arterial hypotension or increased intracranial pressure can result in lowered cerebral perfusion pressure. Either ischemia or luxury perfusion occur at different post-trauma periods (Nichols, Beel & Munro, 1996). Sudden increases in blood pressure can be transmitted to the brain's microcirculation, contributing to secondary hemorrhage and edema. Loss of autoregulation may occur in some areas but not others (Miller & Gudeman 1986).

Disruption of Cerebral Autoregulation

Autoregulation is sensitive to both minor and severe traumatic brain injury (Strebel et al., 1997). Lack of cerebral autoregulation has been established after minor head injury, which may increase risk for secondary ischemic neuronal damage. After head injury, autoregulation is absent, reduced, or delayed, leading to moderate or transient hypotension causing ischemia. After impact injury (rat model) there is transient hypertension and increased blood flow, followed by blood flow reduction below control values within minutes (Lam, Hsiang, & Poon, 1997; Muir, Boerschel, & Ellis, 1992). Impaired cerebral autoregulation of vasomotor control occurs after percussion injury (Junger, 1997 et. al.), and is associated with poor outcome even after mild head injury (Zubkov, et al., 1999). Post TBI cardiovascular sequelae include hypertension and numerous other dysfunctions (Labi & Horn 1990). SPECT signs of hypoperfusion have been attributed to loss of cerebral autoregulation after head trauma including minor head injury (Lam, Hsiang, & Poon, W. S., 1997). After head injury and hypoperfusion, cerebral metabolic rate of oxygen tends to be highest very early, decreasing over the first 1-5 days (Robertson, 1996). While blood flow measurements vary with location, the PCS is associated with slowed cerebral circulation for up to 3 years (53)(Alexander, 1995).

Adrenomedullary SNS, CNS effects after , stress and anxiety: Elevated plasma catecholamine levels are associated with SNS stimulation of the adrenal medulla and other postganglionic activity during mental and physical stress: vascular pressor (vasodilation or constriction), myocardial, and blood pressure effects (Catt 1995); (Cryer, 1995). Stress also stimulates norepinephric neurons centrally (locus ceruleus and SNS centers) (Zigmond, Finlay, and Sved, 1995). Over-sensitivity to sympathetic stimulation has been implicated in the cerebral vasospasm associated with subarachnoid hemorrhage. Panic and anxiety result in symptoms suggesting cerebral ischemia (dizziness; unsteadiness; fainting). Sensitive neuropsychological testing is indicated to detect the subtle deficits that could occur after ischemic damage (Junger et al., (1997). Thrombosis or embolism can occur due to trauma, resulting in ischaemia or infarction (Hughes & Brownell, 1968; Teman, Winterkorn, & Lowell, 1991).

Cerebral vasoreactivity is under varied control: SNS through complex CNS circuits (medulla oblongata; pons; hypothalamus), *feedback* through the extracellular fluid (electrolytes; hormones), *temperature*, and *negative feedback baroreceptor mechanism* of the *tractus solitarius* (Landsberg & Young, 1992). Cerebral vasospasm can be relieved through electrical stellate or cervical ganglia blocks (Jenkner, 1995, pp. 63-73). In a personal communication (Fritz Jenkner, M.D., Vienna, Austria) it was reported that hemispheric flow measured by electrical resistance ("rheoencephalography") increased towards normal levels after stellate block in 11 patients (varied etiology including head trauma).

Trauma and Cerebral Circulation

Vascular Damage and Vasospasm

Early and late *vasospasm* is considered to be a significant entity in head trauma (Chestnut 1996; Zubkov, 1999), occurring in up to 25% of patients (Batjer, Giller, Kopitnik, & Purdy 1993). Cerebro-arterial spasm is caused by sudden traction on the carotid artery sheath at the base of the brain, with symptoms of vascular type headaches, and feeling of being dazed or stunned (Goldstein 1991). Vasospasm is described as occurring after 48 hours. Brainstem damage or subarachnoid hemorrhage is associated with vasospasm independently of dysregulation. Posttraumatic posterior cerebral vasospasm may be responsible for brainstem dysfunction Indeed, one third of head-injured patients with anterior circulation vasospasm also had posterior circulation vasospasm, with unfavorable outcomes (citing Harshall, et al., 1978, 1995).

Ischemia

Even after mild traumatic brain injury (MTBI), in the presence of injury to other systems, deficits of cerebral vascular autoregulation may cause *cerebral ischemia* in the event of decrease of blood pressure, or cerebral edema, consequent to increase in blood pressure (Labi & Horn 1990). Vasospastic ischemia is most common after injury but can occur throughout the acute recovery period (Cherian, Robertson, & Goodman, 1996). Ischemia (associated with vasospasm or mass effects) impairs the metabolic needs of the brain, setting into motion multiple mechanisms of toxic metabolite formation and cell destruction. Blunt trauma can cause cerebral hypoperfusion (45)(Dewitt and 5 others 1997). The location of the hypoperfusion, as revealed by SPECT, in cases where reliable information is obtained concerning the mechanics of the trauma, does not correspond to the site of impact ("coup") or contra-lateral site ("contre-coup").

Arterial Injury

Vasospasm involving the large basal intracranial arteries (ICA; middle cerebral; basilar) occurs in 25-40% of head trauma patients. This association is statistically stronger for the most severely injured patients (Martin and 12 others, 1995). The internal cerebral artery may be damaged from stretching, tearing, or compression, without a blow (Chandler, 1990). It can also be damaged by direct damage to neck structures, i.e., impact, stretching, tearing or compression of the ICA and other cervical vessels (Nordhoff, Murphy & Underhill, 1996); Chandler, 1990) caused by impact or hyper-extension/hyper-reflexion and rotation in various planes ("whiplash"). Injury to the carotid artery is indirect and may not be recognized when there is no penetrating wound of the neck. There is an effect upon the corresponding cerebral hemisphere. The most common finding after non-impact injury to the carotid is a thrombosis of the internal carotid artery 2 cm distal to its origin with an associated intimal tear (Chandler, 1990). Carotid artery obstruction may be falsely attributed to direct injury to the brain or spinal cord: left sided deafness; facial weakness; hemiplegia; hemianesthesia; left homonymous hemianopsia with defective conjugate movement of eyes to the left; expressive aphasia. A traumatic thrombosis may not produce permanent neurological sequelae if the nondominant vertebral artery is involved or collateral circulation exists due to congenital defects of the circle of Willis (Teman, Winterkorn, & Lowell, (1991).

Concussion and Reduced Cerebral Circulation

Concussion is associated with reduced or slowed cerebral circulation. When amateur sportsmen who did and did not box were compared with psychometric tests and SPECT, the non-boxers performed more efficiently on psychometric tests, and those with fewer bouts better than the more experienced boxers. The non-boxers had fewer regions of reduced cerebral perfusion (Kemp et al., 1995). Measurements one week to three years after injury of patients (those with law suit or unsettled insurance claim excluded) manifested reduced blood flow volume, as shown by increased circulation time and decreased amplitude. Initial lack of symptoms, and normal circulation time, may be followed 3 days later with complaints of postural dizziness and headache, when circulation time is reduced. There may be a parallel symptom display and increased circulation time for several weeks. Symptoms mostly abate when circulation time returns to normal. It was speculated that the cause was increased arteriolar vasomotor tone (Taylor and Bell, 1966). Referring to damage to the lowest 4 cranial nerves (Davies, 1997), vascular aetiology has been proposed, suggesting brain stem ischaemia secondary to vertebral artery spasm or compression. Unilateral dysfunction of nerves IX and X results in a unilateral paralysis of the larynx and soft palate, the aetiology usually being vascular, but also following trauma.

Late Vascular Disorders
After severe head injury (GCS between 4-8) mean blood flow velocities in the basilar and middle cerebral arteries gradually increased beginning on day 2 post-injury and peaked in the 4th-5th day after injury. This is considered evidence for vasospasm (Hadani et al., 1997).

Reperfusion Injury to Neck and Cerebral Vessels
Reperfusion following resolution of ischemia or vasospasm leads to additional neurological injury: Phagocytic damage to the endothelium and surrounding tissues; Nemeth, Kakatos, Moravcsik, Radak, Vago & Furesz (1997); release of oxygen-derived free radicals (Kirsch, Helofaer, Loange, & Traystman (1992). This creates damage to vascular, neuronal, and glial membranes, with excitotoxic, intracellular calcium overload, and excitatory amino acid release, i.e., glutamate (Hall, 1996).

Death may occur a considerable time after the injury due to occult vertebral arterial damage in the form of a dissecting hematoma. *Carotid blood flow* is also reduced with head rotation. Carotid cavernous fistula is the most common injury, often resulting from blunt trauma, and patients present with frontal headache, proptosis, diplopia, and visual dysfunction (Zafonte, & Horn, 1999).

CIRCADIAN RHYTHMS

Circadian rhythms organize numerous behavioral and physiological rhythms that express adaptive functions throughout the day. Their basis is both neurological (e.g., the hypothalamic suprachiasmic nucleus [SCN]), and peripheral tissue pacemakers. The SCN is the endogenous circadian pacemaker. It plays a critical role in the sleep-wake cycle, diurnal variations in thermoregulation, feeding, drinking behaviors; and regulation of endocrine rhythms, such as secretion of melatonin by the pineal gland (Berne & Levy, 1998, p. 350). Rhythmic body functions create neural, immunological, hormonal, and cellular messages. Food is used differently at different stages of the circadian cycle, and even influences and influences the host's tolerance of drugs (Cornelissen & Halbert, 1992).

Virtually every homeostatic function has a circadian rhythm (Fisch, 2001): Thermoregulation; endocrine; drug metabolism; pulmonary (bronchoconstriction); gastrointestinal (acid secretion, liver function),immunological, neoplasia (resistance and susceptibility to chemotherapy and radiotherapy), and DNA synthesis); also slow-wave sleep, skin temperature, and calcium excretion (Kupferman, 1991). Circadian rhythms affect the cycle of rest-activity, variations in psychomotor performance, sensory perception, secretion of hormones, and regulation of core body temperature (Moore, 1999). Since disturbances of the sleep cycle are common after injury, it is important to be alert for disturbances of the numerous glands that secrete on a circadian cycle.

The Pineal Gland – Melatonin

The pineal gland is one of the *circumventricular organs* that provide an interface between the brain, the cerebral circulation and the CSF of the ventricular system, that is free of a blood-brain barrier (Guyton & Hall, 2000, p. 714). Fibers receiving information concerning the external light-dark cycle arise from retinal ganglion cells, traverse the optic nerve and chiasm, and project bilaterally to the hypothalamic SCN. This is the pathway by which external light controls pineal gland activity.

The pineal gland coordinates the endocrine circadian rhythms, and regulates the reproductive system. It plays an important *immunoregulatory role* (Maestroni & Conti, 1992). It enhances the anti-body response counteracting various effects of acute stress. This is interpreted as protecting the immune system against the unavoidable injuries of stress and/or infectious events. Deranged pineal functioning could lead to precocious aging of the immune system with early appearance of degenerative diseases (autoimmunity, chronic infections, cancer). Addition hormones that are secreted on a circadian basis include: *Prolactin (PRL), Growth hormone (GH), Thyroid releasing hormone (TRH), ACTH, Cortisol, and Arginine vasopressin (AVP), Menstrual* (cyclic, predictable menses is a function requiring the integration of the hypothalamus, and the ovaries, pituitary, thyroid and adrenal glands (Bulun & Adashi, 2003).

Melatonin is the major secretory product of the pineal. Its main function seems to be synchronizing the organism in the photo period, playing a role in reproduction, metabolism, seasonality, thermoregulation, immunity and possibly aging. It has also been associated with sleep disorders, epilepsy (Maestroni, 2001), and with effecting gonadotrophin secretion and multiple sites of the reproductive axis (Fuller & Fuller, 2002). It has some affect upon suppressing human puberty by acting upon the hypothalamus and pituitary to inhibit gonadotropin secretion.

HORMONE SYSTEM

Hormonal Action (Baxter, 2004)

The classical definition of a hormone is a substance produced in a gland, secreted into the blood, and delivered to a target gland. One type, polypeptide hormones, convey information among cells and organs, controlling growth, development, reproduction and maintenance of metabolic homeostasis. They act on distant organs by being transported through the blood stream as well as being cell-to-cell communicators. The latter function is exemplified by their secretion within neurons of the central, autonomic, and peripheral nervous systems, where they serve as neurotransmitters (Habener, 2003).

The hypothalamus is a hormonal signaling tool responding to an integrated assessment of the system. It is designed for a long-distance or generalized systemic response by relatively specific tissues. This has been described as a the efferent arm of the visceral brain, receiving information from the periphery, which it integrates with that of the internal milieu, in order to adjust important functions such as sympathetic activity and endocrine glands (Brown & Zwilling, 1906). Hormone action is very complex. The substances are secreted by the central nervous system and by neural elements that develop during ontogeny in connection with the derivatives of the primeval gut. During evolution it became useful for the concentration of hormones at particular tissues for specific purposes, (e.g., testosterone's effect upon spermatogenesis in the testis) glands developed at areas distant from the ANS. The means of control of these glands evolved in close proximity to the CNS, i.e., *releasing hormones* released in the hypothalamus that stimulate intermediate hormones in the anterior pituitary gland (Frohman & Felig, 2001). Their cell bodies are in nuclei surrounding the third ventricle. Capillaries, outside the blood brain barrier coalesce into *portal veins* which carry releasing and inhibiting factors to the *troph cells* that actually secrete the anterior pituitary hormones. These substances integrate hormonal and neural mechanisms by acting both as secretagogues for anterior pituitary hormones and as extrapituitary peptide neurotransmitters (Menzaghi et al., 1993).

Hormone secretions activate behavioral traits in three major ways (Wingfield, Jacobs & Hillgarth, 1997): 1) Hormones that are secreted in a paracrine fashion (affect nearby cells) can act as neurotransmitters or neuromodulators; 2) true endocrines are secreted into the bloodstream, enter the CNS, and organize or activate behavior; 3) in a combination of 1 and 2, a blood-borne hormone can act on neurotransmitters or neuromodulators to regulate behavior. Since hormonal signals are appropriate only for restricted intervals during development, it may be inferred that disruption of endocrine secretion interferes with behavioral signalling, activation, and organization, as well as effects upon physiology and morphology. The body's more than 100 hormones are capable of interacting with more than one cell type distributed in various tissues (Kahn et al., 1998).

Physiological responses result from the coordination of many different cell types and organs. Multiple hormones cooperate in the coordination of development, reproduction and homeostasis. Particular hormones act at multiple sites. There are a variety of receptors for a given hormone, located in different organs and issues, whose response determines the hormone's biological effect. Each hormone can multiple responses, summating to give the overall effect (Jameson, 1996). Hormone and related substances are secreted all over the body, not merely in the classical endocrine glands. Particular hormones act at multiple sites. There are a variety of receptors for a given hormone, located in different organs and issues, whose response determines the hormone's biological effect. Each hormone can multiple responses, summating to give the overall effect.

System Interactions

Almost all hormones influence brain activity. Neural and endocrine factors influence the immune system, while cytokines (secretions of lymphocytes, monocytes, vascular elements) modulate both the neural and endocrine functions. The immune, neuroendocrine, and CNS systems have reciprocal effects on paracrine, autocrine, and endocrine control of release of cytokines, hormones, and growth factors (Ferrari et al., 2000). These regulate the complex multidirectional communications among these systems. Both nerve and endocrine cells have a secretory and electrical potential capacity (Reichlin, 1998).

Endocrine Maintenance of Homeostasis

Hormonal secretion is stimulated by changes in hormonal balance, with the hormonal products acting on the respective target organ to reestablish homeostasis. The is controlled by inhibitive (negative) feedback from the target organ. Endocrine regulation is complex, and multiple glands may respond, e.g., a dozen after a meal (Habener, 2003). The most important hormones maintaining homeostasis are (Jameson, 2001): *Thyroid* hormone - controls about 25% of basal metabolism in most tissues; *Cortisol* - exerts a permissive action for many hormones, in addition to its own direct effects; *PTH* - regulates calcium and phosphorus levels; *Vasopressin* - regulates serum osmolality by controlling renal water clearance; *Mineralocorticoids* - control vascular volume and serum electrolytes ($Na+$ and $K+$) concentrations; *Insulin* - maintains euglycemia in the fed and fasted states.

PTSD and Hormonal Feedback

PTSD symptoms might fluctuate due to varying physiological functioning. It is necessary to tightly regulate glucocorticoid secretion since their excess can be damaging. This is accomplished via multiple feedback loops. Fast negative feedback turns off pituitary secretion of ACTH by inhibiting hypothalamic corticotropin releasing hormone(CRH) secretion. This is accomplished by hippocampal efferent pathways to the paraventricular nucleus of the hypothalamus. Loss of glucocorticoid feedback occurs in depression and animals exposed to chronic stress. In contrast, PTSD is associated with enhanced negative feedback. Stress response may cause increased hippocampal glucocorticoid receptors (upregulation) that contribute to the fast negative feedback sensitization created by earlier stress exposure (Liberzon, Krstov, & Young, 1997). Although there may be periods of non-responsiveness, a contrasting mechanism may be severe, episodic increases in HPA axis levels of glucocorticoid feedback. This could be *inadequate negative feedback control* with episodic reactivation of the stress response (Michelson, 1995).

Brain Trauma and Endocrinological Dysfunction

Persons who have been injured in accidents may also have incurred damage to the CNS and peripheral structures which contribute to persistent stress. Many somatic symptoms are attributed to TBI and persistent stress. The physiological mechanism could be endocrinological, e.g., weakness, tiredness, vague, gastrointestinal discomfort, and weight loss or gain (Frohman & Felig, 2001).

Extremes of HPA Axis Activity (Appels, 2000)

Increased activity seen in chronic stress is associated with melancholic depression, panic disorder, diabetes mellitus, central obesity, Cushing's syndrome, elevated excretion of cortisol and immunosuppression. *Decreased activity* occurs after prolonged exposure to stress, and is associated with adrenal insufficiency, atypical depression, chronic fatigue syndrome, fibromyalgia, nicotine withdrawal, decreased free cortisol secretion, and increased activation of inflammation.

Some symptoms of HPA axis activity: *Connective tissue* (poor wound healing, thinning of the skin, easy bruising); *bone* (inhibit bone formation and contribute to net bone resorption); calcium metabolism (decreased calcium absorption and increased urinary calcium excretion resulting in disabling osteoporosis); growth and development (inhibit growth in children by a direct effect on bone cells, although glucocorticoids do accelerate the development of a number of systems and organs in fetal tissues); *blood cells and immunological function* (decrease the migration of inflammatory cells to sites of injury, a major mechanism of its anti-inflammatory actions and increased susceptibility to infection following chronic administration); *immunologic and inflammatory responsiveness*, which affect the hypothalamic-pituitary-adrenal axis. They inhibit release of effector substances such as interleukin-1, which presumably reduces secretion of CRH and ACTH.

Glucocorticoid Effects upon the CNS: Excess and Withdrawal

The brain is an important target for glucocorticoids: Euphoria; with prolonged exposure, a variety of psychological abnormalities occur, including irritability, emotional lability, depression; apathy and lethargy; psychosis, hyperkinetic or manic behavior is less common, although overt psychoses occur in a small number of patients. Other effects are claimed impairment in cognitive functions, most commonly memory and concentration; increased appetite, decreased libido, and insomnia, with decreased REM sleep and increased Stage II sleep) (Aron et al., 2004; Stewart, 2003). The corticoid withdrawal syndrome is characterized by headache, lethargy, nausea, vomiting, anorexia, abdominal pain, fever, myalgia and arthralgia, postural hypotension, etc. (DeAngeles et al., 2001). Accident victims often exhibit some of these.

Hypopituitarism

Head trauma can cause defects ranging from isolated ACTH deficiency to panhypopituitarism with diabetes insipidus (Molitch, 1996). Any suggestion of damage to the sella turcica should initiate study of pituitary function, which may take years to develop. Symptoms of hypopituitarism may be total or partial (D'Angelica et al., 1995; Grossman & Sanfield (1994). Panhypopituitarism is rare, and is associated with alterations in arousal and awareness. Hypopituitarism is clinically evident after 70-75% destruction of the adenohypophysis. Total loss of pituitary secretion requires 90% glandular destruction and may accompany prolonged coma. Recovery of pituitary function usually parallels neurological improvement. Residual impairment is not uncommon (Frohman, 1995). Prompt treatment is essential after suspicion of a pituitary injury. *Hypothalamic anovulation* is a result of disorder of the production of LHRH in the arcuate nucleus of the hypothalamus and its secretion into the portal vessels from the median eminence. It can be caused by head trauma or any other disorder of the CNS interfering with this process (and feed back by gonadal steroids mediated by brain neuromodulators such as norepinephrine, dopamine and β-endorphin). It is also related to stressful events and vigorous exercise (Bulun & Adashi, 2003).

Hypopituitarism Symptoms

Polyuria, polydipsia, thirst (diabetes insipidus is associated with reduced levels of vasopressin after severe head trauma (Ganong & Kappy, 1993), but may occur after minor head trauma (hypothalamus, hypophysectomy, retrograde degeneration of axons into the supraoptic and paraventricular hypothalamic nuclei (Kern & Meislin, 1984; Robertson, 1995). With delayed onset, permanent antidiuretic hormone insufficiency is expected (Hadani, Findler, Shaked, & Sahar, 1985). Panhypopituitarism (Liau et al., 1996); (Attie et al., 1990; Ferrari & Crosignani, 1986; Grossman & Sanfield, 1994; Reichlin, 1992; Shaul et al., 1985). Excessive and inappropriate secretion of antidiuretic hormone (SIADH); thyroid dysfunction (Bontke, Zasler, & Boake, 1996). Galactorrhea, amenorrhea, and hirsutism (Rebar, 1996), and inhibition of gonadotropin secretion resulting in secondary hypogonadism in boys (Matsumoto, 1996) may indicate hypothalamic damage with hyperprolactinemia. Loss of axillary and pubic hair (Woolf, 1992); growth failure; acquired gonadotropin deficiency (Ferrari & Crosignani, 1986); hypothyroidism; ACTH deficiency (D'Angelica et al., 1995); transient hypogonadotrophic hypogonadism (Woolf et al., 1986) or permanent hypogonadotrophic hypogonadism (Ferrari & Crosgnani, 1986); reduced thyroid function, possibly associated with a stress-related sympathetic discharge of catecholamines (Woolf, Lee, Hamill, & McDonald, 1988); hyponatremia (cerebral salt wasting, or natriuresis (syndrome of inappropriate antidiuretic hormone secretion (vasopressin or ADH) (*SIADH*)(Kokko, 1996); myxedema; dwarfism; obesity; hypothermia; bradycardia (Treip; 1970); dermatological (waxy or dry skin; wrinkling around eyes and ears); anemia; psychiatric disturbance (mental slowing; apathy; delusions; paranoid psychosis); hypoglycemia; weakness; lethargy; cold intolerance; decreased libido; constipation; bradycardia; hoarseness; myxedema; increased, decreased menstrual flow and amenorrhea; delayed resumption of menstruation) (Bontke et al., 1996).

HOMEOSTASIS AND ALLOSTASIS

Homeostatic Set-Points

Homeostatic set points are a set of physiological functions, occurring in different organs and using varied means of communication. They are designed to maintain an organ's output within a narrow range. This has been described as "time unqualified feedback" (Halberg et al., 2000). Temperature and oxygen level are examples. Homeostasis implies that there is a *body set-point*, i.e., an optimal level for each physiological system, to which functions are returned through bodily mechanisms. This has been described as "time unqualified feedback" (Halberg et al., 2000). Examples of set-points are osmoregulation (Robertson, 2001) under posterior pituitary control, heat regulation (Guyton & Hall, 2000, pp. 826-830), and oxygen level. This traditional view is incomplete: The *set point varies* with (a) circadian rhythms, (b) the interaction between the relative period of the cycle for the two systems (biological or environmental events that may have a different rhythm, shorter or longer (see Chapter on Endocrine Functions), (c) anticipation of future events (a short-lived process that may become self-sustaining.

Endocrine Participation in Homeostasis and Metabolism (Jameson, 2001; Marks, Marks & Smith, 1996, Chapter 45)

Hormones are divided into anabolic (insulin) and counterregulatory (contrainsular), i.e., opposed to the actions of insulin: glucagon; epinephrine; norepinephrine; cortisol; somatostatin; growth hormone; thyroid hormone. Hormonal secretion is stimulated by changes in hormonal balance, with the hormonal products acting on the respective target organ to reestablish homeostasis. The is controlled by inhibitive (negative) feedback from the target organ. Endocrine regulation is complex, and multiple glands may respond, e.g., a dozen after a meal (Habener, 2003). The most important hormones maintaining homeostasis are (Jameson, 2001): *Thyroid* hormone - controls about 25% of basal metabolism in most tissues. Controls about 25% of basal metabolism in most tissues. It increases the rate of fuel consumption, and increases the sensitivity of target cells to other insulin counter-regulatory hormones; *Cortisol* - exerts a permissive action for many hormones, in addition to its own direct effects; *PTH* - regulates calcium and phosphorus levels; *Vasopressin* - regulates serum osmolality by controlling renal water clearance; *Mineralocorticoids* - control vascular volume and serum electrolytes (Na+ and K+) concentrations; *Insulin* - maintains euglycemia in the fed and fasted states. *Insulin*: The primary anabolic hormone. It maintains euglycemia in the fed and fasted states. It is the major anabolic hormone: Promotes storage of nutrients in liver, muscle and adipose tissue; inhibits fuel mobilization; and stimulates synthesis in various tissues of over 50 proteins, some of which contribute to growth (functions similar to insulin-like growth factors). *Glucagon*: A contrainsular hormone (pancreas). Its target is the liver where its functions include the formation of glucose and ketogenesis (a metabolic process found when fatty acid levels are elevated, e.g., fasting, starving, and high fat, low carbohydrates diet, of interest to those who consider this approach to poorly controlled seizures. *Cortisol* - exerts a permissive action for many hormones, in addition to its own direct effects. *Parathyroid hormone (PTH)*: Regulates calcium and phosphorus levels; *Vasopressin* - regulates serum osmolality by controlling renal water clearance; *Mineralocorticoids*: Control vascular volume and serum electrolytes (Na+ and K+) concentrations.

Stress as Dysregulation of Homeostasis

Homeostasis is controlled through feedback loops from the endocrine glands that maintain hormone levels rather precisely by feeding back to the hypothalamus and the pituitary.

Stress is an *alarm reaction* when there is a profound disturbance of *homeostasis*. Although homeostasis is a term used by physiologists to mean maintenance of static or constant conditions in the internal environment (Guyton & Hall, 2000, p. 3,4), we shall see that this incompletely describes even normal functioning. Stress has been conceptualized as a significant change of emotional and physiological homeostasis, in a situation in which the person is unable to cope and restore the changed equilibrium. Although homeostasis is a term used by physiologists to mean maintenance of static or constant conditions in the internal environment (Guyton & Hall, 2000, p. 3,4), it incompletely describes even normal functioning. The clinician is concerned with threats to adaptation that are of longer duration and more intense than the usual level and range of physiological functions so that they constitute interference with homeostasis. A more comprehensive view of orderly physiological functioning is allostasis. Homeostasis has an honorable history but it is now a component of a more comprehensive concept that reflects diurnal and stress factors, i.e., allostasis. Homeostasis implies that there is a body setpoint, i.e., an optimal level for each physiological system, to which functions are returned through bodily mechanisms. Allostasis implies that there is a variable set point for physiological phenomena that varies with time of day, with adjustment in anticipation of future events, and with increased demand of normal and frequent stressors.

Metabolism

Change of weight after injury or illness is common, occurring primarily in either direction or fluctuating around the initial value. Impaired persons characteristically lose *stamina*, considered as capacity to exert effort over a useful period of time at its former level. The variables are appetite, fuel metabolism, and absorption, transport, and oxidation of foodstuffs (Marks, Marks, & Smith, 1996).

Hypothalmic or Pituitary Stalk Damage

Hypothalamic stalk damage differs from pituitary insufficiency (Reichlin, 1998). Pituitary secretion is regulated by complex, multi-layered controls. This complicates assessment of hormonal events at hypothalamic and higher centers through assay of pituitary hormone blood levels. Further, there may be loss of the normal circadian rhythmic secretion of corticotropin (ACTH). Hypophysiotropic levels cannot be measured directly since pituitary hormone secretion is regulated by multi-level controls. Assay of pituitary hormones in the blood does not necessarily lead to information concerning the condition at the hypothalamus and higher levels. Responses to physiological stimuli can be paradoxical. Hypothalamic injury does not cause effects identical to primary pituitary insufficiency. The results are decreased secretion of most pituitary hormones but also hypersecretion of hormones normally under inhibitory control (PRL). Also, precocious puberty can be caused by the loss of normal restraint over gonadotropin maturation (Cone et al., 2003). Inhibitory control over the neurohypophysis leads to inappropriate vasopressin secretion, i.e., syndrome of inappropriate antidiuretic hormone (*SIADH*). The clinical features are water retention, i.e., water intoxication with hypotonicity and hyponatremia (Strewler, 1998).

Hypothalamic influence is positive in all instances except secretion of prolactin (PRL), so that damage causes a release of PRL (Molitch, 1996. Hypothalamic damage interferes with maintenance of body homeostasis (Treip, 1970). Hypothalamic-pituitary damage is caused by blunt trauma, mass effects causing compression of the hypothalamo-hypophyseal portal vessels (Graham, 1996), shearing movements of the brain tearing the pituitary stalk (Molitch, 1996), and bullet wounds outside the brain (D'Angelica, Barba, Morgan, Dobkin, & Pepe, 1995). Basilar skull fractures that tear the pituitary stalk rupturing the neural connections to neurohypophysis and vascular connections to the adenohypophysis, disrupt delivery of releasing or inhibiting factors to the pituitary. A severe enough lesion of any part of the HPA leads to loss of endocrine homeostasis, by disturbing excitatory and inhibitory stages of endocrine signalling to the hypothalamus and pituitary gland (Molitch, 1995). Damage to the hypothalamic-pituitary axis commonly causes secondary hypopituitarism, expressed as somatic, sexual, and developmental problems. The degree of hormonal reduction reflects the severity of the trauma (D'Angelica et al., 1995). The hypothalamus is a hormonal signaling tool responding to an integrated assessment of the system. It is designed for a long-distance or generalized systemic response by relatively specific tissues. This has been described as a the efferent arm of the visceral brain, receiving information from the periphery, which it integrates with that of the internal milieu, in order to adjust important functions such as sympathetic activity and endocrine glands (Brown & Zwilling, 1996).

After head injury, the most important endocrine complication is anterior pituitary failure, and from the published reports, this may take months or years to develop. Severe head injury with poor prognosis is associated with reduced levels of glucocorticoids, PRL, and TSH response to TRH (Edwards & Clark, 1997). From a behavioral point of view, one may wonder if lesser injuries are associated with some reduced levels of these endocrine substances with obscure emotional consequences. *Abnormal thyroid levels*, derived from trauma, are characterized by thymus deficiency, i.e., *thymulin* (Mocchegiani, Santarelli & Fabris, 1994).

Reproductive Axis

The reproductive axis is inhibited at all levels by various components of the HPA axis, e.g., glucocorticoids, inflammatory cytokines. The effect is bidirectional.

Infertility in the absence of anatomical abnormalities was associated with psychological stress profiles (Lemack, Uzzo, & Poppas, 1998). Various components of the HPA axis and cytokines inhibit the reproductive axis. CRH and glucocorticoids inhibit gonadotropin releasing hormone (GnRH), pituitary gonadotrophs, the gonads, and target tissues. Ovarian steroids in particular target the CRH gene, leading to potential *gender differences* in the stress response. *In women* physical, psychological, metabolic, and pharmacological stresses may result in reversible reproductive axis suppression. They are believed to act by inhibiting the GnRH pulse generator output as a final common mechanism. After cues are processed by brainstem and higher CNS pathways, are integrated and interpreted, output information is directed by hypothalamic nuclei. Anxiety or perceived threat can result in reversible suppression of the hypothalamic GnRH network, which directs gonadotropin secretion and mediates feedback control via ovarian steroid and glucoprotein signals. Various stressors affect GnRH release, including surgical trauma, psychiatric disorders, infectious disease, and strenuous exercise. Low levels of plasma estrogen cause of accelerate health problems, e.g., osteoporosis and subsequent fractures after menopause (Rivest & Riviere, 1993). Suppression of luteinizing hormone (LH) and follicular stimulating hormone (FSH) causes relative quiescence of ovarian function with reduction of sex hormone steroid secretion, diminished gonadal steroid feedback control of the hypothalamo-pituitary unit, and *hypothalamic amenorrhea* (Rivest & Riviere, 1993; Veldhuis, Yoshida, & Iranmanesh, 1998). *Endometriosis* is associated with impairment of the immune system (Di Stefano, Provinciali, Muzzioli, Garzetti, Ciavattini, & Fabris (1994). *In men*, stress, including surgical stress, induces hormonal changes (including LH/FSH secretion) leading to reduced *testosterone*. Stress increased concentrations of norepinephrine, epinephrine, and serotonin may induce *altered testicular metabolism* or *testicular vasoconstriction*. *Anger and depression* are associated with enhanced stress, and therefore higher sympathetic tone and smooth muscle contraction, resulting in reduced capacity for erection. Related to this concept, abnormal levels of circulating norepinephrine and epinephrine contract penile cavernous tissue, reducing the capacity for arterial inflow, which may underlie *erectile failure during stress* (Lemack, Uzzo, & Poppas, 1998).

Dysfunctions of Sexual Development

The hypothalamic-pituitary endocrine axis contributes to development and homeostasis. Normal development is the outcome of integrated physiological functioning. Growth, for example, is contingent upon thyroid secretions, growth hormone, insulin, glucocorticoids, catecholamines, CNS biogenic amines, inhibitory effects of the CNS independent of sex steroids, and reduced sensitivity of the hypothalamus to inhibitory effects of sex steroids and CNS inhibition (MacGillivray, 1995). Juvenile hypothyroidism causes severe reduction of linear growth, with delayed sexual maturation and onset of puberty. The child appears much younger than the chronological age. Precocious puberty and galactorrhea occur rarely. Intellectual performance is more but not as severe as cretinism (Larsen Reed, 2003).

Indications for a Child or Adolescent Endocrinological Examination
Growth retardation (Yamanaka et al., 1993; Eichser, Frisch, Eichler, & Soukop, 1988; lack of achievement of puberty; precocious puberty (defined as the onset of secondary sexual characteristics before age 8 in girls and 9 in boys (Towbin, Charron, and Meza, 1996), with growth acceleration and skeletal maturation, or dilation of the third ventricle (Woolf, 1992) consequent to a tear of the hypothalamus (Attie et al., 1990) which may commence within a few months of injury (Shaul, et al., 1985); GnRH release in girls due to hypothalamic damage (Rosenfield, 1996); interference with inhibition of gonadotropin secretion by the mass effects of head trauma due to hypothalamus damage (Styne, 1996); growth hormone deficiency (Attie et al., 1990) that may commence within a few months of injury (Shaul, Towbin, & Chernausek, 1985); absent secondary sexual development consequent to hypopituitary

insufficiency (Miller et al. 1980; Pescovitz, 1992); gonadal failure with loss of libido, impotence, amenorrhea (Cytowic, Smith, & Stump, 1986), amenorrhea and sexual infantilism consequent to hypothalamic insufficiency (Grossman & Sanfield, 1994).

BRAIN

Blood-Brain Barrier (BBB) and Blood Cerebrospinal Fluid (CSF) Barrier

The BBB is more than a filter: It is an active regulator of the internal environment of the brain. The initial proof of such a barrier involved came from the coloring of all body tissues except the brain, eyes and gonads blue after injection of a dye (Goldmann, 1909 cited by Somjen). That the effectiveness of this function includes the gonads, which is not reported in the ubiquitous statements about the BBB, is more a matter for psychoanalysts than neuroscience. The brain's surrounding liquid, CSF, is secreted by the choroid plexus and also moved by active transport (not passive filtration as in other tissues) through the BBB of the capillary walls into the interstitial space of CNS tissue. Lipid soluble. The product of endothelial secretion is the interstitial fluid of the CNS. The regions of the brain where the endothelium is leaky are the circumventricular organs (see below) (Somjen, Chapter I). The major compartments of the brain, i.e., the CNS and CSF, are separated from a third compartment, the blood. The three fluid compartments of the brain are extracellular (interstitial), intracellular, and CSF. The BBB is designed to create a stable environment for neurons to function effectively. In the brain there are two types of surfaces between liquids and the brain parenchyma: Blood vessels and the ventricles. In the lateral ventricles The capillary beds of the brain are non-fenestrated (tight junctions between the cells lining the endothelium (lining of the blood vessels and lymphatic vessels). The choroid plexus is a capillary network surrounded by a lining or epithelium. The endothelium at the choroid plexus is somewhat structurally different, but some compounds may not penetrate. Thus blood-brain and blood--CSF barriers have similar physiological effects (Greenberg & Atmar, 1996), although the BBB has 5000 times the surface area of the blood-CSF barrier (Parent, 1996, p. 17). The BBB excludes many toxic substances and prevents momentary interference with neuronal functioning by circulating transmitters such as norepinephrine and glutamate whose blood level can increase greatly in response to ·stress or food. Cells lining the capillaries that create the BBB differ from ordinary capillaries: tight intercellular junctions and relative lack of transport of circulating chemicals. The BBB is permeable to certain substances, e.g., lipids in proportion to their solubility, and gases such as O_2 and CO_2). There are other mechanisms as well that transport substances across the BBB (Laterra & Goldstein, 2000).

Cerebrospinal Fluid (CSF) is secreted by the choroid plexuses, which are found in the walls of the lateral ventricles and the roofs of the third and fourth ventricles. 70% of the CSF is secreted by the choroid plexus, and 30% comes from the capillary bed of the brain and metabolic water production. These structures are the carrier of solutes that evade the BBB. CSF is filtered from the blood by the choroid plexus in the lateral, third and fourth ventricles. CSF exits the fourth ventricle through the foramina of Lushka and Magendie to the arachnoid villae of the subarachnoid space which absorb the CSF back into the bloodstream (Blessing, 2002). CSF removes waste products of neuronal metabolism, drugs, and other substances diffusing into the brain from the blood. As it streams over the ventricular and pial surfaces of the brain, it drains solutes and carries them through the arachnoid villi into the venous blood. It integrates brain and peripheral endocrine functions. Hormones or hormone releasing factors from the hypothalamus are secreted into the extra cellular space, or directly into the CSF. They are carried to the median eminence and thence into the hypophyseal portal system (Parent, 1996, pp. 14-15).

Trauma and the BBB

Animals models of TBI (impact and acceleration) have demonstrated perturbation of the BBB. Disruption leads to exudation of substances from the blood into the brain. Experimental fluid percussion of animals creates bilateral permeability change in neocortex, dorsal hippocampus, subcortical white matter, and throughout the brainstem. Lateral percussion appears to evoke more unilateral change involving the same anatomic sites. The perturbation of the BBB appears to be transient, resolving in the first days after injury (Povlishock, 1996). *Traumatic subarachnoid hemorrhage* results in production of oxygen radicals, which cause an increase in BBB permeability, delayed vasospasm, acute hypoperfusion, and excitatory amino acid release (Hall, 1996). Lactate accumulation at high concentrations has a deleterious effect on brain cells, including a breakdown of the BBB (Hovda, 1996).

Circumventricular Organs

Some substances that are excluded from the brain due to the blood brain barrier (BBB) (e.g., peptides, cytokines, hormones, etc.) are admitted through the circumventricular organs which lack the BBB. They are secretory midline tissues in the (third ventricle) whose tissues and capillaries are permeable, therefore permitting the diffusion of large molecules from the general circulation (Aron, Findling, Tyrell, 2004). Some of these nuclei are major regulating systems. CVO capillaries (and those of peripheral organs) have specialized functions for movement of substances into the cell, as well as permitting passive diffusion. The CVO include the subfornical organ; organum vasculosum of the lamina terminalis [OVLT - supraoptic crest); the median eminence; the neurohypophysis; the pineal body; the subcommissural organ; and, the area postrema (group of cells on the dorsal surface of the medulla oblongata). These tissues seem permeable to proteins and peptides (Parent, 1996, p. 23). The area postrema sends signals widely within the brain stem, particularly to the parabrachial nuclei which integrates visceral afferent information and autonomic function. Cells lining the ventral surface of the medulla are especially sensitive to its hydrogen ion concentration (pH) (Blessing, 2002).

Cerebral Homeostasis

A lesion in a pathway to a cortical region can create *hypometabolism*, i.e., diaschisis (Caselli et al., 1991). Homeostatic considerations are cerebral blood flow (CBF), blood pressure and cerebral metabolic rates of glucose, lactate, and oxygen CMR_{O_2}. Cerebral perfusion pressure (CPP) is the difference between mean arterial pressure and intracranial pressure (ICP). Increased ICP is common after moderate to severe head injuries, but its measurement and control is a neurosurgical concern. Nevertheless, the outcome of head injuries (no matter what their intensity) is adversely affected by secondary pathophysiological insults (e.g., changes of pressure and fever) which create chemical cascades into the extracellular fluid (Miller, Piper & Jones, 1996). Conversely, in normal individuals, CBF is closely coupled to CMR_{O_2}. Local CBF increases or decreases according to the tissue metabolic requirements. In such altered physiological states as seizures, changes in brain temperature, and some types of anesthesia, CBF remains coupled to CMR_{O_2}. This coupling is mediated by various metabolic products and nitric oxide (NO) and is adjusted to local cerebral metabolism. The calibre of the cerebral vessels may be influenced by acidosis.

Cerebral Dysregulation

Cerebral metabolic requirements (CMR) are reduced after a head injury. However, hemoglobin concentration may be reduced, so that actual oxygen delivery may be lower for a given CBF value. Head injury results in dysregulation of cerebral homeostasis. Different measurements are taken for global and regional blood flow. The lower the CBF Within the first 6 hours global hypoperfusion can occur; after 6 hours global ischemia is uncommon except when it is associated with secondary injuries. CMR_{O_2} is highest early after the injury, decreases over the first 1 to 5 days, and then increases later in patients who improve neurologically. Increased extraction of oxygen compensates for reduced CBF resulting in maintained CMR_{O_2} (*hypoperfusion pattern*). When further decreases in CBF cannot be compensated for by increased oxygen extraction, the patient has exhausted the brain's compensatory mechanism for maintaining cerebral metabolism. The reduced CMR_{O_2} and increased lactate production produces the *ischemia pattern*. After a while irreversible ischemia or infarction develops (*infarction pattern*) (Robertson, 1996).

AUTONOMIC NERVOUS SYSTEM (ANS)

The ANS maintains a constant internal environment (homeostasis) during ordinary activities, and alters the pattern of functioning during demand and danger. The three divisions are the sympathetic (SNS), parasympathetic (PSNS) and enteric nervous systems (see below). The SNS and PSNS generally counterbalance the alternate function, but each have independent activities. Some afferent fibers may trigger reflexes, and others evoke sensory experiences (pain; hunger; thirst; nausea; visceral distention, and chemical senses). The GI tract is under a very diffuse and complex control of higher centers and the brain stem via the PSNS and SNS which stimulate the enteric nervous system. This may account for the lack of close association between stress and gut dysfunctioning discussed below). The GI tract has direct SNS stimulation. PSNS control is via ganglia which are part of the enteric NS. Within the gut are the mucosal, submucosal, and myenteric plexes. There is a feedback loop to the brain stem (nucleus tractus solitarius; dorsal motor nucleus, see diagrams [Parent, 1996, p. 303; Snape, 1996, p. 681]). The ANS's effectors are smooth muscle, cardiac muscle, and glands. When CNS stimulation indicates that regulation of the body's internal environment is required, autonomic outflow leads to compensatory functions. The CNS component of the ANS, hypothalamus and other portions of the limbic nervous system, are involved with behaviors such as emotion, and others having survival value: emotions, d such viscera behaviors as feeding, drinking, thermoregulation, reproduction, defense, and aggression.

The ANS's functions are directly tied with disturbances of homeostasis and allostasis which are described as consequences of injury and stress. After severe brain injury *dysautonomia* has been reported: Hypersudation, tachycardia, arterial hypertension, muscle hypertonia, hyperthermia and increased respiration rate (Cuny, Richer & Castel, 2001).It participates in maintaining a constant internal environment (homeostasis) during ordinary activities, and alters the pattern of functioning during demand and danger.

Enteric Nervous System (ENS)

The ENS plays a crucial role in the maintenance of homeostasis (Parent, 1996, p. 302). Its neurons outnumber by far all the rest of the autonomic nervous system (Parent, 1996, p. 302). The ENS is a complex neuronal network within the substance of the GI tract. It extends its full length. It has more neurones that the ANS, and its anatomical and functional complexity is second only to the ENS. It is composed of sensory neurones responsive to tension of gut wall and chemical environment, and interneurons and motor neurons controlling muscles of the gut wall, vasculature, and secretions. It controls the function of the gastrointestinal tract, pancreas, and gallbladder (Iverson et al., 2000).

IMMUNE SYSTEM

The function of the immune system is multiple: to recognize foreign proteins, viruses, and bacteria as non-self; to set forth signals that lead other components of the immune system to destroy non-Self (phagocytes (macrophages) that engulf microorganisms and trauma-related substances. LHRH neurons migrate from the medial olfactory epithelium into the basal forebrain. Failure of this migration results in suppression of the pituitarygonadal axis. The physiological development of an operative HPG system requires the presence of an intact immune system (Marchetti et. al., 2001).

The immune system has been considered to be a sensory organ analogous to the nervous system, i.e., it recognizes "non-cognitive stimuli" such as bacteria, viruses, and tumors. The immune and neuroendocrine system shares common signal molecules and receptors. These immune-related chemicals are involved in brain function includes processes such as behavior, neuro-endocrine activity, sleep, neurodegeneration, fever, and depression. *Psychoimmunology* is the study of the bidirectional communication between the CNS and the immune system, specifically anatomical, physiological, and psychological (Kemeny, Solomon, Morley, & Herbert, (1992).

The usual description of the IS that it is stimulated by *foreignness*, i.e., it discriminates between Self and Non-Self. A more recent overview suggests that the IS more concerned with entities that are *dangerous*, i.e., do damage rather than are foreign. *The IS is brought into action by alarm signals from injured tissues, rather than the recognition of non-self* (Matzinger, 2002).

Only molecules foreign to the host are immunogenic (Parslow, 2001. Carrying out a variety of immune responses is consequent to cross-talk between immunocompetent cells, and the expression of different receptors. To regulate immunity, a complex network of communicating signals is used, e.g., cytokines, chemokines, and growth factors (Luger et al., 2003). Capacity to distinguish between self and non-self is the particular quality of the adaptive immune system.; failure to follow instructions taught to T cells produces the anti-self response (autoimmune disease, e.g., systemic lupus erythematosus) (Kong et al., 2003). Injured tissue from trauma as well as disease carriers are examples of non-self substances. Autoimmune diseases are consequent to the immune tissues mis-reading ordinary tissues as foreign. The immune system is subject to neural and hormonal modulation, including that stimulated by stress. *Neuroimmunology* refers to immune reactions involving brain, nerves and muscles, while *neuroimmunomodulation* refers to the interaction of the nervous and immune systems (Reichlin, 1998).

THE INFLAMMATORY SYSTEM

Inflammation is a localized protective response, elicited by tissue injury or destruction, which destroys, dilutes or sequesters the injurious agent and the injured tissue, protects against infection, and regulates the activities of tissue cells that repair the injured tissue. Since inflammation is triggered not only by microbial infection, but also by blunt trauma, radiation injury, lacerations, thermal or chemical burns, it is not considered as an immune reaction. However, immune and inflammatory reactions are closely linked, and often promote and enhance one another. *Tissue injury*, as caused by trauma, bacteria, chemicals, heat, etc., is followed by the release of multiple substances that cause dramatic secondary changes in the tissues, i.e. *inflammation* (Guyton & Hall, 2000, p. 397). CNS effects stemming from cytokines that penetrate the brain, or are produced within it, can promote peripheral inflammation (Lipton et al., 1994). The delicate balance between pro- and anti-inflammatory cytokines is easily disrupted by adverse conditions. The severity of trauma, and the duration of hypotension, will determine whether tissue repair will be initiated by a localized inflammation or whether there will be a systemic induction of a generalized inflammatory process. Massive stress also results in a significant activation of the antiinflammatory cytokine force of TNF, and various interleukins, representing either immunosuppression or immunoparalysis. Immunodeficiency (depressed immune function) in trauma victims is associated with enhanced concentrations of inflammatory cytokines (Faist, Angele & Wichmann, 2004). Under physiological conditions, reactions are maintained by cells that circulate or are tissue-resident. Severe and protracted injury causes proliferation of fibroblasts and endothelial cells at the site which form a permanent scar. Many inflammatory events are controlled by cytokines and other small regulatory molecules called *inflammatory mediators*. They are secreted by injured or distressed host cells while others are byproducts either of tissue injury per se (e.g., fragments of collagen) or of the host's reaction to it. Thus, the inflammatory response is triggered by molecules that signify tissue damage, regardless of its specific cause. The changes in inflamed blood vessels attract cells of the immune system into an injured or infected tissue. The dilatation and incased permeability of vessels near injured issue results in part from a spinal reflex: Pain receptors stimulated by the injury transmit afferent signals to the spinal cord, where they act on autonomic motor neurons to cause relaxation of arteriolar smooth muscles at the injured site. A neural independent component of the vascular response is triggered by substances produced at the injured site which act directly on the local vessels. Among the *vasoactive mediators* are histamine, prostaglandins, and leukotrienes (Parslow & Bainton, 2001). The pathways and events vary according to the inciting stimulus, portal of entry, and characteristic of the host. Some outcomes are detrimental. While inflammatory reactions have evolved to inactivate or eliminate injurious substances or limit their spread, these same reactions can injure host tissues or interfere with normal functions (Terr, 2001).

TISSUE INJURY

Trauma is a multi-system reaction (Zellweger, Schwacha,& Chaudry, 2001). After, an injury the inflammatory and immune humoral systems are expressed and interact, frequently using the same chemical messengers and intra-cellular processes. Their complexity is comparable to that of the central nervous system. In addition, there is a bidirectional interaction between the immune and neuroendocrine systems. The molecular basis for communication are shared regulatory mediators: steroid hormones, neuropeptide, and cytokines) and their receptors (Crofford, 2002). Neuroendocrine control of a wide range of immune responses occurs via neuropeptides and neurohormones (Brown & Zwilling, 1996). Although the inflammatory and immune systems function together, they are presented separately. Cell and chemical types frequently referred to is offered in the Glossary.

Systemic: After a head injury, the acute reaction includes hypotension, hypoxia, hyperglycemia, anemia, sepsis and hyperthermia, increased systemic and intracranial pressure, and also hypoperfusion with hypoxemia, and hypercarbia (Dietrich & Bramlett, 2004; Marion, Sharts, & Tyler-Kabara, 2004). The systemic effect includes: the acute-phase response, increased energy expenditure (hypermetabolism) in severely injured patients, hypometabolism up to 10 days for a period of up to 10 days in experimental animals (Hovda, 1996), hypercatabolism, increased protein turnover, altered vascular permeability, altered mineral metabolism, increased cytokine and hormone levels in the blood, urine and cerebrospinal fluid (which peptides may be involved in secondary neuronal injury, e.g., IL-1, IL-6, and TNF), depressed immune function despite requirement for the body to defend itself against infection (Young & Ott, 1996), hyperdynamic cardiovascular state, gastric ulceration, altered glucose metabolism. Hyperglycemia may cause secondary injury to the brain. Hypoxia secondary to TBI and mild hypotension affects neurotrauma and outcome (Dietrich & Bramlett). *Average energy expenditure* increases 40% after brain injury; another estimate is 40-100% (Dwyer, 2001). The period of increased *metabolic rate* after brain injury may extend for as long as one year. Increased metabolic rate may be mediated by hormonal surge (serum insulin; cortisol; glucagon; catecholamines), cytokine increase, or brain inflammation. Severely brain injured persons lose weight, i.e., decreased muscle mass and visceral protein turnover. The *gut* expresses delayed gastric emptying, decreased pH, and increased gut permeability. The *liver* stimulates hepatic acute phase responses (enhanced and decreased synthesis of particular proteins); elevated liver function tests (probably caused by inflammatory cytokine effects) and altered gene expression leading to altered rates of synthesis of various substances mediated by various cytokines (Young & Ott, 1996).

Soft Tissue Injury

Soft tissues refer to muscle, tendon, or ligament. Their injuries reflect a range of dysfunctions, fibrositis, fibromyalgia, back or neck strain, sprain, etc. *Fibromyalgia* essentially is a history of widespread pain, and pain in 11 of 18 tender spots on digital palpation (American College of Rheumatology criteria, detailed in Romano, 1999) and axial pain over the sternum and spine (Fischer, 2002a). A *strain* refers to overwork or over stretch of tissue due to excessive effort or undue force. There may be localized pain and swelling. *Sprain* refers to a partial tear with localized pain and swelling, or to an injury to issues about a joint in which some of the fibers of a supporting ligament are torn away from the bone (ruptured), but the continuity of the ligament remains intact (Margoles, 1999a). A *jump sign* is a response to an unanticipated painful stimulus, with wincing, crying out, etc. An *active myofascial trigger point* is a focus of hyperirritability in a muscle or its fascia, referring to a pattern of pain at rest and/or in motion. It is always tender, prevents full lengthening of the muscle, weakens it, usually refers pain on direct compression, and often produces specific referred autonomic phenomena in its pain reference zone. A *latent myofascial trigger point* is a focus of hyperirritability in a muscle or its fascia that is painful only when palpated. It may have all the other clinical characteristics of an active trigger point. *Paresthesias* are abnormal sensations in the affected area, usually difficult to describe, with the patient often using metaphorical expressions like "crawling" or "running water" (Margoles, 1999b).

THE POSTCONCUSSION SYNDROME (PCS)

The PCS consequent to a mechanical injury (Parker, 2001) inevitably is accompanied by somatic injuries. Little attention has been paid to the differential diagnosis between neurological disorders (e.g., TBI and cranial nerve damage), and obvious somatic disorders such soft tissue and vertebral column injuries, and systemic reactions of the immune, inflammatory and hormonal systems due to disruption of the circadian cycle and sleep disorders. Diagnostic difficulties exist for depression, anxiety, and other mood disorders, fatigue and loss of stamina, sensitivity to loss of sleep, anxiety, impaired memory, decreased concentration, and insomnia, diabetes insipidus due to damage to the hypothalamic-pituitary stalk, and numerous others. Here as in other syndromes, the potential for appropriate treatment and compensation is lost due to lack of consideration for the etiology of the symptom.

HEALTH

Fatigue

Fatigue has been considered from a variety of perspectives: Pollution of the interior milieu, an energy problem, breakdown of the nervous system, motivational self-assessment regarding the demands of a task. It was related to neurasthenia, which is characterized by the fatigability of body and mind, organic in origin, resulting from environmental factors, treated by rest, and common to the educated and professional classes (Beard, cited by (Appels, 2000).

It is asserted that this state is currently described as fibromyalgia or chronic fatigue syndrome although the present writer is more sympathetic to a physiological mechanism (Appels, 2002). A major depressive episode may be accompanied by decreased energy, tiredness, and fatigue incurred without physical exertion (American Psychiatric Association, 2000, p. 350). Fatigue is common in persons with head and somatic injury after mechanical accidents. *Hypothyroidism* may be accompanied by decreased cardiac output (secondary to a drop in heart rate and contractility) and decreased basal metabolic rate. Symptoms include mild lassitude, fatigue, slight anemia, constipation, apathy, cold intolerance, menstrual irregularities, loss of hair and weight gain (Larsen & Reed, 2003).

Burnout is a concept that evolved from occupational and social psychology. It is the endpoint of a long-lasting stress process resulting in a negative state of physical, mental and emotional exhaustion, i.e., disillusionment. When there is PTSD in the context of the person's inability to obtain a respite from the job, the condition may be magnified and complicated by *"burnout"* (Burke & Richardson, 1996).

REFERENCES

Alexander, M.P. (1995) Mild traumatic brain injury: Pathophysiology, natural history and clinical management. *Neurology*, 35, 1253-1260.

American Psychiatric Assssociation. (2000). *Diagnostic and statistical manual of mental disorders, 4th ed.: Text revision)*. Washington, DC: Author.

Appels, A. (2000). *Encyclopedia of Stress (Vol. 3)* (pp. 598-605). San Diego, CA: Academic Press. In G. Fink (Ed.). *Encyclopedia of Stress (Vol. 2)* (pp. 108-110). San Diego, CA: Academic Press.

Aron, D. C., Findling, J. W., & Tyrell, J. B. (2004). Hypothalamus and pituitary gland. In F. S. Greenspan & D. G. Gardner (Eds.). *Basic and clinical endocrinology, 7th Ed, (pp. 106-175)*. New York: Lange Medical Books.

Attie, K. M., Ramirez, N. R., Conte, F. A., Kaplan, S.L., & Grumbach, M.M. (1990). The pubertal growth spurt in eight patients with true precocious puberty and growth hormone deficiency: evidence for a direct role of sex steroids. *Journal of Clinical Endocrinology & Metababolism*, 71, 975-983.

Baxter, J. D., Ribeiro, R. C. J., & Webb, P. (2004). Introduction to endocrinology. In F. S. Greenspan & D. G. Gardner (Eds.). *Basic and clinical endocrinology, 7th Ed, (pp. 1-37)*. New York: Lange Medical Books.

Berne, R. M. & Levy, M. N. (1998). *Physiology: 4th Ed.* St. Louis: Mosby.

Blessing, W. W. (2002). Brain stem. In V. S. Ramachandran (Ed.). *Encyclopedia of the human brain, Vol. I,* (pp. 545-567). Boston: Academic Press.

Brontke, C. F., Zasler, N. D., & Boake, C. (1996). Rehabilitation of the head-injured patient. In R. J. Narayan, J. E. Wilberger, & J. T. Povlishock (Eds.). *Neurotrauma* (pp. 841-858). New York: McGraw-Hill.

Brown, D. H. & Zwilling, B. S. (1996). Neuroimmunology of host-microbial interactions. In H. Friedman, T. W. Klein, & A. L. Friedman (Eds.). *Psychoimmununology, stress, and infection* (pp. 153-172) Boca Raton, FL: CRC Press.

Bulun, S. E. & Adashi, E. Y. (2003). The physiology and pathology of the female reproductive axis. In P. R. Larsen et al., *Williams Textbook of Endocrinology, 10th Ed.* (pp. 587-664). Philadelphia: Saunders.

Burke, W. H., Zencius, A. H., Wesolowski, and Doubleday, F. (1991). Improving executive function disorders in brain-injured clients. *Brain Injury*, 5, 241-252.

Caselli, R. J. and Yanagihara, T. (1991). Memory disorders in degenerative neurological diseases. In, T. Yanagihara and R.C. Petersen, (Eds.). *Memory disorders* (pp. 369-396). New York: Marcel Dekker.

Catt, K.J. (1995). Molecular mechanics of hormone action: control of target cell function by peptide and catecholamine hormones. In P. Felig, J.D. Baxter, & L.A. Frohman (Eds.). *Endocrinology and metabolism*, 3rd Ed., pp. 713-748). New York: McGraw Hill.

Chandler, W. F. (1990). Trauma to the carotid artery and other cervical vessels. In R. Youmans (Ed.) . Neurological Surgery, vol 4, pp 2367-2376. Philadelphia: Saunders.

Cherian, L., Robertson, C. S., & Gloodman, J. C. (1996). Secondary insult increase if injury after controlled cortical impact in rats. *Journal of Neurotrauma*, 13, 371-383.

Chesnut,R. M. (1996). Treating raised intracranial pressure in head injury. In R. K. Narayan, J. E. Wilberger, & J. T. Povlishek (Eds.). *Neurotrauma*, 445-469. New York: McGraw-Hill.

Cone, R. D., Low, M. J., Elmquist, J. K., Cameron, J. L. (2003). Neuroendocrinology. In P. R. Larsen et al., *Williams Textbook of Endocrinology, 10th Ed.* (pp. 81-176). Philadelphia: Saunders

Cornelissen, G. & Halberg, F. (1992). Toward a 'Chron-sensus' on n*euroimmuno*modulation, with 'modulation' operationally and inferentially defined. In N. Fabris et al., (Eds.). *Ontogenetic and phylogenetic mechanisms of neuroimmunomodulation* (pp. 60-67). Annals of the NY Academy of Sciences, Vol. 650.

Cryer, P. E. (1995). Diseases of the sympathochromaffin system. In P. Felig, J. D. Baxter, & L. A. Frohman (Eds.). *Endocrinology and metabolism*, 3rd Ed. pp. 713-748. New York: McGraw-Hill.

Cytowic, R. E., Smith, A., & Stump, D. (1986). *New England Journal of Medicine*, 314, p. 715.

D'Angelica, M., Barba, D.A., Morgan, A.S., Dobkin, E.D., and Pepe, J.L. (1995). Hypopituitarism Secondary to Transfacial Gunshot Wound. *Journal of trauma: Injury, Infection, and Critical Care*, 39, 768-771.

Davies, M. J. (1997). M. J. Davies & King, T. T. Cranial nerve injuries (I, V and IX-XII). In R. Macfarlane & D. G. Hardy (Eds.). *Outcome after head, neck and spinal trauma*, (pp. 55-63). Oxford: Great Britain.

DeAngelis, L. M. Delattre, J-Y & Posner, J. B. (2001). Neurological complications of chemotherapy and radiation therapy. In M. J. Aminoff (Ed.). *Neurology and general medicine, 3rd Ed.*, (pp. 437-458). New York: Churchill Livingstone.

Dewitt, D.S., Smith, T.G., Deyo, D.J., Miller, K. R., Uchida, T., & Progh, D.S. (1997). *Journal of Neurotrauma*, 14, 223-233.

Di Stefano, G., Provinciali, M., Muzzioli, M., Garzetti, G. G., Ciavattini, A., & Fabris, N. (1994). Correlation betweenm estradiol serum levels and NK cell activity in endometriosis. In N. A. Fabris et al., (Eds.). *Immunomodulation: The state of the art* (pp. 197-203). Annals of the New York Academy of Sciences, Vol. 741.

Dietrich, W. D. & Bramlett, H. M (2004). Basic neuroscience of neurotrauma. In W. G. Bradley et al. (Eds.). *Neurology in clinical practice, 4th Ed. Vol. 2*, (pp. 1115-1126). Boston: Butterworth-Heinemann.

Dwyer, J. (2001). Nutrition. In E. Braunwald, et al., (Eds.). *Harrison's Principles of internal medicine, 15th ed.* (pp. 451-455). New York: McGraw-Hill.

Eichser, I., Frisch H., Eichler H.G., and Soukop W. (1988). Isolated Growth Hormone Deficiency After Severe Head Trauma. *Journal of Endocrine Investigation*, 11, 409-411, Abstract.

Faist, E., Angele, M., & Wichmann, M. (2004). The immune response. In E. A. Moore, et al., (Eds.). *Trauma (5th Ed.)* (pp. 1383-1396). New York: McGraw-Hill.

Ferrari, S. & Crosignani, P. G. (1986). Ovarian failure without gonatotropin elevation in a patient with post-traumatic isolated hypogonadotropic hypogonadism. *European Journal of Gynecology & Reproductive Biology*, 21, 241-244.

Ferrari, E., Fioravanti, M., Magril, F., & Solerte, S. B. (2000). Variability of interactions between neuroendocrine and immunological functions in physiological aging and dementia of the Alzheimer's type. In Conti, A. Et al. *Neuroimmunomodulation: Perspectives at the new millenium.* Annals of the NY Academy of Sciences, Vol. 917, pp. 582-586.

Fink, G. (2000). Feedback systems. In G. Fink (Ed.). *Encylopedia of Stress, (II)*, (pp. 124-137). San Diego, CA: Academic Press.

Fisch, B. J. (2001). Neurological aspects of sleep. In M. J. Aminoff (Ed.). *Neurology and general medicine, 3rd Ed.*, (pp. 509-535). New York: Churchill Livingstone.

Fischer, A. A. (2002b). New injection techniques for treatment of musculoskeletal pain. In E. S. Rachlin & I. S. Rachlin (Eds.). *Myofascial pain and fibromyalgia: Trigger point management* (pp. 403-419). St Louis: Mosby.

Frohman, L. A. (1995). Diseases of the anterior pituitary. In P. Felig, J.D. Baxter, & L.A. Frohman (Eds.). *Endocrinology and metabolism, (3rd Ed.)*, pp. 289-384). New York: Mcgraw Hill.

Frohman, L. A. & Felig P. (2001). Introduction to the endocrine system. In P. Felig & L. A. Frohman (Eds.). *Endocrinology and metabolism, 4th Ed.)*, pp. 3-17. New York: McGraw Hill.

Fuller, C. A. & Fuller, C. M. (2002). Circadian Rhythms. In V. S. Ramachandran (Ed.). *Encyclopedia of the human brain* Vol. I (pp. 793-812). Boston: Academic Press.

Ganong, C. A. & Kappy, M. S. (1993). Cerebral salt wasting in children. *American Journal of Diseases of Children*, 147(2), 167-169.

Goldstein, J. (1991). Posttraumatic headache and the postconcussion syndrome. *Medical Clinics of North America*, 75, 641-651.

Granner, D. K., (1993a). Pituitary and hypothalamic hormones. In R. K. Murray, D. K. Granner, P. A. Mayes, and V. W. Rodsell (Eds.). *Harpers Biochemistry* (pp. 499-508). Appleton & Lange: Norwalk, CT.

Greenberg, S. B & Atmar, R. L. (1996). Infectious complications after head injury. In R. J. Narayan, J. E. Wilberger, & J. T. Povlish0ock (Eds.). *Neurotrauma* (pp. 703-722). New York: McGraw-Hill.

Grossman, W. F. & Sanfield, J. A. (1994). Hypothalamic atrophy presenting as amenorrhea and sexual infantilism in a female adolescent: A case report. *Journal of Reproductive Medicine*, 39, 738-740.

Guyton, A. G. & Hall , J. E. (1996). *Textbook of medical physiology, 9th Ed.* Philadelphia : Saunders.

Guyton, A. C. & Hall, J. E. (2000). *Textbook of medical physiology, 10th Ed.* Philadelphia: W. B. Saunders.

Habener, J. F. (2003). Genetic control of peptide hormone formation. In P. R. Larsen et al., *Williams Textbook of Endocrinology (10th Ed.)* (pp. 17-34). Philadelphia: Saunders

Hadani, M., Bruk, B., Ram, Z., Knoller, N., & Bass, A. (1997). Transiently increased basilar artery flow velocity following severe head injury: a time course Transcranial Doppler study. *Journal of Neurotrauma*, 14, 629-636.

Hall, E. D. (1996). Free radicals and lipid peroxidation. In R. J. Narayan, J. E. Wilberger, & J. T. Povlishock (Eds.). *Neurotrauma* (pp. 1405-1419). New York: McGraw-Hill.

Hovda, D. A. (1996). Metabolic dysfunction. In R. J. Narayan, J. E. Wilberger, & J. T. Povlishock (Eds.). *Neurotrauma* (pp. 1459-1478). New York: McGraw-Hill.

Hughes, J. T. & Brownell, B. (1968). Traumatic thrombosis of the internal carotid artery in the neck. *Journal of Neurology, Neurosurgery and Psychiatry*, 31, 307-314.

Iverson, S., Iverson, L., & Saper, C. B. (2000). The autonomic nervous system and the hypothalamus. In E. R. Kandel et al., *Principles of neural science, 4th ed.* (pp. 960-981). New York: McGraw Hill.

Jameson, J. L. (1996). In inherited disorders of the gonadotropin hormone. *Molecular and cellular endocrinolog*, 125(1,2), 143-149.

Jameson, J. L. (2001). Endocrinology and metabolism. In E. Braunwald, et al., (Eds.). *Harrison's Principles of internal medicine, 15th ed.* (pp. 2019-2029). New York: McGraw-Hill.

Jankovic, B. D. (1994). Neuroimmunomodulation: From phenomenology to molecular evidence. In N. A. Fabris et al., (Eds.). Immunomodulation: The state of the art (pp. 1-38). Annals of the New York Academy of Sciences, Vol. 741.

Jenkner, F. L. (1995). *Electrical pain control.* New York: Springer-Verlag.

Junger E. C. & 8 others (1997). Cerebral autoregulation following minor head injury. Journal of neurosurgery, 86, 425-432.

Kahn, C. R., Smith, R. J., & Chin, W. W. (1998). Mechanism of action of hormones that act at the cell surface. In J. D. Wilson et al., *Williams textbook of endocrinology, 9th Ed.*, pp. 95-143. Philadelphia: Saunders.

Kemeny, J. E., Solomon, G. F., Morley, J. E., & Herbert, T. L. (1992). Psychoneuroimmunology. In C. B. Nemeroff (Ed.). *Neuroendocrinology*, pp. 563-591. Boca Raton, FL: CRC Press.

Kemp, P. M., Houston, A. S., MacLeod, M. A., & Pethybridge, R. J. (1995). Cerebral perfusion and psychometric testing in military amateur boxers and controls. *Journal of Neurology, Neurosurgery, and Psychiatry*, 59, 368-374.

Kern, K. B., & Meislin, H. W. (1984). Diabetes insipidus: Occurrence after minor head trauma. *Journal of Trauma*, 24, 69-72 (abstract).

Kirsch, J. R., Helfaer, M. A., Lange, D. G., & Traystman, R. J. (1992). Evidence for free radical mechanisms of brain injury resulting from ischemia/reperfusion-induced events. Journal of Neurotrauma, 9, Supplement 1. (Central nervous system trauma Status Report: 1991) (pp. S157-S163).

Kong, P. L., Odegard, J. M., Bouzahzah, F., Choi, J-Y, Eardley, L. D, Zielinski C. E., et al. (2003). Intrinsic T cell defects in systemic autoimmunity. In N. Chiorazzi et al. (Eds).

Immune mechanisms and disease (pp. 60-67). Annals of the New York Academy of Sciences, Vol. 987.

Kupferman, I. (1991). Hypothalamus and limbic system: Motivation. In Kandel, E.R., Schwartz, J. J., and Jessell, T. M. (Eds.). Principles of Neuroscience, 3rd Ed., pp. 750-760. New York: Elsevier.

Labi, M. L. C., & Horn, L. J. (1990). Hypertension in traumatic brain injury. *Brain Injury*, 4, 365-370.

Lam, J. M. K., Hsiang, J. N. K., & Poon, W.S. (1997). Monitoring of autororegulation using laser Doppler flowmetry in patients with head injury. Journal of Neurosurgery, 86, 438-445.

Landsberg, L. & Young, J. B. (1992). Catecholamines and the adrenal medulla. In J. D. Wilson & D. W. Foster (Eds.). *Williams textbook of endocrinology*, 8th ed.. pp. 621-705. Philadelphia: Saunders.

Larsen, P. R. & Davies, T. F. (2003). Hypothyroidism and thyroiditis. In P. R. Larsen et al., *Williams Textbook of Endocrinology, 10th Ed.* (pp. 423-456). Philadelphia: Saunders

Laterra, J. & Goldstein, G. W. (2000). Ventricular organization of cerebrospinal fluid: Blood-brain barrier, brain edema and hydrocephalus. In E. R. Kandel et al. (Eds.), *Principles of neural science, 4th ed.* (pp. 1288-1300). New York: McGraw Hill.

Lemack, G. E., Uzzo, R. G., & Poppas, D. P. (1988). Effcts of stress on male reproductive function. In J. R. Hubbard & E. A. Workman, Eds. *Handbook of stress medicine: An organ system approach* (pp. 141-152). Boca Raton, FL: CRC Press.

Liau, L. M., Bergsneider, M., & Becker, D. P. (1996). Pathology and pathophysiology of head injury. *Neurological Surgery*, 4th Ed. (pp. 1549-1594). Philadelphia: Saunders.

Liberzon, I., Krstov, M., & Young, E. A. (1997). Stress-restress: Effects on ACTH and fast feedback. *Psychoneuroendocrinolgy*, 6, 443-453.

Luger, T. A., Scholzen, T. E., Brzoska, T., & Böhm, M. (2003). New insights into the functions of alpha-MSH and related peptides in the immune system. In R. D. Cone (Ed.) *The melanocortin system* (pp. 133-140). Annals of the New York Academy of Sciences, vol. 984. New York, NY.

MacGillivray, M. H. (2001). Disorders of growth and development. In P. Felig & L. A. Frohman (Eds.). *Endocrinology and metabolism, 4th Ed.* (pp. 1265-1316. New York: McGraw-Hill.

Maestroni, G. J. M. & Conti, A. (1992). The pineal-immuno-opioid network. In N. Fabris et al., (Eds.). *Ontogenetic and phylogenetic mechanisms of neuroimmunomodulation* (pp. 56-59). Annals of the NY Academy of Sciences, Vol. 650.

Maestroni, G. J. M. (2001). Melatonin and immune function. In R. Ader et al. *Psychoimmunology, 3rd Ed., Vol. 1.* (433-443). San Diego: Academic Press.

Marchetti, B., Morale, M. C., Gallo, F., Lomeo, E., Testa, N. Tirolo, C., Caniglia, S., & Garozzo, G. (2001). The hypothalamo-pituitary-gonadal axis and the immune system. In Ader, R., Felten, D. L., & Cohen, N. *Psychoneuroimmunology, Vol. 1,* 3rd Ed., (pp. 363-385). San Diego: Academic Press.

Marion, D. W., Sharts, M.C., & Tyler-Kabara, E. C. (2004). Craniocerebral trauma. In W. G. Bradley et al. (Eds.). *Neurology in clinical practice, 4th Ed. Vol. 2*, (pp. 1127-1147). Boston: Butterworth-Heinemann.

Marks, D. B., Marks, A. D., & Smith, C. M. (1996). *Basic medical biochemistry.* Baltimore: Williams & Wilkins.

Martin, N. A., Doberstein, C., Alexander, M., Khanna, R., Benalcazar, H., Alsina, G., Zane, C., McBride, D., Kelly, D., Hovda, D., Becker, D., McArthur, D., & Zaucha, K. (1995). Posttraumatic cerebral arterial spasm. *Journal of Neurotrauma*, 12, 897-906.

Mathew, R. J. (1995). Sympathetic control of cerebral circulation: Relevance to psychiatry. *Biological Psychiatry*, 37. 283-285.

Matzinger, P. (2002). The Danger Model: A renewed sense of self. *Science*, 301-305.

Menzaghi, F., Heinrichs, S. C., Pich, E. M., Weiss, F., & Koob, G. F. (1993). In Y. Taché & C. Rivier (Eds.). *Corticotropin-releasing factor and cytokines: Role in the Stress Response* (pp 142-154). Annals of the New York Academy of Science, vol. 691.

Michelson, D., Licino, J. & Gold, P. W. (1995). Mediation of the stress resonse by the hypothalamic-pituitary-adrenal axis. In M. J. Friedman, D. S. Charney, & A. Y. Deutch (Eds.). *Neurobiological and clinical consequences of stress: From normal adaptation to PTSD* (pp., 225-238). Philadelphia: Lippincott-Raven.

Miller, J. D., Piper, I., R., & Jones, P., A. (1996). Pathophysiology of head injury. In R. J. Narayan, J. E. Wilberger, & J. T. Povlishock (Eds.). *Neurotrauma* (pp. 61-69). New York: McGraw-Hill.

Miller, W. L., Kaplan, S. L. and Grumbach, M. M. (1980). Child abuse as a cause of post-traumatic hypopituitarism. *New England Journal of Medicine*, 302, 724-728.

Miller, J. D., & Gudeman, S. K. (1986). Cerbral vasospasm after head injury. Vasospsm: Occurrence in conditions other than subarachnoic hemorrhage . In R. H. Wilkins (Ed.). *cerebral arterial spasm,* pp. 476-479. Baltimore: Williams and Wilkins.

Mocchegiani, E., Santarelli, L.,& Fabris, N. (1994). In N. A. Fabris et al., (Eds.). *Immunomodulation: The state of the art* (pp. 115-123). Annals of the New York Academy of Sciences, Vol. 741.

Molitch, M. E. (1995). In P. Felig et al., Neuroendocrinology. In *Endocrinology and Metabolism, 3rd ed.*, 221-288, New York: McGraw-Hill, 1995.

Moore, R. Y. (1999). Circadian timing. In M. J. Zigmond et al., (Eds.). *Fundamental Neuroscience*, 1189-1206. San Diego, CA: Academic Press.

Muir, J. K., Boerschel, M., Muir, J., and Ellis, E. F. (1992). Continuous monitoring of posttraumatic cerebral blood flow using Laser-Doppler flowmetry. *Journal of Neurotrauma*, 9, 4, 355-362.

Nemeth, K., Kakatos, Z. Moravcxik, E., Radak, Z., Vago, A., & Furesz, J. Reperfusion tissue injury during coronary bypass surgery. Poster. International Congress of Stress, Budapest, 1997).

Nordhoff, L. S., Murphy, D., & Underhill, M. L. (1996a). Diagnosis of common crash injuries. In L. S. Nordhoff, Jr., (Ed). *Motor vehicle collision injuries*, pp. 1-69. Gaithersburg, MD: Aspen.

Parent, A. (1996). *Carpenter's human neuroanatomy, 9th Ed.)*. Baltimore: Williams & Wilkins.

Parker, R. S. (1995a). Enhancing information-gathering after mild head injurhy in the acute and chronic phases. *Journal of Neurological and Orthopaedic Medicine and Surgery*, 16, 118-125.

Parker, R. (1995b). The Distracting Effects of Pain, Headaches, and Hyper-Arousal Upon Employment After 'Minor' Head Injury. *Journal of Cognitive Rehabilitation 13 (3)*, 14-23.

Parker, R. S. (2001). *Concussive brain trauma*. Boca Raton, FL: CRC Press.

Parker R. S. (2002). Recommendations for the revision of DSM-IV diagnostic categories for co-morbid posttraumatic stress disorder and traumatic brain injury. *NeuroRehabilitation*, 17, 131-143.

Parslow, T. G. (2001). Immunogens, antigens & vaccines. In T. G. Parslow, et al., (Eds.) *Medical immunology (10th Ed.)* (pp. 72-81). New York: Lange.

Pescovitz, O. H. (1992). Pediatric neuroendocrinology: Growth and puberty. In, C.B. Nemeroff, (ed.). *Neuroendocrinology*, pp. 473-500. Boca Ratan: FL.

Povlishock, J. T. (1996). An overvew of brain injury models. In R. J. Narayan, J. E. Wilberger, & J. T. Povlishock (Eds.). *Neurotrauma* (pp. 1325-1326). New York: McGraw-Hill.

Reichlin, S. (1998). Neuroendocrinology. In G. D. Wilson et al. (Eds.) *Williams textbook of endocrinology, 9th ed.* (pp. 165-248). Philadelphia: Saunders.

Reichlin, S. (1992). Neuroendocrinology. In J. D. Wilson & D. W. Foster (Eds.). *Williams textbook of endocrinolology* (8th Ed.), pp. 135-219. Philadelphia: W. B. Saunders.

Reis, D.J.& Golanov, E. V. (1996) Cerebral circulation. In D. Robertson, P. A. Low, & R. J. Pollinsky, (Eds) *Primer in the autonomic nervous system* (pp. 56-58). San Diego: Academic Press.

Rivest, S. & Rivier, C. (1993). Central mechanisms anmd sites of action involved in the inhibitory effects of CRF and cytokines in LHRH neuronal activity. In Y. Taché & C. Rivier (Eds.). *Corticotropin-releasing factor and cytokines: Role in the Stress Response* (pp 117-141). Annals of the New York Academy of Science, vol. 691.

Robertson, C. S. (1996). Nitrous oxide saturation technique for CBF measurement. In R. J. Narayan, J. E. Wilberger, & J. T. Povlishock (Eds.). *Neurotrauma* (pp. 487-501). New York: McGraw-Hill.

Rosenfield,, D. B. (1997). Stuttering. In S. C. Schachter & O. Devinsky, Eds. *Behavioral neurology and the legacy of Norman Geschwind* (pp. 101-111). Philadelphia: Lippincott-Raven.

Shaul, P.W., Towbin, R.B., and Chernausek, S.D. (1985). Precocious puberty following severe head trauma. *American Journal of Diseases of Children*, 139, 467-469.

Snape, W. J., (1996). Disorders of gastrointestinal motility. In J. C. Bennett & F. Plum (Eds). *Cecil textbook of medicine* (pp. 680-688). Philadephia: Saunders.

Somjen, G. G. (2004). *Ions in the brain.* New York: Oxford University Press.

Stewart, P. M. (2003). The adrenal cortex. In P. R. Larsen et al., *Williams Textbook of Endocrinology (10th Ed.)* (pp. 491-551). Philadelphia: Saunders

Strebel, S., Lam, A. M., Matta, B. F., & Neswell, D. W. (1997). Impaired cerebral autoregulation after mild head injury. *Surgical Neurology*, 47, 128-121.

Strewler, G. J. (1998). Humoral manifestations of malignancy. In J. D. Wilson et al., *Williams textbook of endocrinology, 9th Ed.*(pp. 1693-1710). Philadelphia: Saunders.

Taylor, A. R., and Bell, T. K. (1966). Slowing of cerebral circulation after concussional head injury: A controlled trial. *The Lancet*, 7/23/66, 178-180.

Teman, A. J., Winterkorn, J. S., & Lowell, D. M. (1991). Traumatic thrombosis of a vertebral artery in a hypoplastic vertebrobasilar system: Protective effect of collateral circulation. *New York State Journal of Medicine*, 9, 314-315.

Terr, A. I. (2001). Inflammation. In T. G. Parslow et al. (Eds.). *Medical immunology (10th Ed.)* (pp. 189-203). New York: Lange.

Veldhuis, J. D., Yoshida, K., & Iranmanesh, A. (1998). The effects of mental and metabolic stress on the female reproductive system and female reproductive hormones. In J. R. Hubbard & E. A. Workman, Eds. *Handbook of stress medicine: An organ system approach* (pp. 115-140). Boca Raton, FL: CRC Press.

Yamanaka, C., et al., (1993). Acquired growth hormone deficiency due to pituitary stalk transaction after head trauma in childhood. *European Journal of Pediatrics*, 152, (2) 99-101 (Abstract).

Young, B. & Ott, L. 1996). Nutritional and metabolic management of the head-injured patient. In R. J. Narayan, J. E. Wilberger, & J. T. Povlishock (Eds.). *Neurotrauma* (pp. 345-363). New York: McGraw-Hill.

Margoles, M. (1999a). Soft tissue pain problems: Introduction. In Michael S. Margoles & R. Weiner (Eds.). *Chronic pain: Assessment, diagnosis, and management* (pp. 91-92). Boca Raton, FL: CRC Press.

Zafonte , R. D. & Horn, L. J. (1999). Clinical assessment of posttraumatic headaches. *Journal of Head Trauma Rehabilitation*, 14(1), 22-33.

Zellweger, R., Schwacha, M. G., & Chaudrey, I. H. (2001. Immunologic sequelae of surgery and trauma. In R. Ader et al., (Eds.) P*sychoneuroimmunology*, 3rd Ed., Vol 2. (pp. 291-315). San Diego: Academic Press.

Zigmond, M.J., Finlay, J.M., & Sved, A.F. (1995). Neurochemical studies of central noradrenergic responses to acute and chronic stress. In M. J. Friedman, D.C. Charney, & A.Y. Deutsch, Eds.). *Neurobiological and clinical consequences of stress* , pp. 45-60. Philadelphia: Lipincott-Raven.

Zubkov, A. Y., Pilkington, A. S., Bernanke, D. H., Parent, A. D., & Zhang, J. (1999). Posttraumatic cerebral vasospasm: Clinical and morphological resentations. *Journal of Neurotrauma*, 16, 763-770.

In: Trends in Posttraumatic Stress Disorder Research
Editor: Thomas A. Corales, pp. 101-127
ISBN 1-59454-135-3
© 2005 Nova Science Publishers, Inc.

Chapter 5

POST-TRAUMATIC STRESS SYMPTOMS IN CUBAN CHILDREN AND ADOLESCENTS DURING AND AFTER REFUGEE CAMP CONFINEMENT

Eugenio M. Rothe

University of Miami School of Medicine

ABSTRACT

Objectives

Two cohorts of Cuban refugee children and adolescents who migrated with their parents by sea and were later confined to refugee camps were assessed for symptoms of Post-traumatic stress disorder during refugee camp confinement. A third cohort of children and adolescents was assessed for Posttraumatic Stress Disorder four to six months after release from the refugee camps, and assessed for the presence of internalizing and externalizing behaviors by their teachers.

Methods

A clinic population of 285 children and adolescent refugees who had left Cuba by sea in the summer of 1994, undergoing their sixth month of confinement, was assessed in the military field hospital inside the camps for the presence of PTSD with the Posttraumatic Stress Disorder Reactive Index. A second cohort of 79 children and adolescents who had taken an alternative exit route out of Cuba and had been transferred from a camp in another country were assessed using DSM-III-R criteria for PTSD. A third cohort of 87 children and adolescents were assessed for PTSD with the PTSDRI, and for the presence of internalizing and externalizing behaviors by their teachers, using the Child Behavioral Checklist-Teacher Report Form.

Results

The majority of children and adolescents in the clinic population reported very severe symptoms of PTSD. The rates of pre-existing medical conditions such as Asthma and Epilepsy, and pre-existing psychiatric conditions such as Learning Disabilities and Behavior Dis-control Problems, were found to be double than those found in the general population. The type of posttraumatic symptoms and the effects of particular stressors showed variations by sex and gender. The subjects that were transferred from a camp situated in another country also showed elevated rates of PTSD symptoms. However, these were not as sever as those found among the clinic population. The majority of the children and adolescents that were studied after release from the refugee camps reported moderate to sever PTSD symptoms. The most common symptom clusters were avoidance, regressive behaviors, re-experiencing the traumatic events somatic symptoms and hyper-arousal. A statistically significant dose-effect relationship was found between the number of stressors and the severity of self reported PTSD symptoms. Teachers' overall ratings of internalizing and externalizing behaviors did not produce clinically significant findings.

Conclusions

The psychological effects of multiple stressors on child and adolescent refugees are discussed. The role of mental health professionals in treating child and adolescent refugees and their families during refugee camp confinement, the psychological effects on mental health workers, the role of political agendas and the adaptation issues of the refugees to the host country are also addressed. PTSD symptoms among refugee children and adolescents may continue unabated after the stressors have been removed. The symptoms may be experienced subjectively and go unnoticed by adults.

INTRODUCTION

A new literature is emerging that describes psychic trauma in refugee children and adolescents. In the past decade, a number of studies have addressed the traumatic experiences of child and adolescent refugees subjected to war, famine, and political struggles in Cambodia, Vietnam, Tibet, and the countries of the former Yugoslavia (Kinzie et al., 1990; Sack et al., 1993; Mollica, Poole and Son, 1997; Weine et al., 1998; Becker et al., 1999). In the last three decades, war, famine and political struggles have also caused an increase of forced migrations worldwide. Even though statistics regarding refugees are extraordinarily inaccurate, it is believed that by the end of 1970 there were approximately 2.5 million refugees in the world. This increased to 8.2 million in 1980 and with wars in the former Yugoslavia, the current estimate is around 17 million. A second problem is the number of "internally displaced persons" that migrate within a country, when other countries refuse to accept them. These estimates are placed at 21.8 million. Combined, these numbers add up to close to 40 million forced migrants worldwide, or one of every 135 people alive (World Refugee Survey, 2003).

Baum and Davidson (1986) have studied the effects of human made disasters on children and adolescents and have found that these effects can be more psychologically devastating than those of natural disasters. Sack, Seely and Clark (1997) have found that the diagnosis of posttraumatic stress disorder (PTSD) in children and adolescents transcends barriers of culture and language.

This chapter addresses the experience of children and adolescents and their families who left Cuba by sea in the summer of 1994, with the goal of reaching the United States, but who were intercepted by the U.S. Coast Guard and confined to refugee camps located outside the U.S. mainland. It will also describe the experience of those who cared for them and how these child and adolescent refugees fared psychologically after they were released from the camps and admitted to the U.S.

HISTORY OF CUBAN MIGRATIONS BY SEA

January 1st, 1959, marked the beginning of political events in the island of Cuba that culminated with the ascension to power of a communist totalitarian government (Thomas 1986, Suchlicki 1990). Since this date, it is estimated that more than 2 million people (19% of the population) have abandoned the island (Castro, 2002). The phenomenon of the Cuban "rafters" (balseros) began in the year 1959 and during the first two decades of the Cuban revolution, individuals that were captured attempting to leave the island were sentenced to death by firing squad. In the last two decades, punishment has lessened to jail terms, social ostracism, and acts of public humiliation perpetrated by government supported civil repression groups. Individuals who are caught leaving or planning to escape the island are automatically ceased from their jobs and the children are forbidden to attend school, turning the entire family into "social pariahs" and forcing them into internal exile. The government inmediately confiscates all the personal belongings, including the person's home. (Clark, 1992). According to Ackerman and Clark (1995), the "rafter phenomenon" is characterized by a six-step cycle: 1) Beginning of the crisis: due to general discontent among the population, as a consequence of political and financial reasons; 2) The Cuban government "amplifies" the crisis: this way individuals who disagree with the government are identified. This step usually culminates with an opening of the Cuban borders followed by a massive exodus by sea; 3) "Demonization" of those who depart: Which includes the confiscation of all personal belongings and the person's home, followed by social ostracism directed against close relatives who stay behind; 4) The focus of the problem is deflected and blame is placed on the United States: this is usually accomplished by mobilizing a strong international media campaign; 5) Cuba and the United States negotiate to stop the exodus: In this process, there are always benefits to the Cuban government, including the elimination of internal dissenters; 6) Closing of the cycle: after an accord is reached between the two government.

Ackerman and Clark (1995) propose that each decade of the Cuban revolution has generated a massive exodus by sea: Port of Camarioca 1965, Port of Mariel 1980, Guantanamo U.S. Naval Base 1994. The City of Havana is located only 95 miles (152 km) south of Key West, the U.S.'s southernmost point and the preferred exit route of the Cuban rafters.

Taking into account the voyage preparations, Cuban rafters have been divided into three groups: 1) The water taxi mode: Individuals with money who can pay for illegal transport in large, fast boats which originate in Miami or the Bahamas and secretly pick up the passengers in Cuba or adjacent small islands. These comprise only 5% of the total. 2) The betting mode: Individuals with elaborate rafts powered by oars, sails or motor, some fundamental knowledge of navigation and sufficient supplies (50-60% of the total); 3) The "do or die" mode: These are desperate individuals who set to sea in crafts composed of empty barrels, inner tubes or plastic objects without propulsion and without knowledge of navigation, supplies or equipment and which are carried by the currents (30-40% of the total) (Ackerman and Clark 1995).

History of the Cuban Exodus of August 1994

Deteriorating financial and political conditions in Cuba reached an unprecedented state in the summer of 1994. They resulted largely as a consequence of the collapse of the Soviet Union in 1991, which interrupted financial supplies and commerce with Cuba, plunging the island's economy into the worst crisis since 1959. These events were followed by civilian protests, kidnapping of boats and ferries, and violent confrontations with government authorities. Fearing the possibility of a civil war, on August 12th. 1994, the Cuban government opened its borders, allowing all the discontented individuals to leave the island. This announcement culminated with a massive exodus of several thousand people leaving the island by sea using boats, rafts, and other small crafts in order to reach the United States (Ackerman and Clark 1995). Approximately 32,408 people were intercepted at sea by the U.S. Coast Guard and taken to refugee camps located at the Guantanamo U.S. Naval Base in eastern Cuba and other Caribbean locations. Termed "Operation Able Vigil", the U.S. Coast Guard employed 56 vessels to implement the largest naval operation since the Korean War (Ackerman and Clark 1995).

It is unclear how many died at sea but, based on studies of previous exoduses, only 25% survive the crossing (Clark, 1975). It is believed that the massive rescue operations, which were mobilized during the summer of 1994 by the U.S. authorities, may have contributed to dramatically decrease these rates (Ackerman and Clark 1995). The refugees were confined to detention camps located inside the naval base. On October 17th. 1994, three months into the camp detention, the psychological conditions of the refugees were found to be so dismal, that the U.S. government announced the unconditional acceptance of all children younger than 18 years old and the members of their nuclear families into the U.S. (Alvarez 1994). In spite of this government decree, the slow bureaucratic process carried out by U.S. immigration authorities often delayed the process for up to more than a year.

A total of approximately 2,500 children and adolescents were rescued at sea by U.S. Coast Guard by August and September of 1994 (World Relief Organization 1995). They were exposed to a series of traumatogenic events of consistent intensity and prolonged duration (Rothe et al. 1998, 2000, 2002 a-b).

Traumatogenic Events during the Ocean Crossing

The Cuban exodus of August and September 1994 consisted of families leaving the island by sea, using flimsy homemade rafts, a few boats and other small crafts, the majority without motors or navigational instruments (Ackerman and Clark 1995). Children and adolescents described witnessing people passing out and dying on board from starvation and thirst, and floating corpses devoured by sharks. Others witnessed storms at sea and the sinking of boats and rafts. The refugees intercepted at sea were taken to larger U.S. naval vessels, where they slept on deck for as many as five days prior to being transferred to the refugee camps (Rothe et. al 1998, 2000, 2002 a-b).

Conditions in the Refugee Camps

In August of 1994, prior to the arrival of Cuban refugees, the U.S. Naval Base at Guantanamo housed 7,000 Haitian refugees in an area of 42 square miles. An additional 20 refugee camps were built to house the incoming Cubans, including one camp for criminals and the chronic mentally ill. Also, another camp was designed for agitators and Cuban government agents, who had been placed among the refugees in order to sabotage the process. Members of these subgroups were identified and separated from the general refugee population. All of the camps were surrounded by barbed wire and guarded by U.S. military personnel carrying automatic weapons. At its highest point in January of 1995, 32,000 Cuban refugees were living in 20 camps. Approximately 7,000 of these refugees had been initially detained in camps located in Panama, where riots broke out among the refugees; and the Cayman Islands, where the Cuban refuges were mistreated. These events culminated with the transfer of these two sub-groups to Guantanamo (World Relief Organization 1995). The refuges inhabited tents of 8 to 14 occupants having to share a small amount of space with strangers and having very little opportunity for privacy. The children witnessed riots, multiple acts of violence, suicide attempts, and surprise searches conducted in the middle of the night by armed military personnel looking for weapons. Sexually explicit language and sexual activity by adults was commonplace. Poor sanitary conditions, a monotonous diet, heat, dirt, mosquitoes, and blaring noise and music created tension among the refugees, who faced the idleness of confinement and the inability to go elsewhere. Rumors that the refugees would be deported back to Cuba, where they would face political repression and incarceration, were an everyday occurrence. Parents affected by the camp conditions became easily irritated, frequently using corporal punishment with the children when they engaged in minor transgressions.

On November 13, 1994, Tropical Storm Gordon blew away tents and flooded the camps, destroying personal belongings, frightening the refugees and leaving them temporarily homeless (Rothe et. al. 1998, 2000, 2002 a-b and Oller 1995).

Lack of Adequate Planning for the Refugees

The psychological effects of the accumulation of traumatic events and the experience of mass confinement on the refugees were grossly underestimated and practically ignored by government authorities and military personnel initially responsible for organizing the camps. In October of 1994, one month after the exodus, a military psychologist and a psychiatric social worker found themselves as the only mental health professionals serving a growing population of 28,000 people; they were overwhelmed by a deluge of psychotic, depressed, and suicidal patients who numbered in the hundreds.

Volunteers Come for Help

Help arrived in the form of the "Miami Medical Team", a volunteer multidisciplinary disaster relief organization based in Florida. The team consisted of professionals of every medical specialty who paid their own way and volunteered their services to the refugees on the base. The members of the team provided medical and psychiatric services to the refugees, until a military "combat stress team arrived six months later. The author organized an improvised child and adolescent psychiatry clinic in one of the two military field hospitals adjacent to the refugee camps. The staff was composed of the author, a military psychologist and several Cuban psychiatrists and psychologists, who were found among the refugees. The Medical Commanding Officer of the base, Col. Jerry Rose, grew alarmed at the psychological conditions in the camps. He encouraged the author to help document the status of the child and adolescent refugees. The author, along with the members of the clinic staff, collected the first 72 case histories of children and adolescents who presented to the clinic seeking services and drafted a document, which Col. Rose sent to the Pentagon. This, along with many other efforts, including those of several human rights organizations, resulted in the government issuing a decree liberating all the children and adolescents and their nuclear families from the camps after six months of confinement and freeing them to go to the United States. Some children and adolescents, however, spent up to a year in the camps because of the slow bureaucratic process of classifying the refugees-a task conducted by the immigration and naturalization service.

REFUGEE CHILDREN AND ADOLESCENTS INSIDE THE CAMPS

Study I. Post-Traumatic Stress Symptoms in a Clinic Population of Children and Adolescents inside the Refugee Camps

Methods

The population examined in this study consisted of the first 301 children and adolescents, ages 3 to 19 years old, who sought psychiatric services in the two Aero-transportable hospitals (ATH's) adjacent to the refugee camps. This sample represented approximately 11% of the total population of Cuban children and adolescents who were interned at the Guantanamo refugee camps. The interviews took place between December 1994 and March 1995, when the refugees were undergoing the fourth to sixth month of confinement. The subjects had been referred to the psychiatric clinic by one of three avenues: by military pediatricians after receiving primary medical care, or they were identified inside the camps as needing psychiatric services by one of the three psychiatrists and two psychologists, refugees themselves, who volunteered there services in the ATH's. Some of the subjects were also seen after their parents heard about the services and brought the children themselves. Except for two emancipated adolescent girls who were accompanied by their husbands, all other subjects were accompanied to the interviews by their parents or guardians.

Sixteen subjects were dropped from the study due to incomplete data. The final sample consisted of 285 subjects, 153 boys and 132 girls, which were grouped in three age categories: 1) Pre-schoolers (3 to 6 years old), in this age the questions were answered by the children with the parents present. The parents offered clarification when the child was unable to answer. 2) School age (7 to 12 years old) and, 3) Adolescents (13 to 19 years old). Owing to the racial mix of the Caribbean islands and the inherent difficulty in classifying subjects by ethnicity, this task was not undertaken.

The subjects were interviewed in Spanish, by members of the clinic staff and were asked to answer a demographic questionnaire and a standardized instrument, the Post-traumatic Stress Disorder Reactive Index (Frederick, Pynoos and Nader, 1992). This instrument has 21 questions that assess the degree of PTSD in children and adolescents and can be divided into six categories of questions addressing, avoidance, hyper-arousal, somatization, re-experiencing symptoms, regressive behavior and acting out behaviors. It has a reliability of .91, and the items conform to the DSM-III-R. The PTSDRI yields a numerical score that is then translated to five degrees of severity of traumatic stress, characterized as: 1) none, 2) mild, 3) moderate, 4) severe and, 5) very severe. The instrument was translated into Spanish using the method described by Breslin (1986). In addition, the subjects were asked to respond (affirmatively or negatively) to whether they experienced a list of eight symptoms of PTSD (DSM-VI, 1994) and to rate which was the most severe, of three stressors they had endured: the ocean crossing, their confinement in the camps or Tropical Storm Gordon. Finally, the parents were asked about any pre-existing medical or psychiatric, suffered by the children before leaving Cuba.

Summary of Results

Pre-School Children (3 to 6 years old)
The majority of children in these age group reported daily episodes of: 1) crying, 2) nightmares, 3) decreased appetite, 4) difficulty with sleep and 5) aggressive behavior. In addition, 88% of the boys and 87% of the girls reported 6) bedwetting (at least three times a week) and 26% of the girls and 3% of the boys 7) soiling (fecal incontinence) at least once a week, there were no reports of 8) suicidal ideation or attempts in this age group.

Girls appeared to be slightly more affected than boys in all of the symptoms except, aggressive behavior and bedwetting.

In the PTSDRI (Frederick et al., 1992), the majority of the preschool children scored in the "Very Severe" category of Post-traumatic stress symptoms, with girls (84%) appearing as slightly less affected than boys (91%).

In the pre-school group, a slight majority of boys (51%), and girls (52%), reported that "life in the camps", was more stressful than "the ocean-crossing" and then "tropical storm Gordon".

School-Age Children (7 to 12 years old)
The majority of children in this age group reported: 1) crying, however, this symptom decreased by 25% in girls and by 46% in boys, compared to the girls and boys in the pre-school group. Other symptoms such as 2) nightmares, 3) decreased appetite, 4) difficulty with sleep and 5) aggressive behavior, 6) bedwetting and 7) soiling were reported in comparable rates to the pre-school group. However, 8) suicidality began to appear in this group at the rate of 25% in girls and 14% in boys.

In the PTSDRI (Frederick et al., 1992), the majority of children in this age group scored in the "Very Severe" Post-traumatic stress symptoms category, with school-age girls being the most affected among all the age groups.

In the school-age group, the majority of boys and girls rated "the ocean crossing" as the most stressful moment of their ordeal, followed by "life in the camps" and "tropical storm Gordon".

Adolescents

In this age group, the rates of crying, nightmares, appetite disturbance, difficulty with sleep and encopresis decreased considerably, when compared to the school-age group. However, suicidality increased by 6% in boys and bedwetting was reported in 48% of the adolescent girls and 45% of the adolescent boys. Aggressive behavior was found to be 7% higher in girls than in boys.

In the PTSDRI (Frederick et al., 1992), the majority of adolescents scored in the "Very Severe" category of Post-traumatic stress symptoms, with girls appearing more severely affected than boys. However, these scores were lower than the other two groups.

The great majority of adolescent girls (89%) and boys (64%) rated "life in the camps" as the most stressful experience of their ordeal, followed by "the ocean-crossing", and tropical storm Gordon".

Other Findings

The majority of children had arrived in the camps with both parents. Pre-school girls had the highest rate of intact families (81%) and school age boys the lowest (58%). However, the majority (54% left at least one grandparents in Cuba and an even larger number (74%) left behind aunts, uncles and other members of the extended family network system. Half of the population of all the age groups spent less than 48 hours at sea before being rescued by the U.S. Coast guard, while the remaining group spent between two to five days at sea.

Pre-Existing Medical and Psychiatric Conditions

Pre-existing history of asthma was found to be elevated in the adolescent girls (12%) and the pre-school girls (11%). A pre-existing history of epilepsy was reported in 11% of the female and 10% of the male adolescents, as well as 11% of the pre-school girls and 7% of the pre-school boys. In terms of pre-existing psychiatric conditions, 30% of the school age boys and 22% of school age girls had consulted a psychiatrist in Cuba prior to arrival in the camps. Adolescent girls reported the least prior contact with a psychiatrist in Cuba at 11%.

Projective Drawings

During the interview, children and adolescents were invited to "draw anything that comes to mind" and were offered paper and crayons. Some children and adolescents depicted idyllic scenes of their homes in Cuba, but the majority were inclined to depict scenes from the camps or from the ocean crossing. Some drew pictures of small boats and rafts being battered by large waves as well as sinking boats with people drowning and floating corpses being devoured by sharks; others drew rescue scenes in which a helicopter recovers passengers from a sinking raft; some drew pictures of the coastguard ship, to which the refugees were transferred after being intercepted at sea. Scenes from the camps included endless rows of tents surrounded by barbed wire and patrolled by armed guards; others drew riots in which guards beat up civilians as crying mothers watched in horror. One adolescent drew a row of multicolored portable toilets and the truck used to suction the contents.

Study II. Post-traumatic Stress Symptoms in a Sub-Population of Children and Adolescents Confined to a Special Refugee Camp

Methods

This non-clinic population consisted of the totality of children and adolescents, ages 5 to 17 years old (N=138), of a sub-group of Cubans that left the island by sea in the summer of 1994. This sub-group of 1,200 children and adults, who comprised approximately 3% of the total population of refugees in Guantanamo, left Cuba traveling south, towards the Cayman Islands. A voyage of 280 nautical miles which is three times longer and more perilous than the one taken by the majority of the refugees that usually travel north, towards Key West U.S.A., where most of the U.S. Coast Guard rescue ships were concentrated. After being rescued at sea, or after arriving to the Cayman Islands by their own means, these refugees were confined to detention camps situated on these islands, where they were mistreated and underfed (Ackerman and Clark, 1995). As a result of protests by human rights groups, they were transferred to U.S. custody by the government of the Cayman Islands and transported to the Guantanamo U.S. Naval Base, where they were placed in a special camp, selected specifically for this sub-group. Owing to the trying conditions of the camps, which affected the refugees, the military and the volunteer medical people alike, and due to the unavailability of standardized research instruments to measure degrees of PTSD during the initial months of confinement, the authors designed a self report questionnaire with a list of 32 diagnostic symptoms of PTSD based on the DSM-III-R (1987). The symptoms were subsequently divided in six categories: 1) cognitive functions, 2) mood, 3) appetite, 4) sleep, 5) somatic symptoms and 6) conduct symptoms. The children were interviewed in Spanish, inside the camp by the second author of this study, Cuban psychiatrist and refugee himself, who resided in an adjacent camp. The parents of these children were also interviewed and asked about the duration and perils of their voyage, the quality of their voyage preparations, the size and type of sea craft that was used, the monetary cost of the provisions and of the craft employed. Cuban refugees using this exit route out of Cuba had never been studied before (Rothe, Castillo-Matos, Brinson and Lewis, 2000).

Results

Cognitive Symptoms

This area of functioning was the most affected, with 88% of the subjects reporting intrusive recollections of the voyage, 81% feared that these events would occur again, 75% reported fear of recalling the traumatic events and active avoidance of these memories and 67% reported difficulty with concentration.

Mood

The most commonly reported mood change was generalized anxiety, which was reported by 66% of the subjects, frequent crying (on a daily basis) 52%, separation anxiety by 49%, irritability by 38%, and depressive feelings by 35% of the subjects.

Conduct Problems

The most commonly reported symptom was aggressive behavior in 73% of the subjects, interpersonal conflicts 60%, use of profanity and verbal abuse 51% and increase in motor activity 32%.

Somatic Symptoms

Headaches were reported by 52% of the subjects and diaphoresis 23%.

Appetite and Elimination Disturbances

The subjects reported weight loss in 61% of the sample and loss of appetite in 46%, while bedwetting was reported by 36% of the subjects.

Sleep Disturbances

Turbulent sleep was reported by 62% of the subjects, insomnia by 56% of the subjects.

The demographic characteristics of the children and parents that immigrated south towards the Cayman Islands, where similar to the ones of the group that immigrated north, towards the U.S. However, the average cost of the voyage per sea craft was the equivalent in Cuban currency to $4,670.00 for the boat and $6,160.00 for the equipment and provisions of each boat. All the boats were larger than 20 feet in length, only one of the boats had a sail, all the others were powered by a motor and none of the survivors used rafts as a means of exiting Cuba.

Study III. Post-Traumatic Stress Disorder among Cuban Refugee Children and Adolescents After Release From a Refugee Camp

The authors compared the self-reported symptoms of PTSD in a cohort of Cuban children and adolescents with assessments of internalizing and externalizing behaviors by the children's teachers.

Methods

Eighty-seven children who had left Cuba by sea in the summer of 1994 and who had been confined to refugee camps for eight months or more before arriving in the U.S. were evaluated four to six months later. A questionnaire was administered to the parents in Spanish to obtain demographic information about the children and their families. The children and adolescents were administered the PTSDRI. The children were also asked seven questions about the degree of exposure to traumatic events, such as "Did you leave in a raft or a boat?" "How many days did you spend at sea?" and "Did you see sharks during the ocean crossing?" None of the children in this sample had presented to the mental health clinics in the camps seeking services during their refugee confinement. The distress of these children had been contained within their family unit, in contrast with the children in Study I, which were drawn from a highly symptomatic clinic sample.

The children were interviewed in Spanish with the PTSDRI by three psychiatrists, one school psychologist and one educator (school principal), and rated by their eleven Spanish speaking teachers using the Child Behavioral Check List-Teacher Report Form (CBCL-TRF) (Achenbach and Edelbrock, 1986), while they attended a network of several transitional schools, sponsored by the Catholic Archdioceses of Miami, Florida for the purpose of helping the children and adolescents transition into the American school system.

Because of the relatively small sample in this study and to make results more understandable; the five categories of the PTSDRI were collapsed into 1, none (never or a few times), 2, moderate (sometimes or many times); and 3, severe (all the time). To examine the individual questions of the PTSDRI, the questions were grouped into five categories: re-experiencing phenomena, avoidance, increased arousal, regressive behavior, and, for items that did not fit into the other categories, miscellaneous.

The CBCL-TRF consists of 113 questions and computes scores for profiles in ten separate categories: internalizing behaviors, externalizing behaviors, aggression, anxiety-depression, attention problems, delinquent behavior, social problems, somatic complaints, thought problems and withdrawn behavior.

Results

The average age of the children and adolescents was 14.9 years, with a range of six to 17 years. Forty-five (52 percent) were six to 12 years old, of whom 24 (27 percent) were boys and 21 (24 percent) were girls, and 42 (48 percent) were adolescents (13 to 17 years old), of whom 26 (30 percent) were boys and 16 (18 percent) were girls. Eighteen of the children and adolescents (21 percent) had left their father behind in Cuba, 11 (13 percent) had left their mother behind, 20 (24 percent) had left a brother or sister, 58 (69 percent) had left one or more grandparents behind, and 66 (79 percent) had left an aunt or an uncle.

On the PTSDRI, 37 of the children and adolescents (43 percent) showed no evidence of PTSD, 28 (32 percent) showed evidence of moderate PTSD, and 22 (25 percent) showed evidence of severe PTSD. Thus 50 children (57 percent) were considered to have PTSD according to the PTSDRI. Correlations of the CBCL-TRF with the PTSDRI and exposure to stressors were non-significant. A significant positive correlation was found between the total number of stressors to which a child was exposed and the score on the PTSDRI ($r=. 34$, $p<. 01$).

We evaluated the effects of age, gender, months spent in the camp, and responses to the yes-or-no questions about exposure on scores on the behavioral scales of the CBCL-TRF and the PTSDRI. All equations were non-significant—that is, the overall F test was non-significant, except for trends found for the withdrawn scale on the CBCL-TRF ($p<. 09$) and the score on the PTSDRI ($p<. 09$). For the withdrawn scale, feeling that one would die at sea and witnessing acts of violence at the camp were the only significant predictors. For the score on the PTSDRI, age ($t=2.06$, $p<. 05$) was the only significant predictor; the effect of witnessing acts of violence at the camp approached significance ($p=. 06$).

THE CONCEPT OF POST-TRAUMATIC STRESS DISORDER

In spite of it's long history, Post-Traumatic Stress Disorder (PTSD) did not figure as an official psychiatric diagnosis until the publication of the Statistical Manual of Mental Disorders (DSM-III) in 1980. Since that time, much work appeared in the psychiatric literature dealing with trauma in adults. However, in comparison, relatively little attention was paid to the impact of trauma experiences on children (Eth and Pynoos 1985). This began to change with the appearance of the work by Lenore Terr in the Chowchilla School Bus Kidnapping (1979, 1983). Terr (1991) has described the importance of psychological trauma as a crucial factor in the genesis of psychopathology in children and adolescents. She differentiates between two categories of trauma. Type I: Acute, brief, characterized by a single event, and Type II: Chronic, sustained, of prolonged duration. The second one usually has more devastating long-term consequences. Baum et al. (1983) have studied the effects of human-made disasters in children and adolescents and have found that these can have more devastating psychological effects than natural disaster. McNally (1993) explains that in children, PTSD is more likely to occur following events that are sudden, unexpected, life threatening and violent in nature. Newman (1976), Green et al. (1994) and Kiser et al. (1998) have explained that the child's response to trauma varies according to the parental response and to the degree of life threat. Bloch et al. (1956) in an earlier paper noted that the effect of psychological trauma in children and adolescents increases in severity if the victim or family member has been injured. Breslau et al. (1991) explain that the vulnerability to psychological trauma increases in individuals with pre-existing anxiety, depression or parental loss. Helzer et al. (1971) estimate that the prevalence of PTSD in the general population is around 1%.

According to DSM-IV (1994), PTSD involves the development of certain characteristic symptoms following the exposure to traumatic events in which 1) "The person experienced, witnessed, or was confronted with an event or events that involved actual or threatened death or serious injury, or a threat to the physical integrity of the self or others", and 2) "The person's response involved intense fear, helplessness, or horror". In children this may be expressed by agitated and disorganized behavior (Gurwitch et al. 1998). Over the past decade, investigators have increasingly recognized that children's reactions to trauma fall into a pattern which is consistent with the diagnosis of Post-Traumatic Stress Disorder in adults; albeit, with a few variations.

A new literature is emerging addressing the gap of knowledge about the manifestations, diagnosis and treatment of PTSD in pre-school-children (Scheeringa et al. 1995, 2001, 2003). These investigators highlight that pre-school children unmistakably develop symptoms of PTSD, which include re-experiencing, avoidance, numbing and hyper-arousal. However, detecting their presence may be more difficult because diagnostic criteria for PTSD were developed based on verbal reports. These investigators advocate for a modified criteria, more developmentally sensitive to this age group, based on behavioral observations. Most of the research child and adolescent literature on refugees has included children, but mostly adolescent victims of war and genocide.

In summary, the research findings in child and adolescent refugee populations are as follows:

1   Proximity to the traumatic events, duration of exposure, and intensity of traumatic experience can affect psychological response (Jensen and Shaw, 1993; Weine, Becker McGlashan, Vojvoda et al., 1995; Mollica et al. 1997; Becker et al. 1999)

2   Children and adolescents are likely to be influenced by the responses of others to such trauma-family, peer, community, and cultural environments-during and after the traumatic experience. Younger children tend to be better protected from traumatic events, as they tend to remain closer to their families, where as adolescents tend to be more exposed (Sack et al., 1993; Sack et al., 1994; Weine, Becker, McGlashan and Vojvoda et al., 1995; Becker et al., 1999).

3   The general finding that trauma exposed adolescents tend to be less symptomatic and demonstrate better social functioning than their adult counterparts may point to a relative resilience conferred by this particular stage of development (Sack et al., 1994; Weine, Becker, McGlashan, Laub et al., 1995; Weine, Becker, McGlashan, Vojvoda et al., 1995; Becker et al., 1999)

Most of the children and adolescents in the camps were accompanied by both parents and by some members of their extended family. In the chaotic conditions of the refugee camp confinement, the family unit became a strong anchoring point offering the children and adolescents nurturance, safety, and support. Younger children frequently refused separate from their parents and adolescents expressed feeling "closer than ever" to their relatives-perhaps a protective factor for both age groups-and had their emotional distress contained within the family unit. However, increased closeness to the family could interfere with the adolescent's strivings for autonomy and self-definition. The significance of this finding on a long-term basis is yet to be determined, and follow up studies of this population are needed. Another important finding was that more than two thirds of the children and adolescents had left at least one grand parent in Cuba. This represents an important emotional loss in a culture that places great value on the extended family network system and in which the grandparents play an important role in raising the children when parents are at work (Bernal, 1982)

The majority of the children and adolescents in both of the studies conducted inside the camps spent more than tow days at sea. Duration of the ocean crossing as a risk factor was not studied in detail, as separating the impact of this stressor from the multitude of other stressors of prolonged duration would have been impossible. In addition, the extremely elevated rates of PTSD and post-traumatic stress symptoms reported by both refugee subgroups made the quantification of dose-response impractical.

EVIDENCE OF PRE-EXISTING VULNERABILITY TO TRAUMA

Pre-existing medical and psychiatric conditions in this group were found to be elevated over what would be expected in the general population. For example, the prevalence rate of child and adolescent refugees diagnosed with epilepsy and treated with medication in Cuba was more than double of that of U.S. adolescents (Hauser, 1996). Owing to the unavailability of an electroencephalographic machine in the camps, and because of the vague and inconclusive histories of seizures given by children and by the adolescents and their parents, the diagnosis of epilepsy could not be confirmed in these patients. The significance of these findings remains to be determined; however, we speculate that one possible explanation may have been that anti-epileptic medication is sometimes used to control aggressive behavior and that this group of children and adolescents may have been identified as "problematic" before arriving at the camps. Bronchial Asthma-a medical condition with psychosomatic roots-was found to be elevated as well. The asthma rate in the children and adolescents was similar to that of Puerto Rican youth living in Puerto Rico, but was double than that of Cuban-American children and adolescents living in the United States and that of non-Hispanic U.S. children (Carter-Pokras and Gergen, 1993). Rates of pre-existing psychiatric conditions (e.g., ADHD, learning disabilities and other DSM-IV diagnoses) were slightly higher than those of British adolescents in the Isle of Wight Study (Rutter, 1989),

TYPOLOGY OF POST-TRAUMATIC STRESS
SYMPTOMS IN CHILDREN AND ADOLESCENTS

The symptom checklist showed approximately one quarter of the school age girls and one fifth of the adolescents of both sexes had entertained suicidal ideas and that more than half of the sample reported symptoms characteristic of hyper-arousal, including irritable-aggressive behavior, crying, nightmares and sleep and appetite disturbances. The great majority of the pre-school and school age children and almost half of the adolescents of both sexes reported bedwetting, and a smaller number encopresis-revealing a possible pituitary-hypothalamic and autonomic nervous system dysregulation caused by the ongoing stress. This phenomenon has also been described by other investigators in children exposed to natural disasters such as tornados (Bloch, Silver, and Perry, 1956) and the Buffalo Creek Flood (Gleser, Green, and Winget, 1987)

The rates of PTSD were slightly higher in girls of all age groups than in boys-a universal finding in the PTSD literature (Shaw, 2000). It is interesting that the rate of aggressive behavior was slightly higher in the adolescent girls than in the boys. This may have been due to cultural variables affecting reporting; as expressing aggressive behavior is usually more acceptable for boys than for girls, boys may not have considered their own behavior noteworthy, or it may not have represented a change from baseline. For girls, however, becoming aggressive represents a departure from the norm, and discovering this behavior in themselves, girls may have a tendency to over report it. Suicidal thoughts began to appear in the school age group and increased in frequency in the adolescents. There were no records of the number of suicide attempts in the camps, but these were a frequent cause for visits to the psychiatrist. On clinical observation, the attempts that were made seemed to have had a low level of lethality and could be more accurately characterized as suicide gestures, indication a "cry for help". Interestingly, suicide attempts seemed to be more common among adult women than among adolescents of both sexes.

In the PTSDRI (Frederick et al., 1992) the great majority of the children and adolescents rated themselves in the "very severe" (highest) category of PTSD symptomatology for the instrument, with girls showing slightly more symptoms than boys, except among the pre-school group, where boys reported slightly higher severity than girls. This finding, although not statistically significant, is contrary to the to the PTSD literature, which reports that school age and adolescent girls are more vulnerable to developing PTSD symptoms than boys (Shaw, 2000). There is a scarcity in the literature of PTSD with regards to pre-school children (Scheeringa 1995, 2001, 2003), so the significance of this finding in unclear and may merit investigation in future studies.

The children and adolescents in the second study, who had initially immigrated to the Cayman Islands and were later transferred to Guantanamo (a non-clinic population), they were compared to the children and adolescents of the first group, who had traveled towards Florida (a clinic population).

The children in the second group (Cayman Islands) also showed elevated rates of Post-traumatic symptoms, however, the frequency rates were a third to a half less than those children in adolescents in the clinic population. Accurate comparisons between the two groups could not be made given that, due to difficult conditions in the camps, the Cayman Islands group was interviewed using a non-standardized instrument. It is possible that the frequency of post-traumatic stress symptoms reported in the Cayman Islands group was more representative of the entire population of refugee children and adolescents in camps, than the more symptomatic clinic population reported in the first study.

INTERACTION OF SYMPTOMS WITH LIFE IN THE CAMPS

Children and adolescents frequently reported wanting to avoid places that reminded them of the trauma-such as the ocean-and many refused to go on field trips organized by the workers of the World relief Organization to two small beaches located on the base. Another frequent complaint was how certain smells-such as those from the "food wagon", which for months provided the same daily diet of rice sausage and beans-made the children "nauseated just at the sight of the truck". Hyper-arousal symptoms were reported in the form of nightmares, irritability, and frequent physical altercations, which broke out among the children and adolescents, or between the children, adolescents and their parents. Other environmental factors, such as the overcrowded conditions of the camps, the blaring music and noise, and the mosquitoes, also contributed to increasing the irritability and aggressive behavior among the child and adolescent refugees- a phenomenon that was also described by Vitiello and Stoff_(1997) as an important factor contributing to aggression in humans. The military weekly target practice, which produced a series of explosive noises and which was part of the routine on the base when the refugees first arrived, had to be terminated after several weeks of vociferous complaints on the part of the volunteer organizations, who reported how this practice frightened the refugee population. The re-experiencing of symptoms was reported by the children and adolescents in the form of frightful omens such as panic reactions in the presence of rain and thunder, which reminded them of Tropical Strom Gordon, which had devastated the camps one month after the arrival of the refugees.

Regressive Symptoms

Re-experiencing also took the form repetitive, unformed persecutory nightmares and the "apparitions" of dead relatives "carrying messages for the beyond". These occurred mostly at night, in the absence of other distracting stimulation. Regressive behaviors included thumb sucking, bedwetting, and encopresis, as well as separation anxiety from parental figures. Many children and adolescents refused to attend the schools organized in the camps by the World relief Organization and preferred to stay close to their families. -A decision that many adult family members supported. Somatic symptoms, mostly gastrointestinal disturbances, were reported in almost every visit by the children and adolescents and represented a diagnostic challenge to the clinician, as, in addition to the stress, the poor hygienic conditions and the hyper caloric diet in the camps could also account for these symptoms.

Behavior Problems

Acting out behaviors where also quite common among the child and adolescent refugees. Many adolescent boys formed small groups and escaped the confines of the barbed wire, penetrating the military section of the base. On multiple occasions, the military police intercepted the adolescent refugees in the pinball arcade inside the shopping mall or the hamburger fast food restaurant, which held a particular fascination for the Cuban adolescent refugees, who were intrigued by U.S. dietary habits and popular culture. The acting out behavior of sexual promiscuity and whirlwind romances was frequently expressed by adolescent girls, especially given that becoming pregnant increased the girl's chances of being evacuated from the camp and being admitted to the United States. Acting out behavior in the younger children was characterized by an increase of aggressive behavior, which manifested by frequent arguments with parents and physical fights with siblings and peers. In the adolescents, acting out behaviors appeared more as an attempt to break form the confining circumstances of the camps in an effort to defend against the shame of dependency, to exert their autonomy, and to defend against the regressive pull against parental figures.

Ratings of the Most Stressful Experiences

When asked to choose which was the "most stressful moment since you left Cuba?" there were marked differences according to age group. The majority of pre-school boys and girls reported that "life in the camps" was more difficult than "the ocean crossing" and having survived "Tropical Strom Gordon", where as the school age boys and girls reported that "the ocean crossing" had been the most difficult. In contrast, the majority of the adolescent boys, and a greater majority of the adolescent girls reported that "life in the camps" was the most difficult part of the entire experience. The pre-school children complained about missing their school, home and grandparents and feeling confined in the camps and appeared somewhat unaware of the dangers of the ocean crossing and the tropical storm. The school-age children expressed more concern about the dangerous circumstances they had endured during the ocean crossing, which included witnessing people drowning, surviving storms at sea and seeing floating human corpses being devoured by sharks. In contrast, the adolescents complained about the confinement of the camps. The adolescent boys complained about the quality of camp life, the boredom, lack of autonomy that the repetitiveness of the experience. The adolescent girls, in turn, complained about feeling unsafe and under threat of being physically or sexually assaulted by males. These difficulties and fears are understandable, especially when the developmental considerations of each particular age group are taken into account.

Role of Drawing

The invitation to draw-offered to the children and adolescents during or at the end of each interview-proved to be a very useful clinical tool for establishing a therapeutic alliance when the children and adolescents. The majority of the pre-school and school-age children spontaneously produced pictures of their environment in Cuba or of certain events in the exodus, conversing with the clinician as they did so. Some adolescents initially dismissed the invitation to draw as "silly", but eventually engaged in the activity as well. The theme of the drawings also served as an anchor to the interview, permitting the clinician to explore aspects of the child or adolescent's history that may not have been spontaneously volunteered by direct questioning. A pictorial mode of expression also allowed for non-verbal and strongly affect laden aspects of the traumatic experience to emerge, facilitating it's perception by conscious awareness and helping the children or adolescents to bind their anxiety, develop a more organized narrative of events, and thus enhance their ego strength. Many adolescents demonstrated remarkable artistic talent and joined up with several well-renowned Cuban artists among the refugees to establish an art gallery in the camps. An impressive collection was generated and taken on tour throughout the United States to lobby for the release of the refugees. Adolescents also took part in publishing two newspapers, a literary magazine and the multiple musical and theatrical productions organized by the refugees-all of which served as an important form of sublimation-in dealing with the chaotic and uncertain surrounding circumstances.

In conceptualizing treatment for the children and adolescents during the refugee camp confinement, we found that treatment began with the initial interview. Children and adolescents expressed great relief at being able to talk about their experiences, because the adults that had cared for them had thought that not talking about them would be beneficial and would make the children and adolescents "forget" the events. The validations of feelings, perceptions and negative aspects of the refugee experience-as well as the encouragement, and hope offered by the clinicians-proved to have a powerful therapeutic effect and helped cement the therapeutic alliance. All the therapists spoke fluent Spanish and were familiar with Cuban history and cultural nuances. This culturally syntonic experience facilitated a goodness of fit between the children and adolescents and the clinicians.

Meaning Ascribed by the Children and Adolescents to the Refugee Experiences

Clinicians also observed that many children ascribed magical explanations, rooted in egocentric causality to the experience, and to both, children and adolescents, the exodus from Cuba was invested with deep personal meaning. Some adolescents believed that the experience was a "necessary passage in order to deserve freedom"; while others attributed a multitude of magical explanations to the events; still others expressed anger and rage at the perceived injustice of the confinement. We identified the personal significance that each adolescent attributed to the migratory experience as an important component of the individual's personal narrative and internal representational world and one that would carry a strong relevance in the adolescent's future life experience. However, owing to the trying conditions in which the interviews took place, it became difficult for clinicians to explore these aspects more in depth with the adolescents. We hoped that the adolescents would someday be able to integrate the meaning of the refugee experience in an adaptive manner that would not produce developmental interferences but instead promote psychic growth. Because of the tense atmosphere inside the camps during the early weeks of the confinement, the author felt threatened, while visiting the camps alone, by the potential of mob violence and physical assault. Inside the camps, men and women, as well as adolescents, tended to gather in groups and become aggressive and belligerent. A totally different experience took place when the refugees were interviewed alone or accompanied by members of their families.

The adolescents, in particular, complained that inside the camps they felt "dehumanized" and "treated like cattle". All the refugees were required to wear a black-plastic magnetized wristband that, when passed through an electronic sensor, revealed the refugee's serial number and demographic information. Many adolescents, in defiance, refused to wear the bands. In the words of one adolescent, "It's like the Americans are the nazis, these are the concentration camps, and we are the Jews who are being sent to the Holocaust".

In contrast with many of their other experiences as refugees, most of the school-age children and the adolescents found the interview with mental health professionals to be a humanizing experience and found that the clinic provided a safe place away from the chaos of the camps. We hypothesized that the clinic provided a "holding environment" for them. Teenage patients returned many times to chat with members of the commission of volunteers or to "hang out" outside the two tent hospitals.

Impact of Working with the Refugees on Mental Health Professionals

Strong counter-transference issues and worker fatigue were common among the mental health professionals serving the refugees. Cuban-American clinicians frequently found themselves holding back tears, in the middle of an interview, as the children and adolescents narrated an ordeal that very closely resembled those endured, years earlier, by the clinician and/or his family in their own attempt to leave Cuba.

Identification with the plight of the refugees, with a tendency towards the blurring of boundaries, and with the rage directed towards the authorities responsible for the confinement were common themes found among the clinicians. Also, suspicion, paranoia, and rage directed at certain refugees thought to have been politically connected to the Cuban regime were commonly experienced. Feelings of depression, longing and nostalgia abounded at the end of every workday, when clinicians retreated to their quarters at the military base. This appeared to be especially true among the Cuban-American members of the medical team, who engaged in melancholic recollections of their former life in Cuba. Highlighting their sense of loss was the fact that, for the first time in decades, they had been allowed to set foot on the island. Many clinicians filled jars with Cuban soil and took them home so they could feel closer to their homeland or to offer them as presents to relatives. Cuba-American clinicians, many of whom were children and adolescents when they left Cuba and had been assimilated into American society, reported feeling "more Cuban than ever"-having discovered a common denominator with the refugees by which suffering was experienced as a value shared by other Cubans. Their past suffering and the refugees current suffering were viewed as validating a national and cultural identity under siege and in danger of being diluted by four decades of exile in the United States. In some ways, the trans-generational experience of the Guantanamo boatlift was similar to that of a younger Jewish-American generation and their encounters with survivors of the Holocaust in that national identity and cultural history are deeply connected to suffering and the struggle for emancipation. These values are passed down from one generation to the next and serve to maintain a strong sense of national and cultural identity ad cohesion in a community that is separated from its homeland (Herz and Rosen, 1982).

The Role of Political Agendas

Political agendas played a central role not only in the Guantanamo exodus but also in the subsequent immigration of refuges to the United States. The rational behind diverting the refugees to the camps at the Naval Base was based on the U.S. government's previous negative experience involving the 1980 Mariel Boatlift, in which Cuban authorities vacated jails and psychiatric hospitals on the island and mixed several thousand antisocial and chronically mentally ill patients with the refugees, all of whom arrived by surprise on the U.S. shores (Sandoval, 1985). However, once confined to camps in order to be screened prior to entry in the United States, the Guantanamo refugees' experience was compounded by lack of a clear policy on the part of the U.S. government as to the ultimate destiny of the refugees; lack of appropriate preparations in terms of hygiene, general welfare and mental health issues; and the refugees' prolonged confinement and poor conditions.

Inadequate planning for health care and mental health care continued after the refugees arrived in Florida. The state of Florida, in order to save money on Medicaid state funds, contracted with a health maintenance organization (HMO) that set up offices outside the processing centers in Miami. As the refugees completed the process of registration, they were immediately brought into the next office and enrolled in the HMO. Unfamiliar with the U.S. medical system, children, adolescents and families who arrived seeking psychiatric treatment at the public hospital were denied payment by the HMO. The issue was further complicated by the fact that the HMO did not offer child and adolescent psychiatric services. "Dis-enrolling" from the HMO in order to obtain these services covered by Medicaid, proved to be a complicated bureaucratic nightmare beyond the reach and understanding of the newly arrived refugees. The result was that the children and adolescents in need of psychiatric treatment were left in a medical limbo. After many efforts to alert Florida's authorities in charge of refugee affairs of the problem, the author was told confidentially by an officer of the organization an officer of the organization told the author confidentially that state policy towards the Cuban refugees was for them to accomplish a "quiet and rapid assimilation into the community in order not to upset the taxpayers (Rothe 1999). All efforts to develop treatment programs for the refugees were met with equal amounts of resistance. Over a period of some weeks and months, Cuban adolescent refugees began to appear in a number of clinical settings in the greater Miami area, including the special education programs at the public schools as well as the community mental health centers. On the positive side, child and adolescent refugees, for the most part integrated rapidly into the strong, mostly bilingual, and welcoming Cuban-American community in South Florida-which validated their cultural and ethnic identity as well as their refugee experience.

Long Term Effects

Traumatic events such as fleeing on an ocean journey with inadequate means; being exposed to death, violence, harsh weather, and poor environmental conditions; and being confined in a military refugee camp can have profound and long-lasting effects on children and adolescents. We examined children and adolescents who left Cuba with members of their families, were rescued by the U.S. military, and were taken to camps at Guantanamo Bay. Up to six months after leaving the refugee camps, a majority of children in our sample reported moderate to severe symptoms of PTSD, including avoidance, regressive behaviors, re-experiencing the traumatic events, somatic symptoms, and hyper-arousal.

Most of the children reported that the refugee experience had severely affected their peers. We found modest significant relationships between self-reported PTSD symptoms and withdrawn behavior with age and exposure to certain stressors, such as violence. However, none of the 11 teachers reported observing any clinically significant internalizing or externalizing behaviors among the children and adolescents.

A majority of the children left Cuba accompanied by intact nuclear families. However, most of them had left behind grandparents and other members of the extended family. This separation constitutes a significant emotional loss to children in a culture that places great importance on the extended family and in which the grandparents and other relatives care for the children when both parents are at work (Bernal, 1982).

The children and adolescents were exposed to multiple stressors during the ocean crossing. These stressors appeared to be less severe than those found among a highly symptomatic population of children and adolescents who were seen inside the camps for psychiatric care (Rothe, Castillo-Matos & Busquets, 2002). However, no statistically significant correlations between the stressors and the severity of self-reported PTSD symptoms were found in that sample.

The global score on the self-report PTSDRI indicated that a majority of the children continued to experience moderate to severe symptoms of PTSD four to six months after they left the camps. The most severe types of symptoms reported were avoidance, regressive behaviors (characterized by separation anxiety and clinging behaviors), and re-experiencing of symptoms. All three clusters of symptoms tend to be less florid and more subjective than the symptoms of hyper-arousal. Therefore, the symptoms may be less likely to result in the child's being singled out as problematic in a group situation, which would make the child's distress less likely to be noticed by the adults responsible for his or her care.

In the cluster of miscellaneous symptoms, a majority of children considered the migratory experience to have had a strong impact on their lives and on the lives of most of their peers.

Somatization was reported by more than half of the cohort and represents a common expression of internal distress in most children. Surprisingly, only a quarter of the sample reported an onset of externalizing behaviors after the migratory experience. This finding reflects a more subjective and less overtly noticeable expression of the traumatic experience among these children.

In the regression analysis we found a trend toward statistical significance for the withdrawn scale of the CBCL-TRF. A feeling that one would die at sea and witnessing acts of violence in the camps contributed to withdrawn behavior. These findings suggest that internal and external factors combined to contribute to withdrawn behavior in our sample. We also found a trend on the total score of PTSDRI. Being older and witnessing acts of violence in the camps were the significant predictors of this self-report measure. Although the experience of witnessing violence contributed to both behaviors, older children may appear more resilient during the actual traumatic situation but be more prone to experiencing delayed reactions once the stressors have been removed. The family usually shelters older children less than younger children, so these older children may suffer more direct exposure to the traumatic situation.

Also, the finding of witnessing violence was consistent across self-report and observation by a caretaker (a teacher). This finding suggests that violence in a chaotic and traumatic situation will be readily apparent to children and adolescents, as well as to their teachers, and that such experiences will have an impact on the various domains of functioning reported by both.

Our findings are similar to those of other investigators (Kinzie, Sack, Angell et al., 1986; Mollica, Pool & Son, 1997), which reveal that after the stressors have been removed, subjective levels of severity of PTSD symptoms among children and adolescents remain high, while social functioning—in our study, functioning in a classroom—remains relatively unaffected. In our study, even though teachers reported that the children exhibited mild difficulties in certain areas, the overall academic and social functioning was found to be largely intact.

Stresses of Acculturation

This form of refugee stress probably has the poorest conceptualization and study of any of the stressors discussed so far, and, until recently, no instrument existed to measure this particular form of stress (Sack, 1998). Grinberg and Grinberg (1994) have described that when children migrate, they leave behind what constitutes their "human environment" (schoolmates, friends and relatives) as well as their "non-human environment" (their home, school, neighborhood, as well as their toys). They add that children rarely participate in the decision to migrate and often times find themselves shocked by the surprise of having been abruptly uprooted without an appropriate warning. This was very much the case among the Cuban refugee boat children at Guantanamo Bay. Rothe et. al. (2000) found that more than 60% of the Cuban children and adolescents that had arrived in the United States had left behind at least one grandparent, and more than 70% had left behind uncles and aunts; an important source of distress in a culture that places a high value on the extended family network system (Bernal, 1982).

Savin et. al. (1996) have pointed out that trauma often occurs with the experience of loss and that, additionally, refugee children and their families have to deal with the depression that accompanies the multiple losses of relocation. Depression in refugee children may express itself in the form of somatization, acting out or regressive behaviors (Mollica et. al. 1997). In our sample of Cuban children, seen four to six months following their arrival in the U.S., we found that 48% of the subjects reported moderate to severe symptoms of somatization (headaches and stomach aches), 31% reported moderate to severe acting out behaviors and 63% reported moderate to severe regressive behaviors in the PTSDRI (Frederick et. al. 1992). Additionally, 39% of the subjects reported that they had felt "guilty" about what had happened, attributing egocentric causality to the refugee experience. In spite of the fact that this was younger children more often reported this, many adolescents had concluded that their parents had chosen to emigrate, in order to provide them with a better future and for this reason, felt guilty over their parents decision.

Upon their arrival in the United States, we also found that parents were often overwhelmed in dealing with issues such as housing, employment, language and culture shock. Family members who already resided in the U.S. were temporarily housing the majority of the families of these children; which, over time, increased tensions between guests and hosts.

Sack et al. (1994), in studying a random community sample of Cambodian adolescent refugees in the U.S., found that 21% met criteria for PTSD and 11% for depression, after six years in the U.S. They pointed out that depression, which is more closely associated with acculturation, declines over time, while PTSD tends to stay the same (Sack et. al. 1993). In our sample, we found it extremely difficult to track down families after they had spent more than six months in the United States. In our child and adolescent refugee sample we found that, at four to six months after arrival in the U.S., more than 60% reported moderate to severe 1) hyper-arousal, 2) avoidant, and 3) re-experiencing symptoms in the PTSDRI (Frederick et. al. 1992), with re-experiencing symptoms being the most severe. Also, 69% reported traumatic reminders and 72% reported intrusive recollections of the events.

After arriving in the United States, the majority of the Cuban families chose to stay in South Florida, where they had relatives and where they found an already well established and supportive Cuban-American community, as well as a predominantly Hispanic population, which facilitated acculturation. However, a very small minority of unaccompanied Cuban refugee adolescents was placed in foster homes in the Midwestern United States. Anecdotal reports gathered from officials of the Catholic Church Services and the Florida Office of Refugee Affairs revealed that these adolescents exhibited severe conduct problems, and were eventually relocated to the South Florida area, where they found a more supportive and culturally syntonic environment (Rothe, 1999).

Methodological Issues

The number of research studies on refugee populations of children and adolescents has increased significantly in the last decade; however, many problems with methodological issues still exist. For instance, Gurwitch et al. (1998) report that there are no appropriate instruments to measure stress on preschool children. In turn, PTSD has been validated across cultural barriers. Sack et al. (1997) in a study of Cambodian adolescent victims of the Pol Pot regime concluded that some studies on refugees are affected by problems with interpreters, which compromise the validity of the data (Sack, 1998).

In our experience with the Cuban child and adolescent boat children, we encountered a series of methodological difficulties; among which were: 1) The instrument used (PTSDRI, Frederick 1992) did not differentiate between the different stressors endured by children, i.e., the ocean crossing, life in the camps or previous political persecution. 2) Our mission in the refugee camps, as members of the Miami Medical Team (a volunteer relief organization), was mainly to provide clinical services. Therefore, research was not a priority. Also, due to the harsh conditions of camp confinement, which affected refugees, volunteers and the military, it was difficult to devote time to developing sophisticated research designs. This became most evident when we examined a refugee subpopulation that emigrated south, towards the Cayman Islands. Even though the results of this study were of value and provided data that had never been studied before, the study lacked a standardized questionnaire and methodological rigor. 3) The first three studies (Rothe et. al. 1995, Rothe et al. 2000 and Rothe et al. 2002-a) were conducted inside the camps, while the traumatogenic conditions of camp confinement continued to take place. Rumors abounded and changed on a daily basis, with regard to whether the refugees would be admitted to the U.S. or would be returned to Cuba, where they would face political persecution. The rumors indicated, at some points in time, that children and adolescents with psychiatric disturbances would be immediately airlifted into the U.S. At other times, it was believed that having a psychiatric disturbance would cause the refugee to be denied admission into the U.S. and to be returned to Cuba. These rumors, based on the uncertainty of the U.S. government policy towards the refugees, which was being decided on a day-to-day basis, may have contributed to the exaggeration or minimization of the symptoms, when the refugees were being interviewed. 4) The psychiatric interview of the refugees was conducted by Cuban-American volunteer mental health professionals, as well as by three psychiatrists and one master's level psychologist. As a team, all members spoke Spanish as a first language and were deeply familiarized with the cultural and political nuances of the refugee population. For this reason, cultural and language distortions were kept to a minimum. 5) Upon arriving in the U.S. the refugees became quickly dispersed into the community, making follow-up studies nearly impossible. 6) Until recently, no instruments existed that could measure resettlement stress in refugee children and adolescents. Sack (1998) has developed a questionnaire to measure resettlement stress in Cambodian adolescents, but it still has not been validated. Based on his work, he has divided refugee stress into categories: a) Traumatic stress, b) Resettlement stress, and c) Inter-current stress. As previously explained, methodological issues in refugee trauma research are still in its infancy and present many challenges to investigators, which are yet to be explored.

CONCLUSIONS

The results of this study are important to parents, educators, mental health professionals, government authorities, and anyone in receiving communities who come into contact with newly arrived child and adolescent refugees. Our findings highlight the difficulties encountered by teachers in identifying psychologically traumatized child and adolescent refugees who need psychiatric treatment. They also suggest that certain characteristics, such as exposure to stressors and exposure to another person's death or attempted suicide and other types of violence, increase the severity of PTSD and have an impact on particular areas of functioning.

The significance of subjective PTSD symptoms with high levels of psychosocial functioning in this population and the long-term prognosis of these children remain to be determined. The results of our study underscore the need for long-term follow-up studies in this population. Despite their relatively intact psychosocial functioning, these children continued to experience subjective psychic suffering and internal distress.

Clinicians should be alert to the presence of PTSD when they encounter refugee children in their practices. Self-report questionnaires, a comprehensive psychosocial history, and a psychiatric interview should be conducted to more accurately identify subjective psychic suffering and to provide appropriate treatment for these children. Finally, our results highlight the importance of developing culturally sensitive, ethnographic research methodology and instrumentation for research among refugees so that research findings can be applied appropriately.

REFERENCES

Achenbach TM, Edelbrock C (1986), *Manual for the Teacher Report Form and Teacher Version of the Child Behavioral Profile.* Univ. of Vermont Dept. of Psychiatry, Burlington, VT.

Ackerman H, Clark J (1995), *The Cuban Balseros: Voyage of Uncertainty* (Monograph) (1995). The Policy Center of the Cuban American National Council, Inc., Miami.

Alvarez L (November 7, 1994), Elated exiles prepare to meet their loved ones: First 10,000 detainees could arrive next week. *The Miami Herald.* P.1-A, Miami, FL.

Baum A, Davidson LM (1986), A suggested framework for studying factors that contribute to trauma in disaster. In: *Disasters and Mental Health*, ed. B.L. Snowder & M.Lystad. Washington DC: American Psychiatric Press,pp.37-48.

Becker D F, Weine SM, Vojvoda D. & McGlashan TH (1999), PTSD symptoms in adolescent survivors of "ethnic cleansing": results from a one year follow up study. *J. Amer. Acad. Child Adol. Psychiat.*, 38: 775-781.

Bernal G (1982), Cuban Families. In: *Ethnicity and Family Therapy* (eds.) M. McGoldrick, JK Pearce, J Giordano. Guilford Pres, New York.

Bloch DA, Silver E, Perry AB (1956), Some factors in the emotional reaction of children to disaster. *Am J Psychiatry* 113:416-422.

Breslau N, Davis GC, Andreski P, Peterson E (1991), Traumatic Events and Post-Traumatic Stress Disorder in an Urban Population of Young Adults. *Arch. Gen. Psychiatry* 48:216-222.

Breslin R (1986), The wording and translation of research instruments. In: Loaner WJ & Berry JW (Eds.) *Field Methods in Cross-Cultural Research.* pp. 17-164. Sage, Beverly Hills, CA.

Carter-Pokras OD, Gergen PJ (1993), Reported asthma among Puerto Rican, Mexican-American and Cuban Children, 1982 through 1984. *Am J Public Health* 83(4):580-2.

Castro M (2002), The New Cuban Immigration in Context. The Dante Fascell North-South Center.UniversityofMiami.*http://www.miami.edu/nsc/publications/Papers&Reports/Immigration&Integr.html-4.3KB*

Clark J (1975*), Exodus from Revolutionary Cuba (1959-1974): A sociological analysis.* Doctoral Dissertation. University of Florida.

_____ . (1992), *Cuba: Mito y Realidad: testimonio de un pueblo.* Saeta Ediciones. Miami.

Diagnostic & Statistical Manual of Mental Disorders (DSM-III-R) (1987). Am. Psychiatric Assn. Wash. D.C.

_____ . (1994). Am. Psychiatric Assn. Wash. D.C.

Eth S, Pynoos RS (1985), *Post-Traumatic Stress Disorder in Children.* Am. Psychiatric Press, Washington, DC.

Frederick CJ, Pynoos RS, Nader K (1992), *Post-traumatic Stress Disorder Reactive Index* (PTSDRI) UCLA Dept. of Psychiatry, 300 UCLA Med. Plaza, Los Angeles, CA 90024.

Green BL, Korol M, Grace MC (1991), Children and Disaster: Age, gender and parental effect on PTSD symptoms. *J Am. Acad. Child Adol. Psychiatry* 30:945-951.

Gleser G, Green BL, Winget C (1981): *Prolonged Psychological Effects of Disaster: A Study of Buffalo Creek.* New York, Academic Press.

Green BL, Grace MC, Vary MG, Kramer TL, Gleser CG, Leonard AC (1994), Children of disaster in he second decade: A 17 year follow-up of the Buffalo Creek Survivors. *J. Am. Acad. Child. Adol. Psychiatry* 33:71-79.

Grinberg L, Grinberg R (1984) *Psychoanalytic Perspectives on Migration and Exile.* Yale Univ. Press.

Gurwitch RH, Sullivan MA, Long PJ (1998), The Impact of Trauma and Disaster in Young Children. *Child & Adol. Psychiatry Clinic of North America.* Vol 7, No. 1 January pp. 19-31.

Hauser WA: (1996), Epidemiology of Epilepsy in Children. *Neurosurg. Clinics of North America* 6(3): 419-29.

Helzer JE, Robbins LN, McEvoy L (1987), Post-Traumatic Stress Disorder in the General Population *N. Eng. J. Med.* 317:1630-1634.

Herz F M, Rosen E J, (1982), Jewish Families, In: *Ethnicity and Family Therapy*, ed. M. McGoldrick, J.K. Pierce & J. Giordano. New York, Guilford Press, pp.364-392.

Howard J, Hodes N (2000), Psychopathology, Adversity and Service Utilization of Young Refugees. *Am. Acad. Child Adolesc. Psychiatry* 39:3, 3680377.

Jensen, PS, Shaw JA (1993), Children as Victims of War: Current Knowledge and Future Research Needs. *J. Am Acad Child Adol Psychiatr.,* 32: 697-708.

Jorge A, Suchlicki J, Leyva de Varona A (1991), *Cuban Exiles in Florida. Their Presence and Contribution* Research Inst. of Cuban Studies. Univ. of Miami Press, Miami, FL.

Kinzie JD, Bohnlein JK, Leung PK, Moore L J, Riley C, Smith D (1990), The prevalence of post-traumatic stress disorder and its clinical significance among southeast Asian refugees. *Amer. J. of Psychiat.,* 147:913-917.

Kinzie JD, Sack W, Angell R, Manson S, Rath B. (1986), The psychiatric effects of massive trauma on Cambodian children I: The children. *J. Amwer.Acad. Child Adol Psychiat.,* 25:307-376.

McNally RJ (1993), *Stressors that produce PTSD in Children. In: Davidson JRT, Foam EB (Eds): PTSD:DSM-IV and Beyond.* Am. Psychiatric Press, Washington, DC.

Mollica RF, Poole C, Son L (1997), Effects of War Trauma on Cambodian Refugee Adolescents' Functional and Mental Health Status. *J. Am. Acad. Child Adolesc. Psychiatry.* 36:1098-1106.

Newman CJ (1976), Children and Disaster: Some observations at Buffalo Creek. *Am. J. Psychiatry* 133:306-312.

Office of the United Nations High Commissioner or Refugees (1991), In: Ahearn FL, Athey JL (Eds). *Refugee Children, Theory, Research and Services.* Baltimore, Johns Hopkins Univ. Press P. xii.

Oller R (1995), *American Purgatory: Cuban Families Behind the Wire* (Documentary film) 90 Miles Films, Miami, Florida.

Pynoos R S (1992), *Scoring and interpretation of the Post-Traumatic Stress Disorder Reactive Index (PTSDRI)* UCLA Dept. of Psychiatry. 300 UCLA Med. Plaza. Beverly Hills, CAL 90024 (1992).

Rothe E M, Castillo-Matos H, Busquets R (2002-a), Posttraumatic Stress Symptoms in Cuban Adolescents During Refugee Camp Confinement. *Adolescent Psychiatry* Vol.26: 97-124.

Rothe E M, Castillo-Matos H, Lewis J, Martinez O, Martinez I (2002-b), Post-Traumatic Stress Disorder Among Cuban Boat Children After Release from a Refugee Camp. *Psychiatric Services* Vol.53, No.8: 970-976.

Rothe EM, Castillo H, Lewis J , Martinez O, Gonzalez M A, Busquets R, Garcia L, Brinson K, Mason D, Martinez I, Barral E, Aranguren E (1998), Sintomatologia post-traumatica En ninos y adolescentes balseros cubanos: una Sinopsis de tres estudios. *Psiquiatria* Vol. 10, No. 1 Enero-Febrero pp. 18-28.

Rothe EM, Castillo-Matos H, Brinson K, Lewis J (2000), La Odisea de los balseros cubanos: sintomas post-traumaticos y caractersiticas de viaje en ninos y adolescentes. *Medico Interamericano*. Vol. 19, No.12: 578-581.

Rothe EM (1999), Personal Communication with Officers of the Catholic Church Services and Florida Office of Refugee Affairs. *Annual Conference of The Assn. of Teachers of English as a Second Language (TESOL)*, New York, March 11-14.

Rousseau CM, Drapeau A (1998), Parent-Child Agreement on Refugee Children's Psychiatric Symptoms: A Transcultural Perspective. *J. Am. Acad. Child Adolesc. Psychiatry* 37:6 629-636.

Rutter M (1989), Isle of Wight revisited: Twenty-five years of Psychiatric Epidemiology. *J. Am. Acad. Child & Adol. Psychiatry* 28:633-653.

Sack W H, Clarke G, Him G, Dickason D, Goff B, Lanham K, Kinzie J D (1993), A Six Year Follow-up Study of Cambodian Adolescents. *J. Am. Acad. Child Adolesc. Psychiatry* 32:431-437.

Sack WH, McSharry S, Clarke G, Kinney R, Seely J, Lewinsohn P (1994), The Khmer Adolescent Project I. Epidemiologic Findings in Two Generations of Cambodian Refugees *J. Nerv. Ment. Dis.* 182:387-395.

Sack W H , Seely J R , Clarke G N (1997), Does PTSD Transcend Cultural Barriers?: A Study from the Khmer Adolescent Refugee Project. *J. Am. Acad. Child Adolesc. Psychiatry* 36:1 49-54.

Sack W H (1998), Multiple Forms of Stress in Refugee and Immigrant Children. *Child & Adolescent Psychiatry Clinics of North America.* Vol. 7, No. 1 January pp. 153-167.

Savin D, Sack WH, Clarke GN, Meas N, Richart I (1996), The Khmer Adolescent Project III: A Study of Trauma from Thailand's Site II Refugee Camp. *J. Am. Acad. Child Adolesc. Psychiatry* 35:3, 384-391.

Scheeringa M S , Zeanah C H , Drell M J , Larrieu J A (1995), Two approaches to the diagnosis of Posttraumatic Stress Disorder in Infancy and Early Childhood. *J. Am. Acad Child Adolsc Psychiatry* 34:191-200.

Scheeringa M S , Peebles C D , Cook C A Zeanah C H (2001), Towards Establishing Procedural, Criterion and Discriminant Validity of PTSD in Early Childhood. *J Am. Acad Child Adolesc Psychiatry* 40: 52-60.

Scheeringa M S , Zeanah C H , Myers L , Putnam F W (2003), New Findings on Alternative Criteria for PTSD in Pre-school children. *J Am. Acad child Adolesc Psychiatry* 42: 561-568.

Shaw J A (2000), Children, Adolescents and Trauma. *Psychiatr. Quart.,* 71:227-243.

Suchlicki J (1990), *Cuba: From Columbus to Castro*. Brassey's U.S. Inc. Washington, D.C.

Terr LC (1979), Psychic Trauma in Children: Observations Following the Chowchilla School Bus Kidnapping. *Am. Journal of Psychiatry* 137:14-19.

_____ . (1983), Chowchilla Revisited: The Effect of Psychic Trauma Four Years After a School Bus Kidnapping. *Am. Journal of Psychiatry* 140:1543-1550.

_____ . (1991), Childhood Trauma: An Outline and Overview. *Am. Journal of Psychiatry* 148:1-20.

Thomas H (1996), *The Cuban Revolution*. Weidenfeld and Nicholson, LTD London, U.K.

United States Seventh Coast Guard District (1995), *Cuban Rescue Statistics: 1981-1995* Public Affairs office, Miami, Florida.

World Refugee Survey (2003), US Committee for Refugees. *http:///.refugees.org/downloads/wrs03/SSKeyStatistics.pdf.*

Vitiello B, Stoff D M (1997), Subtypes of Aggression and their Relevance in Child Psychiatry. *J. Am. Acad. Child Adolesc. Psychiatry.* 36:3, 307-315.

Weine S M , Becker D F , McGlashan T H, Vojvoda D, Hartman S, Robbins J P (1995), Adolescent Survivors of "Ethnic Cleansing": Observations on their first year in America. *J. Am. Acad Child Adol Psychiat.* 43: 1153-1159.

Weine SM, Vojvoda D, Becker DF, McGlashan TH, Hodzic E, Laub D, Hyman L, Sawyer M, Lazrove S (1998), PTSD Symptoms in Bosnian Refugees One Year After Resettlement in the United States. *Am. J. Psychiatry.* 155:4, 562-563.

World Relief Organization (1995), *Statistics of Cuban and Haitian Refugees at Guantanamo Bay U. S. Naval Base, Cuba (1994-1995).* World Relief Offices, Miami, Florida.

In: Trends in Posttraumatic Stress Disorder Research   ISBN 1-59454-135-3
Editor: Thomas A. Corales, pp. 129-156   © 2005 Nova Science Publishers, Inc.

Chapter 6

LOST CHILDHOOD: CHILDREN SURVIVING THE HOLOCAUST

Rachel Lev-Wiesel[*] and Marianne Amir[†]

Department of Social Work, Ben Gurion University, Beer Sheva, Israel

ABSTRACT

The chapter will be focusing on the long-term effects of Holocaust survivors who were children during the war. The data will be based on two previous quantitative and qualitative studies: The first study examined the psychological distress, Posttraumatic Stress Disorder (PTSD), Quality of Life (QoL), Self-identity and Potency among 170 Holocaust survivors who were born after 1926. This sample was divided into four groups based on the setting of their experience during the Holocaust: Catholic Institutions, Christian foster families, concentration camps, and hiding in the woods and/or with partisans. The second study assessed posttraumatic stress disorder (PTSD) symptoms, subjective quality of life (QoL), psychological distress and potency in a group of child Holocaust survivors who did not know their true identity. Twenty-three such survivors were compared to a matched group of 23 child Holocaust survivors who knew their identity.

The results of the first study showed that survivors who had been with foster families scored significantly higher on several of the measures of distress, whereas survivors who had been in the woods and/or with partisans scored significantly higher on several of the positive measures, QoL, potency, and self-identity. The results of the second study showed that survivors with unknown identity have higher somatization and anxiety scores and lower physical, psychological and social QoL than do survivors with known identity.

The discussion will be focusing on the understanding of the different experiences according to developmental theory and sense of control. In addition, the psychological

---

[*]   Address correspondence to: Rachel Lev-Wiesel, Ph.D., is an Associate Professor in the Department of Social Work, Ben Gurion University, Beer Sheva, Israel. Email: rachellv@bgumail.bgu.ac.il
[†]   Marianne Amir, Ph.D., was a Professor in the Departments of Social Work and Behavioral Sciences, Ben Gurion University, Beer Sheva, Israel. Professor Amir died of cancer in January. This chapter is in her memory.

consequences of not knowing one's identity will be discussed in light of the role of resilience. Several illustrations (personal stories of survivors) will be presented.

INTRODUCTION

Following the initial clinical observations of the "survivor syndrome" (Niederland, 1964), most researchers who examined Holocaust survivors of concentration and labor camps focused on adult survivors' PTSD symptoms (Danieli, 1985; Krystal & Niederland, 1968; Yehuda, Kahana, Binder-Brynes et al., 1995; Yehuda, Sartorius, Kahana, Southwick & Giller 1994). Survivors had difficulties persevering work, maintaining relationships, and face new situations. They also had guilt feelings for having survived, bursts of anger, a low frustration threshold, a feeling of helplessness, lack of initiative and interest in life, low self esteem, thoughts of being lost, anxiety attacks and psychosomatic symptoms. Lorenzer (1968) noted that many survivors are using the defense mechanisms of denial and separation excessively (e.g., denial of having lost close family). However, this type of denial helped maintain psychological equilibrium through a rigid fixation (Nathan, Ettinger & Winnik, 1964).

In recent years there has been a greater recognition that a wide range of traumatic events were experienced by individuals in the Nazi-controlled areas, both in concentration camps and while avoiding imprisonment by hiding under false identity in monasteries, orphanages, Christian foster families, woods or barns (Kestenberg & Brenner, 1986). It has become increasingly clear that the age of the victim at the time of traumatic event exposure is of importance in the long-term consequences. For example, Keilson (1992) who examined the relationship between personality traits and extreme traumatic events experienced by children during the Holocaust, found that, child survivors who were younger than four at the end of the SWW suffered excessively from neurotic symptoms than survivors who were older than fourteen. Others who compared Holocaust survivors in concentration camps to those who were in "hiding" during the SWW, pointed out that the age at the time of trauma and cumulative number of stressful events were associated with increased symptoms of psychogenic amnesia, hypervigilence, and emotional detachment (Yehuda, Schmeidler, & Siever, 1997).

The Nazis did not consider children to be useful for work (children did not survive long in the camps) they either killed them with their families prior to arrival to the concentration camps or sent them immediately to the gas chambers upon arrival at the camp. There are no exact statistics concerning the number of children who survived the SWW. After the war, approximately 50,000 settled in Israel, and others immigrated to Canada, the United States, Belgium, and France (Tec, 1993). The Nazi persecution of the Jews and the circumstances of war led to separation of families, physical and psychological suffering, hunger, humiliation, and a constant witnessing of cruelty. Today, more than 50 years after the war, the group of child survivors comprises the "last witness" of the atrocities which took place during the Holocaust. In addition, child survivors have experienced the ongoing influences of a lost childhood, from both a personal and a familial perspective. The aim of this chapter is to present two recent studies conducted by the authors that focused on the psychological long-term effects of the Holocaust traumata in Holocaust survivors who were children during the SWW. The first study focused on the psychological long term effects of Holocaust child survivors in relation to the setting experience of survival: Catholic institutions, Christian foster families, concentration camps, and hiding in woods and/or with partisans. The second study focused on the psychological long-term effects of lost identity in Holocaust child survivors who lost their identity compare to child survivors who retained their identity.

THE PSYCHOLOGICAL CONSEQUENCES OF THE HOLOCAUST EXPERIENCE ON THE CHILD SURVIVORS

Researchers and clinicians regard the Holocaust as being a constellation entailing specific psychological harm which becomes more severe as the person ages (Chodoff, 1963; Davidson, 1992; Lederer, 1963; Niederland, 1964). Bunk and Eggers (1993), Gampel (1992), and Tec (1993) suggested that child survivors are different from adult survivors because they were forced to endure formidable stressors and to function as adults without the benefit of adult coping resources and adaptations. These studies were first to draw attention to survivors who were children during the Holocaust and to the different long term effects of experiencing and enduring the Holocaust atrocities in different developmental stage.

Interviews with survivors who were children during the war, reveal a strong and constant sense of fierce longing for one's lost parents, and an intense desire for ties with significant others from the past. The memories of child survivors are usually filled with painful scenes of being separated from their parents, becoming orphaned, being abandoned, feeling cold, starving, experiencing violence, and being physically unable to move for long periods of time (Kestenberg & Kestenberg, 1988; Krell, 1993; Lee, 1988; Moskovitz & Krell, 1990). Different types of painful memories, those of being separated from the warm foster families whom the children had learned to identify with and trust, are common as well (Valent, 1998). The present family is perceived as a substitute for the lost one (Fogelman, 1992; Krell, 1993; Robinson, Rapaport-Bar-Sever & Rapaport, 1994). As the survivors get older, their level of vulnerability to stress factors, such as retirement, the death of a spouse, children leave the home, and health problems, increases.

Yehuda, Schmeidler, Siever et al. (1997) reported that, while the intensity of PTSD symptoms does not significantly differentiate between survivors of concentration camps and hidden children, the impact of the symptoms does vary. Others (Suedfeld, Fell & Krell, 1998) found that psychogenic amnesia and avoidance were stronger among child survivors, while intrusive thoughts were stronger among the camp survivors. Consistently, several qualitative studies suggested that regardless of the fact that the majority of child survivors live normal and creative lives (Krell, 1993), child survivors still suffer from symptoms of the survivor syndrome (Breiner, 1996; Kestenberg & Brenner, 1996; Mazor & Mendelson, 1998; Moskovitz & Krell, 1990; Robinson, Rapaport-Bar-Sever, & Rapaport, 1994; Tauber & Van-Der-Hal, 1996). Kestenberg (1992, 1993) claimed that child survivors adopt psychological defenses such as numbing of affect, splitting, and identification with the aggressor, and frequently suffer from depression, phobias and distorted self-images. Others emphasized that the most outstanding psychological effects of persecution are the loss of identity and feelings of being worthless (Brenner, 1988; Bunk & Eggers, 1993; Rustow, 1989), accompanied by a lifelong sense of bereavement (Mazor & Mendelsohn, 1998).

There is consensus among mental health professionals that a disturbance in a child's life concerning sense of security and quality of life may have long-term impact. A stable relationship with a parental figure who provides psychological and physical needs is crucial to insure psychological equilibrium during the person's life (Klein, 1974; Krell, 1986, 1993; Winnicot, 1965). These conditions were unattainable for Jewish children from 1939 in Poland, then in Czechoslovakia, France, Holland and Hungary until the end of the war in 1945.

SELF-IDENTITY IN THE SHADOW OF THE HOLOCAUST

The main goal of the psychological warfare employed by the Nazis was the annihilation of the entire Jewish people by destroying the individual's personality and identity, both as a person and as a Jew. A person's identity is the product of identifications and processes that the person undergoes during his or her psychological development. Identity formation begins in infancy and continues to adulthood. According to Erikson (1974), identity develops first within the family, where young children emulate the roles their parents model for them, roles that are in turn derived from the parents' own experiences with larger social groups and from their own childhoods. Throughout the life cycle, alternative or additional roles and identities are presented, or modeled, through a variety of other milieus such as school and community, that force the individual to test, choose from and reconcile with these identities. Based on Tajfel-Turner theory, London and Chazan (1990) suggested that a positive sense of self comes automatically with group identity. The very act of being assigned to or belonging to any group leads inevitably to ethnocentricism, the perception that one's group (the "in group") is superior in some basic way to all other groups (Brown, 1985). Kelman (1977) defined personal identity as one's "personal core" created through three processes by which social influences affect identity- compliance, identification, and internalization which is most important for it is most effective in producing an identity that is stable, well-integrated, and authentic or genuine in terms of reflecting the individual's true values. Jewish identity, according to Kelman, is located at the core of personal identity, and since an individual's ethnic and cultural heritage enters into who and what he or she is, the individual must take his/her cultural as well as biological heritage into account if he/she is to develop a firm personality identity (Kelman, 1977).

The concept of self-identity is defined as an inner sense of security which exists when there is a matching between the person's ability to achieve continuity and wholeness and others' perceptions of him/her (Erikson, 1968). The individual's self-identity is comprised of a number of dimensions: self-evaluation, self-perception, self-control, efficiency and initiative, self-confidence, self-image, self-awareness and the ability to form intimate relationships (Jensen, Huber, Cundick & Carlson, 1991).

The identification system plays a central role in the person's ability to form object relationships (Klein, 1976). Identification is a central component in the inner structure of the ego and the super-ego (Erikson, 1968). If the process of identification is arrested or sabotaged, it can have long-term detrimental effects on the individual. As a results the person may suffer from poor quality of life and a weakened personality. The ability of the individual to maintain an independent and mature self-identity is dependent on his or her ability to maintain inner identifications. This ability is necessary for the maintenance of an inner, constant sense of security and a stable and secure ego, as well as for the growing perception of significant others (Kerenberg, 1989).

Silverman (1986) describes the functions of the operation of two mechanisms of identification in the process of identity formation: identification of the difference between the self and the other, and the psychological unity of the self and the other through identification and imitation. These mechanisms change with development; from a primitive, unconscious impulses (e.g. assimilation and accommodation), to a more mature pattern of identification later on in which they acquire a discriminate character derived from the ego and the super-ego. The success or failure of the identification process depends on the degree of significant construction and internalization processes. It raises the following questions: What mechanisms of identification did the child survivors develop when they were abandoned or separated from their parents, and later on from the families who rescued them? Can a child develop a sense of self-worth if he or she has not experienced a mother's love, oral satisfaction, stability in interpersonal relationships, and a stable environment?

Krystal (1968) and Kestenberg (1972) assert that, during the war, the adults often became dependent on their children and, as a result, were forced to forgo their adult status (for example, children became responsible for finding food for the parents in the ghetto). When the parental image is shattered, the child no longer sees his/her parent as being loving and providing security. Wiesel (1968) claimed that, more than once, a deep psychological inner conflict was created in children due to deterioration in their parents' psychological and physical state. Many children were abandoned by their parents or were given to strangers, in spite of the children's protest. Children were sometimes sent from home to home and were dependent on the people who saved them - who might be kind, apathetic or violent. A number of researchers (Freud & Dann, 1951; Moskovitz, 1985; Thorpe & Swart, 1992) found that child survivors tended to act defensively by expressing distrust in others and avoidance of close relationships. In addition, feelings of inferiority, insecurity and disbelief in personal abilities were found among the survivors. Krell (1993) argued that survivors who were children during the Holocaust are ashamed of their past because they believe having been abandoned by their parents for "not being worthy enough" ("Why did they desert me?"). A very common behavior is survivors' avoidance of talking, being an invisible and silent meant survival (Krell, 1993). What is the impact of the Jewish identity which endanger the child' life on the adult survivor's psychological well-being? What is the significance of silence from the aspect of self-worth? What are the consequences of silence, distrust in others, lack of stable, fostering parental figures and injury of self-identity on one's ability to establish intimate relationships which provides support and growth?

Coping with Trauma, Personal and Social Resources

According to stress theory, individuals' personal and social resources are instrumental to their ability to cope with stressful life events (Ben-Sira 1991; Folkman & Lazarus, 1984). While adequate personal resources help persons to maintain or regain their psychological homeostasis in times of stress, their lack may lead to difficulty coping and vulnerability to stress, breakdown and disease (Folkman & Lazarus, 1984). Evidence indicates that the possession of personal resources such as self-esteem, self efficacy, and social support can predict successful adjustment after being traumatized (Gulliver, Hughes, Solomon, and Dey, 1995). Personal resources can be divided into two types, personality resources - strengths or traits the individual has at his\her disposal such as potency (Ben-Sira, 1993), hardiness

(Kobasa, 1979), a sense of coherence (Antonovsky, 1979), and social resources such as social support.

A number of studies have reported evidence for the stress-buffering effects of personality resources (Ben-Sira, 1985, 1991; Lefcourt, Miller, Ware, & Sherk, 1981; Wheaton, 1985). Others reported that irrespective of the level of stress, personality resources are relatively associated with psychological well-being (Holahan & Moos, 1986; Kobasa, Maddi, & Kahn, 1982; Nelson & Cohen, 1983). Among personal resources, potency seems to be a useful concept in studying well-being, especially in the unique situation that this study addresses, namely abusive experiences during childhood, for it reflects the ability of maintaining one's emotional homeostasis in conditions where other resources lose their effectiveness. It is activated after a previous failure in coping. Potency is defined as an enduring confidence in one's own capabilities, and confidence in and commitment to one's social environment, perceived as characterized by a basically meaningful order and by a reliable and just distribution of rewards (Ben-Sira 1993). Empirical evidence renders inferential support to the stress-buffering and re-adjustment promoting function of potency in society at large and among disabled persons (Ben-Sira, 1985; Lev-Wiesel, 1999; Lev-Wiesel & Shamai, 1998).

Regarding social resources, evidence indicated that social support has a moderating effect on the adverse consequences of traumatic stress exposure (Ren, Skinner, Lee, & Kazis, 1999; Wolff, & Ratner, 1999). Yet, different types of social support have varying beneficial effects on different aspects of health, for example, Ren et al., (1999) found that social support mediated the deleterious effects of non-military traumatic events, whereas the adverse consequences of traumatic events experienced in the military were effected by living arrangements. Others found that social support given during war-trauma and after war mediates the long-term negative effects (Paardekooper, de-Jong, & Hermanns, 1999; Solomon, Neria, & Ram, 1998), and enhances the sense of coherence (Wolff, & Ratner, 1999).

STUDY 1: THE PSYCHOLOGICAL LONG-TERM EFFECTS IN RELATION TO THE SETTING OF SURVIVAL

In this study, Lev-Wiesel and Amir (2000) compared four groups of child survivors according to the type of Holocaust experience setting (Catholic institutions, Christian foster families, concentration camps, and hiding in woods and/or with partisans) in the following variables: (1) Holocaust child survivors' PTSD degrees and psychological distress; (2) self identity; (3) personal resources (potency and self-identity); and (4) quality of life (QoL). Lev-Wiesel and Amir tried to determine whether or not different Holocaust experiences are associated with varying long-term effects with regard to frequency of full or partial PTSD, PTSD symptoms, psychological distress, personal resources, and QoL more than 50 years later.

Method

Sample

The sample consisted of 77 men and 93 women, Holocaust survivors who were born after 1926 in areas which were occupied by the Nazis (Poland, Belgium, and France) during the SWW. Participants were recruited primarily from two "hidden children" organisations' lists of participants in Israel. All participants were. Eighty-two percent were married, 12% were divorced, and 6% were widowers. The mean age was 64.4 ± 4.26 years, ranging from 54 to 73. Forty-eight percent of survivors had 12 or less years of education, and the remaining 52% had education beyond high school. Forty-two percent of survivors were employed, the rest were either retired or unemployed. Regarding types of hiding during the war: Thirty-seven were in Catholic institutions (monasteries or orphanage) (mean age 65.35), 52 were in Christian foster families (mean age 63.07), 35 were in concentration camps (mean age 66.03), and 46 were hiding in the woods or with groups of partisans (mean age 63.56).

Participants were interviewed by a social work student who received special training in interviewing this specific population as well as with analyzing the study scales used. Each participant also completed an anonymous self-report questionnaire. All subjects signed an informed consent.

Instruments

The self-report questionnaire included the following measures:

- *Demographic data.* This included sex, age, education, and the experience setting of the participant during the SWW. If the person had multiple experiences (for example, was first in hiding in a monastery and than later was in a concentration camp,) he/she was asked to write about Following in-depth interviews with child survivors, we devised seven main categories of experience settings as follows: Labor camps, concentration camps monasteries, orphanages, Christian foster families, , hiding in the woods, and partisan groups. Of the 170 survivors participating in the none reported labor camp. Since most of the survivors who were in Catholic institutions reported being both in monasteries and in orphanages we united this into one category, i.e. Catholic institutions. The same applies to those who were hiding in the woods or joined the partisans, which we consequently united into one category, i.e. woods and/or with partisans. This created the four study categories.

- *PTSD-Scale.* The PTSD inventory used in the study is a self-report scale based on DSM-III-R criteria (American Psychiatric Association, 1987), adapted from Horowitz, Wilner, and Kaltreider (1980) and consists of 17 items corresponding to the 17 PTSD symptoms. For each statement, participants were asked to indicate whether or not they experienced the corresponding symptom during the last month. This scale has been used extensively in Israel (e.g. Amir and Sol, 1999) and determines whether or not a participant is suffering from PTSD as well as measuring the intensity of the three symptom groups (intrusion, avoidance and arousal). Following the change DSM-IV criteria change, an item was added which assessed whether or not the response to a threat involved intense fear, feelings of helplessness, or a sense of horror. In order for a participant to receive a diagnosis of full PTSD he/she had to give an affirmative response to this item. This scale can also be used to measure whether or not a participant has subthreshold PTSD (Shalev, 1992) and/or partial PTSD (Carlier and Gersons, 1995) (i.e. he/she endorsed the PTSD symptoms partly, but not strongly enough to qualify for a full diagnosis). Each symptom is assessed according to frequency as follows: 1: does not appear at all 3: sometimes appears 5: appears often 7: appears very often. A score of 5 or 7 on an item is considered to be full expression of the symptom; a score of 3 is considered to be partial expression of the symptom. Full diagnosis of PTSD can be made when a participant gets a score of 5 or 7 on two items from group B (intrusive thoughts), on three items from group C (avoidance), and on one item from group D (hyperarousal). In addition, the participant is given a continuous score for each of the three symptom groups as well as a total score, which is the mean of all 17 items. The total score gives an overall indication of the degree to which the participant suffers from PTSD symptoms. In the present study, the reliabilities, as measured by Cronbach's α, were .90 for the full scale and .84, .83 and .83 for the three subscales of intrusion, avoidance and arousal, respectively. While completing the PTSD-scale, the participants were specifically instructed to respond to the items based only on their experiences during the Holocaust (even if he/she had experienced other additional traumatic events since).

- *SCL-90.* In order to assess psychological distress we used the SCL-90, a self-report scale that determines psychiatric symptoms during the two weeks preceding the assessment and than gives a measure of severity of general psychiatric symptomatology (Derogatis, 1977). The SCL-90 is divided into nine subscales: somatization, obsessive-compulsive problems, interpersonal sensitivity, depression, anxiety, hostility, phobic anxiety, paranoid ideation, and psychoticism.. In addition, we used the Global Severity Index (GSI), which reflects the clinical severity of all symptoms and is computby averaging respondents' answers on the 90 items. The SCL-90's psychometric properties have been consistently reported (Derogatis & Clearly, 1977; Derogatis, Rickles, & Rock, 1976) and the Hebrew version has been used extensively in PTSD research in Israel (e.g. Amir and Sol, 1999). Cronbach's α in the present study was between .80 - .92 for each of the subscales, and was .96 for the GSI.

- *Quality of Life.* In order to assess QoL we used a generic scale, the WHOQOL-Bref (The WHOQOL Group, 1995). This scale, developed simultaneously by 15 academic centers world-wide under the auspices of the World Health Organization, consists of 26 items divided into four broad domains: (I) physical health (e.g. to what degree do you suffer from physical ailments?), (II) psychological health (e.g. to what degree do you suffer from negative emotions such as anxiety, depression), (III) social relations (e.g. to what degree are you happy with the support that you get from your friends?), and (IV) environment (e.g. to what degree are you satisfied with your place of residence?). There are also two questions relating to the participant's general perception of his/her QoL (General). The respondent rates each item on a scale that has 5 levels. In this study, Cronbach's alpha scores were .81, .76, .79, and .82 for domains I, II, III and IV, respectively.

- *Omnibus self-test.* In order to assess self-identity, Jensen et al. (1991) developed this scale based on the developmental approach concerning the self. The scale includes

92 items divided into 13 subscales: Perception of personal mood (10 items), security (10 items), trust in others and disclosure (7 items), honesty (3 items), self esteem (6 items), control (8 items), selfishness (10 items), openness (7 items), self management (7 items), perception of how one's society relates to the self (7 items), self criticism (5 items), identity (5 items), and self reflection (7 items). Choices of agreement with the item range between 1 (not right about me whatsoever) and 4 (completely right). In the present study we used the mean score of the items. A high positive correlation was found between the Omnibus self-test and the Tennessee Self-Concept scale that was developed by Fitts (1968). The scale was translated into Hebrew (with Jensen's permission) for use in the present study according to standards formulated for adapting self-report questionnaires from culture to culture (Kuyken, Orley, Hudelson, & Sartorius, 1994). Cronbach's alpha was .86.

- *Potency questionnaire.* Potency is defined as the level of self-evaluation and control that the person has in his or her life, commitment to society (as opposed to alienation) and perception of the society as being a significant and orderly entity (as opposed to anomie). This potency scale, developed by Ben-Sira (1985), has 19 items that measure the following: self-confidence (3 items), control (6 items), social commitment (5 items), and social significance and order (5 items). The items appear in statement form and the respondent is requested to sort them according to 5 categories that correspond to different degrees of agreement with the statement. The measurement has been found to be reliable and valid in a wide range of studies conducted on different populations in Israel (Ben-Sira, 1985, 1991; Lev & Shamai, 1998; Lev, 1996). In this study Cronbach's α was .86.

Results

Initially, a comparison of the four study groups with regard to the demographic variables of age, education, and marital status, was conducted. A significant difference was found between the groups with regard to age in that survivors who were in concentration camps are significantly older than the other three groups (F $(3, 167)$ = 5.00, p<0.01), and with regard to marital status in that survivors who hid in institutions have the highest proportion of unmarried survivors, and that survivors who were in foster families have the lowest proportion of unmarried survivors (χ^2 (3) = 11.16, p<0.01). In the following analyses these two variables, age and marital status, were held constant.

Table 1 shows the percentage of survivors who were diagnosed with full or partial PTSD (according to experience setting). As some of the cells have very few subjects, we did not consider full and partial PTSD as two separate categories. Results showed that fewer survivors who were in Catholic institutions suffer from some kind of PTSD than the other groups (χ^2 (3)=11.16, p<0.01).

To examine the differences of the measures comparing between groups (according to types of experience), analyses of variance (MANOVA) were conducted separately for PTSD symptomatology, psychological distress symptoms, QoL, self-identity and potency. Scheffe's post-hoc analysis was conducted to compare the differences between the groups. Means, standard deviations, F ratios and the post-hoc analysis of scales which showed significant differences are presented in Table 2.

**Table 1. Percentage of Survivors Suffering from Full and
Partial PTSD according to Holocaust Experience**

	I Catholic Institutes N = 37	II Christian foster families N = 52	III Concentration camps N = 35	IV Hiding or woods N = 46
Full PTSD	10.8	21.2	31.4	17.4
	(4)	(11)	(11)	(8)
Partial PTSD	8.1	28.8	17.1	30.4
	(3)	(15)	(6)	(14)
Full or partial	18.9	50.0	48.5	47.8
PTSD	(7)	(26)	(17)	(22)
No PTSD	81.1	50.0	51.5	52.2
	(30)	(26)	(18)	(24)

From Table 2 it can be seen that only two sub-scales on the SCL-90 did not show any significant differences between the groups: interpersonal sensitivity and psychoticism. From the remaining scales, two trends become apparent: First, survivors who were in Christian foster families scored significantly higher than at least one other group on all of the presented scales. Second, survivors who were in hiding in the woods and/or with partisans scored lower than at least one other group on six of the presented scales.

Regarding the PTSD-Scale, the groups did not differ in the total score or in the avoidance and arousal subscores. However, survivors who were in the woods and/or with partisans had significantly lower degrees of intrusive thoughts than the other three groups.

Regarding the WHOQOL-Bref, survivors who lived with foster families had significantly lower levels of quality of life in the physical domain than survivors who were hiding in the woods and/or with partisans. The other three domains did not show any significant differences between the groups.

Regarding personal resources (self-identity and potency), Table 2 shows that three of the self identity subscales showed significant results as follows: Survivors who were in Christian institutions had significantly lower scores on the scale of "identity" than the other three groups. In addition, they had significantly lower scores on the scale of "disclosure" than those who were in foster families and those who were hiding the woods and/or with partisans. Survivors who were hiding in the woods and/or with partisans scored significantly higher on the subscale of "control" than those who were in concentration camps or Catholic institutions. Survivors who were hiding in the woods and/or with partisans also scored significantly higher than the other three groups on the measures of potency.

Discussion

Consistent with previous evidence (Yehuda, Schmeidler, & Siever, et al., 1997) indicated no difference in the levels of PTSD between survivors who were prisoners in concentration camps and others who were in hiding, the only significant difference found here was that survivors who had been in Catholic institutions suffered less than the other groups from this symptom pattern.

**Table 2. Means, Standard Deviations, F Values, and Differences
between the Four Groups of Survivors according Type of Experience**

	I Catholic Institutes N =34	II Christian foster families N = 52	III Concentration camps N = 35	IV Hiding or woods N = 46	F	Scheffe's comparisons
SCL90						
GSI	0.68	0.78	0.48	0.47	5.15[*]	I>IV[*];
	(0.46)	(0.49)	(0.49)	(0.30)	(3,167)	II>III, IV[*]
Anger-	0.67	0.71	0.34	0.50	4.09[*]	II>III[*]
Hostility	(0.55)	(0.59)	(0.42)	(0.39)	(3,167)	
Anxiety	0.76	0.90	0.52	0.47	5.99[*]	II>III, IV[*]
	(0.59)	(0.49)	(0.47)	(0.41)	(3,167)	
Paranoia	0.77	0.72	0.34	0.49	4.64	I, II>III[*];
	(0.88)	(0.62)	(0.42)	(0.43)	(3,154)	
Obsessive-	0.81	0.83	0.52	0.53	4.99[*]	II>IV[*]
compulsive	(0.51)	(0.59)	(0.51)	(0.40)	(3,167)	
Phobic- anxiety	0.27	0.42	0.29	0.26	4.17[*]	I<III[*]
	(0.37)	(0.49)	(0.74)	(0.33)	(3,167)	II, III>IV[*]
Somatization	0.90	0.99	0.61	0.53	4.15[*]	II>IV[*]
	(0.61)	(0.71)	(0.95)	(0.53)	(3,167)	
Depression	0.78	1.07	0.61	0.58	4.73[*]	II>III, IV[*]
	(0.63)	(0.85)	(0.65)	(0.39)	(3,167)	
Quality of life						
Dom1-	15.44	13.63	15.43	15.91	4.11[*]	II<IV[*]
Physical	(2.43)	(4.25)	(2.83)	(2.45)	(3,167)	
PTSD						
Intrusiveness	4.38	3.75	3.83	2.89	6.93[*]	I, II, III > IV[*]
	(1.59)	(1.52)	(1.52)	(0.93)	(3,167)	
Self Identity						
Control	1.90	2.06	1.87	2.12	3.27[*]	I, III < IV[*]
	(0.47)	(0.42)	(0.50)	(0.42)	(3,167)	
Disclosure	1.61	1.81	2.03	1.99	5.19[*]	I<II, IV[*]
	(0.33)	(0.55)	(0.52)	(0.40)	(3,167)	
Identity	1.45	1.97	2.11	1.98	5.55[*]	I<II, III, IV[*]
	(0.86)	(0.76)	(0.49)	(0.62)	(3,167)	
Potency	3.67	3.57	3.66	4.15	9.19[*]	I, II, III < IV[*]
	(0.59)	(0.71)	(0.64)	(0.46)	(3,167)	

Regarding the intensity of the PTSD symptoms, the only significant difference among the groups was that the survivors who were hiding in the woods and/or with partisans had lower intrusion scores than the other groups. Furthermore, this group had higher scores with regard to personal potency, some dimensions of self-identity, and physical QoL. In addition, the results indicated significant differences between the groups' psychological symptoms of distress in that survivors who lived with foster families had significantly higher levels of psychological symptoms of distress on the scales of depression, anxiety, anger, hostility, paranoia, somatization, obsessive-compulsive problems, and phobic anxiety as well as on the GSI, than at least one of the other groups.

In order to explain the results, understanding of some unique characteristics of each type of experience is essential. Being hidden within groups of orphans in Catholic institutions meant becoming a Catholic and thereforegiving up and constantly hiding one's former religion (Judaism). A survivor who was hiding in a monastery described her experience there as follows: "I tried to remember my parents faces, every night before falling asleep I prayed for Jesus to take care of them … . I cried silently… . I knew I was Jewish, but tried to cling to Jesus… . I had some friends at the convent, no one spoke about his/her former family and religion, we understood we should keep it secret… after the war ended the Jews collected us and tried to teach how to be Jews again". In this specific situation there was no attachment to a substitute person, and temporary comfort was often found in the Catholic religion.

Survivors who were prisoners in concentration camps ceased to hide. The rules of the camp were very clear. Death was often regarded as a good remedy for the horror prisoners had to experience daily. Survivor R, who was a prisoner in Aucshwitz, said: "I was only 12 when first I arrived at Aucshwitz, in no time we became zombies, didn't feel anything. Not feeling was easier than feeling the pain and longing for my parents… in a way, being a zombie saved my sanity. "The present results support the view that to have been in a concentration camp does not necessarily have more abrogating long-term consequences than having been in other settings during the Holocaust. Mental health and medical professionals as well as laymen tend to think of concentration camp survivors as the only "true" Holocaust survivors. The current results, which are similar to the results of Yehuda et al. (1997), support the view that there were many other experience settings during the Holocaust that produce the same long-term effects as concentration camps. Future studies should compare these groups to people that did not participate in the war to further explore this issue. In addition, the type of experiences should be further refined with regard to concentration camp type, length of stay, age of arrival, etc.

Hiding in the woods and/or being with partisans meant being on the run from place to place, suffering from starvation, thirst, and cold, living in a constant uncertainty regarding the present, and endangering life in order to procure basic needs. Survivor C, who was hiding in the woods with her father, and later on joined partisans, said: "I remember myself being constantly alert, we never knew if we would survive the next minute. I was hungry, cold, and afraid of being caught by either the Germans or Ukrainians most of the time. I remember how happy and proud I was when my father and his partisan friends managed to carry out a successful operation against the Germans". In general, it seems that this group did something active, and that, to a certain degree, they were in control of their lives. Doing something active to cope with life threats and succeeding in surviving, help preserve one's self-confidence, self-control, and self-appreciation. Lazarus and Folkman (1984) claimed that problem-focused coping strategies are more useful than emotion-focused coping strategies in preserving individuals' psychological well being. Moreover, several children who were hiding in the woods managed to stay with one or two relatives (parents, siblings, etc.), a fact that prevented them from feelings of desertion by their family. Most of the survivors in hiding managed to retain their original identity (first name, family name, and religion). This way, their sense of belonging remained intact. Nevertheless, it is remarkable that over 50 years later this is still apparent. However, it is possible that the children with more personal resources are the ones who succeeded in hiding in the woods and/or joining the partisans, and what we find today are the same traits of sense of identity, control, and potency that saved their lives in the past. As the current study is a cross-sectional study, we have no way of answering this. Further studies should refine this category by including whether the person was with a close family member etc.

Results showed that having been in a foster family is associated with more long term distress than and has different characteristics from the other types of hiding, as it involves substituting one family for another. Some foster families were nurturing and warm, and providing healthy, happy lives to the children, while others were cruel and harsh, strengthening feelings of fear, loneliness, and helplessness in the children who were dependent on and indebted to them. A survivor who was in a foster family, C, said: "I loved my parents (foster), I felt secure with them especially after I was baptized... . I didn't want to leave them... . I was forced to... later on, my father found me, I told him I know I am a Jew but feel Catholic... ." Contrary to C, U said: " I am sure if my parents knew how bad these people were they would have preferred to take me and let me die with them. I hated them, they didn't want me, just wanted my parents' money... made me their slave. I was only four years old and had to do everything at their home, cleaning, working in the field, watering the cows... . I wanted to die but was afraid to... the only good memory from my childhood is lying by myself in the field during the spring, the sun caressing my face... humming a melody my mother used to sing to me at bed-time... ."

Being given to foster families, often by the child's parents themselves, being forced to accept a new identity, and later, at the end of the war, being forced to become a Jew once again (which was perceived as dangerous earlier,) is likely to have harmed the children's basic sense of belonging and self-identity. Belonging, as well as feeling secure and protected, are basic needs of any human being (Maslow, 1968). Lack in these basic needs is likely to cause high levels of frustration, anxiety, and depression; in the previously described situation it may harm self-esteem and sense of potency, as well as heighten levels of anger and hostility. Attachment theory (Ainsworth, 1969) also explains the importance of the early bond to a permanent parental figure. According to Bowlby and Murray (1970), attachment behavior is elicited whenever a person is sick or in trouble, and is elicited at high intensity when he/she is frightened or when the attachment figure cannot be found. One can speculate that some children in warm foster families developed attachment behavior toward the substitute parental figures, the foster parents. It's also possible that in the foster family there was a sense of belonging and positive attachment for a few years, which in many cases was later injured when the children, at the end of the war, had to separate from the family. This may have caused a re-traumatization experience. A number of relatively recent studies show that multiple traumatic experiences lead to an increase in distress symptoms (e.g. Carlson and Rosser-Hogan, 1994; Vrana and Lauterbach, 1994), so one can speculate that among the survivors in this group, the additional separation may have caused adjunct lifelong damage. As survivor Y described his feelings when a Jewish agency took him bylaw from his Belgian foster parents: "a Jew came and talked to me in Yiddish, I ignored him, he said he would take me by force, would kill my foster parents if he had to... . I was terrified... my parents (foster parents) didn't want to give me up... . I begged him not to take me... . I threatened to kill myself... nothing helped... it might seem awful, but for me being separated from my foster parents was more traumatic than the separation from my parents...". Other children who were given to foster families were not as 'lucky'. The foster families did not really want to care for them, often treated them with cruelty and brutality. Those children could not understand why their parents would give them up, unless they had done something bad or did not deserve their parents love. U said: "rationally I know I should forgive my parents... no, no, understand them for their courageous deed, but inside, I am so angry... they should have let me die with them... ."

From a developmental perspective, the results can be understood in that a frequent change in family system and instability in object figures harm the child's basic trust in both himself/herself and in society, thereby decreasing his/her self-identity, self-esteem, and psychological well-being in adulthood (Erikson, 1968). Possibly, in concentration camps and with partisans, the survivor, despite all the atrocities experienced, withheld his/her original identity and sense of belonging, and may not have had to change his/her attachment figure. Since the present study did not assess whether the survivors who had been in foster families had frequent disruptions is attachment figures, the above are speculations which should be addressed in future studies.

In conclusion, this study showed that the type of traumatic experience setting during the Holocaust influences the well-being of people who were children during the SWW even 55 years after the end of the war. The findings from the present study showed that the most distress is experienced by survivors who were in foster families, and that the highest level of well-being is experienced by survivors who were hiding in the woods and/or with partisans.

STUDY 2: THE PSYCHOLOGICAL IMPACT OF LOST IDENTITY IN HOLOCAUST CHILD SURVIVORS

In this study, Amir and Lev-Wiesel (2001) attempted to shed some light on the extent to which the loss of child survivors' original identity affects their current psychological functioning. This was done by examining the impact of not knowing versus knowing Holocaust child survivors' original identity (i.e., name and biological parents) on PTSD symptomatology, psychological distress, personal resources, and quality of life.

Method

Sample

Participants (n = 46; 23 men and 23 women) were recruited from among the members of two "hidden children" organizations in Israel. All participants were Holocaust survivors who were born after 1930 in areas occupied by the Nazis (Poland, Belgium, and France) during World War II. Participants consisted of two groups: Group 1 included survivors who had lost their original family identity (i.e. did not know their original name or who their biological parents were). Group 2 included Holocaust survivors who had retained knowledge of their original identity. Both groups were approached by telephone by undergraduate students in Psychology and Social Work. If they agreed to participate they were met individually in their home. No significant differences were found between the group means with regard to age, gender, marital status, and place of hiding during the Holocaust (i.e., whether the person had been in a Catholic orphanage, with a Christian family or hiding in the woods). Of the entire sample, 72% were married, 12% were divorced, and 16% were widowed. The mean age was 63.0 years (SD = 4.03 years), and the age range was 60 to 72 years. Regarding education level, 48% of survivors had less than 12 years of education and 52% were academic graduates. In terms of occupational status, 48% of the survivors were employed, and the rest were either retired or unemployed. Two persons with unknown identity who were approached refused to participate and five persons with known identity refused. Data collection was conducted in the spring of 1999.

Instruments

The self-report questionnaire included the following measures: Demographic Data Questionnaire-- information was obtained regarding identity, sex, age, education, marital status and place of hiding during the Holocaust, PTSD Scale (see description in Study 1, Instruments section), Psychological distress (The SCL-90, see description in Study 1, Instruments section), Quality of Life --the WHOQOL-Bref (The WHOQOL Group, 1998), and The Potency Scale (Ben-Sira, 1985 as described in Study 1).

Results

Three analyses were performed in order to examine the impact of retaining versus not retaining one's original identity on PTSD symptomatology, psychological symptoms of distress, and QoL. First the frequency of survivors suffering from full and partial PTSD in the two research groups, was calculated. Following this, the two groups were compared in terms of three groups of psychological variables, PTSD symptoms, QoL and psychological distress. Finally, a hierarchical regression analysis for the whole sample was performed, in which the three groups of psychological variables served as the dependent variables, and the predictors were gender, age, working status (working/not working), education (four levels), level of potency, and identity (whether or not the person had retained his/her original identity).

Frequency of Full and Partial PTSD in Survivors with Known vs Unknown Identity

Table 3 shows the percentage of survivors who fulfilled the criteria for full and partial PTSD in the two groups. Because of the small sample size, we combined survivors with full PTSD and partial PTSD in each group. As it can be seen, there was no difference between the two survivor groups in terms of the frequency of full and partial PTSD symptoms ($\chi2$ (**df**=1, N = 42) = 0.08, p = .76).

**Table 3. Full and Partial PTSD vs. no PTSD among
Survivors with Known and Unknown Identity (n = 42)[a]**

	Group I Unknown Identity n = 20	Group II Known Identity N = 22
Full and partial PTSD	50.0% (10)	45.5% (10)
No PTSD	50.0% (10)	54.5 (12)

[a] For the calculation of the PTSD rates we excluded all questionnaires with any missing values, hence the lower number participants in this analysis.

*Comparisons between Survivors with Known versus Unknown Identity on Measures of
PTSD, Psychological Distress, QoL, and Potency*

Differences between the two research groups (survivors with known identity vs. unknown identity) with respect to PTSD symptomatology, psychological distress, QoL and potency were examined. In each analysis, group (unknown versus known identity) was the independent variable. One-way multivariate analyses (MANOVA) were carried out for the first three measures. The dependent measures in these three analyses were, respectively: (1) The four subscales of the SCL-90 (depression, anxiety, obsessive-compulsive problems and somatization), (2) The four domains on the WHOQOL-Bref (psychological, physiological, social and environment) and (3) The three subscales of the PTSD Scale (intrusion, avoidance and hyperarousal). For the measure of potency, a univariate analyses of variance (ANOVA) was performed. Means and standard deviations are presented in Table 4. The MANOVA for the SCL-90 subscales revealed a trend towards a main effect of group, ($F(4,42) = 2.34$, $p < .07$). The MANOVA for the WHOQOL-Bref yielded a significant main effect of group, ($F(4,42) = 3.40$, $p < .05$). The MANOVA for the PTSD-Scale did not reveal any significant group effects on any of the subscales, nor did the ANOVA indicate any group differences on scores of potency. Means SD and univariate F values and p levels are shown in table 4.

**Table 4. Means and Standard Deviations for the Psychological Variables
among Survivors with Unknown and Known Identity (n = 46)**

	Group I Unknown Identity (n = 23)	Group II Known Identity (n = 23)	F(1,45)
SCL90			
Depression	1.18 (.99)	0.72 (.54)	3.50, *p*<.07
Anxiety	0.93 (.74)	0.61 (.50)	2.59, *n.s.*
Obsessive- compulsive	0.94 (.73)	0.69 (.49)	1.63, *n.s.*
Somatization	1.13 (.93)	0.58 (.43)	5.94, *p*<.02
Quality of life			
Dom 1 - Physical	12.14 (4.10)	15.76 (2.74)	11.60, *p*<.001
Dom 2 - psychological	12.75 (2.98)	14.37 (2.29)	3.96, *p*<.05
Dom 3 - social	13.27 (2.36)	14.78 (3.28)	3.17, p<.08
Dom 4 - Environmental	14.22 (1.72)	14.71 (2.44)	.53 *n.s.*
PTSD			
Arousal	3.45 (1.89)	3.28 (1.34)	.00, *n.s.*
Avoidance	2.71 (1.11)	2.74 (1.37)	.00, *n.s.*
Intrusiveness	3.95 (1.36)	3.96 (1.60)	.11, *n.s.*
Potency	3.56 (.91)	3.64 (.69)	.10, *n.s.*

(two tailed test) SD are in parenthesis.

Predicting Psychological Variables among Survivors with Known versus Unknown Identity

The major objective of the present paper was to explore the association between retaining one's identity in the Holocaust and current mental well-being. In order to achieve this aim we performed hierarchical regression analyses. However as the sample size was relatively small, these regressions can only be considered as preliminary analyses. Prior to conducting these analyses, we calculated the correlation coefficient among the study variables. Table 5 presents these data. As can be seen in table 5 gender was correlated with potency and Qol with female have more potency and more Qol then men has. Work status was found to relate to Qol PTSD and GSI with working participants found to report more Qol, less PTSD and less GSI. Potency was found to be negatively correlated with PTSD and GSI and positively with Qol. Identity found to be related to Qol with participants with unknown identity reporting less Qol.

Table 5. Intercorrelations among Study Variables (n = 46)

	Gender	Age	Work	Education	Potency	QoL total	PTSD-total	GSI
Gender[a]	·							
Age	-.37*							
Work[a]	-.26	.09						
Education	-.28	.10	.65*					
Potency	-.46*	.40*	.27	.40*				
Qol-total	-.48†	.57†	-.58†	.19	.77†			
Ptsd-total	.25	-.15	.71†	.10	-.56†	-.47*		
GSI	.17	-.32*	-.62†	-.37*	-.53†	-.55†	-.72†	
Identity[a]	-.04	-.37*	-.09	-.14	-.05	-.39*	-.05	.17

[a] point-by-serial correlations (gender: 0 = female, 1 = male; work: 0 = working, 1 = not working; identity: 0 = known identity, 1 = unknown identity)
(two tailed test).
* $p < .05$;
† $p < 001$

Table 6 presents the hierarchical regression analyses for three variables; The PTSD-total score, the QoL-total score, and the GSI for SCL-90. In each analysis, demographic variables were entered first into the equation (Block 1). In Block 2, the variable of identity (unknown/known) was entered. Finally, in Block 3 we added the potency score (high versus low according to the median).

Table 6. Hierarchical Multiple Regression Analysis Predicting PTSD-total, QoL and Psychological Distress (n = 46)

Variable	B	SE B	β	R^2
PTSD-total				
Block 1				$R^2 = .64$
Gender	-.16	.40	-.06	
Age	-.24	.06	-.68*	
Working status	-.75	.49	-.31	
Education	.60	.10	.02	
Block 2				$\Delta R^2 = .19$†
Gender	-.29	.28	-.12	
Age	-.27	.04	-.78†	
Working status	-1.46	.38	-.61†	
Education	-.09	.42	-.03	
Identity	-1.40	.33	-.57†	
Block 3				$\Delta R^2 = .01$
Gender	-.24	.28	-.10	
Age	-.22	.06	-.65†	
Working status	-1.65	.41	-.69†	

Table 6. Continued

Variable	B	SE B	β	R^2
Education	.25	.51	.08	
Identity	-1.35	.32	-.55[†]	
Potency	-.25	.22	-.17	
QoL-total				
Block 1				$R^2 = .58$
Gender	-.01	.085	-.00	
Age	.56	.13	.78[†]	
Working status	-1.11	1.02	-.24	
Education	1.38	1.14	.26	
Block 2				$\Delta R^2 = .07$
Gender	-.14	.80	-.03	
Age	.26	.12	.78[†]	
Working status	-1.94	1.05	-.41	
Education	1.92	1.07	.37	
Identity	-1.43	.73	-.30	
Block 3				$\Delta R^2 = .12$[†]
Gender	-.44	.66	-.09	
Age	.28	.13	.39[*]	
Working status	-.66	.95	-.14	
Education	-.00	1.07	.00	
Identity	-1.47	.60	-.31[*]	
Potency	1.60	.50	.54[†]	
Psychological symptoms				
Block 1				$R^2 = .75$
Gender	-.67	.20	-.54[†]	
Age	-.16	.03	-.84[†]	
Working status	-.02	.23	-.02	
Education	-.58	.27	-.43[*]	
Block 2				$\Delta R^2 = .01$
Gender	-.69	.21	-.56[†]	
Age	-.16	.03	-.86[†]	
Working status	-.04	.25	-.03	
Education	-.54	.28	-.40	
Identity	-.12	.17	-.10	
Block 3				$\Delta R^2 = .02$
Gender	-.68	.21	-.54[†]	
Age	-.14	.03	-.74[†]	
Working status	-.17	.27	-.15	
Education	-.31	.32	-.23	
Identity	-.15	.17	-.12	
Potency	-.18	.14	-.22	

[*] $p < .05$;
[†] $p < .01$.
Note: (two taild tests).

As indicated in Table 6, 83% of the variance in the PTSD score was explained by age, working status and identity. The survivor who was younger, working, and knew his/her original identity evidenced the highest degree of PTSD symptomatology. Regarding QoL, 70% of the variance was explained by age, potency and identity. The survivor with a higher level of potency, was older and knew his/her identity had a significantly better QoL. In terms of psychological distress (as measured by the GSI score), 75% of the variance was explained by age and gender. Younger, female survivors suffered more psychological distress.

As psychological well-being is the focus of the present report, an additional hierarchical regression analysis was conducted with Domain II (psychological QoL) of the WHOQOL-Bref as the dependent variable (i.e., using the subtest mean rather than the full-scale mean). Age, gender, education, identity, potency and the identity x potency interaction were entered into the equation as the independent variables (see table 7).

Table 7. Hierarchical Multiple Regression Analysis Predicting Psychological QoL (n = 46)

Variable	B	SE B	β	R^2
Block 1				$R^2 = .73$
Gender	-.96	.98	-.16	
Age	.55	.14	.64†	
Education	.33	.97	.05	
Block 2				$\Delta R^2 = .02$
Gender	-1.22	1.01	-0.21	
Age	.51	.14	.60†	
Education	.26	.97	.04	
Identity	-.95	.87	-.17	
Block 3				$\Delta R^2 = .20^*$
Gender	-1.25	.76	-21	
Age	.22	.13	.25	
Education	-1.07	.80	-.17	
Identity	-1.05	.68	-.26*	
Potency	2.18	.55	.61†	
Block 4				$\Delta R^2 = .06^*$
Gender	-1.14	.68	-.19	
Age	.15	.12	.18	
Education	-1.22	.71	-.19	
Identity	-8.51	2.83	-1.50†	
Potency	1.59	.54	.44†	
Potency X Identity	1.86	.74	1.29†	

* $p < .05$.
† $p < .01$.
Note: (two tailed test).

As can be seen in table 7 from the demographic variables only age was found to relate to QUL with high age positively associate with QUL. Identity entered in block 2 didn't reached a significant main effect predicting QUL but in block 3 when potency was entered we found a positive relation between potency and QUL and the Identity variable become significant negatively associate with QUL (This significant β of Identity means significant differences between knows and unknowns group its like a significant t-test of independent groups). The potency X Identity interaction entered in block 4 also found to be significant.

The significant interaction between Potency and Identity is represented in Figure 1 for this interaction's illustration Potency was divided into high and low scores according to the median.

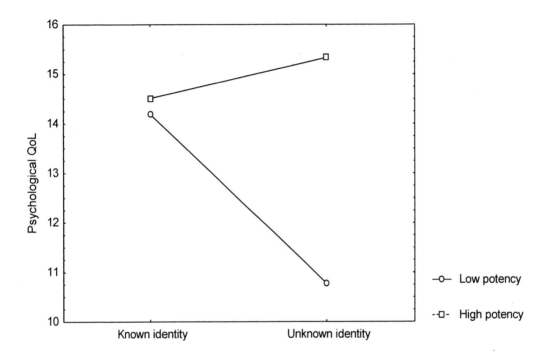

Figure 1. Interaction between Identity and Potency

As can be seen in Figure 1, Identity *moderates* the effect of potency on QUL scores: participants with unknown identity reporting less QUL under condition of low potency then under high levels of potency (i.e. potency serves as a resilience factor among unknown identity participants. The most vulnerable are unknown identities with low potency). Among the known identity participant there is no variability according to their potency levels. Potency found to play an important role in the relation between identity and QUL among unknown participants.

Discussion

The results of this study indicated that losing one's original identity does not lead to greater levels of PTSD. Both survivors who knew their original identity and survivors who did not know their identity evidenced similar levels of full or partial PTSD. Despite this, the two groups of survivors differed significantly in terms of (1) Their levels of somatization, and (2) Physical and psychological quality of life (QoL). Survivors with unknown identity suffered significantly more somatic symptoms and a generally lower quality of life compared to those who had not lost their identity.

Several regression analyses were conducted in order to examine these findings in greater depth. While caution is required regarding the conclusions that can be drawn on the basis of these results due to the small sample size and the large number of variables, knowledge of identity was found to impact several areas of psychological functioning. These analyses indicated that only younger survivors who were currently employed and had retained their original identity suffered more from PTSD symptoms, especially the younger survivors who were currently employed. The results further indicated that QoL among survivors was significantly predicted by with age, identity and potency. Older survivors who retained their identity and obtained high potency scores also reported having a better QoL. Additional analyses indicated that potency, identity and the interaction between these two variables significantly predicted QoL. Survivors with unknown identity experienced a significantly better QoL when they scored high as opposed to low on the potency scale. Retaining or losing one's identity did not appear to affect the degree of psychological distress experienced by the individual.

PTSD and Unknown Identity

The finding that there was no difference between the two child survivor groups in general regarding the frequency and intensity of PTSD symptoms suggests that not knowing one's identity may have different consequences than experiencing traumatic memories and thoughts, which are the essence of the PTSD syndrome. However, the results also suggested that PTSD scores are highest among the younger survivors who know their original identity and were currently employed.

The finding that PTSD scores are higher among younger individuals in general is consistent with earlier work (e.g., Norris, 1992; Green, Grace, Lindy, Gleser & Leonard, 1990). One explanation of this finding may be that when the indivividual does not experience trauma in the sense of being exposed to physical danger (i.e., Criterion A, American Psychiatric Association, 1994), but to one in which the consequences may be less immediately disturbing, but have more pervasive long-term consequences. The outcome may be the development of a different, perhaps more subtle and more serious, pattern of symptoms. Whether this interpretation is correct can only be determined with studies repeated on larger samples and possibly using other measures. Another possibility is that the time in the life of a person at which the trauma occurs may affect how PSTD is evidenced. When survivors are younger, trauma may have more pervasive effects on the personality and psychological functioning and not express itself as traditional PTSD symptoms of intrusive thoughts, avoidance and hyperarousal.

Psychological Impact of Unknown Identity

Not knowing one's identity appears to be associated with an exaggerated focus on physical well being among child Holocaust survivors. This is expressed both in an increased level of somatization symptoms and a lower physical QoL. In order to explain this finding, we must consider the conditions in which child survivors lost their identities. Some were too young to know their parents or their original names at the time they were given to foster families or Catholic institutions such as monasteries and orphanages. Most were unaware of their Jewish identity until after the war. Other children had been given Catholic names in order to protect them from being exposed as Jews. Many of these had either forgotten their original family names or suppressed this knowledge as a result of traumatic events endured.

After the war was ended the Jewish agencies in Israel and abroad gathered these children, sometimes forcing them to separate from their foster parents, in order to return them to the Jewish people. Many were persuaded change there names once again into Hebrew or Jewish names. It was believed that these names would be better fitted to their new destiny – to becoming members of the new Israeli entity.

Paradoxically, being unaware of their original Jewish name and identity spared many survivor children some of the anxieties, worries and agony that Jewish children suffered in order to survive. In general, Jews (and children in particular) had to deny any association to the Jewish people in order to avoid be being exposed and delivered to the Nazis. Children often had to deny any relation to their own parents. Hence, it is possible that losing ones identity may not only have saved the person's life, but also served as a defense mechanism to protect a fragile mental state.

Erikson (1968) emphasized that the use of words representing individual identity (such as "I", and one's first and family names) express a conscious sense of self. Use of such words with respect to the self reflect an unconscious striving for a continuity of personal character, ego synthesis, and a maintenance of inner solidarity with a group's ideals and identity. The need for such words to define the self is well-expressed by B, who said: "I didn't have a name, so I decided to be called Ben-Ami (son of my people)... it was the only identity I was sure of after the war". When self-identity is confused and unclear, the result may be) spoke of painful feelings of personal alienation. Kohut (1977) describes this experience among Holocaust survivors as one in which the person feels terrifying separated from a sense of his own humaness, as if he is a "nonhuman monstrosity".

Physical Well-Being

It is well-known that Holocaust survivors in general exhibit heightened levels of somatic complaints (e.g., Bower, 1994). Other research has shown that high degrees of somatization are often associated with very early psychological injury, such as sexual abuse (Bell, 1994). This suggests that somatizing behavior among adults derives, in part, from childhood. This idea is supported by the findings of Stuart and Noves (1999) on somatizing patients, indicating that display anxious attachment behavior derives from childhood experiences with caregivers. According to them, when under stress as adults, somatizers use physical complaints to elicit care. Conceiveably, not knowing their identity may create a basic, underlying imbalance in Holocaust child survivors' psychological state, anxious attachment behavior and consequent somatization anxiety in adulthood. This internal instability may persist throughout life.

One interpretation of the somatic symptoms experienced by survivor with unknown identity is that they perceive their body as the only continuous, existing identity they have, and so feel it must be guarded with great caution. Somatization may also be intensified among younger survivors because, as suggested by Ford (1997), when children are younger their capacity to communicate psychological experiences is less developed. Hence, it is conceivable that child Holocaust survivors who lost their family identity may symbolically cling to their body as the only clear evidence of their original identity.

The idea that child survivors with unknown identity have a deep need to know who they are is supported by literature on adult adoptee (in general). This line of research has revealed that these individuals are characterized by an obsessive occupation with birth-origin fantasies (Millar-Havens, 1996). These fantasies usually focus on the possible similarity between the adoptee and his/her unknown biological parents, and is expressed behaviorally through compulsively searching for similarity with older people (Hollingsworth, 1998).

Despite their preoccupation with the body, it does not give child survivors any real answers regarding their identity. As U said: "I often wonder whether I resemble my parents in appearance… . My husband teases me that he is one of the few husbands who will never know how his wife will look in the future… . I sometimes look at my daughter and wonder if she looks like my mother. I hope she does… ."

Psychological Well-Being

The results of this study suggest that psychological well-being is determined not only by knowledge of identity, but by feelings of potency. Furthermore, potency and knowledge of identity interact. For the person with unknown identity, the level of potency experienced is crucial to his or her psychological well-being much more than for the person with a known identity. This finding suggests that certain psychological variables, such as feelings of high personal potency, may compensate for one's loss of identity. This hypothesis is in line with other work (e.g. Ben-Sira, 1985) suggesting that potency is partly an inborn trait that enhances wellbeing in a wide range of situations.

In conclusion, this study's findings suggest that knowing one's identity is essential to the psychological well-being of survivors who were children during the Holocaust. The consequences of not knowing their identity seems to last a lifetime, and appears to be mediated by their personal resources.

CONCLUSIONS

An attempt was made to review the literature focusing on the long-term psychological effects of the Holocaust traumata on Holocaust survivors who were children during the Second World War. Two recent studies conducted by the authors were presented. The first focused on the survivors' personal resources, psychological distress and quality of life, in relation to the survival setting experiences. The second study focused on the impact of losing one's identity on his/hers psychological well-being.

The findings of these studies provide a somewhat broader understanding of the Holocaust diverse impact on survivors. It indicates that Holocaust child survivors should not be perceived as a unite group of people who had experienced similar horrific events, suffer from the "survivor syndrome", but rather as individuals whose traumatic experiences could have been different, therefore need different, appropriate, specific approach. This line of thought does not, by all means, reduce the unbearable suffering of the Jewish people as a group.

REFERENCES

Ainsworth, M. D. (1969). Object relations, dependency and attachment: A theoretical review of the infant-mother relationship. *Child development*, 40, 969-1025.

American Psychiatric Association (1987). *Diagnostic and statistical manual of psychiatric disorders (3rd ed., rev.).* Washington DC: Author.

_____ . (1994). *Diagnostic and statistical manual of psychiatric disorders (4th ed.).* Washington DC, Author.

Amir, M. & Lev-Wiesel, R. (2003). Time does not heal all wounds: Quality of life and psychological distress of people who survived the Holocaust as children 55 years later. *Journal of Traumatic Stress,* 16(3), 295-300.

Amir, M., & Sol, O. (1999). Psychological impact and prevalence of traumatic events in a student sample in Israel: The effect of multiple traumatic events and physical injury. *Journal of Traumatic Stress,* 12, 139-154.

Amir, M., Kaplan, Z., and Kotler, M. (1996). Type of Trauma, Severity of Post-Traumatic Stress Disorder Core Symptoms and Associated Features. *Journal of General Psychology,* 123, 341-351.

Bell, I. R. (1994). Somatization disorder: Health care costs in the decade of the brain. *Biological Psychiatry,* 35, 81-83.

Ben-Sira, Z. (1985). Potency: A stress buffering link in the coping stress disease relationship. *Social Science and Medicine,* 21, 397-406.

_____ . (1991). *Regression, stress and readjustment aging: A structured, bio-psychosocial perspective on coping and professional support.* New York: Praeger.

Bower, H. (1994). The concentration camp syndrome. *Australian and New Zealand Journal of Psychiatry,* 28, 391-397.

Bowlby, J., & Murray, C. (1970). Separation and loss within the family. In: E. J. Anthony, & C. Koupernik (Eds.)., *The child in his family.* New York: Wiley.

Bowman, M. L. (1997). *Individual differences in posttraumatic response: Problems with the adversity - distress connection.* New Jersey: Lawrence Erlbaum Associates Inc.

Breiner, S. J. (1996). Children in and outside the concentration camp. *Journal of Psychohistory,* 23, 415-426.

Brenner, I. (1988). Multisensory bridges in response to object loss during the Holocaust. *Psychoanalytic Review,* 75, 573-587.

Bunk, D., & Eggers, C. (1993). Importance of psychodynamic reference factors in psychpathogenesis in persons persecuted by the Nazi regime in childhood. *Fortschritte der Neurologie Psychiatrie,* 61, 38-45.

Carlier, I. V. E., & Gersons. B. P. R. (1995). Partial posttraumatic stress disorder (PTSD): The issue of psychological scars and the occurrence of PTSD symptoms. *Journal of Nervous and Mental Disease,* 183, 107-109.

Carlson, B., & Rosser-Hogan, R. (1994). Cross-cultural response to trauma: a study of traumatic experiences and posttraumatic symptoms in Cambodian refugees. *Journal of Traumatic Stress,* 7, 43-55.

Danieli, Y. (1985). The treatment and prevention of long-term effects and intergenerational transmission of victimization: A lesson from Holocaust survivors and their children. In: C.F. Figley (Ed.), *Trauma and its wake: The study and treatment of post-traumatic stress disorder* (pp. 295-313). New York: Brunner/ Mazel.

Derogatis, L. R. (1977). *The SCL-90-R manual 1: Scoring, administration and procedures for the SCL-90.* Baltimore: Johns Hopkins University, School of Medicine.

Derogatis, L.R. & Clearly, P.A. (1977). Confirmation of the dimensional structure of the SCL-90: A study in construct validity. *Journal of Clinical Psychology,* 33, 981-989.

Derogatis, L.R., Rickels, K. & Rock, A.F. (1976). The SCL-90 and the MMPI: A step in the validity of a new self-report scale. *British Journal of Psychiatry*, 128, 280-289.

Eaton, W.W., Sigal, J.J., & Weinfeld, M. (1982). Impairment in Holocaust survivors after 33 years: Data from an unbiased community struggle. *American Journal of Psychiatry*, 139, 773-777.

Eitinger, L. (1973). Morality and morbidity after excessive stress. *Ceskoslovenska Psychiatrie*, 69, 209-218.

Erikson, E. H. (1968). Identity: Youth and crisis. New York: Norton.

Fitts, W. H. (1968). *Tennessee Self-Concept Scale*. Nashville, TN: Counselor Recording and Test.

Fogelman, E. (1992). Intergenerational group therapy: Child survivors of the Holocaust and offspring of survivors. *Psychiartria Hungarica*, 7, 255-269.

Ford, C. V. (1997). Somatic symptoms, somatization and traumatic stress: An overview. *Nordic Journal of Psychiatry*, 51, 5-14.

Freud, A., & Dann, S. (1951). An experiment in group upbringing. *Psychoanalytic Study of the Child*, 6, 127-141.

Friedman, M. J., Schnurr, P. P., & McDonagh, C. A. (1994). Posttraumatic stress disorder in the military veteran. *Psychiatric Clinics of North America*, 17, 265-277.

Gampel, Y. (1992). I was a Shoah child. *British Journal of Psychotherapy*, 8, 390-400.

Green, B. L., Grace, M. C., Lindy, J. D., Gleser, G. C., & Leonard, A. (1990). Risk factors for PTSD and other diagnoses in a general sample of Vietnam veterans. *American Journal of Psychiatry*, 147, 729-733.

Hollingsworth, L. D. (1998). Adoptee dissimilarity from the adoptive family: Clinical practice and research implications. *Child and Adolescent Social Work Journal*, 15, 303-319.

Horowitz, M., Wilner, N., & Kaltreider, N. (1980). Signs and symptoms of posttraumatic stress disorder. *Archives of General Psychiatry*, 37, 85-92.

Jensen, L.C., Huber, C., Cundrick, B., & Carlson, J. (1991).Development of a self theory and measurement scale. *Journal of Personality Assessment*, 57, 521-530.

Kerenberg, O. (1989). *Psychodynamic psychotherapy of borderline patients*. New York: Basic Books.

Kestenberg, J. S. (1972). How children remember and parents forget. *International Journal of Psychoanalytic Psychotherapy*, 1, 103-123.

Kestenberg, J. S. (1972). Psychoanalytic contributions to the problem of children of survivors from Nazi persecutions. *Israel Annals of Psychiatry and Related Disciplines*, 10, 311-325.

_____ . (1992). Children under the Nazi yoke. *British Journal of Psychotherapy*, 8, 374-390.

_____ . (1992). Children under the Nazi yoke. British Journal of Psychotherapy, 8, 374-390.

_____ . (1993). Child victims of persecution and after-effects in later life. *Psyche: Zeitschrift fuer Psychoanalyse und ihre Anwendungen*, 47, 730-742.

Kestenberg, J. S., & Brenner, I. (1986). Children who survived the Holocaust: The role of rules and routines in the development of the superego. *International Journal of Psychoanalysis*, 67, 309-316.

_____ . (1986). Children who survived the Holocaust: The role of rules and routines in the development of the superego. *International Journal of Psychoanalysis*, 67, 309-316.

Kestenberg, M., & Kestenberg, J.S. (1988). The self belonging and altruism in children who survived the Holocaust. *Psychoanalytic Review*, 75, 533-560.

Klein, H. (1974). Child victims of the Holocaust. *Journal of Clinical Child Psychology*, 2, 44-47.

Klein, M. (1976). *Contributions to psycho-analysis*. London: Hogarth Press.

Kohut, H. (1977). *The restoration of the self*. New York: International Universities Press.

Krell, R. (1986). Therapeutic value of documenting child survivors. *Annual Progress in Child Psychiatry and Child Development*, 281-288.

_____ . (1993). Child survivors of the Holocaust: strategies of adaptation. *Canadian Journal of Psychiatry*, 38, 384-389.

Krystal, H. (1968). *Massive psychic trauma*. New York: International Universities Press.

Krystal, H., & Neiderland, W. C. (1968). Clinical observation on the survivor syndrome. In: H. Krystal (Ed.)., *Massive psychic trauma*. New York: International Universities Press.

Kuyken, W., Orley, J., Hudelson, P., & Sartorius, N. (1994). Quality of Life Assesment Across Cultures. *International Journal of Mental Health*, 23, 5-27.

Lazarus, R. S., & Folkman, S. (1984). *Stress, appraisal and coping*. New York: Springer.

Lee, B. S. (1988). Holocaust survivors and internal strengths. *Journal of Humanistic psychology*, 28, 67-96.

Lev, R. (1996). *Uncertainty, forced relocation and community role in coping with stress*. Ph.D. dissertation, The Hebrew University: Jerusalem (Hebrew).

Lev-Wiesel, R. & Amir, M. (2000). Posttraumatic stress disorder symptoms, psychological distress, personal resources and quality of life in four groups of Holocaust child survivors. *Family Process*, 39(4), 445-460.

Lev-Wiesel, R. & Shamai, M. (1998). Living under the threat of relocation: Spouses' perceptions of the threat and coping resources. *Contemporary Family Therapy*, 20, 107-121.

Lieblich, A., & Josselson, R. (1994). Exploring identity and gender. In A. Lieblich & R. Jsselson (Eds.), *The narrative study of lives*, Vol. 2. Thousand Oaks, CA: Sage.

Maslow, A. H. (1968). *Toward a psychology of being*. Princeton: Van Nostrand.

Mazor, A., & Mendelsohn, Y. (1998). Spouse bereavement processes of Holocaust child survivors: Can one differentiate a black frame from a black background? *Contemporary family Therapy: An international Journal*, 20, 79-91.

Miller-Havens, S. (1996). Grief and the birth origin fantasies of adopted women. In D. Klass, P. R. Silverman, & S. L. Nickman (Eds.), *Continuing bonds: New understandings of grief: Series in death education, aging, and health care* (pp. 273-294). Washington DC: Taylor & Francis.

Moskovitz, S. (1985). Longitudinal follow-up of child survivors of the Holocaust. *Journal of American Academy of Child Psychiatry*, 24, 401-407.

Moskovitz, S., & Krell, R. (1990). Child survivors of the Holocaust: Psychological adaptations to survival. *Israel Journal of Psychiatry and Related sciences*, 27, 81-91.

Niederland, W. (1964). Psychiatric disorders among persecution victims. *Journal of Nervous Disorders*, 52, 139-458.

Norris, F. H. (1992). Epidemiology of trauma: Frequency and impact of different potentially traumatic events on different demographic groups. *Journal of Consulting and Clinical Psychology*, 60, 409- 418.

Reijzer, H. M. (1995). On having been in hiding. In H. Groen-Prakken, A. Ladan, & A. Stufkens (Eds.), *The Dutch annual of psychoanalysis 1995-1996: Traumatization and war*, Vo. 2 (pp. 96-117). Amsterdam: Swets & Zeitlinger.

Robinson, S., Rapaport Bar Sever, M., & Rapaport, J. (1994). The present state of people who survived the Holocaust as children. *Acta Psychiatrica Scandinavica*, 89, 242-245.

Rustow, M. W. (1989). From Jew to Catholic and back: Psychodynamics of child survivors. In: P. Marcus & A. Rosenberg (Eds.)., *Healing their wounds: Psychotherapy with Holocaust survivors and their families.* (pp. 271-286). New York: Prager.

Shalev, A. (1992). Posttraumatic Stress Disorder among injured survivors of a terrorist attack. Predictive value of early intrusion and avoidance symptoms. *Journal of Nervous and Mental Disease*, 180, 505-509.

Silverman, M. A. (1986). Identification in healthy and pathological character formation. International. *Journal of Psychoanalysis*, 67, 181-192.

Solomon, Z. (1989). A three year prospective study of posttraumatic stress disorder in Israeli combat veterans. *Journal of Traumatic Stress*, 2, 59-73.

Solomon, Z., Ginzburg, K., Neria, Y., & Ohry, A. (1995). Coping with war captivity: the role of sensation seeking. *European Journal of Personality*, 9, 57-70.

Stuart, S., & Noves, R. (1999). Attachment and interpersonal communication in somatization. *Psychosomatics*, 40, 34-43.

Tauber, Y. (1996). The traumatized child and the adult: Compound personality in child survivors of the Holocaust. *Israel Journal of Psychiatry and Related Sciences*, 33, 228-237.

Tauber, Y., & Van-Der-Hal, E. (1997). Transformation of perception of trauma by child survivors of the Holocaust in group therapy. *Journal of Contemporary Psychotherapy*, 27, 157-171.

_____ . (1997). Transformation of perception of trauma by child survivors of the Holocaust in group therapy. *Journal of Contemporary Psychotherapy*, 27, 157-171.

Tec, N. (1993). A historical perspective tracing the history of the hidden child experience. In: J. Marks (Ed.), *The hidden children: The secret survivors of the Holocaust* (pp. 273-291). New York: Fawcett Columbia.

The WHOQOL Group (1995). The World Health Organization Quality of Life Assessment (WHOQOL): Position Paper from the World Health Organization. *Social Science and Medicine*, 41, 1403-1409.

_____ . (1998). The World Health Organization Qol assessment (WHOQOL): development and general psychometric properties. *Social Science and Medicine*, 46, 85-1569.

Thorpe, M. B., & Swart, G. T. (1992). Risk and protective factors affecting children in foster care: A pilot study of the role of siblings. *Canadian Journal of Psychiatry*, 37, 616-622.

Valent, P. (1998). Resilience in child survivors of the Holocaust: Toward the concept of resilience. *Psychoanalytic Review*, 85, 517-535.

Vrana, S., & Lauterbach, D. (1994). Prevalence of traumatic events and posttraumatic psychological symptoms in a nonclinical sample of college students. *Journal of Traumatic Stress*, 7, 289-302.

Wiesel, E. (1968). *One generation after.* New York: Bard Books.

Winnicot, D. W. (1965). *Maturational processes and facilitating environment.* New York: International Universities Press.

Yehuda, R., Kahana, B., Binder-Brynes, K., Southwick, S. M., mason, J. W., & Giller, E. (1995). Low urinary cortisol excretion in Holocaust survivors with posttraumatic stress disorder. *American Journal of Psychiatry*, 152, 982-986.

Yehuda, R., Sartorius, N., Kahana, B., Southwick, S. M., & Giller, E. L. (1994). Depressive features in Holocaust survivors with and without posttraumatic stress disorder. *Journal of Traumatic stress*, 7, 699-704.

Yehuda, R., Schmeidler, J., Siever, L. J., Binder-brynes, K., & Elkin A. (1997). Individual differences in Posttraumatic stress symptom profiles in Holocaust survivors in concentration camps or in hiding. *Journal of Traumatic Stress*, 10, 453-463.

_____ . (1997). Individual differences in Posttraumatic stress symptom profiles in Holocaust survivors in concentration camps or in hiding. *Journal of Traumatic Stress*, 10, 453-463.

In: Trends in Posttraumatic Stress Disorder Research   ISBN 1-59454-135-3
Editor: Thomas A. Corales, pp. 157-183   © 2005 Nova Science Publishers, Inc.

Chapter 7

RETHINKING THE ROLE OF POSTTRAUMATIC STRESS DISORDER IN REFUGEE MENTAL HEALTH SERVICES

Stevan M. Weine

International Center on Responses to Catastrophes
Department of Psychiatry
University of Illinois at Chicago
Chicago, IL

Schuyler W. Henderson

Columbia University,
New York, New York

ABSTRACT

This chapter rethinks the role of the Posttraumatic Stress Disorder (PTSD) diagnosis in mental health services for refugees. It reviews four research studies conducted with Bosnian refugees in Chicago that investigated services issues related to PTSD. The summary findings were: (1) Persons presenting for services had higher levels of PTSD symptoms, but also depression symptoms and other distinct demographics and service exposure characteristics associated with vulnerability; (2) Assessment and educational activities of providers did not adequately reflect the high prevalence of PTSD in refugee populations; (3) Although nearly all patients treated for PTSD received psychiatric medication and supportive counseling, treatment patterns varied with demographic characteristics; (4) Providers' discourse on refugees was highly oriented towards services issues with a focus on service access problems. Overall, these studies demonstrate that PTSD is an important construct for refugee mental health services, but because PTSD alone does not explain the range or context of refugees' mental health needs, a services perspective on PTSD is necessary.

On the basis of empirical evidence, this chapter delineates a *Services Mental Health* ⟵ *Approach to Refugee Trauma (SMART)* to facilitate building services for refugees with PTSD and related mental health problems. The major claims of this approach are as follows: (1) PTSD should be regarded as one of multiple causes of suffering amongst a heterogeneous refugee population to be addressed by mental health services; (2) PTSD and mental health related information for communities and families, and training for providers, must be more comprehensive and culturally synchronous in order to facilitate better help-seeking and services; (3) Provision of specific interventions in refugee mental health services should be guided by scientific evaluation and clinical observations of targeted outcomes in real life contexts; (4) Refugee mental health services should have as a primary goal facilitating access to a range of mental health, health, social, occupational, child, and family services. Specific implications for interventions and policy-aimed research regarding mental health services for refugee trauma are described.

THE ROLE OF PTSD IN REFUGEE MENTAL HEALTH

The realization that exposure to life-threatening events can result in long-lasting mental health impairment and loss of pre-exposure functioning has produced a series of diagnoses, from war neurosis and shellshock to the current understandings of Post Traumatic Stress Disorder (PTSD), first codified in 1980 in DSM-III (American Psychiatric Association, 1980) and revised for DSM-IV (American Psychiatric Association, 1994). PTSD has since been used in research, policy development and clinical practice to measure and assess mental health sequelae of traumatic experiences including war and displacement (Lamberg, 2003), terrorism (Bleich, Gelkopf & Solomon, 2003), natural disasters (Goenjian et al., 2000), sexual assault (Clum, Calhoun & Kimerling, 2000) and medical illness (Mundy, 2004).

PTSD is the diagnosis that defines the current psychiatric approach to refugee trauma. Although some have argued that PTSD is largely a contemporary, culture-bound diagnosis (Jones et al. 2003; Bracken, 2002), it has nevertheless been used in measuring psychopathology in a wide range of displaced populations, including populations from Europe (Turner, Bowie, Dunn, Shapo & Yule, 2003), Central America (Sabin, Cardozo, Nackerud, Kaiser & Varese, 2003), Asia (Hinton, Hinton, Pham, Chau & Tran, 2003) and Africa (McCall & Resick, 2003). The high prevalence of PTSD has been demonstrated in multiple studies of refugees from different populations, with estimates ranging as high as 95% (Friedman and Jaranson, 1994; Mollica & Caspi-Yavin, 1991; Kinzie et al, 1984).

Refugee mental health has largely focused on clinic-based initiatives that utilize clinical interventions to address PTSD and other trauma related mental health problems of individual survivors (Kinzie & Tran, 1980; Westermeyer, 1991; Garcia-Peltoniemi & Jaranson, 1989). Research, however, has implicated the roles of torture and diminished social support (Holtz, 1998), forced separation from family and exile (Hauff & Vaglum, 1995) and psychosocial difficulties such as unemployment (Lavik, 1996) in the high prevalence of PTSD and psychological distress in displaced populations. The extent to which these psychosocial community-wide factors, and the types of human rights violations that have been experienced prior to or during forced migration (Momartin, Silove, Manicavasagar & Steel, 2003), result in the poor functioning, illness and suffering associated with PTSD remains unclear.

The research presented in this paper examines the mental health services experiences of a population of Bosnian refugees living in Chicago from a perspective that acknowledges both the importance and limitations of the diagnosis of PTSD. Over two million people were forced to flee the Balkans during the wars and genocide in the 1990's (UNHCR, 2002). Between 1990 and 1998, over 83,000 Bosnians arrived in the United States as refugees (INS, 2001). Many have successfully adapted to their lives in the United States, but many have met criteria for the diagnosis of PTSD (Weine et al, 1995) and have sought mental health treatment. Several studies with Bosnian refugees have investigated interventions for PTSD including medications (Smajkic et al, 2001), testimony (Weine et al, 1998) and multi-family groups (Weine et al, 2004). These studies demonstrated the potential of several interventions for reducing PTSD symptoms, but also revealed that refugees present many challenges concerning mental health treatment that PTSD neither explains or addresses.

THE NEED FOR A SERVICES INQUIRY CONCERNING PTSD

With increasing recognition of the importance of trauma mental health services for refugees, there has been heightened pressure upon provider organizations to reexamine existing models for intervention, training, and evaluation (Waldman, 1999). In psychiatry, there has also been a call to demonstrate the effectiveness of services, including services for PTSD (Rosenheck and Fontana, 1999). A mental health services research approach may help to improve mental health services for refugees.

As part of a program of research concerning family-focused mental health services with refugee families, our university/community collaborative services research team conducted multiple services related investigations of Bosnian refugees in Chicago. These studies were guided by a central question of services research: "What works for whom under what circumstances and why?"(Hohman and Shear, 2002).

Services research is oriented towards real life contexts. It recognizes that refugees are persons in profound social, cultural, economic, familial and psychological transitions (Weine, 2001a). Thus, a services research perspective claims that it is important not to consider PTSD diagnosis or symptoms as the exclusive variables, but to inquire as to what other "real world" variables are important in relation to mental health treatment.

Services research recognizes that the delivery of refugee mental health care in urban centers such as Chicago involves the interactivity of multiple types of providers, positioned at different types of service organizations for a heterogeneous population of refugees. It is certainly not true that all refugees have PTSD, or that PTSD is equivalent in all those who do have it. From a services perspective, it is not even presumed that we know the practical significance of PTSD in refugee's lives. For example, PTSD may be an important construct in Western psychiatry, but when refugees talk about trauma in their lives they often frame it in more collectivist terms as a family or a ethno-national experience (Weine, 1999).

Another matter of concern from a services research perspective is that little is actually known about providers' knowledge and attitudes towards and the role of PTSD. Refugee resettlement workers and primary medical care providers play major roles in assessment, education and referral for mental health care. Refugee mental health service providers are involved in the direct delivery of mental health services. All providers bring to their work a diversity of life experience, ethnocultural identity, education and training, disciplinary affiliation, and philosophy. Providers' own knowledge of and attitudes towards trauma would be expected to play an important role in shaping their delivery of refugee mental health services. However, there are no known studies of refugee providers' trauma knowledge, attitudes and activities, although some of the issues are touched upon in the clinical and programmatic literature (van der Veer, 1992).

From the vantagepoint of services, several specific questions should be considered for research on refugees with PTSD:

Who Presents for Mental Health Services?

Services researchers have identified that the decision to seek care is not simply a matter of the presence or severity of psychopathologic symptoms, but also needs to be understood in terms of help-seeking, strength of social networks, family processes, and cultural norms regarding mental health). These processes have rarely been investigated in the area of refugee mental health. A study of Iranian torture survivors relocated to Germany found that those refugees who sought treatment had higher levels of PTSD but were less fluent in German (Priebe & Esmaili, 1977). Those who sought treatment may have had lower levels of acculturation into the new society as well as fewer sources of social support within their new surroundings. No other known published studies have investigated this issue in refugees.

What do Providers and Families Know about PTSD?

Mental health researchers have investigated provider's attitudes and approaches concerning diverse health issues (Montenegro, 1999; Singh et al, 1998). For example, Westen looked at providers' attitudes and approaches towards personality disorders (Westen, 1997) and found significant departures from accepted standards in the actual practice patterns of providers. Within the field of refugee mental health, it is clear that what is known about Post Traumatic Stress Disorder (PTSD) as a diagnostic construct exceeds what is known about how this construct is actually being deployed by providers in their service activities.

What Kinds of Treatments do Persons with PTSD Receive?

Refugee mental health clinics provide services that are organized around the construct of PTSD. But no prior studies have documented what types of services are actually being used with persons with PTSD, including the roles of psychotherapies and psychiatric medications. Another important but often overlooked consideration in the provision of refugee mental health services is treatment dropout or cessation.

What are Providers Talking about when They Talk about Refugees' PTSD and Mental Health Needs?

Although PTSD is a clearly a dominant construct in refugee mental health services, it is also important to consider to what extent providers who work with refugees are struggling with and reflecting upon other dimensions of mental health. Qualitative research investigating clinical treatments have analyzed providers' statements so as to describe important constructs, factors, or narratives that may not yet be represented in the official professional discourse. However, there are no existing studies on refugee service providers or other trauma mental health providers, including qualitative studies that would help to elaborate such a discourse.

SITES OF INVESTIGATIONS

This chapter reports on a series of studies that were conducted by various members of our collaborative, multi-disciplinary services research team based at the International Center on Responses to Catastrophes at the University of Illinois at Chicago. The team consists of American, Bosnian, and Croatian professionals with multiple years of experience working both in Bosnia-Herzegovina and in the Bosnian Diapsora. For each study, interviewers were bilingual/bicultural members of the Bosnian community who received specific training by the services research team. Cultural and language issues in measurement were addressed through processes involving translations, back translations, piloting, think-aloud interviews and consensus decision making.

Many urban centers that receive large numbers of refugees have established service programs to address refugee's mental health needs. Chicago is home to over 40,000 Bosnians, one of the largest group of Bosnians in the U.S. A refugee mental health program for Bosnians was formed at the Heartland Alliance in Chicago, in collaboration with the State of Illinois Department of Human Services and the University of Illinois at Chicago (with the first author as psychiatrist). This program drew upon many of the recommendations made on the basis of examination of previous mental health services for refugees, including trained bicultural staff and an appealing and non-threatening environment. Services being provided include psychopharmacology, individual and group psychotherapies, testimony, creative arts and massage therapy.

All of these studies concern Bosnian refugees in Chicago. Each study is based upon the analysis of a different data set. However it should be noted that these data sets are presenting different perspectives upon the same experience. That is to say, through these studies we investigated what refugees presented, how they were assessed, how they were treated, and what providers thought. For all four studies the subjects gave informed consent in accordance with procedures and consent forms that were approved by the University of Illinois at Chicago.

Each study had limitations. They had small sample sizes that were not necessarily representative of all refugees or providers. These studies faced cultural and linguistic boundaries that always present the potential for misunderstandings. Nonetheless, we believe that the samples were fairly heterogeneous and that together these four studies help to document and analyze important issues in refugee mental health. Note, this chapter provides summary reports of the statistical and qualitative analyses.

For each of the four studies, we present the research aims, methods, results, and discussion. Then we interpret the results of the four studies from the perspective of the proposed *Services Mental Health Approach to Refugee Trauma* framework and consider intervention and policy research implications.

STUDY ONE: REFUGEES WITH PTSD PRESENTING FOR SERVICES

Research Aims

This study aimed to describe the service use patterns among refugees by comparing the symptomatic, demographic and service exposure characteristics of those who did and those who did not seek mental health services amongst a sample of Bosnian refugees in Chicago. It addressed the following research questions: 1) Did Bosnian refugees who sought mental health services have different symptomatic, demographic and service exposure characteristics than those who did not? 2) Can we construct statistical models out of symptom, demographic and services factors that predict who presented for services? 3) What do the results help us to understand about refugees presenting for mental health services?

Methods

The overall group in this study was Bosnian refugees who were survivors of ethnic cleansing and who resettled in Chicago. Most had co-morbid PTSD and depression and reported very low rates of substance abuse. Most had no prior psychiatric history and no psychiatric hospitalizations. There were a very small minority who did not present with PTSD and depression, who were most often persons with severe, chronic mental illnesses, such as schizophrenia or bipolar disorder. These individuals were not included in this study.

The first group (know hereafter as *Presenters*), was comprised of Bosnian clients who began receiving mental health services at the Bosnian mental health program from September 1, 1997 to March 30, 1998. Network sampling was used to obtain a second group of adult Bosnian refugees who had not sought refugee mental health services in the United States (hereafter known as *Nonpresenters*). The network sampling was begun at the Bosnian Refugee Center and two other contacts in the Bosnian refugee community. Subjects were asked to identify three Bosnians they knew (but who were not in their family), and one was randomly selected to be interviewed. All of those identified who met study inclusion criteria (i.e., PTSD) and were invited to complete the survey agreed to participate. The sample of *Nonpresenters* was stratified in order to obtain more balanced representations for gender, age (i.e., young, middle, and older adulthood), and employment status. The decision to stratify was not based upon survey statistics of the overall Bosnian refugee population in Chicago, because none exist. Rather, it was based upon our experience living and working in that community, which strongly supports the following presumptions about this refugee population: 1) there are approximately equal numbers of men and women; 2) there are approximately equal distributions of age; 3) the majority of adults are employed.

The subjects in each group were assessed via trained interviewers doing semi-structured interviews that gathered their responses to forced response items. *Symptom variables* were assessed with a checklist of traumatic events, the PTSD Symptoms Scale (Foa, 1993), and the Center for Epidemiological Studies Depression Scale (Radloff, 1977). *Demographic variables* were assessed with questions on age, sex, education level, marital status, family composition, employment status, and time in U.S. *Service exposure* was assessed via an instrument developed by the first author (SMW) that contained checklists of specific items concerning: 1) prior experience with and attitude toward mental health services; 2) prior family mental health services; 3) prompts for mental health services; 4) family talk about mental health services; 5) family attitudes about mental health services. Sum scores were made for each checklist.

Data analyses included computation of descriptive statistics for respondents' symptom, demographic and service exposure characteristics with comparisons made by t-test and chi square analyses. Then symptom, demographic and services exposure variables were entered into a systemic logistic regression modeling process so as to construct a parsimonious model describing the characteristics that significantly distinguish presenters and non-presenters.

Results

Of the 41 Bosnians identified in the network sampling who did not present for services, 28 subjects (70%) met symptom criteria for PTSD diagnosis in the *DSM-IV* as determined by the PTSD Symptom Scale. This group was compared with the sample of 29 Bosnian refugees with PTSD who presented for mental health services.

The group of *Presenters* reported statistically significant: 1) higher trauma exposure (p<.05); 2) higher PTSD symptom severity (p<.001); 3) higher depression symptom severity (p< .001). Data analyses revealed significant differences between the two groups of refugees on three demographic variables. The group of PRESENTERS was significantly: 1) less educated (p<.05); 2) more recent arrivals in the U.S. (p<.05); 3) less likely to be employed (p<.001).

Concerning mental health service exposure, *Presenters* had significantly higher ratings on three of the five factors: 1) Prior individual mental health services (p<.001); 2) Prior family mental health services (p<.05); and 3) Family talk about mental health services (p<.05). The group of *Presenters* was significantly more likely to be receiving disability.

A step-wise logistic regression was conducted with three blocks of variables: (1) symptoms; (2) symptoms and demographics; (3) symptoms, demographics and services. At each step, only the statistically significant variables were retained. The three resulting models included the following variables: Model I (Symptoms): depression and traumatic stress; Model II (Symptoms and demographics): depression and years in U.S.; Model III (Symptom, demographic, and services): depression, years in U.S., disability entitlement, prior exposure and family prior exposure. All three models were found to be significant at the p<.001 level. Model I (Symptoms) accounted for 51% of the variance. Model II (Symptoms and demographics) accounted for 68%. Model III (Symptom, demographic, and services) accounted for 84%.

Discussion

This study found that demographic and service use patterns do impact upon presentation for mental health services and therefore should be considered along with PTSD. It found that symptom, demographic and service exposure characteristics were better able to predict who presented for services than symptoms alone. Depression as well as PTSD was significantly different amongst presenters. In the logistic regression models, the symptom factors of traumatic exposure and traumatic stress were left out, whereas depression remained. This suggests that depression, more than traumatic events and PTSD, explains services related behavior.

Although employment dropped out of the statistical model, we cannot overlook the findings that refugees who sought services were significantly less likely to be working at a job for pay. In fact, none of the refugees who sought services were employed, compared to *Nonpresenters*, among whom half were working. Being unemployed may render a person more vulnerable to traumatic stress and depressive symptoms. But it also could be that those who are working, but suffering, are encountering obstacles that prevent them from accessing services.

We also found that Bosnian refugees who sought mental health services were not as highly educated. While it is known that level of education has generally been shown to influence services utilization, most existing studies of non-refugees indicate an opposite pattern of results; persons with higher levels of education are more likely to use mental health services. It is possible that those refuges who are less educated are more vulnerable to the social, economic and cultural hardships of resettling in an urban metropolis. It is also possible that the mental health services being offered are not appealing to the more highly educated refugees.

The importance of the family context is indicated by the finding that having an actual experience with services in the family seems to weigh more heavily than being told about services. It could be that the refugee experience affects multiple family members in such a way that more than one person seeks treatment. It could also be that when one family member has sought mental health treatment, others in the family are required to provide assistance and support to their ill family member and thus more likely to seek treatment themselves.

In conclusion, this study showed that persons presenting for services had higher levels of PTSD symptoms, but also depression symptoms and other distinct demographics and service exposure characteristics.

STUDY TWO: REFUGEE MENTAL HEALTH PROVIDERS PTSD KNOWLEDGE, ATTITUDES, AND BEHAVIORS

Research Aims

This study looked at providers working with Bosnian refugees in Chicago. They were either community social service providers, primary medical providers, or mental health service providers. The overall research question was: What are providers' knowledge, attitudes and activities regarding PTSD? In particular, this study investigated providers to characterize and understand their: 1) knowledge of PTSD; 2) attitudes towards the prevalence of PTSD; 3) attitudes as reflected in spoken advice on PTSD to the refugees; 4) assessments for PTSD; 5) mental health intervention recommendations; 6) educational activities.

Methods

The subjects were providers who had at least 6 months experience working with Bosnian refugees, and were then working at one of the programs in the Chicago area that provided services for Bosnians. The organizations involved were all primarily refugee service organizations (as opposed to mainstream social service or health care), and included: a refugee social center, refugee resettlement organizations, primary medical care clinics, refugee mental health clinics. Providers were divided into three types: 1) primary medical care providers (PMCP); 2) community social service providers (CSSP); 3) refugee mental health service providers (RMHSP). For each organization, program administrators were first contacted, told about the study, and asked to facilitate their employees' participation in the interviews. All organizations agreed to participate. They provided names of all potential subjects within their organization, and then names were randomly chosen. All individuals chose to participate. A total of thirty interviews were performed.

None of the demographic differences between the three groups achieved significance but there were some notable trends. The primary medical providers were older (47.7 years) than the other groups (38.8 years for CSSP and 39.6 for RMHSP). Regarding gender, there were more females amongst the primary medical care group (5 of 6). The highest percentage of

Bosnians was found amongst community social service providers (9 of 12), then mental health service providers (5 of 11), with none amongst the primary medical care providers. There was a high proportion of medical doctors amongst both the primary medical care providers (5 of 7) and the mental health service providers (6 of 11). The latter reflects a trend towards hiring physician refugees as mental health counselors. Primary medical care providers had worked at their organization the longest (41.1 months compared with 33.3 months for PMCP and 24.1 months for RMHSP).

An assessment instrument was developed based upon the principal investigator's (SMW) six year experience as a provider of refugee mental health services, a thorough review of the refugee mental health literature, ethnographic interviews with refugee mental health service providers, and review of other relevant research on service providers (Lynch, 1986; Westen, 1997). The instrument addressed the following areas: 1) Demographic information; 2) Knowledge and attitudes about PTSD and trauma mental health; 3) Assessment of PTSD; 4) Intervention recommendations concerning PTSD; 5) Spoken advice to refugees regarding PTSD; 6) Educational activities concerning PTSD. The instrument consisted of standardized probes, forced response items, and open-ended questions. The data was analyzed via chi-square and one-way ANOVA tests.

The interviews were performed in one meeting lasting approximately one hour. The interviews were conducted at the work place of the subject, at the University of Illinois of Chicago, or at a place of mutual convenience. The interviews were performed by a member of the research team, which consisted of two American psychiatrists (one in training), and a Bosnian psychiatrist in training. Each interviewer participated in orientation sessions and was thoroughly familiar with the relevant constructs, the research instruments, and the need to protect the confidentiality of patients and research subjects. All were under the supervision of the PI.

Results

The majority of providers (87%) reported knowing about PTSD, however this rate was significantly lower (57%) amongst primary medical care providers (p<.05). Primary medical care providers, in comparison with the other two groups received significantly less training and education on PTSD (14% verses 78%; p<.05). They also had less traumatic life experiences (71% v. 83%) and less treatment experiences (14% v. 30%), although these differences were not statistically significant.

Providers were asked to estimate the percentage of Bosnians in Chicago with PTSD and the percentage of Bosnians in Chicago who needed trauma treatment. Their estimates for the percentage of Bosnians in Chicago with PTSD were: community social service providers (51.6%, SD=33.9), primary medical care providers (65.3%, SD=10.8), mental health service providers (53.8%, SD=13.6). Their estimates for the percent of Bosnians in Chicago who needed trauma treatment were: community social service providers (60.6%, SD=31.3), primary medical care providers (63.2%, SD=30.6), mental health service providers (74.7%, SD=21.1). A difference between the estimates of who had PTSD and who needed treatment was calculated for each group. Mental health service providers showed the greatest margin of difference between higher perceived percentages of those needing treatment (75%), and a lower perceived percentage of those with PTSD (54%), which was of borderline significance.

Although all providers report having a routine interview, far fewer use either self-report or interviewer administered questionnaires. Most refugee mental health service providers reported using questions from the D.S.M.-IV to evaluate for PTSD, but this was significantly less in the other two groups (82% v. 26%; p<.05). When asked if they looked for PTSD in the last 5 new Bosnian refugees they saw, the answers were affirmative for all the mental health service providers, but significantly less in the other two groups (100% v. 58%; p<.05).

Providers were asked to think of the last five new refugees they saw, and to indicate which recommendations for treatment or other psychosocial interventions they made (possibilities were zero, one or more than one). The top three recommendations overall were in rank order: 1. Psychotherapy; 2. No intervention; 3. Psychiatric evaluation. Psychotherapy was the recommendation made most often by mental health service providers. Community social service providers' top interventions were referral for either psychiatric evaluation or to their agency social worker. Primary medical care providers mostly chose no intervention.

A majority of mental health service providers told refugees that they should accept mental health treatment, in comparison to half as many other providers (73% v. 37%; p<.1). The rates at which psychiatric medications were recommended are comparable (64% v. 37%). However, refugee mental health service providers were not likely to tell the refugees that something was wrong with them, that they had a mental disorder, or that they were suffering the signs and symptoms of an illness.

Primary medical care providers were the most likely to tell them that they were suffering the signs and symptoms of an illness (43 % v. 26 %) and that they had a mental disorder (29% v. 13 %). Only a minority of all providers reported telling the refugees that there was something wrong with them (13%).

Mental health service providers reported doing far more talking with refugees about the psychiatric consequences of trauma than the other provider groups (82 % v. 42%; p<.05). Overall, slightly over half (53%) of all the providers spoke with families about refugees' condition. This was highesthighest in the RMHSP (63%) and lowest in CSSP (42%). Regarding speaking with refugee individuals or groups outside of the provider organizational context, the rates were highest amongst community social service providers (75 %) in comparison with the two other groups (44 %).

Discussion

This study found a low rate of knowledge about PTSD amongst primary medical care providers. This is of concern given their important role in assessment and referral. It appeared that they had received less education and training on PTSD, and had less personal life experiences with trauma and less experience in psychotherapy.

The PTSD prevalence questions revealed a higher disparity amongst the mental health service providers between the belief that many need treatment and that fewer have PTSD. It suggests that even amongst this group, presumably the most sophisticated in terms of their knowledge of PTSD, the PTSD diagnosis was not consistently being linked to the need for treatment.

Providers' attitudes were also reflected in their spoken advice when they told the refugees about their conditions and what they should do. Overall, the mental health service providers were recommending treatment at higher rates, but were not presenting a rationale that was based on the perception of an illness or disorder, let alone PTSD. The primary medical care providers were more inclined to speak to refugees about the presence of an illness or disorder, but overall were recommending treatment at a lower rate. This again suggests that the connection between knowledge of PTSD and providers' attitudes towards trauma mental health treatment was not as strong as one might expect.

We found deficiencies in the areas of systematic assessment for PTSD. This is of particular concern in locations where specialized refugee mental health services are openly available (such as Chicago). The imperative of doing assessments is less clear in situations where those services do not exist, as is often the case in refugee communities, both in the United States and abroad.

The primary medical care providers' tendency to make mostly no recommendations for treatment can be seen as contributing to the larger access problem, which may possibly be addressable through enhancing primary medical care providers' knowledge of PTSD. The mental health service providers tended to recommend psychotherapy first and foremost. However, only a subset of refugees can or will accept individual psychotherapy, due to many obstacles, not the least of which is stigma. Furthermore, individual psychotherapy can be one important intervention for refugees, but it cannot possibly serve as the treatment of choice in a fiscally constrained refugee mental health system obligated to social suffering and public health.

In the area of education, we found another item of concern. Not speaking with refugee families is effectively ignoring what is arguably the most important resource for refugees – the family. Within Bosnian culture, the family plays a central role in providing support and structure, especially when there is suffering and hardship. Clinical experience and ethnographic inquiry with Bosnian families demonstrate that families clearly play an important role in help-seeking, including for mental health services. The activity of joining with and educating families is supported by multiple health and mental health studies which document the critical role of the family in help-seeking and in the outcome of health interventions (Weine, 1998).

In conclusion, this study showed that assessment and educational activities of providers did not adequately reflect the high prevalence of PTSD in refugee populations.

STUDY THREE: TREATMENT FOR REFUGEES WITH PTSD

Research Aims

Although the service utilization of minority communities has been studied (Alvidrez, 1999; Cooper-Patrick et al., 1999), there has been limited research into the service utilization of refugee populations (Howard, 2000). Much of the research on refugee trauma has focused on the epidemiology of trauma-related mental health problems in refugee populations and little is known about the types of mental health treatment that refugees receive in refugee mental health service organizations. The purpose of this retrospective chart review was to examine the factors associated with treatment patterns in a sample of refugees who had presented for mental health services.

Methods

The subjects of the chart review were 84 Bosnian refugees who were receiving services at the mental health program for Bosnians located in Chicago at the Heartland Alliance.

We reviewed all the cases opened in this clinic between August 1996 and August 1998. The subjects had arrived in the United States between January 1993 and July 1998. The subjects were 54 females (65%) and 30 males (35%). The mean age of the subjects was 48.4 years old (standard deviation 10.7, range 18-77). 54 (65%) were married and living with a spouse and 30 (35%) were divorced, widowed, separated or never married. 32 (39%) had graduated from high school or pursued higher degrees than high school (which we defined as a 'high level of education') whereas 43 (51%) had not finished or attended high school (a 'low level of education'). At the time of presentation 5 (6%) were reported as employed and 78 (94%) were not. 20 (24%) had lost a primary relative (parent, child, sibling or spouse) in the war, whereas 64 (76%) had not.

Before presenting to the clinic, 56 (66%) had received no prior mental health services, and 28 (33%) had received prior mental health services in one or more countries (n=28). That further breaks down into 9.5% receiving services in Bosnia-Herzegovina, 6% in the U.S., 5% in another country (mostly Germany), 1% in Croatia, 12% in more than one of these countries. 18 of the subjects (22%) were self-referred and 61 (78%) were referred by family, members of the community, or a resettlement agency. 58 (69%) had a co-morbid medical condition recorded in the chart, including diabetes, hypertension and heart disease.

This retrospective chart review was conducted using a questionnaire that was developed to collect demographic data (as reported above) and to identify the mental health treatment received. The types of services provided to subjects included psychiatric evaluation, supportive counseling, medication management, individual psychotherapy and group psychotherapy. The subjects were divided into two sub-groups: those who received "Basic Services" and those who received "Psychotherapeutic Services". We defined "Basic Services" as a psychiatric evaluation, supportive counseling, and psychiatric medication management. All patients received at least Basic Services. We defined Psychotherapeutic Services as Basic Services plus individual and/or group psychotherapy.

The instrument collected data concerning the patients' frequency of services use by documenting the number of visits per sequential 3-month periods. We defined "Low Frequency" as including 3-month periods without receiving any services plus 3-month periods with 2 or fewer sessions per month; and we defined "High Frequency" as more than 2 sessions per 3-month period with no periods missed.

Results

Forty-six (55%) of the patients received only Basic Services and 37 (44%) received Psychotherapeutic Services. Of the latter, 24 received group psychotherapy only, 22 received individual psychotherapy only and 9 received both individual and group psychotherapy. 25 subjects (31%) received other types of non-psychotherapeutic intervention, including translation services and interviews for Social Security Disability. While fewer than half of the patients received group or individual therapy, 81 (96%) received psychopharmacologic medication management (particularly with Selective Serotonin Reuptake Inhibitors and anxiolytics).

We found that compared to those who received Basic Services, those who received Psychotherapeutic Services were more likely to have lost a primary relative (p<.05) and to be self referred (p< .05). There was a borderline association with higher number of children.

A model for Psychotherapeutic Services was derived through a backwards elimination process that started with five independent variables, and after eliminating three variables, consisted of two variables: loss of relative and self-referral. The overall model was found to be significant (p < .01). It was able to predict presentation for engagement at an accuracy of 50.1%. All the factors within that model achieved statistical significance.

Receiving group psychotherapy was significantly associated with loss of a primary relative (p<0.043). Receiving individual psychotherapy was significantly associated with lower level of education (p<0.05); borderline associations were found with loss of primary relative.

A model for individual psychotherapy was derived through a backwards elimination process that started with five independent variables, and after eliminating three variables, consisted of two variables: number of children and self-referral. The overall model was found to be significant (p < .01). It was able to predict presentation for engagement at an accuracy of 62.3%. All the factors within that model achieved statistical significance. Using a backwards elimination process, no model for group psychotherapy could be derived.

We looked at the patterns of involvement during the first year of services for each subject (at the time of data collection, those who had arrived in 1998 had only received one full year of services). We found that patients going from high frequency use to low frequency use was associated with not receiving group psychotherapy (p<0.05) and with case closure (p<0.001). Going from high to low frequency usage also showed borderline associations with not receiving individual psychotherapy and with not receiving any psychotherapeutic services. No other demographic or services characteristics showed an association with changing levels of services frequency. In terms of frequency of usage, we found that low frequency use was associated with case closure (p < .01). Otherwise we found no predictors of frequency of services use amongst demographic and service use variables.

Discussion

In this refugee mental health clinic, psychotherapeutic services were being provided to those who appeared to have both higher motivation (self-referral) and higher vulnerability. The latter included loss of a relative, lower level of education, and unemployment.

Loss of a relative may lead to greater vulnerability to psychological stressors (Fuchs, 1999). Complicated bereavement, inability to mourn or perform culturally appropriate rituals, the exacerbation of psychiatric conditions due to the worsening stress, and the lack of that relative's support in the patient's social environment can contribute to greater suffering; loss of a relative may also indicate increased proximity to traumatic events and thus more exposure, although it is not clear that there is a dose-dependent relationship between trauma and subsequent mental health problems (Kroll, 2003). Nevertheless, separation and fear of separation has been demonstrated to be a prominent cause of distress in refugee populations (Sourander, 2003).

Persons with lower levels of education may lack certain adaptive and language skills, rendering them more vulnerable to the stressors of resettlement. Although research with Viet Nam veterans has shown that a history of academic weakness may be a predictor for the development of PTSD after exposure to trauma (Watson et al, 1998), Hermansson et al (2002) found that a higher level of education was correlated with lower levels of mental health in a study of 44 war-wounded refugees. As Brewin, Andrews & Valentine (2000) demonstrated, it can be difficult to ascertain which sociocultural factors improve resilience and which lead to increased vulnerability and studies can produce contradictory results.

Similar to Study One, only 6% of the patients were reported as employed. Employed refugees might be less vulnerable to stressors either by virtue of their employment or their employability (e.g. higher language skills and more social contacts). Drozdek (1997) did not find loss of family, separation, education or social functioning to be either protective or a risk factor for the onset and exacerbation of PTSD but found that social contacts seemed to have been the only protective factor. The social support and integration provided by employment may account for the paucity of employed patients seeking mental health services. However, it is also possible that heavy working hours may prevent presentation for services.

Although these characteristics of loss, lower level of education and unemployment in a traumatised population appear to offer an "ecological niche" (Hacking, 1998) for psychotherapy, it is not known whether these are the persons who can benefit most from psychotherapy interventions. Given that psychotherapy resources are limited, it is important to consider: who stands to gain the most from psychotherapy? It does not appear that there is any empirical basis for deciding this in the field of refugee mental health. Because this study did not address severity of symptoms, we cannot conclude from this chart review that patients who have worse symptoms are the ones receiving Psychotherapeutic services rather than Basic Services.

Overall, the data suggest that the diagnosis or PTSD and pharmacological management of PTSD was nearly universal in this patient population, and that social support and functioning were significant factors in deciding treatment options. Although some factors did not appear significant statistically, further study to evaluate the roles of gender (Sideris, 2003), age and types of experiences the subjects went through (Momartin et al., 2003) would be valuable.

Regarding treatment use patterns, we noted two other trends that, although not reaching statistical significance, appeared interesting. While almost a third of subjects went from high to low levels of involvement over the course of the year, no patients who were identified as having low initial levels of involvement increased their level of involvement. Of nine persons living alone, only two were low frequency users, again suggesting that services are being used by the more socially vulnerable.

In conclusion, this study showed that although nearly all patients treated for PTSD received psychiatric medications and supportive counseling, treatment patterns varied with demographic characteristics associated with vulnerability.

STUDY FOUR: PROVIDERS' DISCOURSE ON REFUGEE SERVICES

Research Aims

The aim of this study was to elaborate a services approach to refugees based upon the narratives of providers working with Bosnian refugees in Chicago. As in study two, these providers were either refugee resettlement providers, primary medical providers, or mental health service providers.

Methods

The subjects and the interviews were the same group of providers that were described in study two. This study focused upon qualitative data obtained from the subjects narrative responses to the following open-ended prompts and questions:

- "Tell me what you think are the most important things to know about trauma mental health for Bosnians".
- "Tell me what you think are some of the questions or problems that have come up for you in doing the work that you do".
- "How do you tell who is in need of trauma treatment?"
- "What are the reasons that Bosnians in Chicago who need trauma mental health treatment do not receive it?"
- "Tell me what you think would make the work that is being done for Bosnians' mental health better".
- "What actions do you think would help to make trauma mental health treatment more available for Bosnian refugees in Chicago?"

Textual coding and analysis was conducted using ATLAS/ti in accordance with standard procedures of qualitative research (Miles & Huberman, 1994; Strauss & Corbin, 1998). Texts were coded using a "start list" of descriptive codes that was created on the basis of ongoing community immersion and fieldwork and previous studies with Bosnian refugees. To establish smaller "sets, themes and constructs" pattern coding was conducted using Atlas/ti's query tool. Pattern coding examines the relationship between codes in order to identify overarching themes and patterns of variation.

Throughout pattern coding, memoing was performed to concisely describe and analyze the pattern coding results. Memoing involved writing short descriptive statements based upon the quotations identified through the pattern coding to summarize the meanings and processes reflected in the quotes. Provisional overall services issues were identified through scanning and sorting those descriptive statements into clusters and categories. Next, the organized groupings of descriptive statements were interpreted from the vantagepoint of key concepts derived from the aforementioned scientific and professional literatures. Lastly, to check for other explanations and contrary evidence, the analysis was re-reviewed by the entire research team.

Results

In the narratives we found numerous differences between provider groups that are important to understand in devising a services approach that considers systemic dimensions. These define three overall sub-discourses differentiated by provider type:

- *Primary Care Providers: Diagnostic Focus:* Primary care providers are able to detect the presence of overt symptoms and are inclined to speak to refugees about the presence of an illness or disorder. However, they are the least inclined to recommend any specific mental health intervention, especially because of lack of knowledge or concern over stigmatization. For example, they said: "You see all sorts of symptoms from your evaluation. Depression, Anxiety, and sleeplessness"; "They don't like to be psycho. Some of them are in self denial so it's very hard to get the information out of them"; "Very often I don't know. I think that's the key problem".

- *Refugee Resettlement Providers: Adjustment Focus:* Refugee resettlement providers are highly attuned to the social and cultural complexities of the refugee experience. They are the most experienced at how to understand and help in refugees' daily lives. However, they are also the least informed about the assessment and treatment of mental health problems. For example, they said: "I try to make them feel at ease"; "You can tell by the behavior, and how their communication is, how the body language is"; "We caseworkers do not recognize their symptoms"; "Most of them are afraid to come because they are afraid they will have in their history they received mental health treatment."

- *Refugee Mental Health Providers: Trauma Psychotherapy Focus:* Refugee mental health providers are the strongest advocates for mental health treatment. However, they are more highly focused on individual psychotherapy than on any other treatments. They also do not communicate with others a rationale that is based on the perception of an illness or disorder. For example, they say: "Trauma it shows in many different ways"; "This is a normal response to horrible events they survived. I always believe that treatment is very helpful, very effective, and there are few side effects, which are not even worth comparing to the benefits of treatment"; "I guess they feel better to come and talk".

The differences between provider groups that we identified are not surprising given that they work in different systems. However it is concerning that there are obvious disconnects between these three perspectives, and that there is the absence of a broader vision of refugee mental health to guide the overall development of services for refugees. At present, there is no articulation of a vision that comes close to addressing the concerns that the providers themselves expressed about the needs of refugees. These providers' narratives suggest that such a vision would have to be far more highly attuned to the worldview and behavior of providers and their organizations, as well as to the interactions between different provider types and different organizations.

Although providers did not articulate a specific services perspective, the qualitative evidence derived from them was highly oriented towards services issues. Their discourse on services was divided into four categories that contained between three and twelve subcategories. All the items listed were mentioned repeatedly by service providers. They encompass problems or issues that are directly related to PTSD but that also were related to other mental health, social, cultural, economic, and familial problems. The four categories are as follows:

- **Problems and Needs of Refugees:** Providers reported that traumatic stress symptoms are important, but they are but one area of concern, and should be seen as a part of a larger complex of refugee's problems and needs. Specific problems prominently mentioned by providers included: alcohol and illegal drugs, cultural adjustment, depression, family problems, financial problems, school problems, social isolation, thought disorder symptoms, trauma related disabilities, traumatic stress symptoms, traumatic memories, work problems
- **Services Access Problems:** Providers expressed strong concerns about refugees' access to services, including mental health, but also social, cultural, educational, legal, and financial services. Access problems mentioned by the providers included: avoidance, denial, rear, lack of family support, lack of information, lack of time, inability to trust, language problems, retraumatization, and stigmatization. They were concerned that very little professional attention was paid to how to help providers to address access problems.
- **A Spectrum of Outcomes:** Providers articulated that it was necessary to target not only improvement in PTSD and other psychopathological symptoms, but also to consider other outcomes. Specific outcomes prominently mentioned included: access to services, coping abilities, family functioning, knowledge and attitudes, other mental health symptoms, daily functioning, social support and social network, work and finance.
- **A Range of Services Interventions:** Providers said that more types of services interventions were necessary in addition to clinical interventions. These included community education and access interventions that were supportive of mental health interventions must be developed. Prominently mentioned were interventions that would address the needs of children and youth and interventions that would address persons who were having problems progressing out of low-wage work.

Discussion

Overall, we found that many issues articulated by refugee mental health providers are services issues. Providers' statements reflect a fairly broad consideration of the services questions we initially asked: What kinds of care, for what persons, seeking what help, towards what outcomes? The four overall areas emphasized in this framework are consistent with the major themes in the services research on combat veterans, such as those identified by Rosenheck and Fontana (1999): the relative fit of clinical services with survivors' needs and resources; the barriers to accessing services; and the effectiveness of services.

Their emphasis and obvious concern regarding these services issues stands in contrast to the existing literature on refugee mental health, which has not made mental health services an area of appreciable focus. A services framework is about making interventions work within the real-life needs, strengths, meanings and constraints of the refugees' worlds. The specific concerns articulated by providers can serve as a preliminary blueprint for further development of new interventions for refugees, as will be discussed below. However, the strong presence of services-concerns amongst providers is not matched by their articulation of any kind of services-related conceptual approach that would assist in understanding or managing the services problems facing refugees (e.g. family theory or social network theory). Instead, providers tend to fall back on medical, clinical psychiatric, psychotherapeutic approaches.

In conclusion, this study showed that providers' discourse on refugees was highly oriented towards services issues with a focus on service access problems.

A SERVICES MENTAL HEALTH APPROACH TO REFUGEE TRAUMA (SMART)

We began with the claim that there is an overall need for applying a mental health services approach to refugee trauma. Next we reported on four studies of Bosnian refugees in Chicago that examined PTSD through a mental health service lens. The summary findings were: (1) Persons presenting for services had higher levels of PTSD symptoms, but also depression symptoms and other distinct demographics and service exposure characteristics associated with vulnerability; (2) Assessment and educational activities of providers did not adequately reflect the high prevalence of PTSD in refugee populations; (3) Although nearly all patients treated for PTSD received psychiatric medication and supportive counseling, treatment patterns varied with demographic characteristics; (4) Providers' discourse on refugees was highly oriented towards services issues with a focus on service access problems. Overall, these studies demonstrate that PTSD is an important construct for refugee mental health services, but because PTSD alone does not explain the range or context of refugees' mental health needs, a services perspective on PTSD is necessary.

On the basis of the empirical evidence presented in these four studies, we propose a *Services Mental Health Approach to Refugee Trauma* to facilitate building services for refugee trauma. The major claims of this approach are as follows.

(1) *PTSD should be regarded as one of multiple causes of suffering amongst a heterogeneous refugee population to be addressed by mental health services.* Study one demonstrated that it is especially important to recognize the role of depression amongst refugees. Study three indicated several factors associated with vulnerability that included loss, low education level, and unemployment. Study four identified that many refugees have a range of other mental health, social, and cultural problems that should also be considered. We believe that special attention should be paid to mental health problems in children and adolescents, given that this was a concern of refugees, and has important implications for the future of families and communities. This range of different types of mental health problems requires the development and implementation of spectrum of targeted mental health services.

(2) *PTSD and mental health related information for communities and families, and training for providers, must be more comprehensive and culturally synchronous in order to facilitate better help-seeking and assessment.* Study two revealed that providers, communities, and families were not adequately informed about how to

address the mental health consequences of the refugee experience. They need information and communication strategies that fit with the cultural and social worlds of their particular refugee group. The overall aim should be to facilitate help-seeking for necessary and appropriate mental health services

(3) *Provision of specific interventions in refugee mental health services should be guided by scientific evaluation and clinical observations of targeted outcomes in real life contexts.* Study three demonstrated that psychiatric treatments may be filling an ecological niche created by the refugee experience (e.g. psychotherapy for those who lost loved ones). Although interventions must certainly be aware of and responsive to vulnerability, interventions must be subject to rigorous conceptual and empirical processes that seek to explain intervention change processes. There is a need for scientific studies of whether or not interventions work, as well as evaluation of the experiences of those who are treated with the intervention. It is also important that interventions focus not only upon vulnerability but also upon enhancing strengths and resilience, especially in families and communities (Walsh, 1998).

(4) *Refugee mental health services should facilitate access to a range of mental health, social, family, and health services.* Study four demonstrated that refugees have a broad range of mental health, social, economic, and cultural needs and that they confront many obstacles to getting services that may address these needs. Study one showed that employment appears to be an obstacle to accessing mental health services. We believe that mental health services should function as an overall access intervention that aims to improve refugees' access to services, including mental health, but also health, social, educational, legal, and employment services.

This SMART framework can be used to promote and guide necessary changes in the field of refugee mental health. It provides a basis for rethinking refugees' interactions with services, including issues of access, treatment, adherence, support and education, in a way that is more oriented to the daily realities facing refugees. It provides a theoretical basis for building interventions and for conducting policy aimed research.

IMPLICATIONS FOR INTERVENTIONS

This framework can help to specify implications for interventions for refugee trauma.

Access Interventions

An access intervention helps people obtain the services they need to address their problems. Access interventions are needed for sub-group of refugees who are not likely to present for mental health services but who are suffering. Access interventions should also address other pressing service needs of refugees such as accessing health, school and legal services. In addition, mental health services should be designed to be as accessible as possible; they should be responsive to the specific obstacles that refugees report, such as employment and no prior experience with mental health services.

Systematic Assessment

Providers and their organizations should accept that systematic assessment of PTSD and depression and other common mental health problems is a necessary element of refugee mental health interventions. This should be taught and practiced at all three types of provider sites. This would require the development of resource materials that pose the least possible burden upon providers and refugees. It is also essential to understand that screening itself is an intervention and requires a sense of safety, trust, and caring if it is going to be helpful. To be truly useful, screening for trauma related mental health problems must also be accompanied by the appropriate recommendations. Needless to say, assessment is not useful if there are no available treatment services.

Training Mental Health Providers

Mental health providers for refugees require more training in PTSD and related mental health treatment issues. This is important not only because of their direct role in providing services but also because of their roles interacting and communicating with non-mental health service providers and with refugee families and communities. Thus this training must address cross-cultural issues and contextual issues, gender issues, children, and interventions.

Training Primary Care Providers

More could be done to help primary medical care providers be more effective in addressing PTSD. The aim could be to enable primary medical care providers to intervene confidently in a systematic manner with their refugee trauma patients. This could be accomplished through developing targeted educational program and resource materials concerning PTSD and related mental health problems. This intervention must deal with the realistic limitations of time availability, and linguistic and ethnocultural differences (Kroll, 2003; Hinton et al., 2003; Fox, 2003). It must be grounded in the existing research on education and training programs for health care workers in related areas (Cook et al, 1998; Harwell et al, 1998).

Familial and Occupational Interventions

There is a need to go beyond individual psychotherapy and psychiatric medications in mental health clinics to develop innovative interventions which better address some of the broad range of problems and needs of refugees. This should include occupational interventions aimed at job placement and advancement. It should also include family preventive interventions aimed at addressing high-risk behavior and school problems in youth as has been done in other populations facing adversity such as urban families (Weine et al, 2004; McKay, 2002).

Educating Refugees

Education of refugee families concerning trauma mental health and its treatment must be seen as an essential activity for all providers. Refugees often have neither prior experience with trauma mental health problems nor treatment, and so may often have high levels of stigma, shame, and fear. In order to help them to utilize mental health services, refugees and their families need information; they need help talking about that information in families; and they need help to build their trust in service providers and institutions. It is important to ground an educative approach to refugees in the resilience and strengths inherent in a refugee group's ethnocultural experience and community resources.

IMPLICATIONS FOR POLICY AIMED RESEARCH

The family nursing researchers, Feetham and Meister, claim: "The evaluation of [a] program should guide the development of policies to sustain the program." (p. 251). In the field of refugee mental health, the researchers have tended to be clinicians and the research itself has centered on the link between science and clinical practice rather than between science and policy. It could be argued that the policy of central concern in the refugee mental health field has been the policy of justifying clinical treatment programs for refugee survivors of trauma. The preponderance of research on PTSD and traumatic stress serves this policy aim (albeit in a narrow sense), but does not serve policy for refugee mental health services in a broader sense.

We propose that one way to shift the policy-aimed research in refugee mental health in a more services oriented direction would be to make the refugee family the central focus. Targeting refugee families necessarily directs attention to issues other than PTSD, and implies that the knowledge base the research is attempting to build must address a broader range of concerns related to families. Feetham's criteria for family research can be usefully applied to services research for refugee families. Several criteria with clear implications for services research with refugee families include:

(1) there is a family conceptual and theoretical framework;
(2) there is an explicit conceptualization of the family;
(3) the definition of the family is consistent with the conceptualization, design and methods;
(4) the findings add to the knowledge of family functioning and family structure.

Gathering data on the individual members of families does not mean that the work is genuinely family focused. It is necessary for the researcher to grapple with established or innovative ways of organizing one's ideas about refugee families and then letting those ideas guide the research process, from the initial stages of identifying research questions all the way through to sampling, measurement, analysis, and reporting. Services research on refugee families should also avoid common clinical biases, especially ones derived from the more individualist approach, such as pointing out what's wrong with families rather than identifying family strengths and resilience and not sufficiently attending to the unique contributions of cultural, social and historical contexts.

Feetham and Meister further recommend that policy-aimed family research initiatives should be concerned with those policies that specifically affect families, such as the health and well-being of other family members, education, employment/income, and poverty/welfare. In an similar vein important policy issues affecting refugee familiesin the current era include: asylum policy; access to health care; welfare reform and welfare to work; costs of the provision of mental health services; and language education policy.

Feetham and Meister provide a framework for moving from the evaluation of interventions to programs of research that are deliberately focused upon policy. They advocate for a "science policy" based upon the guidelines developed for the nursing research of families. It recommends that the research of families:

(1) be conceptually and methodologically rigorous;
(2) focus on circumstances in which families are likely to need help;
(3) contribute to the development and testing of interventions and assessment of strategies;
(4) be conducted in the broadest context of relevance to the individual and family, such as in the community, health system, environment, and social and health policy; and
(5) provide guidance to institutions and agencies.

Services research concerning refugee families has a long way to go. The systems that provide and fund services are for the most part oriented in other directions (especially on individual, psychopathologically-oriented, and psychodynamic therapies). Furthermore, the agencies that provide services are themselves balkanized and resistant to linking into a broader network. The concepts and methodologies for addressing the complex issues involved in family research are not yet a part of refugee mental health system. Because of what we have learned about the limitations of the PTSD approach, we would argue that the struggle to change this is worth fighting for.

CONCLUSIONS

PTSD is an important construct for refugee mental health services, but because PTSD alone does not explain or address the full range of mental health needs of refugees, other services dimensions must be considered. On the basis of empirical research with refugees, this chapter described a *Services Mental Health Approach to Refugee Trauma (SMART)* for helping refugees with PTSD. The major claims of this approach are as follows: (1) PTSD should be regarded as one of multiple causes of suffering amongst a heterogeneous refugee population to be addressed by mental health services; (2) PTSD and mental health related information for communities and families, and training for providers, must be more comprehensive and culturally synchronous in order to facilitate better help-seeking and services; (3) Provision of specific interventions in refugee mental health services should be guided by scientific evaluation and clinical observations of targeted outcomes in real life contexts; (4) Refugee mental health services should have as a primary goal facilitating access to a range of mental health, health, social, occupational, child, and family services. These claims should guide interventions and policy-aimed research regarding mental health services for refugee trauma.

REFERENCES

Alvidrez, J. (1999). Ethnic variations in mental health attitudes and service use among low-income African American, Latina, and European American young women. *Journal of Community Mental Health, 35(6)*, 515-30.

American Psychiatric Association (1980). *Diagnostic and Statistical Manual of Mental Disorders* (3rd Edition) (DSM-III). Washington, DC: APA.

_____ . (1994). *Diagnostic and Statistical Manual of Mental Disorders* (4th Edition) (DSM-IV). Washington, DC: APA.

Becker, D.F., Weine, S.M., Vojvoda, D., & McGlashan, T.H. (1999). Case Series: PTSD symptoms in adolescent survivors of "ethnic cleansing": Results from a 1-year follow-up study. *Journal of the American Academy of Child and Adolescent Psychiatry , 38*, 775-781.

Bleich, A., Gelkopf, M., & Solomon, Z. (2003). Exposure to terrorist attacks, stress-related mental health symptoms, and coping behaviours among a nationally representative sample in Israel. *Journal of the American Medical Association, 290*, 612-620.

Boehnlein, J.K. (1987). A review of mental health services for refugees between 1975 and 1985 and a proposal for future services. *Hospital and Community Psychiatry, 38*, 764-768.

Bracken, P. (2002). *Trauma: Culture, Meaning, and Philosophy*. London and Philadelphia: Whurr Publishers.

Brewin, C.R., Andrews, B., & Valentine, J.D. (2000). Meta-analysis of risk factors for posttraumatic stress disorder in trauma-exposed adults. *Journal of Consulting and Clinical Psychology, 68*, 748-766.

Cardozo, B.L., Vergara, A., Agani, F, & Gotway, C. A. (2000). Mental Health, Social Functioning, and Attitudes of Kosovar Albanians Following the War in Kosovo. *Journal of the American Medical Association, 284 (5)*, 569-577.

Clum, G.A., Calhoun ,K.S., Kimerling, R. (2000). Associations among symptoms of depression and posttraumatic stress disorder and self-reported health in sexually assaulted women. *Journal of Nervous & Mental Disease. 188(10)*, 671-8

Cook, J.A., Horton-O'Connell, T., Fitzgibbon, G., & Steigman, P.J. (1998). Training for state-funded providers of assertive community treatment. In P.W. Corrigan & D.F. Giffort et al. (Eds.) *New Directions for Mental Health Services, Building Teams and Programs for Effective Psychiatric Rehabilitat, 79*. (pp. 55-64). San Francisco, CA: Jossey-Bass Inc..

Corbin, J., & Strauss, A. (1990). Grounded theory research: Procedures, canons, and evaluative criteria. *Qualitative Sociology*, 12, 3-21.

Cooper-Patrick, L., Gallo, J.J., Powe, N.R., Steinwachs, D.M., Eaton, W.W., & Ford, D.E. (1999). Mental health service utilization by African Americans and Whites: the Baltimore Epidemiologic Catchment Area Follow-Up. *Medical Care, 37(10)*, 1034-45.

Drozdek, B. (1997). Follow-up Study of Concentration Camp Survivors from Bosnia-Herzegovina: Three Years Later. *Journal of Nervous & Mental Disease, 185(11)*, 690-694.

Foa, E.F., Riggs, D.S., Dancu, D.V., & Rothbaum, B.O. (1993). Reliability and validity of a brief instrument for assessing post traumatic stress disorder. *Journal of Traumatic Stress, 6*, 459-473.

Friedman, M. J., & Jaranson, J. (1994). The applicability of the post-traumatic Stress disorder concept to refugees. In: A. M. Marsella, T. Bornemann, S. Ekblad, & J. Orley (Eds.) *Amidst Peril and Pain*. Washington D.C.: American Psychological Association.

Fox, S.H. (2003). The Mandinka nosological system in the context of post-trauma syndromes. *Transcultural Psychiatry, 40(4)*, 488-506.

Fuchs, T. (1999). Life events in late paraphrenia and depression. *Psychopathology 32(2)*, 1999, 60-9.

Garcia-Peltoniemi, R., & Jaranson, J. (1989). *A Multidisciplinary Approach to the treatment of torture victims*. Paper presented at the Second International Conference of Centres, Institutions and Individuals Concerned with the Care of Victims of Organized Violence, San Jose, Costa Rica.

Goenjian, A. K., Steinberg, A. M., Najarian, L. M., Fairbanks, L. A., Tashjian, M. & Pynoos, R. S. (2000). Prospective study of posttraumatic stress, anxiety, and depressive reactions after earthquake and political violence. *American Journal of* Psychiatry *157*, 911-916.

Hacking, I. (1998). Mad travelers: Reflections on the reality of transient mental illness. United States of America. Charlottseville, VA: The University of Virginia Press.

Harwell, T.S., Casten, R.J., Armstrong, K.A., Dempsey, S., Coons, H.L., & Davis, M. (1998). Results of a domestic violence training program offered to the staff of urban community health centers. *American Journal of Preventive Medicine, 15(3)*, 235-42.

Hatfield, A.B., & Lefley, H.P. (1987). *Families of the mentally ill: Coping and adaptation*. New York: Guilford Press.

Hauff, E., & Vaglumm, O. (1995). Organised Violence and the Stress of Exile: Predictors of Mental Health in a Community Cohort of Vietnamese Refugees Three Years After Resettlement. *The British Journal of Psychiatry, 166(3)*, 360-367.

Hermansson, A-C, Timpka, T., & Thyberg, M. (2002). The Mental Health of War-Wounded Refugees: An 8-Year Follow Up. *Journal of Nervous and Mental Disease, 190 (6)*, 374-380.

Hinton, D., Hinton, S., Pham, T., Chau, H., & Tran M. (2003). 'Hit by the wind' and temperature-shift panic among Vietnamese refugees. *Transcultural Psychiatry. 40(3):* 342-76.

Holz, T.H. (1998). Refugee Trauma versus Torture: A Retrospective Controlled Cohort Study of Tibetan Refugees. *The Journal of Nervous and Mental Disease, 186(1)*, 22-24.

Howard, M., & Hodes, M. (2000). Psychopathology, Adversity, and Service Utilization of Young Refugees. *Journal of the American Academy of Child and Adolescent Psychiatry, 39(3)*, 368-377.

Immigration and Naturalisation Service (2001). Refugee Arrivals into the United States by Selected Country of Chargeability. Retrieved March 31, 2004 at http://uscis.gov/ graphics/shared/aboutus/statistics/ref01yrbk/ra2001list.htm.

Jones, E., Vermaas, R.H., McCartney, H., Beech, C., Palmer, I., Hyams, K., & Wessely, S. (2003). Flashbacks and post-traumatic stress disorder: the genesis of a 20th century diagnosis. *The British Journal of Psychiatry, 182*, 158-163.

Keane, T.M., Kaloupek, D.G., & Weathers, F.W. (1996). Ethnocultural considerations in the assessment of PTSD. In: Marsella, A., Friedman, M.J., Gerrity, E.T., Scurfield, R.M., &

Friedman, M.F. (Eds.) *Ethnocultural Aspects of Posttraumatic Stress Disorder* (pp. 183-208) Washington DC: American Psychological Association.

Kinzie, J.D., & Tran, K.A. (1980). An Indochinese refugee psychiatric clinic: culturally accepted treatment approaches. *American Journal of Psychiatry 137*, 1429-1432.

Kinzie, J.D., Fredrickson, R.H., Ben, R., Fleck, J., & Karls, W. (1984). Post-traumatic stress disorder among survivors of Cambodian concentration camps. *American Journal of Psychiatry, 141*, 645-650.

Kroll J (2003). Posttraumatic symptoms and the complexity of responses to trauma. *Journal of the American Medical Association, 290(5)*, 667-70.

Lamberg L. (2003). In the wake of tragedy: studies track psychological response to mass violence *Journal of the American Medical Association, 290(5)*, 587-9.

Lavik, N.J., Hauff, E., & Solberg, O. (1996). Mental Disorder among Refugees and the Impact of Persecution and Exile: Some Findings from an Out-Patient Population. *The British Journal of Psychiatry, 169 (6)*, 726-732.

Leaf, P.L., Bruce, M.L., & Tischler, G.L. (1986). The differential effect of attitudes on the use of mental health services. *Social Psychiatry, 21*, 187-192.

Lewis, R. B. (1998). ATLAS/ti and NUD*IST: A comparative review of two leading qualitative data analysis packages. *Cultural Anthropology Methods, 10(3)*, 41-47.

Lynch, M.M. (1986). Needs assessment of the chronically mentally ill: Practitioners and client perspectives. *Administration in Mental Health, 13(4)*, 237-248.

Marsella, A., Friedman, M.J., Gerrity, E.T. & Scurfield, R.M. (Eds.). (1996). *Ethnocultural Aspects of Posttraumatic Stress Disorder*. Washington, D.C. American Psychological Association.

McCall, G.J., & Resick, P.A (2003). A pilot study of PTSD symptoms among Kalahari Bushmen. *Journal of Traumatic Stress. 16(5)*, 445-50.

McKay, M., Harrison, M., Gonzales, J. Kim, L., and Quintana, E. (2002). Multiple-family groups for urban children with conduct difficulties and their families. *Psychiatric Services, 53*, 1467-1468.

Mollica, R., & Caspi-Yavin, Y. (1991). Measuring torture and torture-related symptoms. *Psychological Assessment, 3*, 1-6.

Momartin, S., Silove, D., Manicavasagar, V., & Steel, Z. (2003). Dimensions of trauma associated with posttraumatic stress disorder (PTSD) caseness, severity and functional impairment: a study of Bosnian refugees resettled in Australia. *Social Science and Medicine 57(5)*, 775-81.

Montenegro, R. (1999). Education, training and stigma. *New Trends in Experimental & Clinical Psychiatry, 15(2-3)*, 87-88.

Mundy, E., & Baum, A. (2004). Medical disorders as a Cause of Psychological Trauma and Posttraumatic Stress Disorder. *Current Opinion in Psychiatry 17(2)*, 123-127.

Pescosolido, B. A. (1986). Migration, medical care preferences and the lay referral system: A network theory of role assimilation. *American Sociological Review, 51*, 523-540.

Priebe, S., Esmaili, S. (1977). Long-term sequelea of torture in Iran – who seeks treatment. Journal of Nervous and Mental Diseases 1997; 185, 74-77.

Radloff, L.S. (1977). The CES-D Scale: A self-report depression scale for research in the general population. *Applied Psychological Measurement, 1*, 385-401.

Rosenheck, R., & Fontana, A. (1999). Changing patterns of care for war-related post-traumatic stress disorder at Department of Veterans Affairs medical centers: the use of performance data to guide program development. *Military Medicine, 164(11)*, 795-802.

_____. (1999). Delivery of services for PTSD. *PTSD Research Quarterly, 10*, 1-7.

Sabin, M., Cardozo, B.L., Nackerud, L., Kaiser, R., & Varese, L. (2003). Factors associated with poor mental health among Guatemalan refugees living in Mexico 20 years after civil conflict. *Journal of the American Medical Association, 290(5)*, 635-642.

Shapiro, S., Skinner, E.A., Kessler, L.G, Von Korff, M.,. German, P.S., Tischler, G.L., Leaf, P.J. et al. (1984). Utilization of health and mental health services: Three epidemiological catchment area sites. *Archives of General Psychiatry, 41*, 971-978.

Sideris, T. (2003). War, gender and culture: Mozambican women refugees. *Social Science and Medicine, 56(4)*, 713-24.

Silove, D. (1999). The psychosocial effects of torture, mass human rights violations, and refugee trauma. *The Journal of Nervous and Mental Disease, 187*, 200-207.

Singh, S. P., Baxter, H., Standen, P., & Duggan, C. (1998). Changing the attitudes of 'tomorrow's doctors' towards mental illness and psychiatry: a comparison of two teaching methods. *Medical Education, 32(2)*, 115-120.

Smajkic, A., Weine, S., Bijedic, Z., Boskailo, E., Lewis, J., E., & Pavkovic, I. (2001). Sertraline, Paroxetine and Venlafaxine in Refugee Post Traumatic Stress Disorder with Depression Symptoms. *Journal of Traumatic Stress. 14(3)*, 445-452.

Smajkic, A., Weine, S., Duric-Bijedic, Z., Lacevic, A., Lewis, J., & Pavkovic, I. (2000). Discontinuation of SSRI's in traumatized refugees. *Med Arh, 54(2)*, 111-3.

Sonis, J. (1999). Bosnian Refugee Survivors of Torture in Primary Care [Abstract] *Final Program and Proceedings of the International Society for Traumatic Stress Studies 15th Annual Meeting*, USA.

Sourander, A. (2003). Refugee families during asylum seeking. *Nordic Journal of Psychiatry, 57(3)*, 203-7.

Turner, S.W., Bowie, C., Dunn, G., Shapo, L., & Yule, W. (2003). Mental Health of Kosovan Albanian refugees in the UK. *British Journal of Psychiatry, 182*, 444-8.

United Nations High Commision for Refugees (2002) Global Report 2001, Retrieved on March 31, 2004 at http://www.unhcr.ch/cgi-bin/texis/vtx/home.

van der Veer, G. (1992). *Counseling and therapy with refugees*. Chichester: John Wiley & Sons.

Waldman R (1999). *Psychosocial effects of complex emergencies: symposium report.* Washington, DC: The American Red Cross.

Walsh, F. (1998). Strengthening family resilience. New York and London, The Guilford Press.

Watson, C.G., Davenport, E., Anderson, P.E., Mendez, C.M., & Gearhart, L.P. (1998). The relationships between premilitary school record data and risk for posttraumatic stress disorder among Vietnam war veterans. *Journal of Nervous and Mental Disease, 186(6)*, 38-44.

Weine, S. M. (1998). A prevention and access intervention for survivor families. Grant proposal to the National Institute of Mental Health. (RO1 MH59573-01).

_____. (1999). Services Based Research for Refugee Families. Grant proposal to the National Institute of Mental Health (K01 MH02048-01).

Weine, S.M. (1999). *When History is a Nightmare: Lives and Memories of Ethnic Cleansing in Bosnia-Herzegovina.* New Brunswick and London: Rutgers University Press.

Weine, S.M., Kuc, E., Dzudza, E., Razzano, L., & Pavkovic, I. (2001). PTSD among Bosnian refugees: a survey of providers' knowledge, attitudes and service patterns. *Journal of Community Mental Health, 37(3),* 261-271.

Weine, S. M., Kulenovic, T., Dzubur, A., Pavkovic, I, & Gibbons, R. (1998). Testimony psychotherapy in Bosnian refugees: A pilot study. *American Journal of Psychiatry, 155,* 1720-1726.

Weine, S.M., Razzano, L., Miller, K., Brkic, N., Ramic, A., Smajkic, A., Bijedic, Z, et al. (2000). Profiling the trauma related symptoms of Bosnian refugees who have not sought mental health services. *Journal of Nervous and Mental Diseases. 188(7),* 416-421.

Weine, S. M., Vojvoda, D., Becker, D., McGlashan, T., Hodzic, E., Laub, D., & Hyman, L., et al. (1998). PTSD symptoms in Bosnian refugees One year after resettlement , *American Journal of Psychiatry, 155 (4),* 562-564.

Wells, J.E., Robins, L.N., Bushnell, J.A., Jarosz, D., Oakley-Browne, M.A. (1994). Perceived barriers to care in St. Louis (USA) and Christchurch (NZ): reasons for not seeking professional help for psychological distress. *Social Psychiatry and Psychiatric Epidemiology, 29,* 155-164.

Wells K. (1987). Which Mexican-Americans Underutilize Health Services? *American Journal of Psychiatry, 144,* 918-922.

Westen, D. (1997). Divergences between clinical and research methods for assessing personality disorders: Implications for research and evolution of axis II. *American Journal of Psychiatry, 154(7),* 895-903.

Westermeyer, J. (1991). Frameworks of Mental Health Services. In Westermeyer, J., Williams, C.L., & Nguyen, A.N. (Eds). *Mental Health Services for Refugees* Washington, D.C.: U.S. Government Printing Office

Westermeyer J. (1991). Models of Mental Health Services. In Westermeyer, J., Williams, C.L., & Nguyen, A.N. (Eds). *Mental Health Services for Refugees.* Washington, D.C.: U.S. Government Printing Office.

Yamamoto, J. (1978). Research priorities in Asian-American mental health delivery. *American Journal of Psychiatry, 135,* 457-458.

In: Trends in Posttraumatic Stress Disorder Research   ISBN 1-59454-135-3
Editor: Thomas A. Corales, pp. 185-205   © 2005 Nova Science Publishers, Inc.

Chapter 8

BRIEF THERAPY OF POSTTRAUMATIC STRESS DISORDER IN REFUGEES[*]

Sara Nieves-Grafals

Clinical Psychologist Independent Practice Washington, D.C.

ABSTRACT

Posttraumatic stress disorder is frequently seen among refugees who have been exposed to violence. Delayed onset following migration triggers recurrent nightmares, flashbacks, emotional detachment, and difficulty trusting others. Some people suffer from a pattern of alcoholism, family violence, and somatic illness that is rooted in traumatization. Long-term therapy is rarely practical for overwhelmed clients with multiple needs. This chapter describes an eclectic brief treatment that takes into account cultural factors. The importance of psychodiagnostic assessment is explored. A 4-stage treatment process involving specific tools is described. Contraindications for short-term therapy are also outlined.

INTRODUCTION

The United Nations High Commissioner for Refugees (2002) reported that about one out of every 300 people on our planet is a refugee. Bolton (2003) described how widespread trauma prior to migration places refugees at risk for developing posttraumatic stress disorder (PTSD.) Momartin, et al (2003) documented traumatic sequelae in Bosnian people in exile following migration to Australia. Sabin, et al (2003) noted poor mental health among Guatemalans living in Mexico 20 years after civil conflict. Similar results were noted for Somali immigrants residing in the United Kingdom following trauma-related migration (Bhui, et al, 2003). Yet despite these realities, few research articles have focused on therapy of PTSD with refugees.

---

[*] This chapter is an expanded version based on Nieves-Grafals, S. (2001) Brief Therapy of Civil-War Related Trauma: A Case Study. *Cultural Diversity and Ethnic Minority Psychology*, 7, 387-398.

Understanding the cultural context can help clarify what reactions are related to cross-cultural adaptation and what symptomatology warrants treatment (Alarcón & Foulks, 1995; Comas-Díaz & Jacobsen, 1987; Jenkins, 1996).Therapy that takes into account these factors can work quickly (Macksoud, Aber & Cohn, 1996). Otherwise, the risks of therapeutic failure, non-compliance and drop-out increase. In this chapter, a step-wise approach to brief therapy with refugees is described.

BRIEF THERAPY OF PTSD

A number of brief therapy methods have been used to treat PTSD: dynamic psychotherapy (Marmar, 1991), pharmacotherapy (Friedman, 1998; Hertzberg et al, 1999) supportive work (Prout & Schwarz, 1991), thought control (Warda & Bryant, 1998), eye movement desensitization reprocessing or EMDR (Cahill, Carrigan & Frueh, 1999; McNally 1999; Poole, De Jongh & Spector, 1999; Shapiro, 1989, 1997), and psychosocial treatments (Hembree & Foa, 2003).

Because families provide a natural support network, treatment involving this grouping has received attention (Brende & Goldsmith, 1991; Craine, Hanks, & Stevens, 1992; Miller, 1999; Rabin & Nardi, 1991). Ariel (1999) advocates culturally sensitive family therapy. A combination of didactic and cognitive-behavioral strategies has also been used successfully with trauma survivors individually (Matsakis, 1992), in groups (Lubin, Loris, Burt & Johnson, 1998) and in combination with pharmacotherapy (Otto et al, 2003).

Some mental health professionals have developed culture-specific techniques to treat Latinos. For example, PTSD survivors of natural disasters have benefited from the Mexican technique based on EMDR called the butterfly hug (Jarero, 2001). Chilean psychotherapists developed *testimonios* (Aresti, 1988; Doerr-Zegers, Hartmann, Lira & Weinstein, 1992) to help reintegrate traumatic memories and their significance into the person's identity. The present therapy model combines elements from a number of the aforementioned traditions and applies them to PTSD in a culturally familiar context.

Basics of the Brief Therapy Model

In the present chapter, psychodiagnostic methods used with refugees are outlined (Nieves-Grafals, 1995), followed by a description of a 4-stage treatment model (Nieves-Grafals, 2001). Core factors in the therapeutic process involve: (a) quickly promoting a therapeutic alliance from the initial contact, (b) teaching self-soothing and anxiety reduction skills, (c) confronting traumatic memories, (d) intense re-processing, when necessary, (e) integration of the experience into the person's identity, and (f) relapse prevention.

Because the client's own support network is more powerful than any therapist's interventions, care is taken to enlist the help of that group in treatment, whenever possible. So individual, family or couple's therapy is employed. Fifty minute weekly sessions are used with one exception. When Eye Movement Desensitization Reprocessing (EMDR) treatment occurs, 90 minute sessions are usually employed to allow enough time for catharsis and containment. In the termination phase, sessions may be biweekly or even monthly to gradually end therapy and allow for consolidation of gains. In contrast to traditional approaches where termination is final, indefinite availability to the client in times of need is advocated.

While techniques are important, the quality of the therapeutic relationship is a key ingredient in assuring a positive outcome. Because traumatized refugees have suffered human rights violations, regaining the capacity to trust another human being may be the single most important goal of this type of therapy. Reconnecting to others is a sign of healing and recovery from psychological trauma.

Psychological Testing and Diagnosis of PTSD in Refugees

Although PTSD is widespread in refugee populations, its diagnosis is difficult because the syndrome can remain hidden, or misdiagnosed. Refugees are survivors who thrive on problem-solving. Few dwell on past events. Many have adapted to exposure to violence, since they have had to survive life in a civil war zone. As a result, when refugees are asked about traumatic experiences the response is characteristically a denial. Violence becomes a normal part of daily life in a civil war zone, and unless a survivor is specifically asked (e.g., "Have you lost a family member or friend due to the civil war in your homeland?") important clinical material rarely emerges. It is wise not to rule out PTSD based on this initial denial of traumatic exposure (Davidson & Connor, 1999).

Psychological testing is a useful tool in diagnosing PTSD in refugees. The use of the Rorschach in the assessment of PTSD has been reported in the literature (Frueh et al, 1995; Goldfinger, Amdur & Liberzon, 1998; Holaday, 2000; Levin, Lazrove, & Van der Kolk, 1999). Some reports have specifically focused on culturally diverse clients (Munczek & Tuber, 1998; Nieves-Grafals, 1995).

In this model, testing is used when diagnostic issues are unclear. After cognitive and projective testing using the Rorschach is administered, a clinical interview takes place. Conducting the interview at the end helps the clinician investigate issues that have surfaced during the testing. Also, testing fatigue lowers defenses so the client is likely to be less guarded in making disclosures. Manifestations of PTSD on projective data include images of blood, violence, dismembered bodies as well as percepts mentioning maps and geographical allusions to the person's homeland (Nieves-Grafals, 1995). If these signs are present, questioning to rule-out PTSD takes place.

The author has seen many clients suffering from visual illusions —often associated with blood or dismembered bodies they saw during the war. These memories are engraved in the person's nervous system and surface in frightening images. In a number of cases, refugees have erroneously been diagnosed as schizophrenic, when in reality symptoms stemmed from PTSD. With psychotherapy for PTSD, symptoms have remitted. In some cases, brief pharmacotherapy has also been helpful. While this clinical observation merits empirical investigation, it should be kept in mind in working with refugees that often psychotic-like manifestations of PTSD do not stem from major psychiatric disorders. Psychological testing is especially helpful in making this difficult differential diagnosis, as illustrated in the case that follows.

Clinical Case Using Psychological Testing

Mr. V is a 28 year old single man who comes from a war-torn region in Central America. He is an inpatient at a forensic psychiatric unit. The client was admitted to determine his competency to stand trial following charges of stealing food from a restaurant. On admission, Mr. V presented with paranoid ideation, insomnia and disorientation. He appeared to be responding to visual hallucinations. Nursing staff reported particular concern about the patient's refusal to take a shower, especially since ten days had elapsed since hospitalization. Other residents complained about his body odor.

The patient is monolingual in Spanish, a factor that made communication with him especially problematic for the staff, since no one spoke Spanish. Referral for psychodiagnostic testing in Spanish included a request to evaluate his competency, cognitive capacity and emotional functioning. The treatment team asked for a differential diagnosis between a brief psychotic disorder versus schizophrenia.

Mr. V, a thin man about 5'7 in stature, waited in the testing office on the ward. I entered with my testing briefcase in hand. Immediately, his eyes widened and he retreated in a panic, as if I was coming to hurt him. I realized that in his homeland, women are routinely used to interrogate political prisoners and even torture them, since they are perceived as less intimidating. What to me was a harmless testing kit may have represented hidden torture tools. I quickly opened up the case and showed him the blocks and puzzles, reassuring him that I had come to help him. We chatted in Spanish about the weather and food on the ward, taking time to develop a working relationship before embarking on the task at hand.

Because Mr. V came from a rural area in his country, I assumed that he had a limited formal education. Thus no reading or writing would take place in the assessment.

He confirmed that he had completed only the first grade. His parents stopped sending him to school when his teacher was gunned down during class for his political beliefs.

Testing using the Spanish WAIS (1996) took place. The Digit Symbol and Object Assembly subtests were not used. A Bender-Gestalt, Human Figure Drawings and Rorschach were also administered. Images of blood, dismembered bodies, people getting hurt and references of his homeland pervaded the projective testing protocol.

The clinical interview revealed that Mr. V had farmed in his country to help his parents to support his seven siblings. The family lived in a village where intense warfare had taken place. Gunshots were common at night. On several occasions, the family awoke to find corpses of fellow villagers on the road in front of their house. At times, people had been dismembered. The corpses were left to rot in the heat because no one would claim them for fear that they would be branded as co-conspirators and executed too.

One day, Mr. V found out that one of his uncles had been captured. He went to the police station looking for him. The next day, he was incarcerated. Mr. V was interrogated and tortured, using scalding water. During his detention, he heard the screams of other people as they were tormented by interrogators. After nine months, Mr. V was released and told to leave the country, or he would be killed.

Based on clinical and historical data, the patient's reactions during the session and test data, it became clear that Mr. V was suffering a brief reactive episode of stress induced psychosis. Mr. V suffered from visual illusions related to what he witnessed in his homeland.

His refusal to take a shower on the ward was reformulated as stemming from a combination of survival instinct as well as cultural factors. First, Mr. V had been tortured with scalding water. Traumatic experiences activate survival strategies where the person resolves to avoid exposure to the stimuli that have hurt them in the past. This is an adaptive mechanism that was working well for Mr. V—a sign of resilience. Secondly, Mr. V came from a rural village that lacked running water. People bathed in the river. His unfamiliarity with water coming out of a wall coupled with his association to pain made the sight of steaming water coming out of a pipe seem like a tool of torture. With this understanding in mind, nursing staff worked with Mr. V to use a washcloth and a bucket of tepid water to clean himself in a setting that he deemed safe. Cultural factors and traumatization related to torture explained what had been initially diagnosed as stemming from schizophrenia. Treatment methods would be quite different in both instances, illustrating the importance of clear diagnosis before embarking in treatment.

Brief Therapy Contraindications

When there are serious comorbid disorders, such as borderline personality disorder, or schizophrenia, only stages 1 and 2 of the present treatment model are recommended. Severe pre-existing psychiatric disorders can be exacerbated during the third phase of treatment—reprocessing the trauma— and therefore this is contraindicated. For instance, reactivation of early childhood trauma may result in regression. The present treatment is best used when the patient had a reasonably stable level of functioning prior to exposure to trauma.

For clients who use alcohol and/or drugs, it will be important to work in substance abuse treatment and reach a reasonably stable level of sobriety (about six months) prior to becoming involved in trauma work. Likewise, in families that engage in violence, this symptom needs to be targeted first with anger management and conflict resolution work prior to embarking on therapy for PTSD.

Therapeutic Goals

Refugees tend to be strong people with adaptive capacities that have helped them to save their lives. Through repeated traumatization, the person's resilience has diminished to the point of becoming symptomatic. The therapist needs to find out what methods the client used in the past to survive. Therapy aims to reinforce existing coping skills, nurture the re-emergence of dormant survival strategies and teach new methods of dealing with stress.

The therapist helps the client to regain the ability to trust. Frequently, civil war victims have been hurt by the inhumane actions of people who have caused them to lose the world that they knew. Distrust is an understandable reaction. Clients begin to believe that they are very vulnerable and therefore people will take advantage of them. The negative belief "I am a victim" becomes modified through a positive partnership with the therapist. Instead of engaging in self-protective social withdrawal, the goal is to help the client to use good judgment in deciding whom to trust rather than to refrain from developing attachments. As the capacity for human connection reemerges, the therapist encourages the client to develop a support system.

The therapist endeavors to help reduce barriers to the individual's capacity to function to full potential. One crucial barrier is a lack of familiarity with cultural norms. For example, a client feared that she would be evicted from her apartment because she paid her rent five days after the due date. Ms. D lay awake at night, anticipating that the landlord would throw her belongings on the street any day. An explanation regarding the "grace period" for payment and with laws that protect renters was all the intervention that she needed. Her insomnia remitted immediately. Because the therapist acts as a bridge to the client's adoptive country, a sound knowledge of the client's cultural norms is critical in expediting this adaptation process as well as preventing unnecessary distress.

As soon as symptoms remit and the client has started to develop a support system, client and therapist assess readiness for termination. Once termination takes place, it is not considered final. Unlike traditional termination where client and therapist bid each other goodbye permanently, the author continues to be available to clients indefinitely —much like a small town family doctor. After sessions have ended, the therapeutic connection acts as an invisible safety net that will allow the patient to seek therapy, should the need arise again.

In general, goals of this model are:

- Reduce symptoms as quickly as possible
- Reinforce existing coping skills
- Nurture the reemergence of dormant survival strategies
- Teach new methods of dealing with stress
- Help regain the capacity to trust people
- Foster development of a strong support system
- Expedite adaptation to the host country
- Reduce barriers to the individual's capacity to function to his full potential
- Establish a therapeutic bond that will facilitate future therapy, if needed

STAGE I: BUILDING AN ALLIANCE

Therapy begins with the initial contact. This could mean the telephone conversation where the appointment is scheduled. The telephone contact provides a useful opportunity to begin working on the relationship and teaching the client about therapy. Time and location of the meeting are discussed with sensitivity to the fact that the client may not yet be familiar with the city or locale. Clients are told that the hour is reserved for them and that they will not have to wait. This is helpful in fostering compliance and reducing the possibility of late arrivals. Many people assume that they will wait to be seen for an extended period of time based on past experiences in a doctor's office. In some countries clients are simply seen on a drop-in basis, or on a first-come, first-served system. A client accustomed to that type of system assumes that an appointment time is meaningless. Thus, the telephone contact allows the therapist to explain to the client what is expected to avoid misunderstandings and conflicting expectations. Clarification of parameters—time frames, geographic location—helps the client to feel nurtured and guided. This immediately sets the stage for a positive connection with the therapist.

During the first two sessions, the therapist works very actively to prevent premature drop-out by engaging the client. In contrast to traditional therapy where a listening stance is preferred, an active and involved therapist is reassuring for refugees. A silent professional is generally experienced as distant and uncaring. This can activate the client's distrust and scare them away from treatment. Instead, clients need to feel that the practitioner is involved and open about their thoughts and motives. This openness includes sharing emotional reactions, such as laughing with the client or showing empathic concern through nonverbal behavior as well.

The office setting is also an important aspect of engaging the client and fostering a sense of safety. A lady who had been raped during migration tentatively walked into the office. She took a long look around the room and sank into the sofa, placing a decorative pillow on her lap. With a broad smile, she said: "I feel safe here". It is not uncommon for people to comment on the physical appearance of the office and express their reactions. With clients coming from civil war zones, visual assessment of a situation is a key survival strategy. War survivors learn to reveal little information verbally given the danger of being accused of subversive activity. Instead, visual scanning of situations alerts them to danger. Communicating safety is done by providing an inviting, home-like office setting.

Cross-Cultural Social Norms in Engaging Clients

Many clients have said that their parents and grandparents would counsel them during childhood not to say anything about the family. One young lady recalled how her classmates in El Salvador remained mute when the teacher asked them to say what their parents did for a living. Fearing that the parents would be endangered, the children assumed protective silence, while communicating with each other non-verbally. Thus expecting clients to be self-revealing upon meeting the therapist is unrealistic. Taking the time to reduce anxiety by following socially appropriate approaches will let the client slowly asses the therapist and the safety of revealing information.

Formal respect, yet nurturing warmth need to be communicated to the client. The therapist should be familiar with culturally appropriate greetings. For most cultures, first names are only used amongst family members. So calling a stranger by the first name can be perceived as disrespectful, rather than friendly. South Americans, Puerto Ricans, Cubans and Dominicans will generally prefer to be called by the title and last name or by *Don* or *Doña* and the first name if the person is older. People from Spanish-speaking countries normally have two last names. The first last name is the father's surname, and the second is the mother's last name. Both should be used when referring to a client.

Likewise, the therapist should become familiar with gestures that are used for greetings. A bow or nod, rather than a handshake would be appropriate when greeting a Chinese client. In Brazil, women will kiss each other, and a limp handshake is the norm in the Philippines. Taking the time to learn about these social norms is very important as it conveys understanding and fosters the development of a good working alliance.

Familiarity with thinking style in different countries is also an important ingredient. It can mean the difference between developing good rapport and scaring a client away from treatment if they feel misunderstood, pushed or rushed. In the United States, people value efficiency and speed in delivering services. Thus information is provided by getting to the crux of the matter immediately and then expanding on the subject. In Southern Europe, Latin America and Africa, training involves the opposite cognitive style. Students are encouraged to lay the ground work of a concept and gradually work towards the core idea. A good exposition of ideas will guide the listener to reach core conclusions later in the discourse.

A pyramid model helps to clarify the two world views. In the US thinking style, the tip of the pyramid is reached first: the core idea (see Figure 1). Subsequently, related subjects are explained. The European/Latin/African style inverts the pyramid (see Figure 2), so that the general thoughts are explained first—the foundation— and finally the core concepts are reached. Why are these distinctions important? Clients from other countries need time to present the therapist with the full picture of why they came for treatment, rather than reaching the bottom-line in a matter of minutes. A therapist trained in the US style will instinctively ask key questions of the client immediately. This can cause the client to become guarded and spend more time laying the groundwork before revealing crucial information. A mismatch of cognitive worlds can trigger premature drop-out. Awareness of these differences in cognitive worlds can help the therapist to slow down the questioning, while allowing the natural process to unfold. When clients are pushed, defenses will increase and cognitive disorganization will block progress in therapy. Paradoxically, if the client is allowed to develop their story using the inverted pyramid approach, therapeutic goals will be reached more quickly.

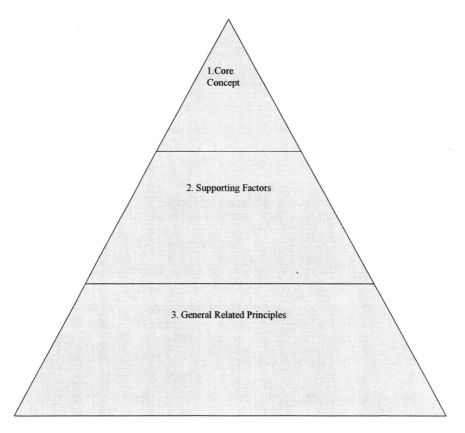

Figure 1. Cognitive Style in the United States

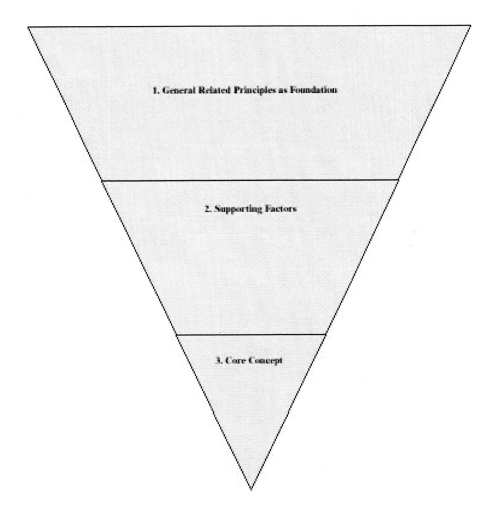

Figure 2. Latin/Southern European/African Cognitive Style

PSYCHOTHERAPY PROGRESSION

Session #1

A supportive/didactic orientation is important in seeking the client's collaboration. In teaching the client about PTSD and the fact that it is very treatable, hope is encouraged. Regaining hope is an integral component of healing.

It is also important to anticipate discomfort, so that people do not abandon the therapeutic process prematurely. During the first meeting, the client is warned that it is common to feel worse after the first two sessions because painful memories have been explored. Teaching the person that re-experiencing pain precedes healing can also be reassuring. Otherwise, the client may simply abandon therapy because they feel worse after sessions: "Why should I bother talking to the therapist if I end up crying every time I see her?"

During the first session, the therapist listens for couple or family themes and decides whether an individual, couple's or family approach makes the most sense. A general rule of thumb is that whenever there is one family member who is suffering, the whole family is likely in distress as well. Whenever possible, working in a family context helps members to support each other's growth and grieving. Otherwise, the focus on the traumatization may prove disruptive to family members who may still be working on the "it's best to forget" principle. At the end of the session, the client is given a homework assignment of formulating goals to pursue if therapy is to begin. In essence, the goals for the first session include:

- Address expectations and assumptions
- Help regain hope
- Communicate an understanding of the client's cultural framework
- Reduce anxiety about psychotherapy
- Teach about PTSD
- Establish a trusting relationship
- Anticipate obstacles to active participation in therapy
- Homework assignment: request client's therapeutic goals.

Session #2

Assessment concludes during the second session and treatment recommendations are discussed. The therapist also aims to seek the client's active involvement. Reactions to the first session are elicited to help tailor the intervention to the client's needs and to prevent premature termination by quickly addressing concerns. For example, if the client expresses guilt about having complained about family members, slower pacing and balancing of information may be indicated so that the person is not scared away. Realistic goals and time frames are discussed. The screening process is completed and —when diagnostic questions remain unanswered—referral for psychological assessment is done. Frequently a Rorschach is administered at this time to make certain that the person does not have severe comorbid conditions that would make the short-term intervention contraindicated. Once there is a clear sense that the person and/or family suffers from uncomplicated PTSD, specific recommendations about appropriate therapeutic modes are made. A verbal contract is agreed upon, usually for ten sessions with the option of an additional ten if needed. Therefore, during the second session the key points to target are:

- Explore reactions to the initial session
- Assess resiliency
- Discuss the homework assignment: the client's goals
- Determine motivation for treatment
- Gauge appropriate pacing for the client
- Refer for psychological testing, if needed
- Formulate diagnostic picture

- Discuss applicable therapeutic modes
- Contract for short-term therapy

STAGE II: CONTAINING THE PAIN AND STRENGTHENING COPING SKILLS

Beginning on the third session, clients are taught how to self-soothe and manage anxiety. This stage of treatment can take between one and four sessions, depending on the client. Unless a client is able to self-soothe and return to a reasonably calm state after confronting painful material, the use of destructive familiar coping skills may surface. This can include acting-out. Therefore working actively to teach healthy coping skills is crucial in fostering healing. As is normally done in the Eye Movement Desensitization Reprocessing—EMDR— protocol (Shapiro, 1989, 1997), the therapist prepares the client to cope with painful and potentially disorganizing affect. The therapist enlists the "survivor self" in the work by eliciting a history of how the client managed to handle stressful situations in the past. Strengths are validated. Often clients take for granted heroic efforts made in emergency situations without recognizing their own stamina. It is helpful and reinforcing to stress the person's coping ability and their potential to use those skills in the future.

Because clients are used to the medical model, they often expect a prescription that will heal them. They want to know how what steps to take so that they can begin feel better. Instead of discouraging this expectation, the therapist uses this motivation for guidance to teach tools that provide some degree of immediate symptom relief. The techniques come from different approaches —mostly cognitive therapies.

Brief self-soothing strategies such as EMDR's "safe place" exercise and the "butterfly hug" are used. Thought-field Therapy (TFT) —a Chinese acupressure based technique developed by Roger Callahan —is also helpful in anxiety reduction. The client taps on a series of points on the body while concentrating on the anxiety-provoking imagery (Callahan, 1995, 1997, Folkes, 2002, Wylie, 1996).

In the "safe place" imagery, the client is asked to think of a place that they associate with peace and tranquility. The person is guided through making the "safe place" real by noticing sensory details like the sounds, colors and scents. Mental visits to this soothing image twice per day between sessions are encouraged. Invariably the setting of the "safe place" changes as treatment progresses. For example, a 24 year old client spoke of her bed as the only safe place that she could think of. She had been assaulted by an acquaintance and also witnessed a violent explosion in her neighborhood during the civil war in her country. As she processed these traumatic images, her safe place evolved to include more of the outside world. Towards the end of treatment, she visualized walking outdoors and feeling safe.

A technique that has been helpful because of its simplicity and soothing effects is the "butterfly hug". In 1997, following a hurricane in Acapulco, Mexico, EMDR practitioner Lucina Artigas (Jarero, 2002) developed this technique. Bilateral stimulation coupled with a self-affirming statement produces a calming response. It is also possible for one family member to apply this technique to another. The client crosses the arms gently over the chest with each hand patting the opposite shoulder alternately in rapid succession, like the wings of a butterfly. Other places in the body such as the knees, thighs, or arms could be used instead.

The person repeats a calming statement such as "I have gone through difficult periods and I have managed to overcome them. I will be fine" or "I am safe", or simply the word "peace", until relaxation takes place. This technique is also used to foster sleep in people who suffer from insomnia and/or nightmares. Because it is easily learned and it can be used anywhere, clients have found it helpful.

Chinese acupressure methods inspired California psychologist Roger Callahan to develop Thought Field Therapy (TFT). Families can perform this calming procedure along with the therapist who demonstrates it by self-tapping on specific pressure points described in a protocol, such as the eyebrow, under the eye and index finger. Prior to tapping, the client rates the level of anxiety related to a particular image on a scale from one to ten —with ten being extreme distress. While concentrating on the stressor, the tapping is done and repeated until the level of emotional discomfort decreases to a level of 2 or 3. This exercise helps clients to gain control of their symptoms when they see how easily they can lower their anxiety in a matter of minutes. The method is also helpful in groups. While no one really knows how or why it works, clients often conclude that they feel better because they have been distracted — even though in reality they are instructed to concentrate on the discomfort. Practically speaking, it has been a helpful tool, regardless of its unknown mechanism of action.

If one of the anxiety symptoms involves ruminating about the past or worrying, recommending "worry periods" is helpful. Clients are instructed to spend scheduled periods of time (between 15 and 20 minutes per day) actively worrying. When concerns crop up during the day, they are deferred to the "worry period". Clients report that this helps to free them while they are trying to accomplish other goals. Frequently, people become bored with the worry periods and unable to worry during the time set aside. Slowly this extinguishes the debilitating symptom.

Another approach that targets worrying involves the use of folk approaches. For instance, Guatemalan paper-clip size "worry dolls" are entrusted with particular concerns on behalf of the owner. The client is instructed to assign a worry to each doll while placing them on the night table prior to sleeping. The dolls "worry" while the owner gets a peaceful night sleep. Native Americans have used worry stones for centuries (Jones & Jones, 1995). The Irish worry stone and Greek worry beads serve the same purpose. The person rubs a small marble stone or beads in a necklace to "release" anxiety. The key is to identify the concern and use a folk instrument to dissociate the issue and free up the sufferer's emotional energy, albeit temporarily.

After clients gain some mastery of anxiety reduction and containments techniques, they are ready to deal with painful traumatic material. The decision to proceed to the next stage of therapy is made jointly. In families, there may be a variety of levels of readiness. Stronger family members are enlisted to help support those who may not be as resilient.

In summary, during the second stage therapy will:

- Reinforce existing constructive coping skills
- Teach self-soothing tools: "safe place" exercise, TFT, "butterfly hug"
- Use folk approaches, such as worry dolls or worry beads, for containment of negative affect
- Determine readiness to confront traumatic material

STAGE III: DEALING WITH THE TRAUMA

During this stage, clients need to be ready to experience and express emotional suffering. Sometimes families become alarmed when one member cries. In fact, one way in which people console each other is to say "Don't cry". The therapist anticipates this and explains that tears are "natural medicine" which provides relief. This instruction prevents blockage of the cathartic process through the client's attempts "to be strong" by not crying.

For some Latin American clients, common wisdom communicated by generations involves hiding painful experiences from the children. This often results in not preparing youngsters to deal with separations. A common occurrence during civil wars involved the need for parents to migrate —often through risky clandestine means— to escape political persecution. Children would wake up one day to find the mother or father missing. Reunification frequently took years. During therapy sessions, family members would often talk for the first time of the painful separation process. Resentments, feelings of abandonment and guilt would invariably surface. Therapists need to be aware of these themes and ready to deal with potentially conflict-ridden and distressing family sessions.

Some families gradually piece together traumatic recollections. However, in other instances people abruptly want to open up all the material that they have been processing in silence. Clients should be protected from overwhelming themselves and their families if they want to deal with too much material too quickly. The therapist slows down the process by reinforcing the effort and breaking it down into manageable pieces. Journaling or audio taping the account between sessions is sometimes used to aid in the processing, but a maximum daily time limit spent on this activity —15 to 30 minutes— is indicated so clients will not be consumed by the process.

Sometimes it is enough to let the clients tell about their horrifying experiences of violence and torture. Family members cry together, validating each others' recollections. Sometimes this "testimonial" process alone helps restore the person or family to a healthier level of functioning. Quickly people begin to speak in amazement about all they went through, while valuing their present safety and strength. In these cases, relief occurs quickly —within two or three sessions. Clients are ready to proceed to termination.

Frequently, recurrent memories of the trauma become more intense and re-processing is needed. EMDR, a method of desensitization used to treat PTSD (Shapiro, 1989, 1997), is employed either individually or within a family or couple's session. Depending on the wishes of the individual who is to undergo the processing, other family members may be present.

Children are not present during the processing. In cases where the children are plagued by fears, one parent asks the child to talk about the source of distress while gently stimulating the child bilaterally by playing hand slapping or tapping of the knees. Depending on the response, one, two, or three EMDR sessions may be used.

Processing of traumatic material is usually stopped ten minutes before the end of the session to allow for closing and containment. Exercises involving cognitive imagery and/or self-soothing along with reinforcement for the work accomplished provide some closure between sessions. Participants are warned not to be alarmed if they are fatigued for up to three days following the sessions. They are encouraged to get more sleep than usual during this healing stage. Clients are also instructed to participate in at least one recreational activity between sessions and to do something positive for themselves at least once daily. Examples of activities include: reading a book, doing nothing for ten minutes, taking a walk, soaking in a bubble bath, listening to music, cooking a special meal, visiting a friend. After the first EMDR session, clients are encouraged to call the therapist the next day to report how they are. This supportive measure helps to assess the client's resilience for treatment planning purposes. If an extra session is needed shortly thereafter, it is scheduled at that time.

Part of helping people to regain control of their lives following trauma, involves the ability to self assess. This includes an awareness of feelings and reactions. Throughout therapy, the client is asked to verbalize how they feel. This practice helps the person to judge readiness for termination. During the eighth session —sometimes earlier— progress is assessed by reviewing presenting symptoms. The decision to proceed with termination or to contract for additional sessions is made. From experiences with this population, positive symptoms, i.e., those that involve hyperarousal and re-experiencing of the event such as nightmares and flashbacks, recede quickly as the client devotes attention to the traumatic material directly. Negative symptoms, i.e., those that involve avoidance and isolation, need more direct intervention than the processing of the trauma as they become a part of the person's defensive make-up. Thus the efforts to rebuild a network are an important indicator of readiness for termination.

Summing up, during the third stage of treatment, the client will:

- Express emotions in connection with traumatic memories
- Revisit traumatic events using testimonials and/or journaling
- When necessary, use EMDR
- Seek support and additional rest following processing of traumatic material
- Self-soothe and use containment exercises to end sessions
- Alternate processing sessions with meetings aimed at consolidating gains
- Engage in recreation and good self-care
- Call the therapist the day after processing to help assess resilience
- Seek contact with outsiders
- Become involved in social activities, such as classes, church or community events
- Integrate positive learning from the traumatic experiences
- Evaluate progress
- Proceed with termination

Termination

Because the therapist is a consultant who aims to remove obstacles to healthy functioning, the ultimate goal of treatment is to become obsolete. In the last number of sessions, clarification of therapeutic gains is made. Although traumatic events are undoubtedly distressing, their growth-promoting effects are acknowledged. When clients recognize that they have gained emotional strength and wisdom from trauma, they signal readiness to work on termination.

If the client took undue responsibility for the traumatization, this needs to be re-visited. If a person indeed bears some of the blame for what happened —as is seen with victims/perpetrators—who tortured others for fear of reprisal, they can be assisted to make plans for reparation. A plan to perform community service or other ways of contributing to society can help with the healing. For people who are religious, spiritual means of atonement can hasten the healing process. For example, clients who are Catholic have availed themselves of the sacrament of Confession and absolution. This ritual is immensely helpful in putting past guilt to rest, as well as in devising a method of reparation.

Natural developmental milestones in adulthood can cause relapse. Transition periods such as relocation, divorce, death of loved ones, the anniversary of migration, retirement and return visits to the homeland can be stressful. Predicting stress points can prevent a recurrence of symptoms. Clients are prepared to take special measures during those times to allow for renewed surfacing of traumatic material. Examples of preventive measures include: awareness of the connection between current events and past trauma, additional social support, recreation, journaling, involvement in goal-oriented activities and use of self-soothing exercises.

During the termination phase, goals are to:

- Assess goals reached during the brief therapy
- Consolidate stress reduction tools
- Integrate traumatic events into personal history
- Incorporate good self-care into lifestyle
- Learn to recognize and anticipate stress triggers
- Distinguish the difference between normal mourning and depression, or PTSD
- Plan for future transition periods so they do not produce relapse
- Develop long-term goals to pursue following termination

Over the years, there are points in life where past trauma may be activated, despite the client's best preventive work. A client may wish to participate in two or three therapy sessions as a "booster shot". Addressing material that may not have been fully worked out and strengthening coping techniques may be very beneficial. In some instances, follow-up contact has involved long-term treatment. Sometimes traumatic issues lie dormant over years despite therapy, only to surface with external triggers, as was the case with the following client.

Clinical Case Involving Reactivation of Trauma

Identifying Data and Reason for Referral

Reverend B, a 44 year old Catholic priest from South America, sought treatment ten years after termination of brief therapy for politically motivated trauma. During his initial treatment with the therapist, he had worked through nightmares, distrust of people and pervasive anxiety following incarceration in his homeland for his teachings. Upon termination, the client had been symptom-free. He had been living in a religious community and teaching in an elementary school in the United States.

Ten years later, he called with a chief complaint of nightmares accompanied by irritability, flashbacks, distrust of people, short-term memory difficulties, poor concentration, anxiety, social withdrawal and insomnia. The precipitating event involved participation in a religious retreat that focused on sexual abuse by the clergy. Following the retreat, Reverend B became focused on reading and hearing about sexual abuse cases. He realized that he had been sexually abused by a priest when he was an adolescent.

When he was 13 years old, Reverend B had served as an altar boy in his parish. A priest had befriended him. The client was very happy with the attention, especially given that his own father had died two years earlier. Reverend B wept as he confessed that on two occasions, he performed oral sex on his mentor. Although he had recalled the incident, he realized that he had convinced himself that he had exaggerated its meaning. But exposure to the subject over three days during the retreat made him recognize that he had been abused. Shame, fear of exposing the older priest and guilt over his own role in the sexual contact made him shy away from confronting it years earlier.

Course of Treatment

Therapy was resumed, with the understanding that it would be open-ended since childhood abuse was involved. The impact of the trauma had impacted Reverend B's character. Thus brief therapy would not be appropriate. Reverend B recognized that he had distrusted people and remained distant from them, especially authority figures, due to anxiety that he would be victimized.

Therapy included sessions detailing the abuse, journaling, and EMDR sessions where Reverend B focused on negative beliefs about himself that he had developed in connection with the abuse. For example, he believed that he was an evil person because of the trauma. Specifically, Reverend B felt that his mouth was unclean and he developed dental pain. During EMDR sessions, he realized that he had blamed himself for what happened. He acknowledged that as a 13 year old youngster who was going through mourning for the loss of his father, he craved paternal attention. It had been difficult for him to believe that a clergyman could take advantage of a child. Reverend B had chastised himself for not protecting himself from his mentor. Initially Revered B would become very distressed and symptomatic following intense processing. Towards the end of treatment, Revered B developed an understanding of what triggered the abuse and stopped chastising himself. Nightmares remitted and he began to develop closer attachments to people in his family and community.

Weekly sessions over 18 months and biweekly meetings for 3 months comprised treatment. Throughout the therapy, Revered B also worked with a spiritual advisor within the church on the issue of forgiveness. This helped to expedite his healing. As part of the therapeutic process, Revered B traveled to his home town to the place where the abuse occurred. It was not possible to confront the perpetrator because he had died years earlier. Nevertheless, Revered B wrote him a letter detailing his feelings about the abuse. He expressed surprise when he realized that the memories no longer triggered emotional distress. When Reverend B said: "These [memories of sexual abuse] are just recollections that can no longer hurt me" we knew that he had healed. During a wrap-up period over four sessions, he recognized that his religious vocation had been fortified as he resolved to work within the church to educate people about abuse and prevent future generations from having to deal with its sequelae.

Clinical Case Using Brief Therapy

Identifying Data and Reason for Referral

Ms. Z is a 50 year old Central American mother of two young adults. She resides alone in her apartment. Her son (age 24) brought her in for therapy following a period when she complained that her neighbors were listening in on her. He became concerned that she was "losing her mind." Additional symptoms involved: insomnia, visual illusions of decapitated corpses, anxiety whenever her daughter (age 22) was not in her presence, nightmares, and an exaggerated startle response. The precipitating event involved her daughter's moving out to live with roommates.

History

The client was the second of nine siblings. She was raised by her mother in a household of limited economic means. Since childhood, she worked to help support her siblings. She began to live with the father of her children at age 15. By the time she was 18, she had two children. When she was 25 years old, a group of men came to her house and set it on fire. Her husband was abducted. Two days later, his decapitated body was dumped on the street. Ms. Z left her children in her mother's care and fled by land to the United States, fearing that she would be killed too. After working as a housekeeper for a number of years, Ms. Z managed to save enough money to send for her children. By that time, her children were adolescents. After their long separation, she vowed never to leave them again. Ms. Z's son was the first to leave the household. The following year, her daughter decided to move with roommates. Ms. Z became symptomatic for the first time.

Course of Treatment

A total of twelve sessions took place. Some of the sessions involved the participation of the son and daughter. After making a diagnosis of delayed onset PTSD, the initial sessions involved a didactic intervention. The family was assured that Ms. Z was not "losing her mind". Instead the nature and triggers of PTSD were explained, along with the formulation that the separation from the daughter had activated PTSD in connection to traumatic losses in their homeland years earlier. TFT and the "butterfly hug" were taught to all family members. They worked on calming and self-soothing skills. Quickly (by the third session) family members were ready to confront traumatic memories.

Family sessions involved testimonials of what occurred during the war. Since migration, Ms. Z and her children had never discussed the traumatic loss of the father or the burning of the house. For the first time, the family cried together. They spoke of their memories: hearing gunshots at night, the horror of masked men breaking into their house and burning it down, the disappearance of the father, and the disbelief and pain of seeing his mutilated body on the street. All family members expressed surprise at the vivid memories described. The mother sobbed while she said that she thought the children had forgotten what happened. The son and daughter told Ms. Z that they never mentioned it to protect her from feeling sad. Therapeutic interventions were limited to witnessing the account and speaking about its emotional impact and the family's strength and courage. The mother's "paranoid" symptoms were reframed in terms of the experiences in a polarized country and multiple losses. The daughter's move triggered the dormant fear that every separation would be the last, as had been the case with the father. Delayed mourning took place in the sessions.

By the ninth session, Ms. Z's symptomatology subsided. She and her daughter began to make plans to return to their native country for a visit, once the mother obtained a green card. Termination sessions focused on steps needed to complete the mourning and prevent relapse. Months after termination, the son called to say that his mother had just returned from a visit to their country of origin. She remained symptom-free and adapting well to living on her own.

Post-Therapy

Because healing and personal growth are life-long processes, therapist and client work together to identify long-term goals. This is a final way to foster hope for the future once the barriers of PTSD are moved. In the final session, a token of the therapeutic work is given to the client as a concrete reminder of what was accomplished. Depending on the client's belief system or cultural group, items such as a certificate of completion of the brief therapy, a guardian angel pin, a blank journaling book, a religious medal, or any small item that is symbolic of the sessions, is given to the client upon embarking on the next stage of life.

It is not uncommon for clients to bring gifts to the therapist as a way of expressing gratitude and a reminder of the work performed. In most cultures, this is a healthy sign of a reciprocal relationship. As long as the gift is a small token of the relationship, it is received and appreciated by the therapist, rather than interpreted —as is routinely done in traditional training. The parting gift allows some closure and connection. It is seen as a sign that some hope and trust in humanity have been restored.

CONCLUSION

As noted in this chapter, psychodiagnostics and brief therapy of PTSD taking into account cultural factors are helpful with a number of refugees. Assessing cultural issues, being aware of the sociopolitical context prior to migration and understanding client's values help to engage clients in a process that can be painful. These are key ingredients in helping refugees.

The information presented in this model is anecdotal since it has not been examined using research tools. Empirical research with different groups of refugees would be a significant contribution to the field. Since the initial article describing the model was published in 2001, mental health professionals from Guatemala, the United Kingdom and Italy have written to report clinical usefulness with refugee populations in their countries. Hopefully, the next generation of researchers will endeavor to test this approach and others, so that this well-deserving population will have access to the treatment that it needs.

REFERENCES

Ariel, Shlomo (1999) *Culturally Competent Family Therapy*, Westport, CT: Praeger.
American Psychiatric Association (1994) *Diagnostic and Statistical Manual of Mental Disorders* (DSM - IV), Washington, D.C.

Alarcón, R. & Foulks, E.F. (1995) Personality Disorders and Culture: Contemporary Clinical Views (Part A). *Cultural Diversity and Mental Health*, 1, 3-17.

Aresti, L. (1988) Political Reality and Psychological Damage. In A. Aron (Ed.), *Flight, Exile and Return: Mental Health and the Refugee*. Committee for Health Rights in Central America, San Francisco.

Bhui, Kamaldeep, Abdi, Abdisakama, Abdi, Mahad, Pereira, Stephen, Dualeh, Mohammed, Robertson, David, Sathyamoorthy, Ganesh & Ismail, Hellena. (2003) Traumatic events, migration characteristics and psychiatric symptoms among Somali refugees: preliminary communication. *Social Psychiatry and Psychiatric Epidemiology*, 38, 35-43.

Bolton, E. (2003) PTSD in Refugees. National Center for Post-Traumatic Stress Disorder, Department of Veterans Affairs Fact Sheet.

Brende, J. & Goldsmith, R. (1991) Post-traumatic Stress Disorder in Families. *Journal of Contemporary Psychotherapy*, 21, 115-125.

Cahill, S., Carrigan, M.H., Frueh, B.C. (1999) Does EMDR Work? And If So, Why? *Journal of Anxiety Disorders*, 13, 5-33.

Callahan, R. (1997) Thought field therapy: the case of Mary. *Traumatology*, 3, 1.

Callahan, R. (1995) A thought field therapy (TFT) algorithm for trauma. *Traumatology*, 1, 1.

Comas-Díaz, L. & Jacobsen, F.M. (1987) Ethnocultural Identification in Psychotherapy. *Psychiatry*, 50(3), 232-241.

Comas-Díaz, L. & Padilla, A. (1990) Countertransference in working with victims of political repression. *American Journal of Orthopsychiatry*, 60(1), 125-134.

Craine, M.; Hanks, R. & Stevens, H. (1992) Mapping Family Stress: The application of family adaptation theory to Post-traumatic Stress Disorder. *American Journal of Family Therapy*, 20, 3, 195-203.

Davidson, J. & Connor, K. (1999) Management of Posttraumatic Stress Disorder: Diagnostic And Therapeutic Issues. *Journal of Clinical Psychiatry*, 60, 33-38.

Doerr-Zegers, O., Hartmann, L., Lira, E. & Weinstein, E. (1992) Torture: Psychiatric Sequelae and Phenomenology. *Psychiatry*, 55, 2, 177-184. Hembree, E. & Foa, E. (2003) Interventions for trauma-related emotional disturbances in adult victims of crime. *Journal of Traumatic Stress*, 16, 187-199.

Folkes, C.E. (2002) Thought field therapy and trauma recovery. *International Journal of Emergency Mental Health*, 4, 99-103.

Friedman, M.J. (1998) Current and Future Drug Treatment for Posttraumatic Stress Disorder Patients. *Psychiatric Annals*, 28, 461-468.

Frueh, B., Leverett, J. & Kinder, B. (1995) Interrelationships between MMPI-2 and Rorschach Variables in a Sample of Vietnam Veterans with PTSD. *Journal of Personality Assessment*, 64, 312-318.

Goldfinger, R., Amdur, R. & Liberzon, I. (1998) Psychophysiologic Responses to the Rorschach in PTSD Patients. *Depression and Anxiety*, 8, 112-120.

Hertzberg, M.A., Butterfield, M.I., Feldman, M., Beckham, J.C., Sutherland, S., Connor, K.M. & Davidson, J.R. (1999) *Biological Psychiatry*, 45, 1226-1229.

Holaday, M. (2000) Rorschach protocols from children and adolescents diagnosed with posttraumatic stress disorder. *Journal of Personality Assessment*, 75, 143-157.

Jarero, I. (2002) The Butterfly Hug: An Update. *Eye Movement Desensitization Reprocessing International Association Newsletter*, 6.

Jenkins, J.H. (1996) Culture, Emotion and PTSD. In Marsella, A.J., Friedman, M.J., Gerrity, E.T. & Scurfield, R.M. (Eds.) *Ethnocultural Aspects of Posttraumatic Stress Disorder: Issues, Research and Clinical Applications*, 165-182.

Jones, R.B. & Jones, G. (1995) *Listen to the Drum: Blackwolf Shares His Medicine.* Salt Lake City, Utah: Commune-A-Key Publishing.

Levin, P., Lazrove, S. & Van der Kolk, B. (1999) What Psychological Testing and Neuroimaging Tell Us About the Treatment of Posttraumatic Stress Disorder by Eye Movement Desensitization and Reprocessing. *Journal of Anxiety Disorders*, 13, 159-172.

Lubin, H., Loris, M., Burt, J. & Johnson, D.R. (1998) Efficacy of Psychoeducational Group Therapy in Reducing Symptoms of Posttraumatic Stress Disorder Among Multiply Traumatized Women. *American Journal of Psychiatry*, 9, 1172-1177.

Marmar, C. (1991) Brief dynamic therapy of Post-traumatic Stress Disorder. *Psychiatric Annals*, 21(7), 405-414.

Matsakis, A. (1992) *I Can't Get Over It: A Handbook for Trauma Survivors*, New Harbinger Publications, Oakland, California.

McNally, R.J. (1999) Research on Eye Movement Desensitization Reprocessing (EMDR) as a Treatment for PTSD. *PTSD Research Quarterly*, 10, 1-7.

Macksoud, M.S., Aber, J. & Cohn, I. (1996) Assessing the Impact of War on Children. In R.J. Apfel & B. Simon (Eds.), *Minefields in their Hearts: The Mental Health of Children in War and Communal Violence* (pp. 218-230). New Haven: Yale University Press.

Melancon, G. & Boyer, R. (1999) How to Prevent Posttraumatic Stress Disorder Before Traumatization Occurs. *Canadian Journal of Psychiatry*, 44(3), 253-258.

Miller, L. (1999) Treating Posttraumatic Stress Disorder in Children and Families: Basic Principles and Clinical Applications. *American Journal of Family Therapy*, 27, 21-34.

Momartin, S., Silove, D., Manicavasagar, V. & Steel, Z. (2003) Dimensions of trauma associated with posttraumatic stress disorder (PTSD) caseness, severity and functional impairment: a study of Bosnian refugees resettled in Australia. *Social Science and Medicine*, 57, 775-781.

Munczek, D.S. & Tuber, S. (1998) Political Repression and its Psychological Effects on Honduran Children. *Social Science Medicine*, 47, 11, 1699-1713.

Nieves-Grafals, S. (1995) Psychological Testing as A Diagnostic and Therapeutic Tool in the Treatment of Traumatized Latin American and African Refugees, *Cultural Diversity and Mental Health*, 1, 19-27.

Nieves-Grafals, S. (2001) Brief Therapy of Civil-War Related Trauma: A Case Study. *Cultural Diversity and Ethnic Minority Psychology*, 7, 387-398.

Otto, M. W., Hinton, D., Korbly, N. B., Chea, A., Ba, P., Gershuny, B.Z. & Pollack, M.H. (2003) Treatment of pharmacotherapy-refractory Cambodian refugees: A pilot study of combination treatment with cognitive-behavior therapy vs. sertraline alone. *Behaviour Research and Therapy*, 41, 1271-1276.

Poole, A.D., De Johng, A. & Spector, J. (1999) Power Therapies: Evidence versus Emotion. *Behavioural and Cognitive Psychotherapy*, 27, 3-8.

Prout, M. & Schwarz, R. (1991) Post-traumatic Stress Disorder: A brief integrated approach. *International Journal of Short-term Psychotherapy*, 6(2), 113-124.

Rabin, C. & Nardi, C. (1991) Treating Post-traumatic Stress Disorder couples: A Psychoeducational program. *Community Mental Health Journal*, 27(3), 209-224.

Sabin, M. E., Lopes Cardozo, B., Nackerud, L., Kaiser, R. & Varese, L. (2003) Factors associated with poor mental health among Guatemalan refugees living in Mexico 20 years after civil conflict. *Journal of the American Medical Association.* 290, 635-642.

Shapiro, F. (1989) Eye movement desensitization: a new treatment for Post-traumatic Stress Disorder. *Journal of Behavior Therapy and Experimental Psychiatry*, 20(3), 211-217.

Shapiro, F. & Forrest, M.S. (1997) EMDR: *The Breakthrough Therapy for Overcoming Anxiety, Stress, and Trauma.* New York: Basic Books.

Stadter, M. (1996) *Object Relations Brief Therapy: The Therapeutic Relationship in Short-term Work.* New Jersey: Aronson.

Warda, G. & Bryant, R.A. (1998) Thought Control Strategies in Acute Stress Disorder. *Behaviour Research and Therapy*, 36, 1171-1175.

Wylie, M. (1996) Going for the cure. *Family Therapy Networker*, 20, 20-37.

In: Trends in Posttraumatic Stress Disorder Research   ISBN 1-59454-135-3
Editor: Thomas A. Corales, pp. 207-227   © 2005 Nova Science Publishers, Inc.

Chapter 9

TRAUMA RECOVERY: BEYOND POSTTRAUMATIC STRESS DISORDER AND OTHER AXIS I SYMPTOM SEVERITY

Tara E. Galovski[*], Ana A. Sobel,
Kelly A. Phipps and Patricia A. Resick
University of Missouri - St. Louis
Center for Trauma Recovery
St. Louis, MO 63121-4499

ABSTRACT

This chapter will offer the reader a brief review on the impact of trauma on domains of psychosocial functioning (occupational, social, recreational/leisure, sexual). Typically, improvements in these areas of psychosocial functioning of trauma exposure may be considered in a tertiary manner or even anecdotally reported in large treatment outcome trials. We will then examine the impact of two empirically validated treatments (Prolonged Exposure and Cognitive Processing Therapy) on impairments in domains of psychosocial functioning of trauma exposure. Specifically, we will explore the effects of these two evidence-based treatments on the various domains of psychosocial functioning (occupational, social/recreational, sexual). Clinically, as will be discussed, changes in these domains are often reported as the most meaningful to the patient.

INTRODUCTION

From the earliest application of cognitive-behavioral interventions in the treatment of Posttraumatic Stress Disorder (PTSD), clinical researchers have consistently reported success in reducing PTSD symptomatology. Specifically, the inclusion of exposure-based

---

[*] Address correspondence to: Tara E. Galovski, Ph.D., Assistant Research Professor, University of Missouri - St. Louis, Center for Trauma Recovery, Kathy J. Weinman Bldg. - lower level, 8001 Natural Bridge Rd., St. Louis, MO 63121-4499, Tel: 314-516-7232, Fax: 314-516-7233, email: galovskit@msx.umsl.edu

components of therapy and cognitive interventions in a variety of trauma recovery treatment packages has strong empirical support. In their review of the PTSD treatment outcome literature, Foa and Meadows (1997) outlined methodological standards for treatment outcome research and applied those "gold standards" to the existing outcome literature for PTSD. The authors concluded that cognitive-behavioral treatments tended to have the most well-controlled outcome studies and were most stringently evaluated.

The overall success of these programs of research has been demonstrated across a variety of treatment packages employing numerous combinations of cognitive-behavioral techniques, and targeting a variety of trauma populations including sexual/physical assault (e.g., Foa, Dancu, Hembree, Jaycox, Meadows, & Street, 1999; Kilpatrick, Veronen, & Resick, 1982; Resick, Nishith, Weaver, Astin, & Feuer, 2002) military combat (e.g., Frueh, Turner, Beidel, Mirabella,& Jones, 1996; Keane, Fairbank, Caddell, & Zimmering, 1989) and populations including multiple types of trauma (e.g., Taylor et al, 2003; Lee, Gavriel, Drummond, Richards, & Greenwald, 2002; Marks, Lovell, Noshirvani, Livanou, & Thrasher, 1998). The primary variable in measuring treatment outcome in the above-mentioned studies and similar large-scale research projects is typically PTSD symptomatology with concurrent manifestations of psychopathology such as depression and panic secondarily considered. However, PTSD and its comorbid disorders represent just one trajectory of possible reactions to traumatic stress (albeit the most common).

This chapter will offer the reader a brief review on the impact of trauma on domains of psychosocial functioning (occupational, social, recreational/leisure, sexual). Typically, improvements in these areas of psychosocial functioning of trauma exposure may be considered in a tertiary manner or even anecdotally reported in large treatment outcome trials. We will then examine the impact of two empirically validated treatments (Prolonged Exposure and Cognitive Processing Therapy) on impairments in domains of psychosocial functioning of trauma exposure. Specifically, we will explore the effects of these two evidence-based treatments on the various domains of psychosocial functioning (occupational, social/recreational, sexual). Clinically, as will be discussed, changes in these domains are often reported as the most meaningful to the patient.

TRAUMA EXPOSURE AND PSYCHOSOCIAL FUNCTIONING

The importance of assessing change within psychosocial domains of functioning is evidenced by the amassing literature demonstrating the clear presence of significant deficits in the major role functioning of individuals exposed to trauma. For instance, Kessler (2000) reports that the effect of PTSD on work productivity alone is the equivalent of 3.6 work days per month. This work loss translates into a societal cost equal to $3 billion dollars annually in the United States. It can thus be surmised that the experience of PTSD impairs work functioning. A selection of studies reviewed, below identified functional impairments observed in traumatized populations in the areas of occupational, social, and economic functioning.

Zatzick and colleagues (1997a, 1997b) evaluated data collected as part of the National Vietnam Veterans Readjustment Study (NVVRS) and found that male and female veterans with PTSD were more likely than veterans without PTSD to report problems with various functional impairments including the ability to function at home, work, or at school; self-reported physical health status, and limitations in leisure activity. Jordon and colleagues (1992) also evaluated data from the NVVRS sample and found that male veterans with PTSD were more likely than non-PTSD veterans to report problems with interpersonal relationships. In a community-based sample, Amaya-Jackson and colleagues (1999) found that individuals with clinically significant PTSD symptoms (but who did not meet full diagnostic criteria) were more likely than those without PTSD symptoms to report impaired social support and inadequate economic resources.

While the previous studies focused on community and veteran populations, other studies have focused particularly on the relationship between interpersonal trauma (i.e., sexual and physical assault) and specific areas of deficit in domains of psychosocial functioning. These studies have identified major role functioning deficits in social adjustment and interpersonal arenas (e.g., Cloitre, Scarvalone, & Difede, 1997; Resick, Calhoun, Atkeson, & Ellis, 1981; Zoellner, Foa, & Brigidi, 1999), intimacy (e.g., Feinauer, Callahan, & Hilton, 1996; Harris & Valentiner, 2002, Thelen, Sherman, & Borst, 1998) and sexual dysfunctions (e.g., Briere,1988; Letourneau, Resnick, Kilpatrick, Saunders, & Best, 1996).

Another psychosocial domain that may be affected by trauma is recreational or leisure activity. Although the importance of leisure activity has been illustrated insofar as it may play an important role in helping individuals to cope with daily and normative stress (Iwasaki & Mannell, 2000), there is an absence of literature documenting the possible relationship of impairments in leisure activity to more life-altering stressors such as sexual or physical assault (Hutchinson, Loy, Kleiber, & Dattilo, 2003).

This brief review of the literature illustrates the relationship between trauma and deficits in psychosocial role functioning, but also highlights a limitation in our ability to truly understand the impact of trauma on psychosocial factors. That limitation is the inability to establish casual relationships due to the use of primarily correlational and retrospective designs. Future research needs to employ prospective designs with extended follow-up using appropriate control conditions to better assess the potential causal relationships between trauma and psychosocial factors. Also crucial to future research is the necessity of assessing whether the empirically supported treatments for PTSD positively impact these psychosocial variables.

Shalev (2000) reviewed many issues regarding measurement in treatment outcome studies of PTSD in an effort to establish the most productive methods for assessing treatment success. He specifically noted the importance of incorporating associated psychosocial behavior patterns of PTSD (e.g., quality of life, social and interpersonal functioning) as important targets of measurement in PTSD treatment outcome studies. Falsetti and colleagues (2003) also posited that the evaluation of functional impairment in other psychosocial domains of functioning is crucial to outcome assessment. They argued that the goal of PTSD treatments is not only to reduce symptoms, but also to improve global functioning. These investigators first evaluated the impact of their treatment (Multiple Channel Exposure Therapy; MCET) on symptoms of PTSD and panic, resulting in the finding that MCET was effective at reducing symptoms and maintaining symptom reduction at the 3- and 6-month follow-up point with female trauma victims (as cited in Falsetti, Erwin, Resnick, Davis, & Combs-Lane, 2003). In their more recent publication (2003), the authors reported their assessment of improvements in various domains of functioning using the same sample. The authors found that participants in the treatment group demonstrated improvements in work, marital, economic, and overall adjustment immediately following MCET; these improvements were maintained at 3 and 6-month follow-up for the treatment group. However, they noted that participants in the treatment group did not differ from the control group on measures of psychosocial functioning immediately following treatment. They indicated that while preliminary, their findings support the importance of continuing to assess change in these domains in order to fully understand the long-term effects of our treatments for PTSD, particularly in domains of psychosocial functioning. Additional studies have also identified improvements in psychosocial domains of functioning including interpersonal functioning and social adjustment (Cloitre, Koenen, Cohen, & Han, 2002; Resick & Schnicke, 1992).

In summary, although there appear to be strong arguments for the inclusion of measures assessing these psychosocial domains of functioning in treatment outcome research, there is a paucity of well-controlled outcome studies specifically targeting and tracking psychosocial change. Given that the efficacy of cognitive-behavioral treatments in reducing PTSD and related symptomatology has been established, it appears necessary to further identify and assess factors associated with both trauma and PTSD that may also be benefited by these treatments.

COGNITIVE PROCESSING THERAPY AND PROLONGED EXPOSURE THERAPY

As in the Falsetti et al. (2003) article, the current study assessed the psychosocial functioning of female survivors of sexual assault before and after they received trauma-focused therapy. The primary goal of the original study from which this data are presented was to evaluate the effects of therapy with regard to symptom reduction. Psychosocial change was targeted secondarily. However, the available data do contribute significantly to the overall literature as discussed below. The women whose data we present participated in treatment-outcome research conducted by Resick, Nishith, Weaver, Astin, and Feuer (2002). The published results of their study have been primarily focused on the diagnoses of PTSD and depression as well as trauma-related guilt. We will report treatment outcome data in this chapter specific to the following domains of functioning: occupational, social/leisure, and sexual/intimacy.

Prior to describing the psychosocial functioning of the participants before and after receiving trauma-focused therapy, Resick et al. (2002) will be briefly reviewed. A randomized, controlled treatment outcome trial was conducted comparing two cognitive-behavioral interventions: Cognitive Processing Therapy (CPT; Resick & Schnicke, 1993) and Prolonged Exposure Therapy (PE; Foa, Hearst, Dancu, Hembree, & Jaycox, 1994). CPT consists of two main components: cognitive therapy and exposure therapy (Resick & Schnicke, 1993). The cognitive therapy component primarily involves the therapist and client engaging in a collaborative effort with the goal of identifying maladaptive cognitions that the client has developed about the meaningfulness of the trauma. For example survivors may blame themselves for the occurrence of the trauma or develop generalized views about the dangerousness of others. The identified cognitions are then explored and challenged for the purpose of helping clients to develop more accurate and balanced views concerning the trauma. The exposure component involves having clients write detailed accounts of their assault. These accounts are read aloud in session and for homework with the goal of enabling clients to confront their distressing memories and to process their emotions.

The main components of PE are imaginal exposures to memories of the traumatic event and in vivo exposures to feared stimuli outside of therapy (Foa & Rothbaum, 1998). The exposures serve to facilitate the emotional processing of the trauma and the reduction of anxiety associated with memories of the trauma and other fear-producing situations. During the imaginal exposures, clients are asked to close their eyes and re-experience the trauma by providing repeated, detailed verbal accounts of the incident. The in vivo exposures involve the clients confronting feared stimuli (which in actuality are not dangerous), beginning with situations that evoke moderate levels of anxiety followed by situations evoking increasing levels of anxiety.

Participants in the study were randomly assigned either to CPT, PE, or a minimal attention waiting-list control condition (MA). Clients in the CPT and PE conditions met with their therapists twice weekly for a total of 13 treatment hours. Clients in the MA, or wait-list control condition were told that therapy would be provided in six weeks. An interviewer called them every two weeks to ensure that they did not need emergency services. After six weeks, the MA participants were randomly assigned to the CPT or PE conditions.

A diagnosis of current PTSD resulting from a sexual assault was required for participation in the study. Participants were not excluded from the study if they experienced other traumatic life events, but they had to have experienced a discrete incident of completed rape in childhood or adulthood. In addition, the rape had to occur at least three months prior to participation in the study. Clients were excluded from participation for current psychosis, developmental disabilities, illiteracy, suicidal intent, current parasuicidal behavior, and current dependence on drugs or alcohol. Women were also excluded from participation if they had been involved in an abusive relationship within the last 6 months or were currently being stalked. Clients prescribed psychotropic medication were included in the study if their medications were stabilized.

Participants were assessed at pretreatment, posttreatment, and 3 and 9 months posttreatment. Although not reported in the Resick et al. (2002) article due to the limited number of data at the time, assessments were also conducted at 5-years post-treatment. At pre-treatment, participants did not significantly differ in PTSD or depression severity between the three conditions. Of the 171 female rape victims with PTSD who were randomized into one of the three conditions, 121 completed treatment. Results indicated that participants in both CPT and PE showed significant reductions in symptoms of PTSD and depression. There were no significant differences between the participants in CPT or PE with regard to a diagnosis of PTSD or major depressive disorder at any of the assessment points. Both treatments yielded significantly superior results to clients in the MA condition. Table 1 shows the percentages of participants by type of treatment who met criteria for PTSD and depression during each of the assessment periods.

In addition to the battery of psychometrically sound outcome measures described below that tap into symptomatology and various domains of functioning, CPT contains another mechanism that enables therapists and researchers to gain a deeper understanding of how traumatic events affect the lives of survivors. This mechanism, termed the Impact Statement, is a written essay in which participants describe the impact of the traumatic event on their lives. The Impact Statement allows the participants to reflect upon the important changes that they observed in their own lives without being limited by specific interview or self-report questions.

Table 1. Percentages of Participants in the Resick et al. (2002)
Study Meeting Criteria for Posttraumatic Stress Disorder (PTSD)
and Major Depressive Disorder (MDD) by Treatment Condition

Assessment Time-point	Treatment Condition			
	CPT	PE	CPT	PE
	PTSD(%)	PTSD(%)	MDD(%)	MDD(%)
Pre-Treatment	100	100	46.3	52.6
Post-Treatment	19.5	17.5	a	a
3-month f-u	16.2	29.5	17.6	22.2
9-month f-u	19.2	15.4	3.8	15.4

CPT = Cognitive Processing Therapy.
PE = Prolonged Exposure Therapy.
a = Percentages were not reported for rates of MDD at post-treatment because depression was not assessed at this time-point.

Research participants were instructed to write an Impact Statement after the first session of treatment, before the final session of treatment, and at their 5-year follow-up assessment. They were given the following instructions:

> Please write at least one page on what it means to you that you were raped. Please consider the effects the assault has had on the beliefs about yourself, your beliefs about others, and your beliefs about the world. Also consider the following topics while writing you answer: safety, trust, power/control, esteem, and intimacy.

Although not specifically instructed to do so, the clients almost invariably reported changes in their everyday functioning far more frequently than changes in specific PTSD symptomatology. These data suggest that perhaps the impact of the trauma within the domains of psychosocial functioning is even more meaningful to the traumatized individual than the specific symptoms of PTSD and comorbid psychopathology. The effectiveness of our treatments of PTSD may be deemed successful not only by decreases in specific symptoms of psychopathology, but in meaningful, observable changes in the traumatized individual's daily functioning. The words of our clients provide further evidence for the importance of targeting psychosocial domains among clients completing PTSD treatment.

The Impact Statement below was included to serve as an example of how participants may describe the effects of the rape on their lives. It was completed by a study participant between the first and second sessions of CPT. As an adolescent, this client experienced repeated incidents of sexual abuse by a teacher, with the final incident being a completed rape after she graduated from high school. It is evident in her essay how the sexual traumas impacted her not only with regard to symptomatology, but also had a profound effect on her psychosocial functioning, particularly in the domains of socializing, leisure activities, health, and intimate relationships.

Up until the time of my assault, I was a normal, fun loving kid. I had always been a tomboy and loved doing anything outdoors. I was pretty outgoing and made friends fairly easy. I did sometimes tend to stay in the background until I knew people a little better.

I was raised to be active in church. My parents didn't fight in front of anyone and didn't raise their voices very often. My dad worked and my mom stayed at home. My parents were loving and always provided for our needs, but they were also a little distant and avoided discussing anything "painful." I had two sets of grandparents. I spent lots of time with both sets.

I have many wonderful memories of my childhood until the age of 13. I was raised to be kind and forgiving and to trust authority figures. I didn't cause much trouble at home or school, but I did struggle in school. My older brothers were very smart. I loved to read. I would rather skip homework and go ride my bike or walk in the woods. I felt happy and safe. I had never questioned my safety until the fall of 1952.

At that point I didn't have many feelings or thoughts about sexual issues, other than wanting a boyfriend. My parents never discussed sex or body issues with us. I didn't have hardly any knowledge base about sex or my own body. I knew my baby brother had a penis, but I was sure it would fall off at some point. I also trusted adults and never questioned what they said, except for the normal 13-year old questioning.

I started my ninth grade year with a new history teacher. He was young and it was his first year of teaching. He had a violent temper. He screamed a lot and said unkind things to students. He would intimidate everyone. He threw objects across the room, banged his fist on desktops, got right in kid's faces, and yelled. I hated going to class. I never questioned him on anything out of fear.

Like I said before, I wasn't a top student. I really had trouble in history and being in history class with him made it worse. After the first month of school he offered to help tutor me after school or between classes or lunch. My first lesson alone with him is when the abuse started. Just a simple touch on my shoulder and I didn't pull away and he must have known he had me snarled in his sick web.

This is when my life changed. Fear overwhelmed me, shame followed my everywhere and secrets haunted my every minute. Trust was gone. I didn't trust other people, and I certainly didn't trust myself any longer. I had so many questions but there were no answers and nobody to talk to.

I was scared to death for my safety, and at times my sanity. I had more fear that he would tell my parents than of him hurting or killing me. I wanted to be that "good girl" my parents had raised. And I wasn't any longer. The fear of disappointing them almost ate me alive. Of course this meant I couldn't tell them.

I felt like I had a scarlet letter branded on my chest. It was so hard to undress in gym class because I thought everyone must know because it somehow showed on my body. I began to have a warped body image because I felt so different from every other girl. Almost like he left his dirty, big handprints all over me. I think what I was feeling were the internal scars he had, and was inflicting on me. I became withdrawn and avoided people. I was sick a lot. I had difficulty taking a deep breath and had lots of headaches. I lost self-confidence and lost that free spirit you have at that age. I couldn't understand why someone wasn't stopping him. I really felt the internal battles in my mind and spirit between what was right and what was happening.

After over a year of the sexual abuse and his mind games, I started to believe his bullshit of how special I was to him. I avoided having a boyfriend because of this. His manipulation had worked on me. I still question what it was, or is, in me that made me the one he picked.

A few days after I graduated I went to his house for the first time. He wanted me to bake a cake, then he raped me on his wife's bed. I never heard from him after that, or until my own children started junior high. I told my best friend about the rape. She hit me in my face and asked me how I could do that. Then I put it away because I wasn't sure how I could have done that.

Sex means pretty much nothing to me other than some physical pleasure. I went through many, many sexual relationships with men. I always felt like sex was expected. That was what I had learned. There were times I enjoyed it and other times I hardly remembered it. I never said "no". Since my parents never discussed sex with me, I just went on what I had learned from my teacher. There isn't much emotion that goes along with sex. You know the saying, "Just Do It." That's me. I don't see love and sex going together. Actually, it's hard for me to understand love with a man. I feel like I had a type of love for my perp but it wasn't a "normal" love. How could a 14-17 year old (I didn't love him when I was 13) love a married man who was abusing her?

I love my children and family, but I don't feel love for a man. It makes me rather sick to think about it. I am very distant in relationships. I need to be in control at all times. If I'm not, I feel like I can't breath. I have let myself get involved with a few men who probably wouldn't be considered the "cream of the crop". I don't feel worthy of being with certain men. I feel like I'm "used goods" and not good enough for the really nice guys.

Even though I feel the need for control I am also an enabler. Men with problems stick to me like glue. Sometimes I think I can fix them but can't fix myself. I need to fix something. I don't choose men wisely. I currently choose men who are in relationships because I can walk away without making any commitment. I don't want the emotional ties. I don't want a man asking me to move in or get married, or tell me how to cook or what to wear. I'd rather be alone than have that. It is a lonely feeling at times but empowering at other times. I don't trust myself to make the right decisions.

Sometimes I sit and watch people. I hear them talk and want to scream at them. I want to tell them how petty they are or how stupid they sound. People can really annoy me. I don't like to be crowded or feel blocked in. I prefer to stay on the sidelines, watching and listening.

I would like to have more female friends, but I have a hard time getting comfortable with them. Sometimes I feel it is because I don't trust myself with their men. It may not bother me to have sex with their boyfriends and think nothing of it, so I don't get too close. People usually like me, but I keep a safe distance. I have one really good girlfriend, but she is single without a boyfriend.

I feel safe in my home to some extent now. I feel pretty safe in my town. I have a gun and would not hesitate to use in on someone trying to hurt me in my home. I grew up target shooting so I feel at home with firearms. I also carry a small knife in my purse. I am careful and watchful of my surroundings, but not phobic about it. I go out by myself at night and just take the normal precautions.

There have been a few times where I just get freaked out and leave where I am because I suddenly feel scared of something. I always drive myself in case this happens. I have some serious fight/flight issues. There have been times in the last two years that I have been very afraid my perp would hurt me again. I also feared my ex-husband. He has a rage disorder and this pushed him over the edge.

I have been really tired a lot and not very motivated in some areas. Sometimes I feel like I have two people living inside of me, the good girl and the dirty bad girl. Actually, I feel like that a lot. The abuse cut me in half, replacing what was once good and pure with a dirty feeling, shameful, numb and damaged young girl. She is still there. It's the numbness and blame that are serious roadblocks in my life.

Basically, I don't trust many people. I don't trust myself. I don't trust men at all (except my dad and son), I like to be alone. I don't want a relationship with a man. I can't get too close or open up to many people. I am tired and unmotivated. I don't hate my life and I don't want to die. I just want to get better and learn to embrace all that is in me. I'm just not sure what "me" is.

The assault made me feel dirty, like I was a bad child, distrustful, and fearful. I kept the secret for so long and put the blame on myself for so long it's hard to shake off. People would rather eat glass than hear about it. I feel like I did at 13, alone. I would like to find out what my flaw is/was that made me such an easy target.

Changes in Psychosocial Functioning

A subsample of the original 121 treatment completers was examined using the available data pertaining to the various domains of psychosocial functioning. Specifically, we chose 70 treatment completers (35 PE and 35 CPT) for whom we have data at three assessment points, pre-treatment, post-treatment, and 9-month follow-up. The sample size was reduced due to the missing data in the domains of interest in the current study. The 3-month follow-up assessment period was excluded because of the lack of measures collected assessing psychosocial functioning at that time point. Demographic information and client variables on these 70 participants are available in Table 2.

Table 2. Demographic Information and Patient Variables

	Mean (SD)	Mean (SD)	Group Differences
Age	32.77 (9.50)	33.61 (11.09)	$t = -.324, p = .73$
Months Since Rape	111.12 (121.12)	126.92 (91.59)	$t = -.618, p = .54$
Total # of Crimes Experience	6.66 (4.98)	5.71 (4.73)	$t = -.813, p = .42$
CAPS PTSD Severity	72.97 (18.33)	73.86 (17.70)	$t = -1.24, p = .84$
	N (% of Total)	N (% of Total)	Group Differences
Race			
Caucasian	29 (40.8)	33 (46.5)	
African American	6 (8.5)	3 (4.2)	$X^2 = 1.24, p = .27$
Major Depressive Disorder			
Current-Yes	16(22.2)	12 (16.7)	$X^2 = .94, p = .33$
No	20 (27.8)	24 (33.3)	
Lifetime-Yes	25 (40.3)	29 (46.8)	$X^2 = .04, p = .85$
No	4 (6.5)	4 (6.5)	
Panic Disorder			
Current-Yes	4 (4.5)	6 (8.5)	$X^2 = .40, p = .53$
No	31 (43.7)	30 (42.3)	
Lifetime-Yes	7 (10.8)	9 (13.8)	$X^2 = .05, p = .82$
No	23 (35.4)	26 (40.0)	
Alcohol			
Lifetime-Yes	0 (0.0)	1 (1.4)	$X^2 = 1.01, p = .31$
No	36 (50.0)	35 (48.6)	
Cannabis			
Lifetime-Yes	8 (12.5)	6 (9.4)	$X^2 = 1.01, p = .31$
No	21 (32.8)	29 (45.3)	
Cocaine			
Lifetime-Yes	3 (4.7)	1 (1.6)	$X^2 = 1.52, p = .22$
No	26 (40.6)	34 (53.1)	

Table 3. Repeated Measures ANOVAs across Time
(Pre-treatment, Post-treatment and 9 month follow-up)

Measure	Assessment Point	Treatment Condition		Statistic
		CPT Mean (sd)	PE Mean (sd)	Main effect of time
Occupational Functioning				
SAS-SR Overall work	Pre	1.95 (.5)	2.15 (.5)	F = 27.6,
	Post	1.52 (.5)	1.67 (.5)	p<.001
	9 month f-u	1.45 (.4)	1.65 (.4)	
Economic	Pre	2.69 (1.4)	2.12 (1.2)	F = 7.55,
	Post	1.93 (1.2)	2.00 (1.0)	p<.001
	9 month f-u	1.93 (1.1)	1.78 (.8)	
Social and leisure functioning				
SAS-SR Social & leisure	Pre	2.82 (.6)	2.74 (.6)	F = 71.3,
	Post	1.99 (.5)	1.94 (.4)	p<.001
	9 month f-u	2.08 (.5)	2.00 (.4)	
CSI Social support	Pre	20.1 (8.8)	20.1 (9.2)	F = 24.88,
	Post	28.03 (8.0)	27.7 (8.4)	p<.001
	9 month f-u	22.3 (9.2)	21.56 (9.5)	
CSI Social withdrawal	Pre	30.03 (7.8)	30.42 (6.97)	F = 86.10 p<.001
	Post	17.88 (5.77)	20.00 (7.13)	
	9 month f-u	16.94 (6.76)	20.39 (8.58)	
SAS-SR Extended family	Pre	2.20 (.5)	2.34 (.6)	F = 24.51,
	Post	1.85 (.8)	1.80 (.5)	p<.001
	9 month f-u	1.78 (.5)	1.81 (.4)	
SAS-SR Family unit	Pre	2.75 (.9)	2.68 (.7)	F = 34.09,
	Post	1.73 (.6)	1.82 (.5)	p<.001
	9 month f-u	1.78 (.7)	1.8 (.4)	
Sexual functioning				
TSI Sexual concerns	Pre	11.61 (6.97)	10.89 (6.3)	F = 76.03,
	Post	4.71 (4.4)	3.81 (3.7)	p<.001
	9 month f-u	3.36 (4.0)	4.33 (4.3)	
TSI Dysfunctional sexual behavior	Pre	5.67 (5.98)	5.33 (6.3)	F = 19.72,
	Post	1.79 (3.6)	1.56 (3.4)	p<.001
	9 month f-u	2.18 (5.4)	2.28 (3.3)	
BDI Item # 21	Pre	1.74 (1.1)	1.51 (1.1)	F = 40.47,
	Post	.49 (.82)	.34 (.73)	p<.001
	9 month f-u	.69 (.96)	.66 (.97)	
FOI	Pre	105.6 (16.8)	106.8 (17.1)	F = 59.19, p<.001
	Post	87.8 (18.8)	92.3 (17.4)	
	9 month f-u	85.7 (19.2)	94.3 (19.0)	

Table 4. Five year Follow-up Analyses

Measure	Assessment Point	Treatment Condition		Statistic
		CPT Mean (sd)	PE Mean (sd)	Main effect of time
Occupational Functioning				
SAS-SR Overall work	Pre	2.13 (.6)	2.25 (.5)	F = 26.4,
	5 yr f-u	1.50 (.5)	1.58 (.5)	p<.001
Economic	Pre	2.38 (1.3)	2.10 (1.3)	F = .07, p<.78
	5 yr f-u	1.91 (1.2)	2.43 (1.3)	
Social and leisure functioning				
SAS-SR Social & leisure	Pre	2.83 (.7)	2.73 (.6)	F = 11.1,
	5 yr f-u	2.12 (.6)	2.54 (.8)	p<.002
CSI Social support	Pre	21.5 (10.6)	21.4 (8.2)	F = .26, p<.614
	5 yr f-u	20.4 (9.9)	24.11 (9.5)	
CSI Social withdrawal	Pre	29.8 (8.5)	29.7 (7.9)	F = 29.32
	5 yr f-u	21.35 (10.9)	19.53 (8.8)	p<.001
SAS-SR Extended family	Pre	2.29 (.7)	2.32 (.8)	F = 5.87, p<.02
	5 yr f-u	1.73 (.6)	2.14 (.9)	
SAS-SR Family unit	Pre	2.74 (1.2)	2.73 (.8)	F = 9.9, p<.004
	5 yr f-u	1.77 (.7)	2.06 (1.0)	
Sexual functioning				
TSI Sexual concerns	Pre	11.39 (7.9)	10.20 (5.4)	F = 14.83,
	5 yr f-u	6.72 (7.2)	6.23 (5.98)	p<.001
TSI Dysfunctional sexual behavior	Pre	6.55 (6.1)	4.05 (5.5)	F = 10.45, p<.002
	5 yr f-u	3.09 (4.4)	2.60 (3.8)	
BDI Item # 21	Pre	1.86 (1.1)	1.20 (1.1)	F = 19.64,
	5 yr f-u	.59 (1.0)	.75 (1.2)	p<.001 Interaction: F = 4.48, p<.05
FOI	Pre	109.3 (16.7)	103.3 (17.1)	F = 20.59, p<.001
	5 yr f-u	93.67 (22.6)	87.9 (16.0)	

Progress within each domain of psychosocial functioning is assessed across this period of time (pre-treatment, post-treatment, and 9 month follow-up). Repeated measures, between subjects MANOVAs were conducted on data in the two domains of psychosocial functioning in which we had multiple measures (social/leisure functioning and sexual functioning). Both yielded a significant main effect of time (p<.001), but neither indicated a significant interaction between treatment conditions. Although we realize we run the risk of substantially increasing experiment-wise error, follow-up univariate tests were conducted on each measure these analyses are exploratory in nature and running multiple analyses will give the reader the best overall picture of the trends seen in the data. The means, standard deviations, and statistics for all measures described below are contained in Table 3. Data are currently being collected on the same participants in an effort to assess treatment gain maintenance five years following the conclusion of treatment. To date, we have data on approximately 53 five-year follow-ups. These data are provided separately in Table 4.

We also attempted to provide the reader with specific examples within each domain of functioning of clients' descriptions of how the trauma has impacted the various areas of their lives. These reports were gathered from Impact Statements collected during treatment from CPT participants. The quotes provided are samples from the many examples we could have chosen. Perhaps even more illuminating than the empirical data, these quotes capture the far-reaching and devastating effects of trauma in the lives of sexual assault victims in their own words. We also included some quotes gathered from Impact Statements written at the conclusion of therapy to provide the reader a qualitative sense of the generalized effects of therapy beyond symptom improvement. It should be noted that these quotes are gathered from the CPT clients only because the Impact Statement is a treatment component unique to that intervention. Unfortunately, there is no parallel mechanism contained in PE from which we could present similar data reflecting change in that treatment condition. Thus the presentation of these quotes does not intend to offer comparative data, but instead a qualitative estimation of the overall impact of trauma on important areas of daily functioning.

Occupational Functioning

"I wonder sometimes what the point is in trying to accomplish something, to build a career, when at any moment someone can come along and rip the foundations right out from under it. Setting goals didn't use to be so difficult – too many puddles to wade through now."

"How can I feel proud of my life and who I am. I am fat, my hair is ugly. I no longer can study in college for my master's, I don't have a job and I don't really want one. I am afraid of failing. Before the rape, I was a star athlete, thin, preppy, a student, fun to party with, included in activities at school, a volunteer in the community…"

The participants were administered the Social Adjustment Scale – Self-Report (SAS-SR; Weissman & Bothwell, 1976). The scale yields an overall adjustment score and six subscales measuring level of functioning over the course of the previous two weeks in the following domains: work, social/leisure, relationships with extended family, marital relations, parental functioning, and relationships within the family unit. There is also a single item querying economic change. With respect to the occupational functioning subscale, respondents completed one of three sections depending on work status: working at home, working outside the home, or student. Items on the subscale measure level of functioning, interest, satisfaction, and quality of work relationships.

A repeated measures ANOVA indicated that participants in both treatment conditions improved similarly in overall occupational functioning. It may be hypothesized that improvements in work functioning may be revealed in improvements in greater economic stability. The economic subscale of the SAS-SR is comprised of only one item asking the respondent if she/he has had adequate finances to care for self and family's financial needs over the last two weeks. A repeated measures ANOVA on this item revealed a main effect of time, indicating that clients reported less financial difficulty at post-treatment and at the 9 month follow-up than at pre-treatment, p<.001. There was no difference in outcome between the two treatment conditions.

Social & Leisure

> "I have lost of all of my friends because of the rape."
> "My guard is always up. I don't have any friends."
> "I have no friends and no one to talk to or get advice from."
> "I constantly feel rejected and left out. I am easily hurt and, in turn, I isolate. I don't feel any kind of closeness or attachment with another adult."

More data were available on the impact of PTSD on socialization and recreation than on occupational functioning because multiple measures were gathered in this domain. As described above, the SAS-SR provides a social and leisure subscale measuring level and type of social interactions, social discomfort and loneliness, and level of interest in hobbies. Similar analyses were conducted to examine changes across time on the social-leisure subscale. Results indicated a similar pattern with both groups improving across time (p<.001) in this domain.

The Coping Strategies Inventory (CSI; Tobin, Holroyd, Reynolds, & Wigal, 1989) was designed to assess particular coping thoughts and behaviors around a specific stressor. It yields a number of subscales, two of which are relevant to the domain of social functioning. These scales include social support (the ability to seek emotional support from social resources such as family and friends) and social withdrawal (the extent to which one withdraws from family and friends especially with respect to an individual's reaction to the traumatic stressor). The ANOVAs indicated similar patterns as emerged on the SAS-SR. Specifically, both treatment conditions demonstrated significant improvements in the ability to generate social support across time, p<.001. Likewise, the two treatment groups decreased their levels of social withdrawal across time, p<.001. There was no significant difference between treatment groups in participant improvement; however as seen in Table 2, there was a trend for treatment decreases in social withdrawal among participants in the CPT condition (relative to the PE condition) to be somewhat better maintained.

The SAS-SR also provides two subscales specifically examining the quality of interactions with family outside the home (extended family) and family inside the home (family unit). Similar analyses revealed the same pattern of improvement: the two treatment conditions improved equally well across time in their interactions with both extended family (p<.001) and within the family unit (p<.001).

Sexual Functioning/Intimacy

> "We haven't made love at all. He can't touch me in any way similar to the way that man touched me."
> "I used to look forward to sex within the bounds of my marriage. Now I can only envision sex as something one-sided and violent. If I ever think about having sex, I think of it as being violent and not nice. I can't feel sexy."

"I am unable to enjoy sex and can't make myself stay in reality the few times I do have sex."

"I sabotage relationships when I start to feel too much. I will imagine they are unfaithful or pick them to pieces and get out of it as soon as real intimacy begins."

Clearly in the case of sexual assault, future sexual functioning can be impaired. The Trauma Symptom Inventory (TSI; Briere, Elliott, Harris, & Cottman, 1995) was developed to tap posttraumatic symptomatology beyond the symptoms of PTSD. The inventory generates a number of subscales including sexual concerns and dysfunctional sexual behavior. The results of the sexual concerns subscale analysis revealed that CPT and PE clients both realized significant decreases in sexual concerns across time. Similarly, the dysfunctional sexual behaviors in the two groups decreased significantly across time. There were no differential treatment outcomes between the two conditions on either scale.

We also looked at item #21 of the Beck Depression Inventory (BDI; Beck et al., 1961) which queries the respondent as to the level of interest he/she has experienced in engaging in sexual relations over the course of the past two weeks. A similar analysis revealed that respondents showed a significant increase in interest in sexual relations across time. The two treatment conditions improved equally on this item.

Finally, we also looked at the Fear of Intimacy Scale (FIS; Descutner & Thelen, 1991) in order to assess the level of participant's anxiety about close, dating relationships. This scale assesses anxiety around dating relationships regardless of the participant's current relationship status. Fear of intimacy [as defined by the FIS is "the inhibited capacity of an individual, because of anxiety, to exchange thoughts and feelings of personal significance with another individual who is highly valued" (p.219)] is not necessarily specific to sexual functioning. However, this analysis was placed here rather than in the social support section because the data refers to fear of intimacy within the dating relationship. The analyses revealed that both groups showed significant decreases across time on fear of intimacy, p<.001. Although there were no significant differential treatment effects, a trend emerged indicating that CPT showed increased treatment gains while PE lost treatment gains at the 9-month follow-up point.

Final Impact Statements

As described above, we ask clients, through the course of CPT, to write a second Impact Statement describing how they feel the trauma impacts their life today (after completing a course of therapy). The client returns to the final session with this completed essay and shares it with the therapist. The therapist then retrieves the original Impact Statement written by the participant after session 1 and re-reads it to the client. The contrast between the two statements is almost invariably very powerful for the client.

The Impact Statement below was completed prior to the final session of CPT by the participant whose initial Impact Statement was included earlier in this chapter. It is evident how treatment helped her to view the meaning of her traumatic experiences in new and different ways. It is also clear how such changes are reflected in more positive cognitions and future planning in the domains of social functioning, intimacy, and health/body image.

The fact that I was assaulted will forever be a part of my life, just as any significant event will be part of my life. It is not something that will simply "go away."

Over these many years it has had an impact on my relationships with friends, family, my children and lovers. Most of the impact was negative. I was fearful of someone finding out and fearful and anxious about how people would view me. I felt betrayed, dirty and ashamed. It was difficult to trust people. I had constructed a thick wall around myself to protect me from being hurt. I was numb to many emotions and feelings. It was easy for me to blame myself for almost anything. As a whole, I felt pretty worthless and unlovable.

After being able to disclose my assault I felt a sense of new strength. I had a mission, a goal to make sure this wouldn't happen to another girl. I devoted all my energy to this. What I had failed to do during this time was to address my own issues regarding the assault.

I have, however, been given the rare opportunity to look deeply into my own beliefs and areas in my life that are/were at a stand still. It has changed my thinking and feeling about myself and my future.

My self-esteem was pretty low. I felt like a branded horse – one who could be easily spotted in a herd. I made a decision without giving much thought to how my decision might affect me. I probably can say I didn't really care too much. I didn't feel worthy of the best for myself. My sexuality was part of me that suffered. Love and sex didn't go hand in hand. Sex was something I could give freely to almost anyone. Love was something I didn't give out too much. I didn't feel safe around myself. I couldn't trust many decisions I made.

Now, I find myself stopping to think. I kept myself so busy before, I didn't have time to think. Being busy allowed me to push negative thoughts in the back of my head, where I thought they belonged. I now have the desire to move ahead, which means taking time for me. The only words I can find to describe this therapy is "eye-opening and kick-ass."

I feel much safer with myself now. I feel that my decision-making skills are greatly improved. I have learned to trust my own instincts and be more in tune with my own beliefs. I have had to take a long, hard look at my own beliefs and actually develop a few. I do believe that I am an important person who deserves better than what I allowed myself to accept before. I know that this may mean there will be times when I am lonely, but that time is worthwhile if it deepens my own respect for myself.

I was ashamed and felt tons of guilt from the assault. I didn't stop to think that it wasn't my fault: it was his. He was the sick person, not me. I am aware, now, that I was a victim that was carrying the weight of the shame on my shoulders. I now feel that weight has lifted and became lighter. I feel I am reclaiming my spirit.

I have had the feeling that my body was different from other female bodies. I could never pinpoint what was different, but I knew it was. I felt it must be and it somehow drew this adult man to me. I began to hate my own body and feel ashamed of any sexual urges. My parents added to this by making me ashamed of masturbation when I was young. I know now that my body isn't different. The man who assaulted me was different and my parents were just uninformed and naïve (as was I). I now feel comfortable with my body.

I realize that I have hidden behind my weight. It was/is a safety device to ward away relationships with men. I am now starting to feel stronger and have a desire to get healthy, which include dropping some of my weight. I know this will be hard, but I have discovered hard things are often worth the effort.

My assault left me with a feeling of helplessness and despair. I felt very alone. I have found people who care about me and my future, lessening this helpless, hopeless feeling. I know I am worth the time others have invested in me and I have invested in myself.

I can't say that I am a totally changed person, but I can honestly say I am changing for the better. I know I want happiness and peace in my life. I want relationships with women and men. At some point I may even want a relationship with one man. I am starting to open up to that possibility. But, if that doesn't happen I will be content with myself.

For years I allowed my abuse to hold me down, kick me in my ass, convince me I was worthless and fill me with shame and guilt. I am ready to knock this stigma, this nasty dirty monkey off my back. I know there will be times of self-doubt and that monkey will hop back on, but I feel I have the tools to put him in the cage where he belongs. I am a work in the making. A new piece of art almost ready to be displayed, full of new lines and colors. There is one road for me now, one straight ahead, not one full of ruts and turns. I am stronger and growing even stronger.

We chose to include some of those quotes gathered from CPT participants at the final session of therapy specifically related to improvements in the domains of functioning of interest to this chapter.

"I am happy and enjoy the relationships I am forming with others."

"I go out now. I don't just sit home and stew."

"I can go to church now, to the park, store, hang out. I'm even looking for a job."

"My attempts to reach out now are usually to reciprocate a favor or a dinner invitation rather than just a lonely phone call at 9-10 pm. I know more about family members and friends now because I ask how they are doing and listen to the details of their lives and jobs. I find their conversations interesting and time passes quickly. Since I bought a home computer, I have begun spending more time writing letters feeling the need to do something more with my time than watching TV or playing solitaire. I want to know that my time here mattered, and one small way that I can make an impact is through my interactions with others."

5 Year Follow-Ups

As mentioned above, we have begun gathering data at a five-year follow-up point on all participants in the original treatment-outcome study. We currently have data on the above mentioned measures on approximately 53 individuals. Repeated measures ANOVAs were conducted in order to ascertain differential maintenance in treatment gains across the entire treated sample comparing the pre-treatment assessment point to the five-year follow-up point on the measures described above. Means, standard deviations and statistics are provided in Table 3. The results of the analyses revealed a main effect of time indicating that all treatment gains were maintained across the entire treated sample on all measures except the CSI social support subscale and the single economic question of the SAS-SR. In the case of both exceptions, the scores at the five-year follow-up point closely resembled those seen at pre-treatment. No significant interactions emerged on the TSI subscales, the CSI subscales or the FOI. On the BDI single item, a significant interaction was found suggesting that a larger decrease in sexual indifference occurred in the CPT sample than in the PE sample.

Some examples from Impact Statements collected at the 5-year follow-up were included to highlight life changes in the various domains of functioning across a longer time period:

"I have since learned to love and fell in love a year ago with my best friend. We are now planning our wedding."

"I have realized that I can use my own traumatic experience as an asset in my career, social life, and education. I have taken the experience and utilized it to help others."

"I have a wonderful man in my life now. I have no problems sharing anything with him and this includes my bed. I have my life back thanks to programs such as these. I thank God for all of you who helped set me back on track."

"I have a relationship with God now and this has helped draw me closer to Him again."

"I am currently in a 1 1/2 year relationship that is healthy, safe, nurturing, and loving for the first time in my life. I feel worthy, respected, and loved. I have a good job that I enjoy, do well at, and get satisfaction from. I am intimate and truthful."

SUMMARY AND CONCLUSIONS

The DSM-IV (Anon, 1994) diagnosis of PTSD requires that the relevant symptomatology be present at a level significant enough to cause impairment in major role functioning (see Criterion F). It may even be argued that it is this very requirement that distinguishes a normal reaction to an extraordinary event from a response indicative of psychopathology. Through the qualitative examination of the Impact Statements presented throughout this chapter, we have demonstrated in this chapter, in the trauma survivors' own words, that the impact of the trauma on these areas of psychosocial functioning is particularly meaningful to the client. Our empirical data corroborates the patients' reports in that it provides some preliminary evidence that treatment (regardless of type) reduces distress in these major domains of functioning. Certainly, we do not minimize the importance of decreases in clusters B (re-experiencing symptoms), C (avoidant symptoms), and D (hyperarousal symptoms). However, we have found, in reviewing the available literature that relatively scant attention has been paid to the remediation of symptom F – the impact of trauma on major role functioning. It is our conclusion that research testing the efficacy of interventions geared toward trauma recovery should begin to place a greater, if not equal, emphasis on assessing change in psychosocial functioning.

Towards this end, improvements in methodology are clearly warranted. There is a need for more prospective study in an effort to more clearly delineate the nature of the relationship between trauma exposure and later deficits in functioning. Particularly, the question needs to be posed, are deficits directly caused by trauma exposure or more indirectly a result of the experience of living with the symptoms of PTSD and its commonly co-occurring Axis I disorders? Such delineation would certainly inform treatment. If the symptoms of PTSD are directly causal in deficits in role functioning, then symptom relief should result in major improvements in such functioning. However, if the exposure to trauma indicates a direct and causal pathway to impairments in functioning, then our interventions may require modification to target these particular deficits and trauma sequelae. Perhaps, the question may best be answered on a case by case basis, in which the best treatment approach may be a more flexible design allowing for specific attention to role functioning deficits if need be.

To reliably measure and evaluate outcomes in these areas, the various domains of psychosocial functioning require more specific definition and more thorough assessment. Administering multiple measures across each domain of functioning would provide more accurate estimations of both levels of pre-treatment deficits and degree of post-treatment improvements. Some of these measures could include objective reports and corroborating testimony from significant others within the clients' lives. Assessments should take into account the variety and complexity of manifestations of traumatic response within each domain. For instance, in estimating marital improvement, one individual may be considered "improved" if she remains married and works out marital differences while another client may be considered "improved" if she finds the strength to leave an abusive marital situation. Assessments of improvements in these domains must take into account these case-specific nuances. This poses a different level of analysis than measuring symptom severity. Decreases on the CAPS or the BDI-II can be considered universally positive, whereas changes in marital status are positive or negative depending on the given situation.

The impact of trauma is far-reaching; research revealing the extent of its devastation can only be imagined. Beyond the domains examined in this chapter, the Impact Statement clearly highlighted further areas that are greatly impacted by exposure to trauma and warrant consistent assessment as well. These include recreational/leisure activity, religiosity and spirituality, etc. Depending on the meaningfulness of specific domains to the trauma survivor, each domain should be included in the assessment and targeted in treatment. As an example, we found through our analysis of the Impact Statements, numerous accounts of lost spirituality and religious conviction following a trauma. In the post-treatment Impact Statements, many people also reported the relief and comfort they had found in reconciling with their God or religion. For at least a subset of individuals, this was perhaps the most important treatment gain.

Possible mediators within the relationships between trauma exposure and deficits in domains of functioning also warrant further investigation. The impact of individual variables such as gender, ethnicity, family of origin, social support, trauma type, trauma exposure length, individual's age at onset of trauma, chronicity of trauma, and time elapsed since trauma exposure are only some of the variables that could potentially impact pathological manifestations within a variety of domains of functioning. Likewise, the same variables could certainly impact the resolution of presenting problems with treatment.

The available literature and our own brief analyses suggest that empirically supported, established treatments are positively impacting trauma survivors' major role functioning. However, as previously indicated, it is less clear whether treatment is directly or indirectly related to symptom improvement in psychosocial functioning. For example, following a course of PE or CPT, one client may experience less avoidance of cues reminiscent of the trauma, such as social situations. Becoming less fearful of socializing may lead to meeting new people and perhaps beginning meaningful relationships. Thus, social functioning is improved secondarily to the improvement in the Cluster C symptomatology. Likewise, this individual may have been performing poorly at work and in danger of losing a job due to problems in concentration perhaps partly stemming from significant sleep loss. Improvements in these specific symptoms could drastically improve job performance. Contrarily, another client may have suffered a severe childhood history of emotional and physical abuse. She may present as having very low self-esteem and sense of self-worth and a resultant poor work and relationship history. Her trauma may be so temporally distal from her current situation that she may not even recognize the possible relationship between the two. Changes in social and occupational functioning may be achieved more successfully by directly targeting cognitions around these current psychosocial impairments than targeting PTSD symptoms per se.

Our review suggests that deficits in major role functioning and their resolution is an understudied area within treatment outcome research. Our data also suggests that we, as researchers, may be remiss in that the impact of trauma on these domains of functioning is clearly a meaningful topic to the trauma survivor. Specifically assessing these areas and educating clients on the potentially far-reaching impact of trauma exposure may serve to increase our knowledge base of the true impact of surviving trauma and certainly may inform our treatment.

REFERENCES

Amaya-Jackson, L., Davidson, J. R., Hughes, D. C., Swartz, M., Reynolds, V., George, L. K., & Blazer, D. G. (1999). Functional impairment and utilization of services associated with posttraumatic stress disorder in the community. *Journal of Traumatic Stress, 12,* 709-724.

Anon (1994). *Diagnostic and Statistical Manual of Mental Disorders. (4th Ed.).* Washington, DC: American Psychiatric Association.

Beck, A. T., Ward, C. H., Mendelson, M., Mock, L., & Erbaugh, J. (1961). An inventory for measuring depression. *Archives of General Psychiatry. 4,* 561-571.

Briere, J., Elliott, D. M., Harris, K., & Cottman, A. (1995). Trauma Symptom Inventory: Psychometrics and association with childhood and adult victimization in clinical samples. *Journal of Interpersonal Violence, 10,* 387-401.

Briere, J. (1988). The long-term clinical correlates of childhood sexual victimization. *Annals of the New York Academy of Sciences, 528,* 327-334.

Cloitre, M., Koenen, K. C., Cohen, L. R., & Han, H. (2002). Skills training in affective and interpersonal regulation followed by exposure: a phase-based treatment for PTSD related to childhood abuse. *Journal of Clinical and Consulting Psychology, 70,* 1067-1074.

Cloitre, M., Scarvalone, P., & Difede, J. (1997). Posttraumatic stress disorder, self- and interpersonal dysfunction among sexually retraumatized women. *Journal of Traumatic Stress, 10,* 437-452.

Descutner, C. J. & Thelen, M. H. (1991). Development and validation of a Fear-of-Intimacy scale. *Journal of Consulting and Clinical Psychology, 3,* 218-225.

Falsetti, S. A., Erwin, B. A., Resnick, H. S., Davis, J., & Combs-Lane, A. M. (2003). Multiple channel exposure therapy of PTSD: impact of treatment on functioning and resources. *Journal of Cognitive Psychotherapy: An International Quarterly, 17,* 133-147.

Feinauer, L. L., Callahan, E. H., & Hilton, H. G. (1996). Positive intimate relationships decrease depression in sexually abused women. *The American Journal of Family Therapy, 24,* 99-106.

Foa, E. B., Dancu, C. V., Hembree, E. A., Jaycox, L. H., Meadows, E. A., & Street, G. P. (1999). The efficacy of exposure therapy, stress inoculation training, and their combination in ameliorating PTSD for female victims of assault. *Journal of Clinical and Consulting Psychology, 67,* 194-200.

Foa, E. B., Hearst, D. E., Dancu, C. V., Hembree, E. A., & Jaycox, L. H. (1994). *Prolonged exposure (PE) manual*. Unpublished manuscript, Medical College of Pennsylvania, Eastern Pennsylvania Psychiatric Institute.

Foa, E. B., & Meadows, E. A. (1997). Psychosocial treatments for posttraumatic stress disorder: a critical review. *Annual Review of Psychology, 48*, 499-480.

Foa, E. B., & Rothbaum, B. O. (1998). *Treating the trauma of rape: cognitive-behavioral therapy for PTSD*. New York: Guilford Press.

Frueh, B. C., Turner, S. M., Beidel, D. C. C., Mirabella, R. F., & Jones, W. J. (1996). Trauma management therapy: a preliminary evaluation of a multicomponent behavioral treatment for chronic combat-related PTSD. *Behavior Research and Therapy, 34*, 533-543.

Harris, H. N., & Valentiner, D. P. (2002). World assumptions, sexual assault, depression, and fearful attitudes toward relationships. *Journal of Interpersonal Violence, 17*, 286-305.

Hutchinson, S. L., Loy, D. P., Kleiber, D. A., & Dattilo, J. (2003). Leisure as a coping resource: variations in coping with traumatic injury and illness. *Leisure Sciences, 25*, 143-161.

Iwasaki, Y. & Mannell, R. C. (2000). Hierarchical dimensions of leisure stress-coping. *Leisure Sciences, 22*, 163-181.

Jordan, B. K., Marmar, C. R., Fairbank, J. A., Schlenger, W. E., Kulka, R. A., Hough, R. L., & Weiss, D. (1992). Problems with families of male Vietnam veterans with posttraumatic stress disorder. *Journal of Consulting and Clinical Psychology, 60*, 916-926.

Keane, T. M., Fairbank, J. A., Caddel, J. M., & Zimmering, R. T., (1989). Implosive (flooding) therapy reduces symptoms of PTSD in Vietnam combat veterans. *Behavior Therapy, 20*, 245-260.

Kessler, R. C. (2000). Posttraumatic Stress Disorder: The burden to the individual and to society. *Journal of Clinical Psychiatry, 61*, 4-12.

Kilpatrick, D. G., Veronen, L. J., & Resick, P. A. (1982). Psychological sequelae to rape: assessment and treatment strategies. In D. M. Dolays & R. L. Meredith (Eds.), *Behavioral medicine: assessment and treatment strategies* (pp. 473-497). New York: Plenum Press.

Lee. C., Gavriel, H., Drummond, P., Richards, J., & Greenwald, R. (2002). Treatment of PTSD: stress inoculation training with prolonged exposure compared to EMDR. *Journal of Clinical Psychology, 58*, 1071-1089.

Letourneau, E. J., Resnick, H. S., Kilpatrick, D. G., Saunders, B. E., & Best, C. L. (1996). Comorbidity of sexual problems and posttraumatic stress disorder in female crime victims. *Behavior Therapy, 27*, 321-336.

Marks, I., Lovell, K., Noshirvani, H., Livanou, M., & Thrasher, S. (1998). Treatment of post-traumatic stress disorder by exposure and/or cognitive restructuring: a controlled study. *Archives of General Psychology, 55*, 317-325.

Resick, P. A., Nishith, P., Weaver, T. L., Astin, M. C., & Feuer, C. A. (2002). A comparison of cognitive-processing therapy with prolonged exposure and a waiting condition for the treatment of chronic posttraumatic stress disorder in female rape victims. *Journal of Consulting and Clinical Psychology, 70*, 867-879.

Resick, P. A. & Schnicke, M. K. (1993). *Cognitive processing therapy for rape victims: a treatment manual*. Newbury Park, CA: Sage.

_____ . (1992). Cognitive processing therapy for sexual assault victims. *Journal of Consulting and Clinical Psychology, 60*, 748-756.

Resick, P. A., Calhoun, K. S., Atkeson, B. M., & Ellis, E. M. (1981). Social adjustment in victims of sexual assault. *Journal of Consulting and Clinical Psychology, 49,* 705-712.

Shalev, A. Y. (2000). Measuring outcome in posttraumatic stress disorder. *Journal of Clinical Psychiatry, 61,* 33-42.

Taylor, S., Thordarson, D. S., Maxfield, L., Fedoroff, I. C., Lovell, K., & Ogrodniczuk, J. (2003). Comparative efficacy, speed, and adverse effects of three PTSD treatments: exposure therapy, EMDR, and relaxation training. *Journal of Consulting and Clinical Psychology, 71,* 330-338.

Thelen, M. H., Sherman, M. D., & Borst, T. S. (1998). Fear of intimacy and attachment among rape survivors. *Behavior Modification, 22,* 108-116.

Tobin, D. L., Holroyd, K. A., Reynolds, R. V., & Wigal, J. K. (1989). The hierarchical factor structure of the Coping Strategies Inventory. *Cognitive Therapy and Research, 13,* 343-361.

Weissman, M. M. & Bothwell, S. (1976). Assessment of social adjustment by patient self-report. *Archives of General Psychiatry, 33,* 1111-1115.

Zatzick, D. F., Marmar, C. R., Weiss, D. S., Browner, W. S., Metzler, T. J., Golding, J. M., Stewart, A., Schlenger, W. E., & Wells, K. B. (1997a). Posttraumatic stress disorder and functioning and quality of life outcomes in a nationally representative sample of male Vietnam veterans. *American Journal of Psychiatry, 154,* 1690-1695.

Zatzick, D. F., Weiss, D. S., Marmar, C. R., Metzler, T. J., Wells, K. B., Golding, J. M., Stewart, A., Schlenger, W. E., & Browners, W. S. (1997b). Posttraumatic stress disorder and functioning and quality of life outcomes in female Vietnam veterans. *Military Medicine, 162,* 661-665.

Zoellner, L. A., Foa, E. B., & Brigidi, D. (1999). Interpersonal friction and PTSD in female victims of sexual and nonsexual assault. *Journal of Traumatic Stress, 12,* 689-700.

In: Trends in Posttraumatic Stress Disorder Research
Editor: Thomas A. Corales, pp. 229-247

ISBN 1-59454-135-3
© 2005 Nova Science Publishers, Inc.

Chapter 10

CRITICAL INCIDENT STRESS MANAGEMENT (CISM) TEAM COORDINATION AFTER A MULTIPLE CASUALTY/MULTIPLE FATALITY INCIDENT IN A MEDICAL/SURGICAL HOSPITAL SETTING[1]

Hope E. Morrow
Marriage and Family Therapist

ABSTRACT

A multiple casualty/multiple fatality incident in a medical/surgical hospital setting will present many challenges to a Critical Incident Stress Management (CISM) Team Coordinator supervising the CISM team's response, as well as to hospital administrators. Mental health professionals, who have not had the opportunity to work in this type of healthcare facility, will likely be unfamiliar with the work environment and agency culture as it exists within these settings. In particular, knowledge of "Code Blue" responses will be crucial to proper assessment of the event's impact on hospital employees and subsequent CISM response planning. In addition, although hospital administrators are skilled in managing hospital operations, including medical and surgical treatment of crime victims, they probably will be unprepared for any situation in which a number of their employees have been injured or killed as the result of a violent crime committed on the premises. Some of the issues that they will face will include the shock that such an event has occurred in their facility, frantic and/or grieving family members, traumatized and/or grieving employees, heightened concerns for safety and security on behalf of frightened employees and their family members, the unprompted arrival of well-meaning but not always properly trained mental health professionals, and a throng of media representatives. The initial hours following the event will be chaotic (at best) and the collaborative efforts of both the hospital's administration, the CISM Team Coordinator and off-site Employee Assistance Program (EAP) and/or Crisis Response Organization (CRO) support personnel will be needed to facilitate the recovery process. This article will review these issues as well as important considerations in the initial and

---

[1] This chapter is adapted (with the permission of the publisher) from the article, "Coordinating a Multiple Casualty CISM Incident Response within a Med/Surg Hospital Setting" (Morrow, 2001).

ongoing assessment of a critical incident in a hospital setting, team member selection, logistics concerns unique to these settings, and the subsequent planning of the CISM response.

INTRODUCTION

A multiple casualty/multiple fatality hospital-based incident will present unique challenges to first-arriving Critical Incident Stress Management (CISM) team members. Unlike stand-alone psychiatric hospitals where ambulance personnel transport the injured away to a nearby hospital, within a medical/surgical hospital setting, hospital staff will respond to treat the wounded. Consequently, having an understanding of "Code Blue" responses and related aspects of the hospital environment will be crucial to properly assessing the impact of the incident on employees and planning the Critical Incident Stress Management (CISM) team's response.

In addition, hospital administrators may be unprepared for an event in which a number of their employees are injured or killed as the result of a violent crime committed on the premises. Some of the issues they will face will include the shock that such an event has occurred in their facility, frantic and/or grieving family members, traumatized and/or grieving employees, heightened concerns for safety and security on behalf of frightened employees and their family members, the unprompted arrival of well-meaning but not always properly trained mental health professionals, and a throng of media representatives. The hospital's administration will need to respond in an effective and timely manner to insure that the hospital continues to function and that employees and their families are to receive proper care. This article will address these issues and is based on "lessons learned" by the author while coordinating a CISM team response after a multiple fatality incident in a Medical/Surgical hospital setting.

IMPORTANT CONSIDERATIONS FOR HOSPITAL ADMINISTRATORS

No employer wants to experience a multiple casualty or multiple fatality incident within his or her own facility; however, should such an event occur, it will be helpful to have pre-planned the response to it and to have all administrative staff (including department heads) acquainted with their roles should the plan need to be implemented. The following are some important considerations.

Bereaved Family Members (and Family Members of the Injured)

Affected family members (of those who were injured or killed) need to be provided with accurate and up-to-date information. The importance of this can not be over-emphasized. It is also important that they receive this information *prior* to its release to the media.

Common Critical Incident Stress Reactions

Initially, hospital administrators and employees will experience shock and disbelief. It will be hard to assimilate all that has happened. During these first hours, they typically will not know how the event is going to affect them until they have completed their first full work shift following the incident.

Critical Incident Stress Reactions

Hospital employees who witness or are victims of a multiple casualty/multiple fatality incident may experience a wide variety of *critical incident*[2] stress reactions in the hours and days immediately following the event. These reactions may include physical, behavioral, cognitive, and/or emotional symptoms (see Table 1; Mitchell et al., 2001; Mitchell & Everly, Jr., 2003). They are normal reactions to an abnormal event in their work environment (Mitchell et al., 2001). For most people, these reactions will subside within a few weeks; however, any physical symptoms (that could indicate the existence of or exacerbation of a serious medical problem) should be evaluated immediately by a physician.

Bereavement

Although medical and social services staff may be very familiar with grief and loss issues, other hospital employees may be experiencing grief for the first time. Another aspect of the CISM team's role will be to bridge this gap by normalizing employees' grief reactions and providing education on the bereavement experience as well as the process of moving through it.

For administrators (and department heads) dealing with grieving employees, it will be important to recognize that their losses extend beyond the death of one or more employees. There will also be secondary losses related to the removal of the deceased employee's personal items from the workplace, the loss of usual routines (disrupted by the traumatic event and the injury or death of co-workers), having to cancel or adjust social plans that were planned to include an injured or deceased employee, the absence of a deceased employee's jokes and sense of humor within the workplace, missing an injured or deceased employee at future staff meetings and team building functions, the hiring of a new employee to fill a deceased employee's position, and other related losses. As the days and months pass after the death(s), employees may periodically be reminded of these additional losses as routine events and celebrations are reestablished within the workplace. Each may trigger a new wave of sadness and/or grief, but with time the intensity should diminish. Depending on the nature of their relationship to the deceased (and other factors), each employee's timetable for working through this process will vary.

---

[2] A *critical incident* is "an event which has the potential to overwhelm one's usual coping mechanisms resulting in psychological distress and an impairment of normal adaptive functioning" (Everly, Jr. & Mitchell, 1999, p. 11).

Table 1. Common Signs and Signals of a Stress Reaction

Physical[*]	Cognitive	Emotional	Behavioral
chills	confusion	fear	withdrawal
thirst	nightmares	guilt	antisocial acts
fatigue	uncertainty	grief	inability to rest
nausea	hypervigilance	panic	intensified pacing
fainting	suspiciousness	denial	erratic movements
twitches	intrusive images	anxiety	change in social activity
vomiting	blaming someone	agitation	change in speech patterns
dizziness	poor problem solving	irritability	loss or increase of appetite
weakness	poor abstract thinking	depression	hyperalert to environment
chest pain	poor attention/ decisions	intense anger	increased alcohol consumption
headaches	poor concentration/ memory	apprehension	change in usual communications
elevated BP	disorientation of time, place or person	emotional shock	etc.
rapid heart rate	difficulty identifying objects or people	emotional outbursts	
muscle tremors	heightened or lowered alertness	feeling overwhelmed	
shock symptoms	increased or decreased awareness of surroundings	loss of emotional control	
grinding of teeth	etc.	inappropriate emotional response	
visual difficulties		etc.	
profuse sweating			
difficulty breathing			
etc.			

[*] Any of these symptoms may indicate the need for medical evaluation. When in doubt, contact a physician.

Note: From *Critical Incident Stress Management: Group crisis intervention* (p. 137), by J. T. Mitchell and G. S. Everly, Jr., 2003, Ellicott City, MD: International Critical Incident Stress Foundation, Inc. Copyright 2003 by the International Critical Incident Stress Foundation, Inc. Reprinted with permission.

Critical Incident Stress Management (CISM) Services

Understanding CISM Services

CISM is a comprehensive multi-component system of crisis intervention that encompasses intervention strategies spanning all three phases of the crisis spectrum: a) the pre-crisis phase, b) the acute crisis phase, and c) the post-crisis phase (Mitchell et al., 2003). The goals of CISM are to reduce the incidence, duration, and severity of stress-related impairment arising from a critical incident and to facilitate the referral for follow-up care, when needed (Everly, Jr. et al., 1999).

Although originally developed for use with emergency services personnel who encountered extremely stressful events, the use of CISM has expanded over the past several years to include the military, hospitals, schools, retail businesses, bank personnel jurors, industrial organizations, aviation companies, and disaster settings (Everly, Jr. et al., 1999). The Occupational Safety and Health Administration (OSHA) has also acknowledged that an "emerging trend is to use critical incident stress management to provide a range or continuum of care tailored to the individual victim or the organization's needs" (Occupational Safety and Health Administration, 1998, p. 8). In its *Guidelines for Preventing Workplace Violence for Health-Care and Social-Service Workers* (Occupational Safety and Health Administration, 2003, p. 9-10), OSHA also states that

> "Post-incident response and evaluation are essential to an effective violence prevention program. All workplace violence programs should provide comprehensive treatment for employees who are victimized personally or may be traumatized by witnessing a workplace violence incident. Injured staff should receive prompt treatment and psychological evaluation whenever an assault takes place, regardless of its severity....
>
> "Counselors should be well trained and have a good understanding of the issues and consequences of assaults and other aggressive, violent behavior. Appropriate and promptly rendered post-incident debriefings and counseling reduce acute psychological trauma and general stress levels among victims and witnesses. In addition, this type of counseling educates staff about workplace violence and positively influences workplace and organizational cultural norms to reduce trauma associated with future incidents."

Accessing CISM Services for Affected Employees

Although many hospitals already utilize CISM services after less tragic critical incidents that occur on a periodic basis within hospital settings, some may not have these services in place yet. If not, hospital administrators and human resources personnel should make sure they become familiar with how to access CISM support services as part of their pre-incident response planning. Typically, they will be available through any of the following:

1   If the employee benefit package includes an Employee Assistance Program (EAP), critical incident stress management services may be available through that program. Depending on the hospital's contract, these services may be (a) completely covered, (b) available for an additional charge, or (c) contracted up to a specified number of service hours (after which additional services are available for a fee).

2   If the employee benefit package does not include an EAP or their EAP does not provide these services, the hospital can contract directly with a Crisis Response

Organization (CRO) to provide them. (Some EAPs will subcontract with a CRO to provide services when their own network of providers is insufficient to handle the response.)

3   Some hospitals may have an in-house CISM team that may be able to provide some assistance; however, these employees may be directly or indirectly impacted. They should *not* be used if they were direct witnesses to the event, provided care to the injured and/or deceased while the incident was ongoing, work in the area where the incident occurred, or are friends and/or family of any of the victims.

Using CISM providers from an EAP and/or CRO has another important advantage over the in-house team. Generally, the level of psychological impact on employees will not be fully known until they return to work for their next shift. An EAP or CRO will have the ability to call in additional providers, if needed, using their own personnel to make the phone calls. This task may be much more difficult for an in-house CISM team attempting to handle this type of incident. Similarly, an independent clinician providing CISM support services may not have a network of properly trained providers to call if additional responders are needed.

If outside (EAP and/or CRO) resources are used in combination with an in-house CISM team, the hospital administration and the outside agency will need to agree on which group will coordinate the overall team. If the number of EAP/CRO CISM providers is low relative to the in-house team's capacity to provide services, it may be best for the in-house team to coordinate services; however, if a large number of EAP/CRO providers are responding, it may be better for in-house team to relinquish that role to an outside response team member. Regardless of the decision, all CISM providers should be clear about the designation of Team Coordinator and accept assignments from that individual.

Handling Volunteer Mental Health Professionals Who Respond

According to (Robinson & Murdoch, 2003), emergency response personnel deal with life and death issues on a regular basis and tend to expect the same immediacy of response in meeting their own needs. Similar expectations may be true of in-house hospital staff; and for this reason, it may be very tempting to accept offers of assistance from local mental health professionals (MHPs) who respond to the scene. However, utilizing the services of MHPs who self-activate themselves may prove to be more problematic than helpful. Unfortunately, most graduate training programs for MHPs do not provide coursework in the management of acute critical incident (or traumatic) stress reactions. Thus, although well-intentioned, many of the volunteer MHPs may not be adequately trained to provide assistance.

It will also be very chaotic during the initial hours following incident and very difficult to assess the qualifications of arriving MHPs. Instead, it may be better to turn them away after collecting their business cards. Later, the business cards can be turned over to the CISM Team Coordinator who can turn them over to the EAP or CRO (who can more easily check qualifications and recall them, if needed).

Immediate Staffing Concerns

After the incident, the hospital's administration may need to find relief staff to keep patient care areas functioning at appropriate levels. Once the crime scene has been secured by law enforcement, employees who witnessed any aspect of the event will need to be interviewed by investigators. This activity may require that they be relieved of their duties temporarily. Additional staff also may be needed to cover the duties of employees who were injured or killed during the incident. Some of the employees who were directly involved in the incident (either as victims or caregivers) may be in shock and have difficulty concentrating. Although these reactions are usually transitory, it may be appropriate to consider relieving these employees of their duties for the remainder of their shift. Others may just want to go home and hug their family members. Whatever the reason, relief staffing will most likely be needed.

Another concern that may impact the need for relief staff is whether or not employees will be provided with a defusing prior to going home for the day. A defusing is a shortened version of the Critical Incident Stress Debriefing (CISD) and is provided on the same day as the incident (Mitchell et al., 2001). Once law enforcement has concluded their interviews, providing a group defusing allows each directly-involved employee to share the story of what happened with other involved co-workers. This has several benefits. Sometimes an employee may have hid where he or she could hear the incident as it unfolded, but could not see what was happening. His or her fantasies may be worse than the actual event. Other employees may lack memory of some aspect of the event. Hearing co-workers share their experience can fill in needed information and reduce anxiety. In addition, a defusing provides the CISM team members with their first opportunity to normalize employees' reactions and to teach new skills for managing those reactions. A defusing also provides an opportunity to do some additional assessment of the initial impact of the event.

Dealing with the Media

Once the media becomes aware of the incident, the hospital can expect to have a swarm of media representatives arrive and begin broadcasting from outside the hospital. While they can be a great resource for disseminating information, unfortunately some reporters in the past have used unethical measures to obtain their stories. Heightened security and proper identification of those who enter the facility after the incident may be necessary to prevent less scrupulous reporters from gaining unauthorized access to the crime scene.

At some point, hospital administrators may be asked to give a statement to the media or they may wish to hold a press conference. The following are some suggestions that may be helpful:

1   Write out your statement in advance and read it during the press conference. This will help you to stay on topic.
2   Decide in advance what is to be said about security concerns and how they are going to be handled. You can expect the press to ask about this issue if you don't address it. (You might want to consult with the hospital's legal counsel and/or a public relations firm prior to making any statements.)

3   Be ready for some difficult questions from the media – it can helpful to anticipate the questions that may be asked. Prepare your responses to them in advance.

4   Press conferences can be very upsetting to the employee(s) designated to participate and answer questions from the press. A CISM team member should be made available to provide support (as needed) after the press conference is over.

THE CISM TEAM RESPONSE

Logistical Concerns

Hazards of Cell Phone Use

Unfortunately the radio frequencies used by some cell phones cause interference with the medical telemetry equipment used to transmit a monitored patient's vital signs (heart rate, blood pressure, and respiratory rate) back to the Nurse's station. For this reason, their use may be prohibited in some Medical/Surgical hospitals.

To deal with this problem, the Federal Communications Commission (FCC) set aside (on June 8, 2000) three sections of radio bandwidth (608-614 MHz, 1395-1400 MHz and 1429-1432MHz) for use specifically on telemetry equipment in order to eliminate this problem (Federal Communications Commission, 2000). On October 16th, 2002, the FCC stopped authorizing new telemetry equipment unless designed to operate on recently designated frequencies; however, it may take several years for older equipment to be replaced (Federal Communications Commission, 2003). Consequently, it will be very important for the CISM Team Coordinator to check with the hospital regarding the appropriateness of using cell phones for communication between team members. In some settings, alternate forms of communication will have to be used. The options include:

- *Beepers*: The Team Coordinator should maintain a list of all on-site team members' pager numbers and update it as new responders arrive. Keep in mind that any team member whose pager is combined with his/her cell phone will NOT be able to use it if cell phone use is restricted within the hospital.

- *House Phones*: House phones are generally very readily accessible at Nurses' Stations and other locations throughout the hospital and can be used by team members to call the Incident Command Center or, in some cases, each other. Each team member should be provided with the telephone extension(s) for the Incident Command Center as well as the beeper numbers of on-scene team members.

- *Overhead Public Address System*: Generally, calling the hospital's PBX operator (by dialing "0"), identifying yourself as a response team member and requesting that a specific team member be paged, will be sufficient to utilize this system. However, this will only work if the other team member is monitoring overhead announcements. This system also should be used sparingly as the PBX operators will be overwhelmed with other incident-related calls.

- *Business Band Handheld Radios*: Another option is to strategically supply specific team members with programmable handheld business band radios that have the CTCSS code squelch. When utilized, the radio will send transmissions with an additional radio frequency code and open its speaker ONLY when it "hears" transmissions that contain that CTCSS code. By setting all radios used by the team to the same code, transmissions by other nearby businesses using the same frequency are screened out. It is important that all team members understand that this feature is NOT the same as encryption and that ALL transmissions can be heard by anyone with another business band radio (either un-coded or set to the same code) or a scanner. For this reason, NO confidential information should EVER be transmitted via radio. Also, a license is also required by the Federal Communications Commission to operate these radios, but a CISM team (or the team's employer) can obtain a single commercial license that will cover all of the radios (call the FCC at 1-800-418-3673 for more information or visit the FCC's website at http://www.fcc.gov/formpage.html and download the required forms; Federal Communications Commission, personal communication, July 20, 2000).

Understanding "Code Blue" Responses

Typically, a *Code Blue* is called using the overhead public address system to give notice to in-house medical personnel to respond because a patient has gone into cardiac arrest. Hospital staff may also *call a Code* when additional emergency medical support services are needed to provide acute care for a deteriorating patient. Nursing personnel (including possibly a Unit Secretary or Ward Clerk) respond with the *crash cart*, containing items needed to restore a patient's airway, breathing and/or circulation (heart function such as tubes for intubation, an *ambu bag*, oxygen, cardiac defibrillator, medications and other related supplies. Additional support personnel will also arrive from other departments: the patient's physician (if in the house at the time), medical residents, security, the nursing supervisor, pharmacy, electrocardiogram (EKG), respiratory therapy, transporters, the hospital chaplain and any others whose services are needed. An in-house incident involving other hospital employees (as victims) will challenge these responders to stay focused while providing emergency medical care to their injured or dying co-worker(s). For all Code Blues called during the incident, the CISM team leader should expect that all of these responders may have been impacted by the experience and they should be provided debriefings specifically designated for caregivers so that they can discuss their experience without traumatizing others who were not present at the scene.

Arriving On-Scene and the Initial Assessment

Gaining Access to the Facility
The contracted first-responder may be confronted with two obstacles to gaining access to the facility:.

As mentioned earlier, the healthcare facility may have been inundated by many local mental health professionals' offers of assistance, making it easy for the contracted responder to be turned away. The contracted CISM team members should arrive with the name, department and phone number of the in-house staff member who authorized or arranged for the team's services. This information will facilitate the first responders gaining access to the facility and initiating the assessment.

If law enforcement is still processing the crime scene, there may be limited access permitted by them until they complete their work. Not only may the CISM responder's entry be denied, the investigation may also result in hospital staff being prohibited from walking to the responder's location. Consequently, first responders should anticipate the possibility of some initial delay in accessing the scene, but should not postpone the response unless instructed to do so.

Initializing CISM Services

The first responder (who is responsible for the initial assessment of the agency's needs) should arrive, if possible, with at least two other team members who can handle any immediate crisis intervention and/or defusing needs.

Important Considerations at the Initial Briefing and Assessment

It is important during the initial briefing to obtain the names of the dead and injured, their respective departments and their past work history (other areas where they have worked and/or have close friends, as well as which shift(s) they have worked). This information will be extremely important when determining which employees are likely to be the most impacted.

If there were injuries, obtain the names of the injured, their current condition (if known) and their current location within the hospital (Emergency Room (ER), Operating Room (OR), Intensive Care Unit (ICU), regular patient room, etc.). If some have been released, which ones? It will also be important to know if affected family members have been notified and if any of them are currently at the hospital. If they are not, when they are expected to arrive? Ask whether staff from the Department of Social Services will be able to greet and assist the families or will the CISM team need to do so?

Be aware that the hospital may express concerns about maintaining the confidentiality of this information, especially in relation to the media; they should be re-assured that the CISM team will keep all of this information confidential.

The "Walk-Through" of the Scene

Walking through an active crime scene (before it has been cleaned up) can be traumatic and should be avoided if it is not necessary for a team member's role. However, it is very important for the Team Coordinator (and, if a different team member, the first-responder responsible for the initial assessment) to be given a tour of the crime scene so that accurate assessment can be made of which staff and which departments are likely to be the most severely impacted. The following information will be important to obtain during the walk-through:

1   Determine the location of each victim within the hospital at the time of the incident and whether each was a visitor, patient or staff member.
2   For which victims was a "code blue" called? Where were those victims located? If there were more than one victim for whom a code was called, was there adequate coverage for all responses? If not, which code was not adequately covered and who were the responders to it?
3   Which patient rooms are located adjacent to each Code Blue site? Were they in their rooms at the time of the incident? Were visitors present?

4   Which departments are located adjacent to each Code Blue site? Which employees were working in those departments at the time of the incident?

5   Were any victims pronounced dead at the scene and if so, how long did the body remain there? Where were those locations? Were bodies still present when relief staff arrived and to what extent were they exposed to the scene(s) while providing patient care? (Note: law enforcement may still be processing the crime scene(s) at the time of the walk-through and the bodies may not have been removed yet.)

6   During medical treatment of the injured, where were they transported and which departments received them?

7   Did any of the victims die while in those departments? If so, were they visitors or employees? If employees, how well were they liked, how long were they employed at the facility and which departments did they work in? Did caregivers know the employee they were treating?

8   Were staff from other departments visiting a crime scene area at the time of the incident (such as to make copies at the Xerox machine, picking up medications at the pharmacy, delivering mail, etc.)? If possible, identify those individuals and their usual work locations.

9   Determine the location of the PBX operators who will have been handling an overwhelming number of phone calls from people outside the hospital. Check on their emotional status and keep in mind that because of the nature of their work, they may need to be relieved to take additional breaks, attend defusings and/or debriefings or to receive one-on-one support.

Keep in mind that the staff member providing the tour of the crime scene may not have time to wait while you gather all of the above information. Ask only the questions that are required to identify the most severely impacted employees. Later, after law enforcement has completed its work and access to the area is easier, you can return to fill in missing information. The Outreach Team (discussed later under "Response Planning") can also be assigned this task.

The provision of CISM services will need to be planned around the shift schedules for each department, so it will be important to obtain specific information about the shifts on which each department operates. Some will be on 12-hour shifts (typically 7A-7P and 7P to 7A) with four days off each week, some on regular weekday business hours, some may be on overlapping eight hour shifts that run around the clock (possibly 6:45A-3:15P, 2:45P to 11:15P and 10:45P to 7:15A) and still others may work a ten-hour shift four days per week. Finding times that will permit the participation of homogenous groups of employees may be difficult and the hospital administration can be very helpful in figuring this out.

Finally, one or more departments may have staff members who do not speak English or from whom it is not their primary language. Determine which foreign languages are spoken within the hospital, the need to provide debriefing and crisis intervention services in these other languages, and which departments will need these services.

Assessment of the Scene

Having gathered all of this information, an assessment can now be made of roughly how many employees and which departments are likely to be the most severely affected. The hospital will have employees and others who will have been impacted in a variety of ways, those *circles of impact* can be roughly defined as follows:

1   Witnesses – including employees, patients and visitors. These individuals may have been targets of the perpetrator who were missed, direct visual witnesses, or just happened to be in the general proximity but with direct line-of-sight of the incident.
2   Employees involved in providing emergency medical treatment to the victims.
3   Staff caring for seriously and/or critically injured victims (especially co-workers) who are unstable and/or are not expected to survive.
4   Employees, patients and/or patients' family members involved in caring for victims who were not seriously injured.
5   Co-workers who were/are also close friends or family members of the victim(s).
6   Long-term co-workers of the victim(s) who have worked with the employee victims, but who are not close friends.
7   Co-workers of the victim(s) who have worked for the hospital for a shorter period of time and do not know the victims through other work settings, but are still impacted by the occurrence of the event within their place of employment.

After organizing the above information, the Team Coordinator can begin planning the response; however, some additional information will need to be collected on the next day.

Additional Assessment Tasks (For Day Two):
As early as possible on the second day, the CISM team leader will need to obtain a list of the following, through the Human Resources Department (or from Department Heads):

1   Names and phone numbers of employees
    (a) who were scheduled to work the day after the incident, but did not show up, or
    (b) who were scheduled off but were present on the day of the incident.
2   Language spoken by each absent employee, if not English.

The Telephone Outreach team (described below) will use this information to contact these employees and make sure they receive any needed support services.

Planning the CISM Team Response
The nature of the CISM Team response will vary depending on the severity of the incident and the degree to which hospital staff are impacted. The following discussion assumes that the provision of CISM services will be provided by a team responding on behalf of an external EAP or CRO.

Initial Defusing
Unless the affected staff has been released from duties, arrange defusing for them prior to their departure. To help reduce the development and propagation of rumors among employees, include an administrator in the FACT stage that can provide accurate and updated information regarding the details of the incident.

Initial Meeting with the Administrator(s):

As soon as possible (and preferably on the day of the incident), arrange a meeting with the hospital's administrator to establish a collaborative relationship between the hospital and the CISM team. The support of this individual will be crucial to the success of the overall operation and creating an expectation of staff participation. The goals of this meeting are as follows:

1. *Response Planning*: Explain that the CISM team's response plan on the next workday following the incident will be based on the assessment of the scene and the present estimate of how many staff members have been affected. As staff arrive for work, this assessment may change as a more accurate determination is made of the emotional impact of the incident. At that time a decision will be made to expand or reduce the number of responding team members, as appropriate. (Note: Some team members should be placed on standby should the operation need to be expanded.)

2. *Explanation of CISM Services*: Based on the current assessment, explain the types of services that appear to be needed for the following day and how the hospital's administration can support the response plan. This should include clearly conveying the administration's expectation to department heads that their affected employees be allowed to attend and providing relief staff to cover these individuals' work duties while they are absent from their units.

3. *Hospital Liaison to CISM Team Coordinator*: Request that the administrator designate a liaison to assist the CISM Team Coordinator with securing rooms for debriefings, department head briefing meetings, the drop-in center and individual sessions, announcing schedule and room changes, arranging for team lunches and/or snacks (if off-site meals are impractical), arranging for snacks for debriefing rooms, setting up signage and other needed tasks. This person should be someone who is minimally impacted by the incident and sufficiently knowledgeable of the hospital's environment to be able to carry out these tasks.

4. *CISM Team Command Center*: To reduce the level of chaos within the staff offices used initially by the first-responders, request that the hospital designate a room for the team to use as a "command center" and team member staging area. Preferably, it should have at least one telephone line (for both in-house and outside phone calls), a desk or table, and extra seating for stand-by and newly arriving team members.

5. *Incident Update Bulletin Board*: This bulletin board can be set up as an additional aid in rumor control; have the administration designate a location and the person responsible for updating it. The CISM team/hospital liaison can also use this board to provide updated information on how to access the team's (or other follow-up) services.

6. *Debriefings for Caregivers*: Designate a time (or leave this for discussion with the department heads) for the debriefing of employees who provided medical care to the injured and/or deceased co-workers (and/or visitors). Explain that it is important restrict initial attendance (for the first couple of days) to only the emergency caregivers involved in the incident so that other employees are not traumatized by hearing graphic details about their friends and co-workers. It will be especially important for the administration to provide additional patient care coverage to relieve staff attending these "caregiver's" debriefings.

7. ***Schedule Department Head Meeting***: Arrange a meeting of department heads, preferably on the same day as the incident, to enlist their support of their employees' participation and to involve them in providing information needed for response planning.

8. ***Department Head Meeting Agenda***: Review the agenda of the initial department head meeting (see below). Explain to administrators the importance of them showing administrative support for employees participating in debriefings, individual sessions, etc. as needed.

9. ***Security Issues:*** Advise the administration that security will be a primary concern of employees when they return to work and encourage them to begin thinking about how they will respond to those inquiries. They will need to decide what additional security measures will be instituted (if any) and how to respond to staff who will want to know what is being done to prevent a re-occurrence; encourage the development of a well thought out response to both issues.

10. ***Confidentiality***: Review the limits of confidentiality vis-à-vis staff debriefing sessions. If potentially identifying information is to be collected for the purpose of generating statistics about services provided, be sure the administration understands the confidentiality of that raw data. Any disagreement about the confidential status of this information should be resolved before any data is collected. The hospital liaison should also be made aware of the confidential nature of this information.

11. ***Patients and Patient's Families***: Clarify whether the hospital would like the team to be available to see hospital patients and/or family members; and, if so, establish the notification process for seeing them.

Initial Meeting with the Administration and Department Heads

The following tasks should be on the agenda for this meeting:

1. ***Confidentiality:*** Review the limits of confidentiality vis-à-vis group debriefings, individual sessions and any data collected for statistical purposes.

2. ***Defusing of Administrators and Department Heads:*** If time permits, provide a defusing for these individuals. This process will provide an opportunity to normalize their initial reactions and teach them how to manage some of the grief and/or critical incident stress related reactions that they (and their supervisees) may be experiencing in the next days and weeks.

3. ***Rumor Control:*** To assist with rumor control, arrange for a bulletin board where staff can get updates and include a question box where employees can ask for verification of information.

4. ***Security Issues:*** Stress that security will be a primary concern of employees when they return to work and have the administrative staff discuss any security changes. Department heads should also be instructed on how much they can say in response to inquiries from employees.

5. ***CISM Services Plan:*** Review CISM services planned for the next day: times and tentative locations, how supervisors can access additional services for their staff, location of Incident Command Center, and how employees will be advised of room and/or time changes.

6. ***Daily Briefing with Administrators and Department Heads:*** These meetings will provide an opportunity for the Incident Coordinator, Administration and Department Heads to exchange information, including updates on the condition of hospitalized survivors, any new information regarding the police investigation, funeral and memorial service plans, previously unidentified needs of employees, patients, and/or patient's families, known CISM needs not yet addressed, planned changes in the level of services provided as the response winds down, CISM services provided to date, and any other issues.

7. ***Debriefing of Administrators and Department Heads:*** Schedule a debriefing specifically for these individuals after the initial crisis period has subsided. Explain the rationale for debriefing them as a separate group later in the response:

   a. As supervisors, they will need to suppress their emotions to stay focused on their jobs of directing the work of others (which may make them less emotionally available for any CISM process, including debriefing, if done during this time).

   b. A separate group will allow them to discuss concerns that would be inappropriate to discuss with subordinates.

   c. And finally, in some employment cultures, the presence of supervisors in debriefings of subordinates may inhibit full participation in the debriefing process; other employment settings may have a very close-knit group of employees (regardless of status) and exclusion of supervisors would be contraindicated. Regardless of the hospital's unique culture, this will be a good time to explain how CISM debriefers will handle this issue should any of them choose to attend other group debriefings (and some may choose to do so). Explain that they will be asked to step outside while the group is polled regarding their comfort level in having supervisors present. Explain that the CISM Team will also observe (and ask group members to observe) confidentiality regarding the identity of any staff member who expresses his or her discomfort with having an administrator and/or supervisor present.

Planning the CISM Response for First Full Day after the Incident

Depending on the needs of the affected hospital, any combination of the services listed below can be set up as part of the team's response:

1. ***Placing Team Members on Standby for Individual Crisis Intervention:*** After the location of the Command Center has been announced to hospital staff and department heads, a stream of individuals (needing crisis intervention) may begin to appear at the door. The Team Coordinator should refer these individuals to team members waiting in the staging area. Two team members (possibly more, depending on the size and severity of the incident) should be designated for these individual sessions and directed to wait in the staging area.

2. ***The Drop-in Center:*** Although providing relief staff will permit impacted nursing staff to attend one or more of the debriefings, their patient care responsibilities may prevent them from taking full advantage of the services provided. The intermittent nature of their work, however, will allow them to get their needs met if a "Drop-in Center" is set up in an empty patient room that is central to all the patient care areas. Nurses will then have additional opportunities for ventilation and support as they use

their break times to visit the center. If some hospital employees are caring for injured employees, it may also be important to set up a separate Drop-in Center for them as they may be dealing with different issues. Depending on the level of utilization, the Drop-in Center should be staffed with at least one team member during all hours of operation. Assigning additional team members to this location will also allow for individual sessions to be conducted. This is an important consideration as this site may also receive individuals in need of crisis intervention. Peer debriefers (see Robinson & Murdoch, 2003), with a background in Nursing, are an excellent choice for staffing this location.

3. ***Support for Nurses and Others Caring for Injured Employees:*** If some hospital employees are caring for injured co-workers, it may also be important to set up a separate support opportunities for them as they may be dealing with different issues.

4. ***Debriefing Groups for Caregivers:*** During the first one to two days, the focus of these debriefing groups should be on those who provided direct medical care to the injured and deceased victims. Encourage the administration to schedule registry staff and/or local hospital mutual aide to relieve affected nursing staff for the purpose of attending these groups. Be sure the administration understands the time required to conduct a debriefing properly and that relief staff are scheduled accordingly. Keep in mind that in some cases, these debriefings may also need to be provided in a language other than English.

5. ***Crisis Intervention (Individual Sessions):*** While the Team Coordinator may be temporarily drawn into providing brief support while an employee is waiting for a free CISM team member to provide crisis intervention services, the Team Coordinator should not be expected to fulfill this role[3]. These services should be provided by staff assigned to the staging area for this specific purpose or by staff in the Drop-In Center. These services may also need to be provided in a language other than English.

6. ***In-House Outreach Teams:*** Outreach teams (consisting of two CISM team members) can be used effectively to make "rounds" throughout the hospital to check on employees who might need additional support or who are not able to get away from their patients for long enough to visit the Drop-In Center. On their first round, they should introduce themselves to Department Heads (or each unit's current supervisor or charge nurse) and let them know that they will be floating throughout the hospital and will check back with them periodically to see how their staff are doing. They can provide individual sessions and/or small group debriefings as needed; but, the Incident Coordinator should be kept advised of activities that will take them out of service. It is also advisable to have some members of the CISM Outreach team remain in this role for at least part of the Night Shift so that their needs are also addressed.

---

[3] The CISM Team Coordinator needs to remain available for coordinating the activities of the CISM team, on-going information collection regarding the hospital staff's needs and regular communication with off-site personnel regarding assessment, response planning and staffing. Off-site personnel may include the hospital's Employee Assistance Program (EAP) representative(s), a Crisis Response Organization's representative(s), or other off-site personnel handling the CISM team staffing needs (and other issues) during the response. The hospital's administration will also be involved with this process, but it may not always be through the CISM Team Coordinator.

7. ***Outreach Team Supervisor:*** To reduce the supervisory responsibilities of the CISM Team Coordinator, it can be very helpful to staff the Outreach Teams with two licensed CISM providers (rather than peers) and to designate one of them as the roving supervisor. This person should be in regular contact with the CISM Team Coordinator, providing updates as needed.

8. ***Outreach—Telephone:*** Due to the varied work schedules characteristic of medical and nursing personnel, some employees, who were involved in or impacted by the incident, may be taking their usual days off beginning the day after the incident. Some others may find it difficult to return to work. Some CISM team members can be tasked with checking on these individuals as part of a "Telephone Outreach team". The team should be provided with a list of these staff members (including phone numbers and language spoken) so that they can be called at home. These calls can also be used as an opportunity to provide telephone defusing (if time allows), assess the impact of the incident on them, and advise them of the services available at work. Translators or bilingual team members should be used for non-English speaking employees.

9. ***Outreach - Home Visits:*** If an employee is having difficulty returning to work, a CISM team member can be designated to visit that person (and his or her family, if needed) at home. Having that same team member available to meet the staff member when he or she returns to work can also be helpful.

10. ***Hospital Liaison (designated hospital employee):*** As mentioned earlier, the Incident Coordinator should have the Hospital Administration designate a minimally or un-impacted staff member to act as a Liaison between the Hospital and the CISM team. This person will be responsible for signage, arranging group room and daily briefing locations, team lunches and snacks (if needed), broadcasting room changes and other necessary information to department heads and/or staff, and any other task that requires knowledge of the hospital's internal workings.

11. ***Department Debriefings:*** As the response to the incident progresses, it may become apparent that there are some departments that need to be debriefed separately, either because scheduling does not allow them to attend the main debriefing sessions or they may prefer to debrief as a separate group. These departments should be identified and a debriefing scheduled through the department head.

12. ***Handling Patient Contacts:*** Unfortunately, it is possible that some patient rooms may have been directly adjacent to one or more of the incident scenes. Debriefing patients who were emotionally impacted by the incident should ONLY be done after a doctor's order has been written on the patient's chart. In some situations, temporary privileges may need to be granted by the hospital before a CISM team member may see a medical patient. After obtaining administrative consent, a letter to the attending physician can be placed on the chart of each affected patient. This letter should advise the doctor that the patient has been exposed to the traumatic event, educate him/her about common reactions to traumatic stress, describe the CISM services that are available to the patient and provide instructions on how to order them for a patient who's condition is stable enough to tolerate the process.

13. ***Patient's family and visitors:*** At the discretion of the hospital administration, the team may be asked to see family members of affected patients and/or others who were in the hospital at the time of the incident. If additional support is needed by any

of these individuals, they should be referred to a local clinician who accepts reimbursement from the local Victims/Witness Program. It can be helpful to obtain a list of these clinicians from the local program office at the beginning of the incident response and keep it in the Incident Command Center so that referrals can be easily provided.

Winding Down the Operation

1. *Release of CISM Team members:* As the need for the team's services declines, members of the team should be released from duty. In deciding which team members to release first, consider the overall hours and exposure each has had as well as their hours of availability for additional assignment. Determine the current staffing requirements of the operation, and retain team members based on their availability, while balancing their need for time off.

2. *Making Recommendations to Administrators for Follow-up:* Determine what resources the hospital has available for assessing an employee's need for additional follow-up and/or referral to Workman's Compensation. Generally, this will be handled by the hospital's Employee Assistance Program or a designated staff member from Human Resources or the Department of Social Services.

3. *Final Meeting with Administration:* In this meeting, the CISM Team Coordinator (or other designated team representative) will officially transfer the responsibility for follow-up care to the hospital's administration. At this time, the administrators will need to make decisions about follow up services and how they will be made available to affected employees. If an EAP is not available, a specific individual will need to be designated to handle inquiries and assist affected employees with the referral process, including workman's compensation. The hospital's employees also need to be made aware of this person's role in the referral process.

Finally, two additional issues may need to be addressed:

(a) If the hospital has not already do so, it may be appropriate to recommend that the administration have a Workplace Violence Risk Assessment done identify risk factors within the hospital.

(b) The Administrative staff may have questions about how to deal with areas of the hospital that have become reminders of the traumatic incident for some staff members. The CISM team representative(s) can make recommendations.

CONCLUSION

Coordinating a CISM team's response to a multiple casualty or multiple fatality incident is an enormous responsibility and a very stressful experience. The author hopes that by sharing these "lessons learned" that CISM-trained clinicians and hospital administrators will be better prepared to respond to this type of incident. The uniqueness of each event will also require that both be flexible and creative in adapting this material to meet the needs of employees impacted by future similar events.

With incidents of workplace violence increasing, it is also becoming more likely that the healthcare industry will occasionally experience this type of tragic event. Hospital administrators (as well as their employees) need to be prepared for this possibility. Utilizing risk assessment services to evaluate their work environment is an important first step. In addition, attention needs to be given to the commonly used "code gray" which alerts available staff to respond because assistance is needed to contain a behaviorally out-of-control individual. This code needs to be augmented with a new code (and the development of an appropriate response policy) that alerts responders to the presence of a lethal weapon. Without this new code, unsuspecting employees are at risk of responding to the designated location and finding themselves directly confronted with an armed and lethally dangerous assailant. Clearly, there will be greater risk to the lives of hospital employees (in both medical and psychiatric facilities) until these protective measures have been developed and implemented. Please, if you work in one of these healthcare settings and your administration has not yet implemented this change, encourage them to do so: your life and/or those of your co-workers may be saved by it.

REFERENCES

Everly, G. S., Jr., & Mitchell, J. T. (1999). *Critical Incident Stress Management (CISM): A new era and standard of care in crisis intervention.* (2nd ed.) Ellicott, MD: Chevron.

Federal Communications Commission. (2000). News Release: FCC establishes new wireless medical telemetry service. Retrieved February 5, 2004, from the Federal Communications Commission Web site: *http://ftp.fcc.gov/Bureaus/Engineering_ Technology/News_Releases/2000/nret0009.html.*

Federal Communications Commission. (2003). About Wireless Medical Telemetry. Retrieved February 5, 2004, from the Federal Communications Commission Web site: *http://wireless.fcc.gov/services/personal/medtelemetry/about/.*

Mitchell, J. T., & Everly, G. S., Jr. (2001). *Critical incident stress debriefing: An operations manual for CISD, defusing and other group crisis intervention services.* (3rd ed.) Ellicott City, MD: Chevron.

Mitchell, J. T., & Everly, G. S., Jr. (2003*). Critical Incident Stress Management (CISM): Group crisis intervention.* (3rd, Rev. ed.) Ellicott City, MD: International Critical Incident Stress Foundation, Inc.

Morrow, H. E. (2001). Coordinating a multiple casualty Critical Incident Stress Management (CISM) response within a medical/surgical hospital setting. *Int.J.Emerg.Ment.Health*, 3, 27-34.

Occupational Safety and Health Administration (1998). *Recommendations for workplace violence prevention programs in late-night retail establishments* (OSHA Publication No. 3153). Washington, DC: U.S. Department of Labor.

Occupational Safety and Health Administration (2003). *Guidelines for preventing workplace violence for health care and social service workers* (OSHA Publication No. 3148). (Rev. ed.) Washington, DC: U.S. Department of Labor.

Robinson, R., & Murdoch, P. (2003*). Establishing and maintaining peer support programs in the workplace.* (3rd ed.) Ellicott City, MD: Chevron.

In: Trends in Posttraumatic Stress Disorder Research   ISBN 1-59454-135-3
Editor: Thomas A. Corales, pp. 249-261   © 2005 Nova Science Publishers, Inc.

Chapter 11

PTSD AND OTHER MENTAL HEALTH PROBLEMS IN ADULTS WHO REPORT HISTORIES OF SEVERE PHYSICAL ABUSE AND NEGLECT

Sharon C. Borger[1,], Brian J. Cox[1,2] and Gordon J. G. Asmundson[2]*

[1] Department of Psychiatry, University of Manitoba, Winnipeg, Canada.
[2] Traumatic Stress Group, University of Regina, Regina, Saskatchewan, Canada.

ABSTRACT

Background and Objective

There is uncertainty in the literature as to whether childhood history of severe physical abuse or neglect meets the requirement of a traumatic event (Criterion A) for establishing a diagnosis of adult posttraumatic stress disorder (PTSD). The purpose of the present study was to examine associations between two forms of recalled childhood maltreatment (physical abuse and serious neglect), and 19 different adult psychiatric disorders, comorbidity of disorders, and suicide variables in a large nationally representative mental health survey.

Method

Participants were from the National Comorbidity Survey (NCS; Kessler, McGonagle, Zhao, et al, 1994). Those who reported childhood physical abuse or childhood serious neglect and indicated physical abuse and neglect as the *most upsetting* traumatic event they had experienced in their lifetime were included ($N = 146$). DSM-III-R psychiatric disorders were assessed by the *Composite International Diagnostic Interview* (CIDI; World Health Organization, 1990). Lifetime prevalence of the psychiatric disorders and odds ratios were calculated by comparisons between physical abuse and neglect (PAN)

---

[*] Address correspondence to: Sharon Borger, PZ-430 PsycHealth Centre, 771 Bannatyne Avenue, Winnipeg, MB, CANADA R3E 3N4. Tel: (204) 787-7078; Fax: (204) 787-4879; Email: UMMOYSE0@cc.umanitoba.ca

respondents and the remainder of the NCS sample (N = 5731), which served as a normative general population comparison group. The appropriate statistical weight was applied and standard errors were re-estimated to reflect the complex sampling design of the NCS.

Results

Almost 76% of the PAN respondents had at least one lifetime psychiatric disorder and almost 50% had three or more disorders. Logistic regressions demonstrated several large significant positive associations between PAN and prevalence of psychiatric disorders, comorbidity, and risk of suicide ideation, planning, and attempts, when compared to the remainder of the NCS sample. The largest effects (odds ratios) were observed for PTSD, the presence of three or more lifetime disorders, and suicidal ideation and attempts.

Conclusion

General population findings suggest individuals who experience PAN may be at a greater risk for subsequent development of psychiatric disorders, particularly multiple comorbid disorders, and elevated risk of suicidal behaviors later in adulthood, even though many of them do not meet current formal diagnostic criteria for PTSD.

RATIONALE

There is inconsistency in the literature as to whether a history of childhood physical abuse or extreme neglect (PAN) qualifies in meeting the requirement for the presence of a traumatic event (Criterion A) in determining a diagnosis of adult posttraumatic stress disorder (PTSD). Because these individuals looked distinct from those with PTSD who do not report *only* childhood PAN, with women reporting more psychiatric problems and men acknowledging less substance abuse, an influential population-based study of the prevalence of PTSD (Bromet, Sonnega, & Kessler, 1998) excluded them from analyses. The purpose of the present study was to examine relationships between childhood PAN, and subsequent adult psychiatric disorders, comorbidity of disorders, and suicide variables in a large nationally representative mental health survey.

BACKGROUND

The National Comorbidity Survey

The National Comorbidity Survey (NCS; Kessler, McGonagle, Zhao, et al., 1994) is a large nationally representative survey of the civilian, non-institutionalized U.S. population, designed to provide data on the prevalence and correlates of DSM-III-R psychiatric disorders. Findings from the NCS have established the most reliable estimates of lifetime prevalence of adult psychiatric disorders, comorbidity of disorders, and other mental health variables to date. Part II of the NCS provides data on the general population epidemiology of DSM-III-R PTSD, and includes estimates of lifetime prevalence of PTSD, comorbidity of PTSD with other psychiatric disorders, and the different types of traumas most often associated with PTSD (Kessler, Sonnega, Bromet, et al, 1995).

Risk Factors for PTSD in the NCS

In a population-based study Bromet and colleagues (1998) examined childhood risk factors associated with PTSD, but excluded those individuals who reported childhood PAN as the *most upsetting* event of their lives, "because of the conceptual overlap between childhood neglect and abuse and the putative risk factors..." (p. 356). Those individuals reporting *only* a history of PAN also presented a different profile from those with PTSD who did not report *only* PAN. Bromet et al. (1998) compared this subsample ($N = 146$) to the remainder of the NCS sample and found that women were more likely to report a history of psychiatric disorders compared to others in the sample, while men were less likely to report a history of substance abuse compared to others in the sample. Those respondents with a history of PAN were excluded from further analyses, although Bromet and colleagues acknowledged that "being physically abused as a child and being seriously neglected as a child, have been conceptualized as precursors of PTSD" (p. 356). A limitation of the Bromet et al study was its sole focus on prevalence of one psychiatric disorder (i.e., PTSD).

Childhood Adversity in the NCS

The relationship between childhood maltreatment and subsequent development of psychiatric disorders in adulthood in population-based samples, has been examined by few investigators (e.g., Kessler, Davis, & Kendler, 1997; Molnar, Buka, & Kessler, 2001). Kessler and colleagues found associations between negative childhood experiences and subsequent psychiatric disorders but, perhaps more importantly, found significant *clustering* among childhood adversities associated with comorbidity of disorders. No evidence was found to support the supposition of *specificity,* between childhood adversities and psychiatric disorders. This study also found high rates of comorbidity among adult psychiatric disorders, in those individuals who had experienced childhood adversities. The authors suggest that future research explore a broader range of childhood adversities, as well as investigate this clustering effect of childhood maltreatment. The present study attempted to address some of these issues by examining two forms of childhood *trauma* which often co-occur - childhood physical abuse and childhood serious neglect.

Current Study

In the present study, data from Part II of the NCS was used to examine associations between childhood PAN and subsequent development of a wide range of psychiatric disorders later in adulthood. Association with mood, anxiety, and substance abuse disorders were evaluated. In addition, associations of childhood PAN with comorbidity of psychiatric disorders, and suicide behaviors were also assessed.

Childhood Maltreatment and Psychopathology

Substantial research exists within the child abuse literature firmly establishing the deleterious effects and negative sequelae associated with early childhood maltreatment. Considerable research suggests a greater risk of psychopathology in children and adolescents who were maltreated, as children (Deykin & Buka, 1997; Kilpatrick, Ruggiero, Acierno, Saunders, Resnick, & Best, 2003; Silverman, Reinherz, & Gianconia, 1996; Van Hasselt, Ammerman, Glancy, Bukstein, 1992). However, there is a paucity of population-based research on the development of psychiatric disorders later in adulthood, among individuals with a history of childhood trauma. With one exception, we are unaware of any studies that have examined the association between a history of PAN, and the development of psychiatric disorders in adulthood in a large, population-based sample. The exception, a study by Kessler et al, (1995) focussed solely on the subsequent development of adult PTSD to the exclusion of other psychiatric disorders.

Molnar and colleagues (Molnar et al., 2001) addressed some of these issues with respect to childhood sexual abuse (CSA). Data from the NCS were used to examine associations between CSA and subsequent psychopathology in adulthood. They found that those reporting CSA showed an increased prevalence of psychiatric disorders in adulthood compared to those not reporting a history of CSA. We felt that a similar systematic investigation of childhood PAN and its correlates, using the NCS, was warranted.

Childhood maltreatment has come to include several different types of child abuse, including, sexual abuse, physical abuse, and serious emotional neglect (Ney, Fung, & Wickett, 1994). Serious childhood neglect, while being the least understood type of abuse, has been posited as the most common form of childhood maltreatment in the United States today (Peerson, 2002). Divergent research has demonstrated physical abuse to be the most common form of childhood maltreatment (Van Hasselt et al., 1992). Some studies have demonstrated a *clustering* effect among childhood adversities (Kessler et al, 1997; Ney et al, 1994), while others support group differences among them with respect to correlates (Bath & Haapala, 1993). Due to high comorbidity among adult psychiatric disorders, . any consideration of *specificity* regarding a single childhood trauma/single adult disorder relationship, should be interpreted with caution (Kessler et al, 1997).

It is difficult to examine one *pure* type of child abuse, as different forms of childhood trauma rarely occur in isolation, and childhood traumas tend to cluster together (Kessler et al, 1997; Kessler et al, 1995; Mullen, Martin, Anderson, Romans, & Herbison, 1996; Ney et al., 1994; Pless, Sibald, Smith, & Russell, 1987; Powers & Eckenrode, 1988). Additionally, certain combinations of childhood maltreatment have been shown to increase the deleterious impact on the individual, with research suggesting the combination of physical abuse, and neglect (verbal abuse sometimes co-occurs) to be the worst combination (Ney et al, 1994).

The current study complements the work on CSA and adult psychiatric disorders in the NCS (Molnar et al, 2001), and extends this analysis to an examination of PAN. Because research on childhood PAN and adult psychiatric disorders in population-based samples is lacking, we felt the current study was timely.

METHOD

Subjects

Data from Part II of the NCS were used in the present study. In Part II of the NCS general population findings were obtained on the epidemiology of PTSD, prevalence of PTSD, comorbidity of PTSD with other disorders, and types of *traumas* most often associated with PTSD ($N = 5{,}877$).

Subjects for the present study included those individuals who reported childhood physical abuse or neglect (PAN) as their *index* trauma when asked to choose from a list of 11 traumatic events ($N = 146$). The index trauma represented the respondent's *most upsetting* traumatic experience in their lives, regardless of whether they had experienced one, or multiple lifetime traumas.

Data obtained were divided into two groups - (1) those who reported PAN, and nominated this type of abuse as the *most upsetting* traumatic event they had experienced in their lifetime ($N = 146$), and (2) the remainder of the NCS sample. The latter group served as a normative comparison group ($N = 5{,}731$). The PAN sample comprised 86 women and 61 men (58.6% and 41.4%, respectively), while the normative group consisted of 2,853 women and 2,877 men (50.2% and 49.8%, respectively). The mean age of the PAN group was 33.64 years ($SD = 9.47$), while that of the comparison group was 33.15 years ($SD = 10.76$).

Procedures

Data collected from Part II of the NCS, a large nationally representative sample of the civilian, non-institutionalized U.S. population, between the ages of 15 -54 years, conducted between 1990 and 1992 was used. In Part I of the NCS respondents were administered the *Composite International Diagnostic Interview* (CIDI; World Health Organization, 1990), a detailed diagnostic interview. The CIDI produced psychiatric diagnoses and information regarding prevalence estimates for 19 psychiatric disorders according to the *Diagnostic and Statistical Manual of Mental Disorders* (DSM-III-R; American Psychiatric Association, 1987). Life-time diagnoses for mood disorders (depression, and dysthymia), anxiety disorders (generalized anxiety disorder, panic disorder, simple phobia, social phobia, and agoraphobia with or without panic disorder), and substance abuse disorders (alcohol abuse with or without dependence, and drug abuse with or without dependence) were made.

Data obtained in Part II of the NCS included a subsample of 5,877 and estimated general population prevalence and correlates of PTSD, as well as traumas most often associated with PTSD. Due to evidence suggesting individuals may be apprehensive and embarrassed to admit to the occurrence of these *traumas*, the trauma-related questions were administered in a booklet format. Included in the list of 11 *traumas* was the experience of *childhood physical abuse* and *childhood serious neglect* (or PAN).

In an attempt to maximize disclosure and minimize embarrassment or stigmatization, Kessler and colleagues (1995) created a list of 11 traumatic events, with the 12th question being an open-ended one, and subjects were asked about each trauma by number only (e.g., "Did you ever experience Event 8 on the list?" or "Did you ever experience Event 9 on the list?"). The items assessing PAN read: "You were physically abused as a child", or "You were seriously neglected as a child". A detailed description of this procedure is published elsewhere (Kessler et al., 1995). Detailed descriptions of weighting procedures and other methods employed in the NCS have been previously published (Kessler et al., 1994, 1995).

Also, the DSM-III-R Criterion A requirement for a diagnosis of PTSD was relaxed to include those events that would otherwise be excluded from qualifying as an *event that is outside the range of usual human experience* (Kessler et al., 1995, p. 1050). This modification, allowing PAN to be nominated as participants' *index* trauma was made in order to determine the extent to which the prevalence of PTSD changed when Criterion A was less stringent. Due to the uncertainty in the literature concerning PAN meeting the current stringent requirement of Criterion A, and Bromet and colleagues' (1998) perspective that there was "conceptual overlap between childhood neglect and abuse and the putative risk factors..." (p. 356), those reporting PAN as their *index* trauma have been excluded from previous research examining prevalence and correlates of PTSD, and other adult psychiatric disorders.

Analysis Procedures

All Analyses Were Computed Using SPSS 11.0 And Appropriate NCS Statistical Weight To Ensure The Data Were Representative Of The U.S. General Population Age 15 - 54 Years. Logistic Regression Was Used And All Inferential Statistics (I.E., Odds Ratios, Confidence Intervals, And *P*-Values) Were Performed Using SUDAAN Software For The Statistical Analysis Of Correlated Data (Research Triangle Institute, 2000). Because Of The Complex Sampling Design Of The NCS, SUDAAN Software Is Needed To Re-Calculate Estimates Of Standard Errors Of Prevalences, Which Were Computed Using The Taylor Series Linearization Method Using The Stratification Information Provided In The NCS Public-Use Data Set Specifically For This Purpose.

RESULTS

Table 1 presents life-time prevalence for mood, anxiety, and substance abuse disorders, among those reporting PAN and those not reporting PAN. Individuals with a history of PAN had elevated prevalence rates for life-time psychiatric disorders, assessed both globally (i.e., mood disorder) and individually (i.e., major depression), compared to those without a history of PAN. Among those physically abused or neglected as children the prevalence of any life-time disorder was 75.8%, compared to 51.5% among those with no history of such abuse (χ^2 = 35.87, $p < 0.001$). Those with a history of PAN also displayed higher prevalence rates for all of the individual psychiatric disorders (i.e., PTSD), when compared to those who did not report these childhood abuses (with the exception of alcohol abuse without dependence). For example, 31.4% of those with a history of PAN had a life-time history of PTSD, compared with 6.7% (χ^2 = 76.78, $p < 0.001$) among those not reporting such childhood trauma (see Table 1).

**Table 1. Multivariate Associations Between Prevalence
(%) of Psychiatric Disorders and Childhood PAN in the NCS**

Disorder	Normative Sample (n = 5731)	Childhood Physical Abuse/Neglect (n =146)	χ^2	Odds Ratios (Confidence Intervals in Parentheses)
Any Lifetime Disorder	51.5	75.8	35.87***	2.96 (1.63, 5.38)***
Lifetime History of Anxiety Disorder	24.7	40.8	17.68***	2.10 (1.34, 3.30)**
Lifetime History of Mood Disorder	18.7	35.7	22.97***	2.43 (1.61, 3.65)***
Lifetime History of Alcohol/Substance Abuse	26.2	42.5	17.63**	2.08 (1.32, 3.27)**
Major Depression	16.5	32.8	22.46***	2.47 (1.61, 3.77)***
Bipolar	1.5	4.2	4.72*	2.88 (1.16, 7.15)*
GAD	4.8	12.7	13.59***	2.89 (1.56, 5.33)***
Dysthymia	6.3	13.6	9.70**	2.33 (1.35, 4.00)**
Non-Affective Psychosis	0.7	2.9	5.62**	4.41 (1.72, 11.27)**
Panic Disorder	3.3	7.6	5.94**	2.40 (1.35, 4.24)**
Panic Attack	7.0	16.1	13.80***	2.58 (1.82, 3.64)***
PTSD	6.7	31.4	76.78***	6.38 (3.92,10.39)***
Simple Phobia	10.9	21.0	12.17**	2.18 (1.37, 3.47)**
Social Phobia	13.2	24.7	13.43**	2.15 (1.25, 3.70)**
Agoraphobia w/ or w/o PD	6.5	7.7	0.32	1.20 (0.72, 1.99)
Agoraphobia w/o PD	5.2	6.1	0.21	1.18 (0.57, 2.43)
Alcohol Abuse w/ or w/o Dependence	22.3	38.0	17.77**	2.13 (1.33, 3.42)**
Alcohol Abuse w/o Dependence	9.4	8.9	0.04	0.94 (0.51, 1.75)
Alcohol Dependence	13.8	30.5	26.17***	2.74 (1.77, 4.25)***
Drug Abuse w/ or w/o Dependence	10.6	24.8	22.68***	2.77 (1.73, 4.44)***
Drug Abuse w/o Dependence	4.4	7.1	2.11*	1.67 (1.09, 2.55)*
Drug Dependence	7.2	19.1	21.40***	3.06 (1.83, 5.10)***

Note: Unless otherwise noted, all disorders are presented without hierarchy.
* p-value < 0.05, ** p-value < 0.01, *** p-value < 0.001. All p-values based on Wald F statistic.

Logistic regressions were performed in order to determine the association between childhood PAN and subsequent adult psychopathology. A history of PAN was significantly and positively associated with each psychiatric diagnostic variable, with the exceptions of agoraphobia with or without panic disorder, and alcohol abuse without dependence.

Table 2 presents associations between PAN and comorbidity of psychiatric disorders. Comorbidity of disorders was significantly higher in those reporting PAN, compared to those not reporting PAN. Logistic regressions confirmed that comorbidity was significantly and positively associated with PAN. For example, among those reporting PAN, 49.2% had three or more disorders, compared with 22.0% for those without such childhood adversities ($\chi^2 = 50.50$, $p < 0.001$). It appears that those with a history of PAN are at greater risk for developing comorbid disorders, particularly two or more, or three or more disorders, as adults.

Table 2. Multivariate Associations Between Comorbidity of Psychiatric Disorders (%) and Childhood PAN in the NCS

Disorders	Normative Sample ($n = 5731$)	Childhood Physical Abuse/Neglect ($n = 146$)	χ^2	Odds Ratios (CI's in parentheses)
Two or more disorders	33.4	58.3	36.95***	2.79 (1.62, 4.81)***
Three or more disorders	22.0	49.2	50.50***	3.43 (2.09, 5.64)***

Note: * p-value < 0.05, ** p-value < 0.01, *** p-value < 0.001. All p-values based on Wald F statistic.

Table 3 presents associations between PAN and prevalence of suicide ideation, suicide plan, and suicide attempts. Those who reported PAN displayed significantly higher rates on each of the suicide variables, compared with those who did not report PAN. For example, the PAN group reported two and one-half times more suicidal ideation, almost four times more suicidal planning, and approximately three times more suicide attempts, compared with those not reporting PAN. Logistic regressions confirmed significant and positive associations between suicide ideation, plan, and attempts, and PAN.

Table 3. Multivariate Associations Between Suicide Variables (%) and Childhood PAN in the NCS

Suicide Variables	Normative Sample ($n = 5731$) (%)	Physical Abuse/Neglect Sample ($n = 146$) (%)	χ^2	Odds Ratios (Confidence Intervals in Parentheses)
Suicidal Ideation	12.3	32.7	16.66***	3.25 (1.97, 5.36)***
Suicidal Plan	3.7	14.0	25.40***	4.29 (2.38, 7.75)***
Suicide Attempts	4.4	13.1	39.74***	3.45 (1.99, 5.98)***

Note: * p-value < 0.05; ** p-value < 0.01; *** p-value < 0.001. All p-values based on Wald F statistic.

DISCUSSION

Almost 76% of those individuals with a history of PAN were diagnosed with at least one life-time psychiatric disorder. The most robust association was between those with a history of PAN, and PTSD. Perhaps even more striking and important, was the finding that approximately 50% of those with a history of PAN had three or more comorbid disorders. Those with a history of PAN also showed elevated prevalence rates for suicidal ideation, plan, and attempts.

General population findings reported here suggest individuals who have experienced childhood PAN, and reported this type of trauma to be the *most upsetting* event to ever occur in their lifetime, may be at a greater risk for subsequent development of adult psychiatric disorders. In addition, high rates of comorbid psychiatric disorders in adulthood appear likely among those with a history of childhood PAN. This finding is consistent with previous research that has shown elevated comorbidity among adult psychiatric disorders in general, and PTSD in particular. Results also indicated a strong association between those with a history of PAN, and suicidal behaviours later in adulthood, even though many of these individuals do not meet the current diagnostic criteria for PTSD. Findings of the present study suggest individuals who have experienced childhood PAN suffer from poor *overall* mental health.

Psychiatric Disorders

Childhood PAN was strongly and positively associated with psychopathology in adulthood. The PAN group displayed higher prevalence rates for mood, anxiety, and substance abuse disorders, assessed both globally and individually, suggesting inferior general mental health.

When assessed for specific psychiatric disorders, childhood PAN was most significantly and positively associated with PTSD, with this group displaying a prevalence rate of 31.4%, compared to 6.7% for the remainder of the sample ($\chi^2 = 76.78$, $p < 0.001$). The PAN group was over four times as likely to develop PTSD later in adulthood, compared to those without a history of PAN.

The fact that childhood PAN was reported as the individual's *most upsetting* trauma, and was robustly associated with a high prevalence of PTSD, addresses current inconsistency in the literature. The existing ambiguity concerns the issue as to whether PAN qualifies in meeting the requirement of the presence of a traumatic event (Criterion A) in the diagnosis of adult PTSD. It may be more accurate and advisable to view these forms of childhood maltreatment as true *traumas,* and expand Criterion A for PTSD in future editions of the DSM to include them.

Results reported here acknowledge previous work using the NCS, on the relationship between childhood sexual abuse (Molnar et al, 2001), and adult psychopathology, and expands this analysis to an examination of PAN. As Kessler and colleagues (1997) suggested, future research should broaden it's scope of childhood maltreatment/adversities, as well as consider a broader range of psychiatric disorders when investigating the relationship between childhood maltreatment and adult psychopathology.

Results demonstrated that those with a history of PAN, not only showed a greater probability for the subsequent development of psychiatric disorders later in adulthood, but also demonstrated that they displayed elevated rates of comorbidity of disorders.

Comorbidity

Evidence from previous research indicates high comorbidity among adult psychiatric disorders (i.e., Kessler et al., 1994, 1995, 1997). For that reason, the present study also investigated the association between PAN and comorbidity of disorders, and results presented here are consistent with those published elsewhere. Previous work on comorbidity in the NCS has not yet examined the relationship between childhood PAN, and prevalence of multiple comorbid disorders. Therefore, the most striking and novel finding of the current study was that those individuals with a history of PAN, displayed significantly higher multiple comorbid disorders, compared to the remainder of the sample. A significant and robust association was demonstrated between PAN and comorbidity, with almost 50% of the PAN group having three or more disorders, compared to the remainder of the NCS sample.

Inconsistency in the literature regarding a *specificity effect* single trauma/single psychiatric disorder association remains a controversial issue, with some work supporting specificity (Mullen et al., 1996), while other research indicates little evidence for specificity (Bath & Haapala, 1993; Kessler et al, 1997; Ney et al, 1994). Results of the present study do not support the *specificity* hypothesis. Although 3/4 of those reporting PAN had a life-time history of at least one DSM-III-R disorder, compared with 51.5% of the remainder of the sample, 58.3% ($\chi^2 = 36.95$, $p < 0.001$) reported two or more disorders, and 49.2% ($\chi^2 = 50.50$, $p < 0.001$) reported three or more disorders. High comorbidity rates such as these do not suggest that specific childhood traumas lead to the subsequent development of specific psychiatric disorders in adulthood.

That being stated, those individuals with a history of PAN displayed the highest prevalence for PTSD over any other psychiatric disorder, and research has demonstrated that comorbidity rates are elevated in subjects with PTSD (e.g., Kessler et al., 1995). The prominent finding that those who experience PAN may be at a greater risk for subsequent development of multiple comorbid disorders in adulthood is even more meaningful given that many of the PAN individuals did not meet the current formal diagnostic criteria for PTSD.

Understanding that childhood traumas, specifically PAN, are associated with high prevalence of comorbid psychiatric disorders in adulthood, makes it difficult to determine which disorder is primary versus secondary. Respondents with a history of PAN who reported more than three disorders may, for example, have five disorders, suggesting symptomatology overlap (e.g., many of criteria C and D for PTSD such as diminished interest, sleep difficulties, restricted range of affect, and difficulty concentrating, overlap with depression symptomatology). It is unclear as to which disorder should be the primary focus of treatment. The finding that almost 50% of the PAN group presented with three or more disorders, is suggestive of overall poor mental health in these individuals. Future research examining childhood PAN would be well-advised to consider the issue of comorbidity and it's treatment implications.

Suicide Variables

Childhood PAN was significantly associated with greater risk of suicide ideation, planning, and attempts. Compared to the remainder of the NCS sample, the PAN group was two and one-half times more likely to report suicidal ideation, almost four times more likely to have made a suicide plan, and approximately three times more likely to have attempted suicide. Since previous research has demonstrated that PTSD is associated with higher rates of suicide ideation, planning, and attempts (Kessler, 2000), attention must be paid to the high prevalence rate of PTSD in the PAN group. It is possible that the high suicide prevalence rates are more a product of PTSD, than of PAN. However, not all the individuals in the PAN group met the current diagnostic criteria for PTSD, and the current results are still higher than those reported elsewhere.

Research has also shown that mood disorders are associated with a greater risk of suicide attempts (Pfeffer et al., 1993); and suicidal ideation and attempts are associated with substance abuse disorders (Borges, Walters, & Kessler, 2000). The high prevalence rate for suicidal behaviors in the PAN group may be confounded by the high prevalence of mood and substance abuse disorders, which were also elevated among the PAN group.

CONCLUSION

The present study's sample has been excluded from systematic analyses in previous population-based research (Bromet et al., 1998) due to conceptual overlap between PAN and risk factors for PTSD, and the fact that there is uncertainty in the literature as to whether PAN qualifies in meeting the formal DSM-III-R requirement of Criterion A, for a diagnosis of adult PTSD. Research has demonstrated that childhood traumas/abuse tend to cluster together and that one form of child abuse rarely occurs in isolation (Kessler et al., 1997; Ney et al., 1994). Childhood physical abuse and neglect may represent the worst combination of childhood maltreatment, and have been shown to produce negative sequelae with respect to subsequent psychological well-being (Ney et al., 1994). Due to the paucity of research on the association between subsequent development of psychiatric disorders in adulthood, and a history of PAN, the present study was warranted. To the best of the authors' knowledge only one study (Kessler et al, 1995) has examined PAN and subsequent development of a *specific* psychiatric disorder - PTSD - in adulthood using a population-based sample, namely, the NCS. The findings of the present study complement the work done on childhood sexual abuse and subsequent psychopathology in adulthood, using the NCS data-set, (Molnar et al, 2001). The objective of the current study was to extend this type of systematic analysis to an examination of PAN.

Childhood PAN is a problem that may lead to serious psychological distress in adulthood evidenced through the symptoms of PTSD, and comorbid psychiatric disorders. General population findings reported here suggest individuals with a history of PAN may be at a greater risk for subsequent development of psychiatric disorders, multiple comorbid disorders, and increased risk of suicidal behaviours in adulthood, even though many of them do not meet current formal diagnostic criteria for PTSD.

The most striking and innovative finding of the present study was the high prevalence of comorbidity of psychiatric disorders, among those individuals with a history of PAN. To understand the mental health profiles of PAN survivors, future research needs to consider comorbidity rather than merely PTSD. Results of the present study clearly showed that while 58.3% of the PAN group had two or more disorders, and 49.2% of the PAN group had three or more disorders, only 31.4% of the PAN group met the criteria for a diagnosis of adult PTSD. Evidently, those individuals with a history of PAN suffer poor overall mental health. This has treatment implications with respect to the difficulty of identifying the primary psychiatric disorder, and the appropriate course of effective treatment.

Limitations of Current Study

The results of the current study were based on a cross-sectional survey (NCS) where trauma was assessed retrospectively, and this could be subject to recall bias. Participants in the NCS were only assessed at one point in time, and there was no way to determine if other disorders intervened between childhood and adulthood.

Future Research

Future research examining PAN, or any childhood trauma, and subsequent psychopathology in adulthood, should consider the implications of high comorbidity of adult disorders. This issue is a crucial one, particularly in terms of treatment implications, and one on which we have hopefully shed some light with the present study.

ACKNOWLEDGEMENTS

Preparation of this article was supported in part by a New Emerging Team Grant PTS-63186 from the Canadian Institutes of Health Research (CIHR) Institute of Neurosciences, Mental Health and Addiction. Sharon Borger was supported by a Natural Sciences and Engineering Research Council of Canada (NSERC) Fellowship Award, PGS-A and PGS-B. (September, 1998 - September, 2002). Dr. Cox is supported by the Canadian Research Chairs Program and the Foundation for Innovation. Dr. Asmundson is supported by a CIHR Investigator Award. We are grateful to Mr. Ian Clara for his assistance with the data analyses. The NCS was sponsored by the U. S. National Institute of Mental Health, the U. S. National Institute on Drug Abuse, and the W. T. Grant Foundation.

REFERENCES

American Psychiatric Association. *Diagnostic and Statistical Manual of Mental Disorders*, Revised Third Edition. Washington, DC: American Psychiatric Association; 1987.
Bath HI, Haapala DA. Intensive family preservation services with abused and neglected children: An examination of group differences. *Child Abuse Negl.* 1993; 17: 213-225.
Borges G, Walters EE, Kessler RC. Associations of substance use, abuse, and dependence with subsequent suicidal behavior. *Am J of Epidemiology.* 2000; 151: 781-789.

Bromet E, Sonnega A, Kessler RC. Risk factors for DSM-III-R posttraumatic stress disorder: Findings from the National Comorbidity Survey. *Am Journal of Epidemiology.* 1998; 147: 353-361.

Deykin EY, Buka SL. Prevalence and risk factors for post-traumatic stress disorder among chemically dependent adolescents. *Am J Psychiatry.* 1997; 154: 752-757.

Kessler RC. Posttraumatic stress disorder: The burden to the individual and to society. *J Clin Psychiatry.* 2000; 61: 4-12.

Kessler RC, Davis CG, Kendler KS. Childhood adversity and adult psychiatric disorder in the US National Comorbidity Survey. *Psych Medicine.* 1997; 27: 1101-1119.

Kessler RC, McGonagle KA, Zhao S, Nelson CB, Hughes M, Eshleman S, Wittchen HU, Kendler KS. Lifetime and 12 month prevalence of DSM-III-R psychiatric disorders in the United States. *Arch Gen Psychiatry.* 1994; 51: 8-19.

Kessler RC, Sonnega A, Bromet E, Hughes M, Nelson CB. Posttraumatic stress disorder in the National Comorbidity Survey. *Arch Gen Psychiatry.* 1995; 52: 1048-1060.

Kilpatrick DG, Ruggiero KJ, Acierno R, Saunders BE, Resnick HS, Best CL. Violence and risk of PTSD, major depression, substance abuse/dependence, and comorbidity: Results from the National Survey of Adolescents. *J of Consul and Clin Psych.* 2003; 692-700.

Molnar BE, Buka SL, & Kessler RC. Child sexual abuse and subsequent psychopathology: Results from the National Comorbidity Survey. *Am Journal of Public Health.* 2001; 91: 753-760.

Mullen PE, Martin JL, Anderson JC, Romans SE, Herbison GP. The long-term impact of the physical, emotional, and sexual abuse of children: a community study. *Child Abuse Negl.* 1996; 20: 7-21.

Ney PG, Fung T, Wickett AR. The worst combinations of child abuse and neglect. *Child Abuse Negl.* 1994; 705-714.

Peerson, S. Adding insult to injury: Special needs of families with abuse and neglect. *Dissertation Abstracts International: Section B. The Sciences and Engineering.* (2002); 62 (8-B): 3811.

Pfeffer CR, Klerman GL, Hurt SW, Kakuma T, Peskin JR, Siefker CA. Suicidal children grow up: Rates and psychological risk factors for suicide attempts during follow-up. *J Am Acad Child Adolesc Psychiatry.* 1993; 32: 106-113.

Pless IB, Sibald AD, Smith MA, Russell MD. Reappraisal of the frequency of child abuse seen in pediatric emergency rooms. *Child Abuse Negl.* 1987; 11: 193-200.

Powers JL, Eckenrode J. Maltreatment of adolescents. *Child Abuse Negl.* 1988; 12: 189-199.

Silverman AB, Reinherz HZ, Giaconia RM. The long-term sequelae of child and adolescent abuse: A longitudinal community study. *Child Abuse Negl.* 1996; 20: 709-723.

Software for the statistical analysis of correlated data (SUDAAN), release 7.5 . Research Triangle Park, NC, Research Triangle Institute, 2000.

Van Hasselt VB, Ammerman RT, Glancy LJ, Bukstein OG. Maltreatment in psychiatrically hospitalized dually diagnosed adolescent substance abusers. *J Am Acad Child Adolesc Psychiatry.* 1992; 868-874.

World Health Organization. *Composite International Diagnostic Interview* (CIDI, Version 1.0). World Health Organization.

In: Trends in Posttraumatic Stress Disorder Research ISBN 1-59454-135-3
Editor: Thomas A. Corales, pp. 263-284 © 2005 Nova Science Publishers, Inc.

Chapter 12

CURRENT STATUS AND FUTURE DIRECTIONS IN THE COGNITIVE-BEHAVIORAL TREATMENT OF PTSD[*]

Steven Taylor and Jaye Wald
University of British Columbia
Gordon J. G. Asmundson
University of Regina

ABSTRACT

Many studies have shown that cognitive-behavior therapy (CBT) is generally effective in reducing posttraumatic stress disorder (PTSD). However, CBT is far from universally efficacious, and so various efforts have been made to enhance or modify treatment protocols. This chapter discusses seven important areas that are currently being investigated, and remain to be further studied, in order to improve the efficacy and availability of cognitive-behavioral interventions for PTSD: (a) To identify the active ingredients of CBT interventions, so that the most effective interventions may be emphasized in treatment packages, while the less effective interventions are de-emphasized or dropped altogether. (b) To develop algorithms for selecting, sequencing, and integrating cognitive-behavioral and other interventions. (c) To better understand and limit the occurrence of side effects and other adverse outcomes. (d) To improve methods for PTSD prevention or early intervention. (e) To enhance treatments for special populations such as children and the elderly. (f) To improve the dissemination of CBT. (g) To draw on new developments in the basic sciences, particularly neuroscience, to guide the refinement of cognitive-behavioral theory and treatment. In the coming years the findings from basic and clinical research are likely to lead to important advances in the treatment of PTSD.

[*] Preparation of this article was ssupported in part by New Emerging Team Grant PTS—63186 from the Canadian Institutes of Health Research (CIHR) Institute of Neurosciences, Mental Health and Addiction. Dr. Asmundson is supported by a CIHR Investigator Award. Address correspondence to Dr. Steven Taylor, Department of Psychiatry, University of British Columbia, 2255 Wesbrook Mall, Vancouver, BC, V6T 2A1, Canada. E-mail: taylor@unixg.ubc.ca.

INTRODUCTION

Cognitive-behavior therapy (CBT) can often reduce posttraumatic stress disorder (PTSD) and associated psychopathology (Taylor, 2004). However, CBT is far from universally efficacious, and so various efforts have been made to enhance or modify treatment protocols. For patients treated with cognitive-behavioral protocols, 15-45% still meet criteria for PTSD by the end of a typical (e.g., 8-12 week) course of treatment (Taylor et al., 2003; van Minnen et al., 2002). Ways of improving treatment outcome include adding interventions to treat comorbid clinical problems (e.g., panic attacks, chronic pain), and adding interventions to treat PTSD itself (e.g., interoceptive exposure, virtual reality exposure therapy, motivational techniques, interventions to reduce expressed emotion in the patient's social milieu). Research is also underway to identify predictors of treatment outcome, in order to identify cases of PTSD that are least likely to be responsive to a given protocol, and then to alter the treatment program to improve treatment outcome.

Drawing on previous work (Taylor, 2004), the present chapter will outline seven important areas that remain to be further investigated in order to improve the efficacy and availability of cognitive-behavioral interventions for PTSD. Further work is required to:

- Identify the active ingredients of CBT interventions, so that the most effective interventions may be emphasized in treatment packages, while the less effective interventions are de-emphasized or dropped altogether.
- Develop algorithms for selecting, sequencing, and integrating cognitive-behavioral and other interventions.
- Understand and limit the occurrence of side effects and other adverse outcomes.
- Improve methods for PTSD prevention or early intervention.
- Enhance treatments for special populations.
- Improve the dissemination of CBT.
- Draw on new developments in the basic sciences, particularly neuroscience, to guide the refinement of cognitive-behavioral theory and treatment.

ACTIVE INGREDIENTS

A number of component studies have been conducted in order to gauge the efficacy of various cognitive-behavioral interventions. Component studies address two questions: (a) Is a given intervention effective, compared to no treatment or compared to a placebo intervention? (b) Is the efficacy of a treatment package improved, for patients in general (e.g., for the average patient), if a given intervention is added to the package? Implicit in question (b) is the assumption that treatment duration is fixed; to add a treatment component means that there will be less therapy time available for other components. For a program of exposure, consisting of 8 hourly treatment sessions, for example, adding cognitive restructuring will mean that there is less time available for exposure. The goal behind question (b) is to identify the most efficient, powerful combination of interventions, for a given treatment duration. An intervention may be effective (compared to no treatment), even though the intervention need not find a place in the most efficient, powerful package of interventions.

Research addressing question (a) has, for example, compared cognitive restructuring plus imaginal exposure to supportive counseling plus imaginal exposure (Bryant et al., 2003). Previous studies have shown that supportive counseling is largely a placebo (e.g., Foa et al., 1991), and so this intervention can be used as a "filler task." Bryant et al.'s study found that the treatment package that included cognitive restructuring was more effective than the package that included counseling. This finding suggests that cognitive restructuring is better than placebo in reducing PTSD, although it does not show that restructuring should be included in the most efficient and effective treatment package.

Studies addressing question (a) have also shown that imaginal exposure, situational exposure, cognitive restructuring, and their combination are more effective than no treatment at all, and are more effective than interventions that are largely placeboes, such as supportive counseling or some forms of relaxation training (e.g., Foa et al., 1991; Marks et al., 1998; Taylor et al., 2003).

Research addressing question (b) has shown that treatments combining imaginal and situational exposure tend to be more effective than treatments consisting of imaginal exposure alone (Devilly & Foa, 2001). Other studies addressing question (b) have generally failed to show, for a fixed treatment duration, that a treatment package consisting of exposure (imaginal and/or situational exposure) can be improved by adding cognitive restructuring or anxiety management techniques (e.g., relaxation training), at least when outcome is assessed in terms of reductions in PTSD symptoms (Foa, 2000; Foa et al., 1991, 1999a; Marks et al., 1998; Paunovic & Öst, 2001; Tarrier et al., 1999). There is some indication that trauma-related guilt is more effectively reduced by combined exposure plus cognitive restructuring, compared to exposure alone (Resick et al., 2002). However, some research has not supported this finding (Marks et al., 1998).

Case studies and a handful of uncontrolled and controlled trials suggest that other interventions can be usefully added to exposure protocols for PTSD, depending on the nature of the presenting problems. The addition of anger management training (Novaco, 1975) is a promising addition for people with PTSD and severe anger (Chemtob et al., 1997). Cognitive-interventions for panic disorder (Taylor, 2000) are useful additions for people with PTSD – either with or without comorbid panic attacks (Taylor, 2004). Interventions for treating substance-use disorders can also be usefully integrated with PTSD treatments for people with comorbid PTSD and substance-use disorders (Brady et al., 2001; Ouimette et al., 2003). Similarly, pain management programs can be usefully integrated with PTSD treatment for people with PTSD and chronic pain (Wald et al., 2004-a). Training in emotion regulation and interpersonal skills is a useful addition to exposure therapy for people with childhood abuse-related PTSD, because these people often report problems with emotion management and interpersonal conflict (Cloitre et al., 2002).

More research is needed to further evaluate the various cognitive-behavioral interventions. A good deal of research attention has been focused on the merits of cognitive restructuring and exposure. Less is known about the value of other component interventions, such as psychoeducation and coping exercises such as breathing retraining.

SELECTION, SEQUENCING, AND INTEGRATION OF INTERVENTIONS

Component studies will eventually enable us to identify the most effective cognitive-behavioral techniques for treating PTSD, which can be assembled into a generic protocol; that is, into a protocol that is optimally effective for the *average* patient, but which may need to be modified according to the problems and needs of specific patients. A range of seemingly useful methods are currently available. But how should the cognitive-behavioral practitioner select the methods to use in treating a specific case? In what order should the interventions be used? Should some methods be used sequentially, or should they be integrated so that they are administered at the same time? An important step in the development of CBT is to devise and evaluate algorithms for selecting, sequencing, and integrating interventions.

Some interventions logically seem to precede others. Breathing retraining or some other method for reducing arousal, for example, is typically implemented prior to exposure exercises. This is so that patients will be able to regulate the degree of arousal they experience during exposure, to prevent them from feeling emotionally overwhelmed. Similarly, training in relapse prevention logically occurs at the end of therapy, once the patient has learned skills in managing or reducing PTSD symptoms.

The ordering of other interventions is less clear. Cognitive restructuring could be implemented before exposure exercises, in order to facilitate exposure. That is, the distress associated with trauma memories can be lessened by restructuring maladaptive, trauma-related beliefs (e.g., "I'm in danger if I ride in a car"). In these circumstances exposure becomes easier to accomplish. Cognitive restructuring could also be performed during exposure. This could be done, for example, by asking the patient to articulate negative thoughts during imaginal or in vivo exposure (the "think aloud" method), which the therapist could then challenge during exposure. Cognitive restructuring could also be performed after exposure. That is, exposure exercises could be used as a means of eliciting dysfunctional beliefs, which then would be targeted with cognitive restructuring.

At the present time, little is known about the best way to combine cognitive restructuring with exposure. Clinicians typically decide on a case-by-case basis (e.g., by beginning with restructuring if the patient appears to have prominent trauma-related dysfunctional beliefs). The development of a working hypothesis or case formulation of the patient's problems can also guide the selection of interventions (for examples of case formulation approaches, see Persons, 1989; Taylor, 2000). Further research into the sequencing or integration of interventions may eventually lead to empirically-derived algorithms for constructing cognitive-behavioral treatment packages.

Algorithms will likely vary with the pattern and severity of the presenting problems. Comorbid or "multimorbid" disorders (e.g., PTSD with chronic pain and substance abuse) or PTSD associated with a complex pattern of traumatic experiences (e.g., multiple traumata) may require different treatment packages than simpler disorders (e.g., single-trauma PTSD without any co-occurring problems). Research on prognostic factors may also eventually shed light on the optimal way to select and combine cognitive-behavioral interventions.

Research on the issue of combining CBT with medications may also lead to advances in treatment outcome. Preliminary evidence, based primarily on case studies, suggests that combined treatment is preferable for patients with PTSD and comorbid chronic pain (Wald et al., 2004-a). More generally, a recent expert consensus recommended that combined CBT and medication be considered when PTSD is comorbid with other disorders (Foa et al., 1999b). Randomized, controlled trials are needed to empirically evaluate this clinical impression. There are currently no published studies comparing cognitive-behavioral treatments with pharmacotherapies, although trials are currently underway. An important question is whether, and under what circumstances, treatment outcome is improved when CBT is combined with effective medications for PTSD, such as selective serotonin reuptake inhibitors (SSRIs).

ADVERSE EFFECTS

Two treatment methods might be equally efficacious but differ in their adverse effects, such as short-term increases in symptoms or longer-term worsening. In developing CBT protocols, the goal is to maximize efficacy while minimizing adverse effects. Most treatments, whether they are psychosocial or pharmacological, have some degree of side effects. Common side effects of CBT include exacerbations in reexperiencing and hyperarousal symptoms. Initial symptom exacerbation can be a result of increased exposure to trauma-related stimuli; as treatment progresses, patients are encouraged to become less avoidant (e.g., through the use of exposure exercises), and so they increasingly come in contact with stimuli that evoke distress and trigger memories of the traumatic event (reexperiencing symptoms). Support for this clinical impression comes from a recent study by Nishith et al. (2002), who used statistical curve estimation methods to identify patterns of symptom change during each of two CBT protocols (imaginal and situational exposure, and imaginal exposure plus cognitive restructuring). For both treatments, rexperiencing symptoms became somewhat worse during the initial phases of treatment, and then declined. Other PTSD symptoms tended to gradually decline without an initial exacerbation.

How frequent and severe are CBT side effects? In a small series of cases selected to illustrate problems with exposure therapies, Pitman et al. (1991) reported that exposure sometimes exacerbated various forms of psychopathology, including trauma-related anger and guilt, anxiety symptoms, and comorbid substance-use disorders. In a randomized, controlled trial of people seeking treatment for PTSD, Tarrier et al. (1999) reported that 31% of patients treated with imaginal exposure experienced a worsening of PTSD symptoms from pre- to post-treatment. The validity of Tarrier's findings has been debated (Devilly & Foa, 2001; Tarrier, 2001). In a study comparing exposure, EMDR, and relaxation training, Taylor et al. (2003) found that symptom worsening occurred in fewer than 7% of patients, and did not vary with the type of treatment. Foa et al. (2002) found that symptom worsening was similarly rare, both during imaginal exposure and during in vivo exposure. Symptom worsening tended to be mild and transient, and was unrelated to treatment dropout. By the end of treatment, patients who had symptom worsening during treatment made comparable treatment gains as patients who did not experience symptom worsening (Foa et al., 2002).

In summary, side effects consisting of symptom worsening sometimes occur during psychosocial treatments for PTSD. Sometimes these side effects are significant (Pitman et al., 1991), but for the majority of patients side effects are mild and transient (Foa et al., 2002; Nishith et al., 2002; Taylor et al., 2003). When side effects or other forms of symptom worsening occur, then cognitive restructuring may be particularly helpful (e.g., cognitive restructuring for exacerbations of trauma-related guilt or anger; Pitman et al., 1991).

It is difficult to predict who is most likely to experience unintended aversive effects of treatment. Patients who have substance-use disorders (either currently or in recent remission) may be at risk for an exacerbation of these disorders during PTSD treatment. Other pretreatment characteristics have generally failed to identify patients who are at risk for symptom worsening. Further research is needed to examine the issue of predicting adverse reactions to CBT, just as further work is needed to identify which patients are most likely to have adverse responses to pharmacotherapies. Therapist skill may be an important factor in limiting CBT side effects (Taylor et al., 2003). Skilled therapists may be better able to guide the pacing and difficulty of exposure exercises. Some lesser skilled therapists might tend push participants to attempt exposure exercises that are too distressing to endure, resulting in aborted (and brief) exposures to intensely distressing stimuli. Such experiences of "failed" exposure may promote future avoidance, and therefore be counter-therapeutic.

PREVENTION AND EARLY INTERVENTION

People who have just experienced a traumatic event are at risk for developing PTSD (American Psychiatric Association, 2000). Accordingly, programs have been developed to prevent PTSD (and other psychopathology) in at-risk populations. There are two ways that have been used to reduce the risk for PTSD. One is to prepare people for dealing with traumatic stressors. Military personnel or emergency services workers, for example, can be educated about what they are likely to witness and about the emotional reactions they may experience (e.g., nightmares). This psychoeducational preparation may be useful in "normalizing" traumatic stress reactions (e.g., "My nightmares over the past few days are a normal reaction to what I've witnessed; there's no need for me to be worried about them"). Such preparation may also help people recognize when they should seek professional help (e.g., "My nightmares have persisted now for two weeks, and I'm feeling jumpy and irritable – it's time I sought professional help"). Unfortunately, little is known about the value of preparatory psychoeducation. Although promising, it remains to be adequately evaluated.

Another, more widely used approach is to intervene shortly after the person has been exposure to a trauma. Among the most widely used interventions are the various forms of psychological debriefing, such as critical incident stress debriefing (Mitchell & Everly, 2000). Debriefing is implemented in a single session, 24-48 hrs post-trauma, either individually or in groups. The trauma survivor is presented with information about common reactions to trauma (e.g., PTSD symptoms), and asked to provide the debriefer with a detailed review of the trauma. The debriefer encourages emotional expression, and encourages the person to discuss the trauma with others. Avoidance of trauma-related stimuli is discouraged, and the person is encouraged to seek further help if symptoms persist.

Despite the widespread use of psychological debriefing, little information about its effects has been available until recently. Research indicates that debriefing, compared to no intervention, is either ineffective or possibly harmful in that it seems to perpetuate PTSD symptoms (Mayou et al., 2000; van Emmerik et al., 2002). A recent meta-analysis of debriefing studies found that there was a trend for the effect sizes of critical incident stress debriefing to be smaller than those for no intervention; symptoms tended to improve after no intervention, but not after debriefing (van Emmerik et al., 2002). Advocates of debriefing may object that not all forms of debriefing have been evaluated (most studies have used the

Mitchell model; Mitchell & Everly, 2000). Even so, the onus is on the advocates of debriefing to demonstrate that their interventions are safe and effective. The available research does not support the current widespread use of psychological debriefing.

A more promising approach is to implement brief (e.g., 4-5 session) CBT programs within 2-4 weeks post-trauma. Methodologically rigorous, controlled studies indicate that such interventions are effective in reducing symptoms and in reducing the risk of developing full-blown PTSD (Bryant et al., 1999; Foa et al., 1995). To illustrate, Foa et al. (1995) compared 4 sessions of CBT with a no-treatment control condition, shortly after assault. Two months post-assault, 70% of the control group met criteria for PTSD compared to only 10% of the CBT group.

Why is CBT effective while debriefing is ineffective or possibly harmful? There are several possibilities. Timing may be important. Intervening too soon may interfere with the natural process of recovery. Debriefing may be too short; longer (e.g., 4-5 session) programs may be required. Early CBT programs are implemented only with people who are symptomatic (and thereby at risk for developing PTSD). In comparison, debriefing is typically applied to all trauma survivors (e.g., all of the staff at a bank after a robbery), regardless of whether the survivors have PTSD symptoms. Debriefing of asymptomatic survivors is no better than no intervention at all, and debriefing with symptomatic survivors appears to perpetuate symptoms, possibly by encouraging rumination over the traumatic event (Mayou et al., 2000). Further research is needed to investigate these possible explanations.

SPECIAL POPULATIONS

Studies indicate that cognitive-behavioral interventions are efficacious for diverse trauma populations, such as survivors of physical and sexual assault (including adult survivors of childhood assault), victims of terrorism and torture, survivors of motor vehicle accidents, and combat veterans (e.g., Blanchard et al., 2003; Ehlers et al., 1998; Foa et al., 1991, 1999a; Ford & Kidd, 1998; Gillespie et al., 2002; Jaycox et al., 1998; Otto et al., 2003; Paunovic & Öst, 2001; Taylor, 2004; Taylor et al., 2001, 2003). However, the effects of CBT in many special populations, as discussed below, have only recently begun to receive empirical scrutiny.

Children and Adolescents

Controlled and uncontrolled trials indicate that cognitive-behavioral interventions can reduce PTSD in sexually abused children and adolescents (Cohen, 2003; Deblinger et al., 1990, 1996; Farrell et al., 1998; King et al., 2000), and that these interventions are superior to waiting-list controls (King et al., 2000). More research is needed on the efficacy of CBT for traumatized children and adolescents who have experienced other forms of trauma. As with adults, there are many outstanding questions regarding optimal treatment components and the benefits of special interventions, such as family-based CBT. The influence of developmental variables (e.g., family, neurobiological, cognitive factors) on PTSD treatment outcome in children and adolescents also requires further inquiry.

Refugees

Many refugees are likely to have experienced a range of traumatic events, such as violence, torture, and other forms of extreme human suffering (e.g., starvation, illness). PTSD has been well documented in refugees across various cultural groups, yet little is known about effective treatments, such as CBT. .Preliminary research indicates that CBT can successfully reduce PTSD in Cambodian refugees (Otto et al., 2003; Paunovic & Öst, 2001) but more treatment research on other refugee groups is needed. Future studies will also need to investigate how treatment protocols can be modified in ways that can incorporate the unique cultural, ethnic, and linguistic needs for specific refugee groups.

Domestic Violence

Domestic violence is associated with high rates of PTSD (e.g., Cascardi et al., 1999; Golding, 1999), yet little treatment research has been done on this trauma group and the effectiveness of CBT is unknown. Domestic violence typically involves chronic victimization via multiple types of trauma (e.g., physical or sexual assault, stalking, psychological abuse), and victims may be exposed to ongoing threats of violence by the batterer (Kaysen, et al., 2003). Also, victims of domestic violence may have complex relationships with the abusive spouse/partner, such as intense, ambivalent feelings (e.g., love combined with guilt or fear). Safety considerations are of paramount importance in deciding how to treat these individuals. It is possible that in some cases the treatment of PTSD could do more harm than good. For example, reducing PTSD in a patient might be associated with a reduction in the fear of the abusive spouse, thereby leading the battered person to return to the abusive relationship. Research is therefore needed to determine whether CBT is safe and effective for PTSD for this trauma population. It seems likely that special interventions may be needed, such as training in interpersonal skills (e.g., assertiveness training) or training in skills for detecting cues to violence (e.g., skills for determining whether a given dating partner is likely to become abusive).

Work-Related PTSD

Workers who experience (or witness) a work accident (e.g., industrial accident), emergency personnel who are traumatized by witnessing others who are badly injured or killed, and employees who are criminally victimized at their workplace (e.g., robbery, assault) are at an increased risk of work-related PTSD (e.g., Asmundson, et al., 1998; Burgess et al., 1996; Corneil et al., 1999; Hennigar et al., 2001). Work-related PTSD can follow a chronic and unremitting course, and concurrent physical injuries, chronic pain, depression, alcohol use, cosmetic concerns (e.g., due to disfiguring injuries), fears of reinjury, and return to work difficulties are common associated features (Grunert et al., 1992; Hull et al., 2002, McDonald et al., 2003).

Only two treatment studies, thus far, have examined the efficacy of comprehensive CBT packages for work-related PTSD. In a study of traumatized police officers with PTSD, Gersons et al. (2000) compared a brief eclectic psychotherapy group (a 16 session manualized protocol that combined CBT and psychodynamic techniques) to a waitlist control group. The intervention group was superior to the waitlist in reducing PTSD, anxiety symptoms, associated comorbidity, and in helping workers return to work. In a consecutive series of workers with PTSD arising from work-related hand injuries, Grunert et al. (1990) examined rates of return to work across four different treatment CBT strategies: (a) imaginal exposure and coping skills training, (b) in vivo exposure that involved returning to the worksite, (c) graded work exposure that involved increasing hours of work each week, and (d) worksite evaluation that involved teaching the individual how to apply and practice learned skills "on the job." These interventions facilitated both a reduction in PTSD symptoms and increased rates of return to work. Graded work exposure produced the highest rate of return to work among the four approaches. At a 6-month follow-up, 61% (74 of 122) workers remained successfully employed with their preinjury employer. More treatment studies are needed to replicate, extend, and improve these promising findings.

PTSD and Chronic Pain

Traumatic physical injuries are often associated with an increased risk of developing PTSD and chronic pain (e.g., Asmundson et al., 1998, 2002; Bryant et al., 1999; Geisser, et al., 1996). Concurrent chronic pain and PTSD often has a chronic, and often escalating, course of distress and disability, yet the etiology and maintenance of these co-existing conditions are not well understood (e.g., Sharp & Harvey, 2001). Individuals with these conditions tend to have poor treatment outcome, and are likely to have additional psychiatric comorbidity, such as major depression and substance abuse (see Asmundson et al., 2002; Sharp & Harvey, 2001). There is some evidence from uncontrolled studies to suggest that targeting the PTSD alone using CBT interventions may be effective (Hickling & Blanchard, 1997; Muse, 1993). However, other research has found that pain symptoms can also interfere with the PTSD treatment by affecting the patient's ability to engage in, and benefit from the intervention (Taylor et al., 2001). These findings warrant the need for alternative treatment strategies such as sequential treatment or concurrent treatment of the pain and PTSD (e.g., through an integrated multi-disciplinary pain management program).

Modified CBT protocols may also be of benefit when pain is present, such as using passive relaxation techniques (exercises that avoid "tense-release" instructions so to avoid pain flareups), brief relaxation exercises between exposure therapy trials, cognitive restructuring of catastrophic pain-related beliefs, or reducing the length of exposure therapy within a session (Wald et al., 2004-a). A recent expert consensus has recommended combined psychotherapeutic and pharmacological therapies for comorbid PTSD and chronic pain disorders (Foa et al., 1999-a) such as the use of SSRIs, nefazdone, and venlaflaxine. Recent advances in pain pharmacotherapy, such as second-generation anti-convulsants (e.g., neurontin, topirimate) will likely lead to more effective treatment options (e.g., Finnerup et al., 2002) and potentially reduce the risk of developing chronic pain (e.g., Schwartman et al., 2001). However, at present, treatment decisions need to be based on a case-by-case evaluation. Controlled trials are needed to determine how CBT protocols can be optimally tailored for these individuals. The merits of various types of medications, CBT, or their combination are yet to be determined.

Clinical Exotica

Another special population that requires further investigation consists of those patients presenting with "clinical exotica"; that is, patients presenting with unusual problems, such as (a) PTSD associated with recovered memories of abuse, (b) PTSD associated with claims of being subjected to unusual traumata (e.g., purportedly witnessing human sacrifice by members of satanic cults), (c) atypical symptoms such as posttraumatic conversion disorder, or (d) PTSD with concurrent psychotic symptoms, such as hallucinations (usually visual or auditory) or delusions.

When considered individually, each form of clinical exotica is rare. Collectively, however, they are not uncommon. For therapists specializing in the treatment of civilian PTSD, for example, it is not unusual to encounter several of these unusual presentations each year. Case studies suggest that cognitive-behavioral interventions can reduce PTSD associated with recovered memories, and can also reduce posttraumatic conversion disorder (Taylor & Thordarson, 2002; Wald et al., 2004-b).Treatment studies on co-existing psychotic symptoms in PTSD have been limited to cases studies, and these reports have generally found that this clinical presentation tends to be largely treatment resistant to both pharmacological and psychosocial interventions (e.g., Bleich & Moskowits, 2000; Chan & Silove, 2000).

Treatment decisions about how to best manage clinical exotica must be made on a case-by-case basis. In some cases traditional CBT for PTSD may be contraindicated; treatment could do more harm than good (e.g., repeated imaginal exposure for a patently false memory may strengthen or enhance the person's belief that the event actually occurred; (Taylor & Thordarson, 2002). Empirical studies of the nature and treatment of clinical exotica should eventually help clinicians to manage these unusual and complex clinical problems.

TREATMENT DISSEMINATION

An effective treatment is of little value if it doesn't reach the people who need it. Accordingly, treatment dissemination is an important issue. There are two types of dissemination; providing practitioners with the education necessary to learn how to implement the treatment, and providing patients with access to treatment services.

Disseminating CBT to Practitioners

Practitioners are unlikely to use CBT for PTSD unless they can obtain the training and supervision needed to become competent and confident in treating trauma survivors with cognitive-behavioral methods. If CBT is to be appropriately disseminated to practitioners, it is also important to identify barriers to dissemination, such as limited training opportunities, and practitioner misconceptions or clinical myths about CBT for PTSD, particularly myths about exposure therapy.

Until recently, little was known about these important issues. (Becker et al. 2004) conducted a survey of clinician's experiences and attitudes about one cognitive-behavioral intervention – imaginal exposure for PTSD. The sample consisted of 852 licensed U.S. psychologists and 50 clinicians from a trauma special interest group. Although roughly half of the larger sample reported being at least somewhat familiar with imaginal exposure, only 17% used it to treat PTSD. The low rate of utilization appeared to arise from a combination of a lack of adequate training (less than a third of practitioners had received formal training in imaginal exposure), and misconceptions about exposure therapy. The latter included clinical myths that imaginal exposure should not be used when patients have comorbid disorders or dissociative reactions (many of the patients treated in randomized, controlled studies have comorbity; e.g., Taylor et al., 2003). Many practitioners also held the misconception that imaginal exposure would cause treatment dropout. However, the rate of attrition from exposure-based therapies is no different from other psychosocial interventions (van Etten & Taylor, 1997; Taylor et al., 2003). Thus, many patients who could benefit from exposure are inappropriately excluded because of practitioner misconceptions. Practitioners were more likely to use imaginal exposure if they had received training in this method and had clinical experience with PTSD. For practitioners with such training and experience, imaginal exposure was used by over 65% of the sample of 852 practitioners and by 65% of the smaller sample of 50 practitioners (Becker et al., 2004).

These findings suggest that cognitive-behavioral advocates should make greater efforts to train clinicians in CBT and to correct misconceptions about this treatment. Training efforts could involve a combination of conference workshops, internships and practica, and information materials (e.g., fact sheets, workbooks, instructional videotapes or CDs). Internet-based information sites could also be developed to further educate practitioners.

Enhancing Patient Access

People living far from major metropolitan centers typically do not have access to specialists trained in the treatment of PTSD. To illustrate the geographic difficulties in providing CBT, consider the Canadian province of British Columbia (BC), which is where CBT is practiced by two of the authors (ST and JW). This province has an area over 900,000 km^2, about the size of France, Germany, and the Netherlands combined. In BC there are few specialists trained in treating PTSD, and almost all are situated in the city of Vancouver, in the far south-western corner of the province. Many PTSD sufferers living in rural areas have to travel for several hours to attend Vancouver clinics.

Treatment accessibility also can be a problem for people with physical disabilities, including those living in urban centers, who may have difficulty traveling to PTSD clinics. PTSD sufferers (including those living in metropolitan centers) may also be reluctant to seek treatment because of shame or embarrassment about disclosing their traumatic experiences (particularly sexual assault), and because of the societal stigma attached to seeking treatment for mental disorders.

A range of strategies have been used to improve patient access to treatment. PTSD workbooks have been developed (e.g., Smyth, 1999; Williams & Poijula, 2002), which patients can use as a form of self-directed therapy, or as an adjunct to treatment with a therapist. Although workbooks have proven useful in the treatment of other anxiety disorders (Taylor, 2000), it remains to be seen whether they are useful in treating PTSD. Given the complexity and heterogeneity of PTSD, it may be that workbooks are more useful as introductions or adjuncts to treatment with a therapist, rather than as stand-alone interventions.

Other approaches to treatment dissemination have arisen from the field of telemedicine. Telephone-based treatment, videoconferencing, e-mail-based treatment, and Internet-provided therapy all have potential value for delivering CBT for PTSD. Internet-based treatment holds particular promise as a means of overcoming obstacles to patient access, and so far has been the only method of telemedicine to be evaluated in controlled research as a means of reducing PTSD symptoms.

In the general population, Internet use has become increasingly widespread in recent years, even for people living in remote regions. Surveys indicate that 50-70% of people in North America have access to the Internet (Harris Interactive, 2003; Nua Internet Surveys, 2002; Victory & Cooper, 2002). Users spend an average of 7 hours per week on online (Harris Interactive, 2003). Internet use is more common among high-income households, although its use is growing rapidly among lower-income groups (Victory & Cooper, 2002). This is probably due to the decreasing costs of computers, and the growing availability of free or low-cost Internet access (e.g., through libraries, community centers, or Internet cafés). Although the Internet is used for a variety of purposes, some of the more common uses include the search for health information, and participation in discussion groups. The majority of adult Internet users (80%) look for health information online, on an average of three times per month (Harris Interactive, 2002). A total of 84% of Internet users have, at one time or other, joined an online group, such as a support group for a medical condition or personal problem (Hoorigan, 2001).

There are a number of potential advantages of Internet-based treatment for PTSD. There is evidence that people interacting with computers (including the Internet) tend to disclose a greater degree of personal information, compared to the information they disclose in a face-to-face format (Alleman 2002; Griffiths, 2001). Thus, it is easier for people to discuss emotional problems such as PTSD symptoms. Most patients express satisfaction with web-based and other computer-assisted forms of treatment (Bailey et al., 2002; Lange et al., 2002). Thus, Internet treatment, compared to face-to-face therapy, may furnish the therapist with more information about the patient, thereby facilitating the development and implementation of treatment strategies. A further advantage of Internet-based treatment is its convenience; people have access to Internet programs 24 hours/day, 7 days/week.

Internet-based mental health programs may contain a variety of components, including psychoeducation, structured exercises, self-scoring quizzes to check the patient's understanding of the material, clinician guidance and feedback, and online symptom measures to monitor treatment progress. An Internet-based program might require that each week participants read a section of the program covering a specific topic, and to participate (e.g., make at least one posting) in a moderated online bulletin board or discussion group. The use of a moderator makes sure that the comments are relevant and keeps the participants on track. Bulletin boards or discussion groups may be open to all patients in a particular treatment program, thereby conveying a degree of social support (e.g., a patient can see that he/she is not alone in grappling with particular problems, and receives support and encouragement from other patients; Weinberg, 2001).

In a series of investigations, Lange and colleagues (2000, 2001, 2002, 2003-a, 2003-b) have shown that Internet-based treatment can reduce PTSD symptoms. Given the increasing number of people with Internet access, Internet-based treatment may come to play an increasingly important role in the treatment of PTSD, perhaps initially as an adjunct to face-to-face contact with a therapist. For some patients, Internet-based therapy might be viable as a stand-alone intervention.

USING BASIC SCIENCE TO GUIDE FUTURE DEVELOPMENTS IN CBT

CBT in a Biological Context

Although we are far from having an integrated biopsychosocial theory of PTSD, great strides have been made in recent years in understanding the etiology of this disorder, including the role of cognitive factors (e.g., encoding and retrieval of traumatic memories, development and activation of dysfunctional beliefs), social factors (e.g., high expressed emotion; see Tarrier & Humphreys, 2004), and biological factors (e.g., the role of the amygdala in emotional memories; see Stowe & Taylor, 2003, for a review).

On a psychological level, PTSD can be regarded as a memory disorder (McNally, 2003), where trauma memories, stored in long-term memory, are hyperaccessible (i.e., readily activated by environmental and other cues) and emotionally charged. The neural correlates of trauma memories include a host of brain structures (e.g., the amygdala, hippocampus, medial frontal cortex), interconnected through a complex network of circuits (Stowe & Taylor, 2003). Trauma memories can be established through fear conditioning, which is mediated through subcortical sensory input reaching the amygdala and other pathways. The amygdala appears to play a role in assigning emotional significance to events (LeDoux, 1995). Hyperreactivity of the amygdala and associated limbic structures in response to trauma-related stimuli has been implicated in PTSD. Extinction of conditioned fear responses appears to involve inhibition of amygdala activity by frontal cortical regions, especially the orbital frontal cortex (Charney et al., 1998). These findings suggest that PTSD can be treated by targeting the neurotransmitter systems that modulate the structures and circuits involved in PTSD (e.g., modulation of amygdala activity), and by psychosocial interventions aimed at either deconditioning emotional reactions that were conditioned by trauma exposure (imaginal and in vivo exposure), or by altering the meaning of the traumatic event (cognitive restructuring).

A strength of CBT has been its links with basic science, particularly cognitive psychology and the animal learning literature. In recent years, however, it seems that CBT (and the allied movement known as "cognitive clinical psychology") has over-emphasized cognitive psychology to the neglect of other important fields of basic science, particularly neuroscience. Important developments in CBT may arise by considering how the findings from neuroscience and related fields can be used to refine or modify CBT for PTSD. In the following sections the potential for using basic science to develop new CBT protocols will be illustrated by three examples: (a) animal research on the role of context in extinction, (b) research on the pharmacological enhancement of fear extinction, and (c) neuroscience research on "memory erasure."

Context and Extinction

The animal learning literature suggests that extinction of emotional responses, such as the reduction of emotional reactions to trauma cues, involves new learning that is stored along with the old learning (Bouton, 2002; LeDoux, 1995). Consider, for example, a person who develops PTSD after being in a building that nearly collapsed during an earthquake. Exposure therapy does not undo the old learned associations (e.g., the associations between buildings and danger); rather, it involves the strengthening of new associations (e.g., the association between buildings and safety). Over the course of exposure exercises, such as repeated trips into tall buildings, the person learns to associate buildings with safety, and this memory representation increasingly inhibits the activation of the memory representation in which buildings are associated with danger.

A consequence is that a given stimulus (e.g., the interior of an office) has two available "meanings" (e.g., dangerous vs. safe) and therefore has the properties of an ambiguous word; its current meaning depends on what the current context retrieves (Bouton, 2002). Contexts can be provided by a variety of background stimuli, including the physical environment, one's internal physical state, and time. The animal learning literature indicates that fear reduction tends to be most complete and enduring if exposure is conducted across multiple contexts (e.g., in different environments and at different times of day; Bouton, 2002). This suggests that treatment for PTSD would be most effective if the person was exposed to many different contexts (e.g., different buildings, and different locations within each building). Similarly, imaginal exposure may be most effective when it is practiced in many different locations and times of day, and under different internal states (e.g., under different baseline emotional or physical states). Cognitive-behavioral practitioners have typically not paid much attention to the contexts in which imaginal exposure occurs. Such exercises are typically practiced either in the therapist's office or in some quiet place in the patient's home. By varying the context of imaginal and in vivo exposure, we may improve the durability of CBT for PTSD.

Pharmacologically-Enhanced Exposure Therapy

Another approach to enhancing the reduction of PTSD symptoms involves the search for pharmacologic agents than facilitate the extinction of emotional responses by strengthening the inhibition of trauma memories. Animal research suggests that amygdala NMDA receptors are important for the expression of conditioned fear responses (Lee et al., 2001; Walker & Davis, 2002). Because NMDA receptors in the amygdala are critical for excitatory fear conditioning, and because extinction, like fear conditioning, is a form of learning, researchers have investigated the possibility that NMDA receptors in the amygdala might also be involved in extinction. In fact, research indicates that NMDA receptors in the amygdala play an important role in conditioned fear extinction. The findings also raise the possibility that NMDA agonists, administered before exposure therapy, might facilitate extinction (Davis, 2002).

One such compound is D-cycloserine, which has been used for years in humans to treat tuberculosis and is not associated with significant side effects. Animal research has shown that this compound facilitates extinction after either systemic administration or intra-amygdala infusion (Walker et al., 2002). D-cycloserine is a widely available and safe compound. It or similar agents might be usefully combined with exposure therapy in the treatment of clinical fear. Studies of D-cycloserine with humans are currently underway (Davis, 2002). Findings so far suggest that this compound may facilitate exposure-related fear reduction and maybe useful as a pharmacologic adjunct to exposure therapy for PTSD (Heresco-Levy et al., 2002; Rothbaum, 2003). The compound could be administered shortly before an imaginal or in vivo exposure exercise in order to facilitate the reduction (extinction) of trauma-related distress.

Memory Erasure

Another approach to fear extinction involves the novel possibility that it might be possible, under some circumstances, to "erase" memories. Learning entails the formation or consolidation of memories. It was once believed that once a memory has been consolidated, then it is resistant to de-consolidation (erasure). In other words, memories – including memories for traumatic events – were thought to be indelible (LeDoux, 1995). Similarly, there is evidence that, under normal conditions, the extinction of acquired emotional responses does not reflect a destruction of the original learning, but rather reflects the inhibition of old learning (LeDoux, 1995).

Recent animal research, however, suggests that memory erasure can occur under particular conditions (Eisenberg et al., 2003). Evidence suggests that when a memory is activated and takes control over the organism's behavior (e.g., by motivating escape or avoidance), then the memory trace undergoes a period of reconsolidation. During this window of time the memory is susceptible to disruption or erasure. Eisenberg et al. demonstrated this, for example, in a fear conditioning paradigm with fish that were trained to associated a light with mild electric shock. Learned avoidance was used as a behavioral expression of the access of a memory trace linking the conditioned stimulus (CS; a flash of light) with an unconditioned stimulus (UCS; electric shock). Once the memory trace had been activated, the fish were exposed to a transient anesthetic. The anesthetic was shown to act like a chemical "memory eraser," weakening the memory trace of the CS-UCS relationship. Extrapolating to humans, it is possible that some chemical compound could have similar effects on traumatic memories. Such a compound could be administered during or shortly after a period of imaginal exposure, in order to weaken the memory trace for the traumatic event. Although research on putative memory erasers is currently confined to animals, it is possible that in the coming years we will see the application of this procedure to humans.

SUMMARY AND CONCLUSIONS

In a study of people with assault-related PTSD presenting to an urban emergency department, Roy-Byrne et al. (2003) found that 81% were interested in receiving some form of treatment; 76% were interested in some form of psychosocial intervention, 62% were interested in medication, and 57% were interested in both. This suggests that, from the perspective of patient preference, psychosocial interventions and medications are both acceptable options. There are many ways of improving the accessibility and efficacy of psychosocial interventions such as CBT. This chapter described a number of important ways of achieving these aims. In the coming years the findings from basic and clinical research are likely to lead to important advances in the treatment of PTSD. This is good news for both patients and practitioners. However, we should not lose sight of the fact that PTSD is part of a broader societal problem. In addition to improving treatments for reducing the psychopathologic effects of traumatic events, we also need to find better ways of reducing the occurrence of events (e.g., interpersonal violence, work accidents) that give rise to PTSD.

REFERENCES

Alleman, J. R. (2002). Online counseling: The Internet and mental health treatment. *Psychotherapy: Theory, Research, Practice, Training, 39*, 199-209.

American Psychiatric Association. (2000). *Diagnostic and statistical manual of mental disorders* (4th ed. text revision). Washington, DC: Author.

Asmundson, G. J. G., Coons, M. J., Taylor, S., & Katz, J. (2002). PTSD and the experience of pain: Research and clinical implications of shared vulnerability and mutual maintenance models. *Canadian Journal of Psychiatry, 47*, 930-937.

Asmundson, G. J. G., Norton, G. R., & Allerdings, M. D. (1998). Posttraumatic stress disorder and work-related injury. *Journal of Anxiety Disorders, 12*, 57-69.

Bailey, R., Yager, J., & Jenson, J. (2002). The psychiatrist as clinical computerologist in the treatment of adolescents: Old barks in new bytes. *American Journal of Psychiatry, 159*, 1298-1304.

Becker, C. B., Zayfert, C., & Anderson, E. (2004). A survey of psychologists' attitudes towards and utilization of exposure therapy for PTSD. *Behaviour Research and Therapy, 42*, 277-292

Blanchard, E. B., Hickling, E. J., Devineni, T., Veazey, C. H., Galovski, T. E., Mundy, E., Malta, L. S., & Buckley, T. C. (2003). A controlled evaluation of cognitive behavioral therapy for posttraumatic stress disorder in motor vehicle accident survivors. *Behaviour Research and Therapy, 41*, 79-96.

Bleich, A., & Moskowits, L. (2000). Posttraumatic stress disorder with psychotic features. *Croatian Medical Journal, 41*, 442-445.

Bouton, M. E. (2002). Context, ambiguity, and unlearning: Sources of relapse after behavioral extinction. *Biological Psychiatry, 52*, 976-986.

Brady, K. T., Dansky, B. S., Back, S. E., Foa, E. B., & Carroll, K. M. (2001). Exposure therapy in the treatment of PTSD among cocaine-dependent individuals: Preliminary findings. *Journal of Substance Abuse Treatment, 21*, 47-54.

Bryant, R. A., Moulds, M. L., Guthrie, R. M., Dang, S. T., & Nixon, R. D. V. (2003). Imaginal exposure alone and imaginal exposure with cognitive restructuring in treatment of posttraumatic stress disorder. *Journal of Consulting and Clinical Psychology, 71*, 706-712.

Bryant, R. A., Sackville, T., Dang, S. T., Moulds, M., & Guthrie, R. (1999). Treating acute stress disorder: An evaluation of cognitive behavior therapy and supportive counseling techniques. *American Journal of Psychiatry, 156*, 1780-1786.

Burgess, E., S., Hibler, R., Keegan, D., & Everly, G. S. (1996). Symptoms of posttraumatic stress disorder in workers' compensation patients attending a work rehabilitation program. *International Journal of Rehabilitation and Health, 2,* 29-39.

Cascardi, M., O'Leary, D., & Schlee, K. A. (1999). Co-occurrence and correlates of posttraumatic stress disorder in physically abused women. *Journal of Family Violence, 14,* 227-249.

Chan, A. O., & Silove, D. (2000). Nosological implications of psychotic symptoms with established posttraumatic stress disorder. *Australian and New Zealand Journal of Psychiatry, 34,* 522-525.

Charney, D. S., Grillon, C., & Bremner, J. D. (1998). The neurobiological basis of anxiety and fear (parts I and II). *Neuroscientist, 4,* 35-44 and 122-132.

Chemtob, C., Novaco, R. W., Hamada, R. S., & Gross, D. M. (1997). Cognitive-behavioral treatment for severe anger in posttraumatic stress disorder. *Journal of Consulting and Clinical Psychology, 65,* 184-189.

Cloitre, M., Koenen, K. C., Cohen, L. R., & Han, H. (2002). Skills training in affective and interpersonal regulation followed by exposure: A phase-based treatment for PTSD related to childhood abuse. *Journal of Consulting and Clinical Psychology, 70,* 1067-1074.

Cohen, J. A. (2003). Treating acute posttraumatic reactions in children and adolescents. *Biological Psychiatry, 53,* 789-795.

Corneil, W., Beaton, R., Murphy, S., Johnson, C., & Pike, K. (1999). Exposure to traumatic incidents and prevalence of posttraumatic stress symptomatology in urban firefighters in two countries. *Journal of Occupational Health Psychology, 2,* 131-141.

Davis, M. (2002). Role of NMDA receptors and MAP kinase in the amygdala in extinction of fear: Clinical implications for exposure therapy. *European Journal of Neuroscience, 16,* 395-398.

Deblinger, E., Lippmann, J., & Steer, R. (1996). Sexually abused children suffering posttraumatic stress symptoms: Initial treatment outcome findings. *Child Maltreatment, 1,* 310-321.

Deblinger, E., McLeer, S. V., & Henry, D. (1990). Cognitive-behavioral treatment for sexually abused children suffering post-traumatic stress: Preliminary findings. *Journal of the American Academy of Child and Adolescent Psychiatry, 29,* 747-752.

Devilly, G. J., & Foa, E. B. (2001). The investigation of exposure and cognitive therapy: Comment on Tarrier et al. (1999). *Journal of Consulting and Clinical Psychology, 69,* 114-116.

Ehlers, A., Clark, D. M., Dunmore, E., Jaycox, J., Meadows, E., & Foa, E. B. (1998). Predicting response to exposure treatment in PTSD: The role of mental defeat and alienation. *Journal of Traumatic Stress, 11,* 457-471.

Eisenberg, M., Kobilo, T., Berman, D. E., & Dudai, Y. (2003). Stability of retrieved memory: Inverse correlation with trace dominance. *Science, 301,* 1102-1104.

Farrell, S. P., Hains, A. A., & Davies, W. H. (1998). Cognitive behavioral interventions for sexually children exhibiting PTSD symptomatology. *Behavior Therapy, 29,* 241-255.

Finnerup, N. B., Gottrup, H., & Jensen, T. S. (2002). Anticonvulsants in central pain. Expert Opinion on Pharmacotherapy, 3, 1411-1420.

Foa, E. B. (2000). Psychosocial treatment of posttraumatic stress disorder. *Journal of Clinical Psychiatry, 61 (Suppl. 5),* 43-48.

Foa, E. B., Dancu, C. V., Hembree, E. A., Jaycox, L. H., Meadows, E. A., & Street, G. P. (1999a). A comparison of exposure therapy, stress inoculation training, and their combination for reducing posttraumatic stress disorder in female assault victims. *Journal of Consulting and Clinical Psychology, 67,* 194-200.

Foa, E. B., Davidson, J. R. T., & Frances, A. (1999b). Treatment of PTSD: The NIH expert consensus guideline series. *Journal of Clinical Psychiatry, 60 (Suppl. 16),* 4-76.

Foa, E. B., Hearst-Ikeda, D., & Perry, K. J. (1995). Evaluation of a brief cognitive-behavioral program for the prevention of chronic PTSD in recent assault victims. *Journal of Consulting and Clinical Psychology, 63,* 948-955.

Foa, E. B., Rothbaum, B. O., Riggs, D. S., & Murdock, T. B. (1991). Treatment of posttraumatic stress disorder in rape victims: A comparison between cognitive-behavioral procedures and counseling. *Journal of Consulting and Clinical Psychology, 59,* 715-723.

Foa, E. B., Zoellner, L. A., Feeny, N. C., Hembree, E. A., & Alvarez-Conrad, J. (2002). Does imaginal exposure exacerbate PTSD symptoms? *Journal of Consulting and Clinical Psychology, 70,* 1022-1028.

Ford, J. D., & Kidd, P. (1998). Early childhood trauma and disorders of extreme stress as predictors of treatment outcome with chronic post-traumatic stress disorder. *Journal of Traumatic Stress, 11,* 743-761.

Geisser, M. E., Roth, R. S., Bachman, J. E., & Eckert, T. A. (1996). The relationship between symptoms of post-traumatic stress disorder and pain, affective disturbance and disability among patient with accident and non-accident pain. *Pain, 66,* 207-214.

Gersons, B. P. R., Carlier, I. V. E., Lamberts, R. D., & van der Kolk, B. A. (2000). Randomized clinical trial of brief eclectic psychotherapy for police officers with posttraumatic stress disorder. *Journal of Traumatic Stress, 13,* 333-347.

Gillespie, K., Duffy, M., Hackmann, A., & Clark, D. M. (2002). Community based cognitive therapy in the treatment of post-traumatic stress disorder following the Omagh bomb. *Behaviour Research and Therapy, 40,* 345-357.

Golding, J. M. (1999). Intimate partner violence as a risk factor for mental disordesrs: A meta-analysis. *Journal of Family Violence, 14,* 99-132.

Griffiths, M. (2001). Online therapy: A cause for concern? *The Psychologist, 14,* 244-248.

Grunert, B. K., Devine, C. A., Matloub, H. S., Sanger, J. R., Yousef, N. J., Anderson, R. C., & Roell, S. M (1990). Psychological adjustment following work-related hand injury: 18-month follow-up. *Annals of Plastic Surgery, 29,* 537-542.

Grunert, B. K., Matloub, H. S., Sanger, J. R., Hanel, D. P., & Yousef, N. J. (1990). Treatment of post-trauma-related stress disorder after work-related hand trauma. *Journal of Hand Surgery, 15A,* 511-515.

Harris Interactive (2002). Harris Poll #21, *Harris Poll Library.* Available at http://www.harrisinteractive.com/harris_poll/index.asp?PID=299. Extracted 30/July/03.

_____ . (2003). Harris Poll #8, *Harris Poll Library.* Available at http://www.harrisinteractive.com/harris_poll/index.asp?PID=356. Extracted 30/July/03.

Hennigar, C., Saunders, D., & Efendov, A. (2001). The Injured Workers Survey: Development and clinical uses of a psychosocial screening tool for patients with hand injuries. Journal of Hand Therapy, 14, 122-127.

Heresco-Levy, U., Kremer, I., Javitt, D. C., Goichman, R., Reshef, A., Blanaru, M., & Cohen, T. (2002). Pilot-controlled trial of D-cycloserine for the treatment of post-traumatic stress disorder. *International Journal of Neuropsychopharmacology, 5,* 301-307.

Hickling, E. J., & Blanchard, E. B. (1997). The private practice psychologist and manual-based treatments: Post-traumatic stress disorder secondary to motor vehicle accidents. *Behaviour Research and Therapy, 35*, 191-203.

Hoorigan, J. B. (2001). Online communities: Networks that nurture local distance relationships and local ties. Available at: www.pewinternet.org/reports/pdfs/PIP_ Communities_Report.pdf. Extracted 30/July/03.

Hull, A. M., Alexander, D. A., & Klien, S. (2002). Survivors of the Piper Alpha oil platform disaster: Long-term follow-up study. *British Journal of Psychiatry, 181*, 433-438.

Jaycox, L. H., Foa, E. B., & Morral, A. R. (1998). Influence of emotional engagement and habituation on exposure therapy for PTSD. *Journal of Consulting and Clinical Psychology, 66*, 185-192.

Kaysen, D., Resick, P., & Wise, D. (2003). Living in dange: The impact of chronic traumatization and the traumatic context on posttraumatic stress disorder. *Trauma, Violence, & Abuse, 4*, 247-264.

King, N. J., Tonge, B. J., Mullen, P., Myerson, N., Heyne, D., Rollings, S., Martin, R., & Ollendick, T. H. (2000). Treating sexually abused children with posttraumatic stress symptoms: A randomized clinical trial. *Journal of the American Academy of Child and Adolescent Psychiatry, 39*, 1347-1355.

Lange, A., Rietdijk, D., Hudcovicova, M., van de Ven, J., Schrieken, B., & Emmelkamp, P. M. G. (2003-a). Interapy: A controlled randomized trial of the standardized treatment of posttraumatic stress through the Internet. *Journal of Consulting and Clinical Psychology, 71*, 901-909.

Lange, A., Rietdijk, D., Hudcovicova, M., van de Ven, J., Schrieken, B., & Emmelkamp, P. M. G. (2003-b). Interapy: Treatment of post-traumatic stress via the Internet. *Cognitive Behaviour Therapy, 32*, 110-124.

Lange, A., Schoutrop, M., Schrieken, B., & van de Ven, J. (2002). Interapy: A model for therapeutic writing through the Internet. In S. J. Lepore & J. M. Smyth (Eds.), *The writing cure: How expressive writing promotes health and well-being* (pp. 215-238). Washington, DC: American Psychological Association.

Lange, A., Schrieken, B., van de Ven, J., Bredeweg, B., Emmelkamp, P. M., van der Kolk, J., Lydsdottir, L., Massaro, M., & Reuvers, A. (2000). "INTERAPY": The effects of a short protocolled treatment of post-traumatic stress and pathological grief through the Internet. *Behavioural and Cognitive Psychotherapy, 28*, 103-120.

Lange, A., van de Van, J., Schrieken, B., & Emmelkamp, P. M. G. (2001). Interapy. Treatment of post-traumatic stress through the Internet: A controlled trial. *Journal of Behavior Therapy and Experimental Psychiatry, 32*, 73-90.

LeDoux, J. E. (1995). In search of an emotional system in the brain. In M. Gazzaniga (Ed.), *The cognitive neurosciences* (pp. 1049-1061). Cambridge, MA: MIT Press.

Lee, H. J., Choi, J. S., Brown, T. H., & Kim, J. J. (2001). Amygdala NMDA receptors are critical for the expression of multiple conditioned fear responses. *Journal of Neuroscience, 21*, 4116-4124.

Marks, I. M., Lovell, K., Noshirvani, H., Livanou, M., & Thrasher, S. (1998). Treatment of posttraumatic stress disorder by exposure and/or cognitive restructuring. *Archives of General Psychiatry, 55*, 317-325.

Mayou, R. A., Ehlers, A., & Hobbs, M. (2000). A three-year follow-up of psychological debriefing for road traffic accident victims. *British Journal of Psychiatry, 176*, 589-593.

McDonald, H., Karlinsky, H., Colotla, V., & Flamer, S. (2003). Posttraumatic stress disorder (PTSD) in the workplace: A descriptive study of workers experiencing PTSD resulting from work injury. *Journal of Occupational Rehabilitaion, 13*, 63-77.

McNally, R. J. (2003). *Remembering trauma*. Cambridge, MA: Harvard University Press.

Mitchell, J. T., & Everly, G. S. (2000). Critical incident stress management and critical incident stress debriefings: Evolutions, effects and outcomes. In B. Raphael & J. P. Wilson (Eds.), *Psychological debriefing: Theory, practice and evidence* (pp. 71-90). NY: Cambridge University Press.

Muse, M. (1986). Stress-related post-traumatic chronic pain syndrome: Behavioral approaches to treatment. *Pain, 25*, 389-394.

Nishith, P., Resick, P. A., & Griffin, M. G. (2002). Pattern of change in prolonged exposure and cognitive-processing therapy for female rape victims with posttraumatic stress disorder. *Journal of Consulting and Clinical Psychology, 70*, 880-886.

Novaco, R. W. (1975). *Anger control*. Lexington, MA: Lexington.

Nua Internet Surveys (2002). How many online? Available at http://www.nua.ie/surveys/how_many_online/index.html. Extracted 30/July/03.

Otto, M. W., Hinton, D., Korbly, N. B., Chea, A., Ba, P., Gershuny, B. S., & Pollack, M. H. (2003). Treatment of pharmacotherapy-refractory posttraumatic stress disorder among Cambodian refugees: A pilot study of combination treatment with cognitive-behavior therapy vs sertraline alone. *Behaviour Research and Therapy, 41*, 1271-1276.

Ouimette, P., Moos, R. H., & Finney, J. W. (2003). PTSD treatment and 5-year remission among patients with substance use and posttraumatic stress disorders. *Journal of Consulting and Clinical Psychology, 71*, 410-414.

Paunovic, N., & Öst, L.-G. (2001). Cognitive-behavior therapy vs exposure therapy in the treatment of PTSD in refugees. *Behaviour Research and Therapy, 39*, 1183-1197.

Persons, J. B. (1989). *Cognitive therapy in practice: A case formulation approach*. New York: Norton.

Pitman, R. K., Altman, B., Greenwald, E., Longpre, R. E., Macklin, M. L., Poire, R. E., & Steketee, G. S. (1991). Psychiatric complications during flooding therapy for posttraumatic stress disorder. *Journal of Clinical Psychiatry, 52*, 17-20.

Resick, P. A., Nishith, P., Weaver, Astin, M. C., & Feuer, C. A. (2002). A comparison of cognitive-processing therapy with prolonged exposure and a waiting condition for the treatment of chronic posttraumatic stress disorder in female rape victims. *Journal of Consulting and Clinical Psychology, 70*, 867-879.

Rothbaum, B. O. (November, 2003). *Discussant's remarks in the symposium, "Predictors of treatment outcome in PTSD"* (M. Creamer, Chair). Presented at the annual meeting of the International Society for Traumatic Stress Studies, Chicago IL.

Roy-Byrne, P., Berliner, L., Russo, J., Zatzick, D., & Pitman, R. K. (2003). Treatment preferences and determinants in victims of sexual and physical assault. *Journal of Nervous and Mental Disease, 191*, 161-165.

Schwartzman, R. J., Grothusen, J., Kiefer, T. R., & Rohr, P. (2001). Neuropathic central pain: Epidemiology, etiology, and treatment options. *Archives of Neurology, 58*, 1547-1550.

Sharp, T. J., & Harvey, A. G. (2001). Chronic pain and posttraumatic stress disorder: Mutual maintenance? *Clinical Psychology Review, 21*, 857-877.

Smyth, L. (1999). *Overcoming post-traumatic stress disorder: A cognitive-behavioral exposure-based protocol for the treatment of PTSD and other anxiety disorders.* Oakland, CA: New Harbinger.

Stowe, R., & Taylor, S. (2003). Posttraumatic stress disorder. *Encyclopedia of life sciences.* Oxford: Elsevier.

Tarrier, N. (2001). What can be learned from clinical trials? Reply to Devilly and Foa (2001). *Journal of Consulting and Clinical Psychology, 69,* 117-118.

Tarrier, N., & Humphreys, A.-L. (2004). PTSD and the social support of the interpersonal environment: The development of social cognitive behaviour therapy. In S. Taylor, S. *Advances in the treatment of posttraumatic stress disorder: Cognitive-behavioral perspectives.* New York: Springer.

Tarrier, N., Pilgrim, H., Sommerfield, C., Faragher, B., Reynolds, M., Graham, E., & Barrowclough, C. (1999). A randomized trial of cognitive therapy and imaginal exposure in the treatment of chronic posttraumatic stress disorder. *Journal of Consulting and Clinical Psychology, 67,* 13-18.

Taylor, S. (2000). *Understanding and treating panic disorder: Cognitive-behavioural approaches.* New York: Wiley.

Taylor, S. (2004). *Advances in the treatment of posttraumatic stress disorder: Cognitive-behavioral perspectives.* New York: Springer.

Taylor, S., Fedoroff, I. C., Koch, W. J., Thordarson, D. S., Fecteau, G., & Nicki, R. (2001). Posttraumatic stress disorder arising after road traffic collisions: Patterns of response to cognitive-behaviour therapy. *Journal of Consulting and Clinical Psychology, 69,* 541-551.

Taylor, S., & Thordarson, D. (2002). Behavioural treatment of posttraumatic stress disorder associated with recovered memories. *Cognitive Behaviour Therapy, 31,* 8-17.

Taylor, S., Thordarson, D. S., Maxfield, L, Fedoroff, I. C., Lovell, K., & Ogrodniczuk, J. (2003). Comparative efficacy, speed, and adverse effects of three treatments for PTSD: Exposure therapy, EMDR, and relaxation training. *Journal of Consulting and Clinical Psychology, 71,* 330-338.

van Emmerik, A. A. P., Kamphuis, J. H., Hulsbosch, A. M., & Emmelkamp, P. M. G. (2002). Single session debriefing after psychological trauma: A meta-analysis. *The Lancet, 360,* 766-771.

van Etten, M., & Taylor, S. (1998). Comparative efficacy of treatments for posttraumatic stress disorder: A meta-analysis. *Clinical Psychology and Psychotherapy, 5,* 126-145.

van Minnen, A., Arntz, A., & Keijsers, G. P. J. (2002). Prolonged exposure in patients with chronic PTSD: Predictors of treatment outcome and dropout. *Behaviour Research and Therapy, 40,* 439-457.

Victory, N. J., & Cooper, K. B. (2002). *A nation online: How Americans are expanding their use of the Internet.* Washington, DC: National Telecommunication Economics and Statistics and Information Administration, US Department of Commerce. Available at: www.ntia.doc.gov/ntiahome/dn/index.html. Accessed 30/July/03.

Wald, J., Taylor, S., & Fedoroff, I. C. (2004-a). The challenge of treating PTSD in the context of chronic pain. In S. Taylor, S. *Advances in the treatment of posttraumatic stress disorder: Cognitive-behavioral perspectives.* New York: Springer.

Wald, J., Taylor, S., & Scamvougeras, A. (2004-a). Cognitive-behavioural and neuropsychiatric treatment of posttraumatic conversion disorder: A case study. *Cognitive Behaviour Therapy*, 33,12-20.

Walker, D. L., & Davis, M. (2002). The role of glutamate receptors within the amygdala in fear learning, fear-potentiated startle, and extinction. *Pharmacology, Biochemistry, and Behavior, 71*, 379-392.

Walker, D. L., Ressler, K. J., Lu, K.-T., & Davis, M. (2002). Facilitation of conditioned fear extinction by systemic administration or intra-amygdala infusions of D-cycloserine as assessed with fear-potentiated startle in rats. *Journal of Neuroscience, 22*, 2343-2351.

Weinberg, H. (2001). Group process and group phenomena on the Internet. *International Journal of Group Psychotherapy, 51*, 361-378.

Williams, M. B., & Poijula, S. (2002). *The PTSD workbook: Simple, effective techniques for overcoming traumatic stress symptoms*. Oakland, CA: New Harbinger.

INDEX